Jan Grabowski

ON DUTY
The Role of the Polish Blue and Criminal Police in the Holocaust

This book was published under the auspices of the
Center for Research on the Holocaust in Poland,
generously supported by the Aaron Gutwirth Fund and the
Danek Gertner Yad Vashem Scholarship.

Jan Grabowski

ON DUTY

The Role of the Polish Blue and Criminal Police in the Holocaust

Translated from the Polish by
Jan Grabowski and Katarzyna Gucio

יד ושם
YAD VASHEM
THE WORLD HOLOCAUST REMEMBRANCE CENTER
THE INTERNATIONAL INSTITUTE FOR HOLOCAUST RESEARCH
The Center for Research on the Holocaust in Poland

Jan Grabowski

Na posterunku

Udział polskiej policji granatowej
i kryminalnej w zagładzie Żydów

Language and Production Editor: Adina Mendelsohn

P.O.B. 3477, Jerusalem 9103401, Israel
publications.marketing@yadvashem.org.il
First published in Polish by Czarne, 2020

ISBN 978-965-308-698-2

Typesetting: Hava Salzman

Printed in Israel by Ayalon Printing

As always, for my father, who survived the hunt

Contents

Preface

The uniformed [Polish] police has had a deplorable role in the "resettlement actions." The blood of hundreds of thousands of Polish Jews, caught and driven to the "death vans," will be on their heads.[1]

Emanuel Ringelblum, Warsaw, late 1943

On January 13, 1943, platoon leader Henryk Mazur from the Stanin detachment of the Polish Blue Police in the Generalgouvernement, filed a report with his superiors in nearby Łuków. The report dealt with Jews fleeing the liquidated ghettos, an issue that was of significant interest to Polish officers from mid-1942:

> I wish to report that on January 11, 1943, in the evening, the [village] elder of Kożuchówka Commune arrested six Jews who were wandering about in the village and brought them to our station. The elder of Janik Commune brought here three Jews and one Jewess. The elder of Sarnów (Tuchowicz Commune) brought three other Jews, and we, ourselves, caught more [Jews] and delivered them to the offices of the Tuchowicz Commune. Finally, there were twenty-three Jews in custody, including two Jewesses. One of the Jews died in jail, so there were twenty-two left. From that number, eleven persons were killed on January 12, 1943. Eleven others were left [alive] because the policemen, due to the poor quality of the ammunition (that's because of many duds) decided not to

1 Emanuel Ringelblum, *Polish-Jewish Relations During the Second World War* (Evanston: Northwestern University Press, 1992), p. 135

> shoot anymore. On January 12, 1943, at 11:00 AM, on my way (together with Constable Wagner) to Łuków to pick up the rifles, I came across a Jew who refused to halt when ordered to. He was shot during an escape attempt in the village of Józefów, Tuchowicz Commune.[2]

Who were these nameless Jewish victims? What were the circumstances of their capture? Why did the village elders hunt down the Jewish refugees, and why did they deliver them to the police stations? What can explain the ruthless and deadly efficiency of the Polish policemen in killing their own countrymen? What had happened during the three years of war and occupation that could possibly explain the transformation of ordinary policemen into ruthless killers? Last but certainly not least, where were the Germans in this horrifying picture?

2 Report, Stanin Police Post, Archiwum Państwowe w Lublinie (AP Lublin), Posterunek Policji Polskiej w Staninie, file 1035.

Introduction

In the late fall of 1939, shortly after the conquest of Poland, the Germans created the Blue Police. It was officially known as the Polish Police of the Generalgouvernement (Polnische Polizei im Generalgouvernement in German), and it mainly consisted of prewar Polish police officers. Within a few short months, the "Blues"—after the color of their uniform—were responsible for the enforcement of the many anti-Jewish regulations issued by the occupiers. Soon after, they also took part in the liquidation of the ghettos and in the extermination of Polish Jews.

Several years ago, while writing about the Holocaust in southeastern Poland, I became increasingly aware of the number of robberies, rapes, and murders committed by Polish policemen on their hapless Jewish victims. The scale of this complicity was astounding: The efficiency of the blue-clad murderers matched that of their German overseers—the gendarmes and the Schupo (Schutzpolizei, the German uniformed protection police). In her book *Our People: Discovering Lithuania's Hidden Holocaust*, Lithuanian author Rūta Vanagaitė described the participation of ordinary Lithuanians in the murder of their Jewish neighbors during the Holocaust in the following words:

> *Žydšaudys* [Jew-shooter] only refers to the people who pulled the trigger. But I think we need to invent additional words to cover the other categories of those who particpated in the process: like *žydgaudys* (Jew-catcher)...and *žydvedys* (transporter of Jews), and maybe even *žydvagis* (thief of Jewish belongings).[1]

1 Rūta Vanagaitė and Efraim Zuroff, *Our People: Discovering Lithuania's Hidden Holocaust* (Lanham, MA: Rowman & Littlefield, 2020), p. 110.

There is no doubt that the expressions used by Vanagaitė—*žydšaudys*, *žydgaudys*, *žydvedys*, and *žydvagis*—also describe the attitudes and behavior of Polish policemen during the war.

Another surprising observation about these policemen concerned their peculiar modus operandi. The Polish policemen secretly murdered the Jews—oftentimes their former neighbors, people whom they knew well from the old times—without informing their German superiors. The operations against the Jews were conducted on the policemen's own initiative and not infrequently as a gesture of solidarity with members of the local community who pleaded with the Blue policemen to remove the cumbersome and unwanted "citizens of Jewish origin," to quote the language of postwar court documents. More often than not, the Germans were kept in the dark. It was not that they would have objected to the murders, but once a report about a discovered or executed Jew had been filed, the response of the Germans was hard to predict. They could, for instance, inquire about the identity of the Poles involved in sheltering Jews, or they could ask questions about property left behind by the victims. Most often, this property had already been transferred into more "deserving" Polish hands. Undoubtedly, it was much more expedient to "solve" the problem without informing the Germans.

Facing the courts after the war, the Polish policemen claimed that murdering Jews allowed them to shield the local peasants from German terror, and their deeds should thus be considered acts of patriotic sacrifice. They argued that once the Germans had apprehended the Jews, the occupying forces could have executed any Poles suspected of providing shelter to the Jews. The occupying forces frequently administered reprisals on a collective basis, bringing suffering to several households or even to the entire village. According to the policemen, the murder of Jews was a form of self-defense by the Polish collective and an attempt to preserve the national substance.

A third surprise stemming from the study of such wartime documentation concerns the dual role of the Polish Blue policemen and their colleagues, officers of the Polish Criminal Police (Polnische Kriminalpolizei in German, and Polska Policja

Kryminalna in Polish).[2] Often, the murderers of the Jews simultaneously played an important role in various organizations of the Polish Underground State or in the Polish resistance. Some of them served in the mainstream Home Army (Armia Krajowa, AK), while others belonged to the left-leaning People's Army (Armia Ludowa, AL) or the nationalist National Armed Forces (Narodowe Siły Zbrojne, NSZ). All of them were ready to sacrifice their lives and die for an independent Poland. According to many policemen as well as other members of the resistance, killing the Jews and fighting for a free Poland were not, however, mutually exclusive concepts. As the popular saying in Poland goes, "Hitler committed frightful crimes, but at least he freed Poland of the Jews!" And if Hitler himself could not complete this task, one had to help him. Józef Górski, a fervent nationalist and an estate owner from the village of Ceranów near Treblinka, wrote the following:

> Today's propaganda presents Jews as part of the Polish nation and claims that the Germans murdered 6 million Poles. This is just another lie among the many we are fed. The Jews have never been Poles. For centuries they have been a polyp on our organism, which, due to our impotence, we have been unable to get rid of.[3]

Another issue is the scale of the involvement of the Blue Police in *Aktionen* conducted against the Jews. From the very first months of the occupation, the Blue Police was one of the most important instruments used for the implementation of German anti-Jewish policies and measures. The fate of the Jews largely depended on the zeal with which the Polish police officers enforced these regulations, most important among them were the new laws forcing Jews to wear white armbands with a blue Star of David, a host of restrictions placed on their mobility, measures against smuggling food from the "Aryan" side into the ghettos, and other

2 The Polnische Kriminalpolizei is also referred to as the Polish Kripo in this volume.

3 Józef Górski, "At the Turn of History," ed. by Jan Grabowski, *Holocaust Studies and Materials: Journal of the Polish Center for Holocaust Research* (2008), p. 310.

regulations instituted by the occupying forces. Without question, these policies can be described as a prelude to the Holocaust. This leads to another question: To what extent were the Polish policemen responsible for the detection of Jews in hiding on the Aryan side?

The policemen, however, were not acting without local assistance. They performed their duties within a well-defined social context, and they relied on networks of informers as well as on the assistance given by the voluntary firefighters' brigades and the omnipresent bystanders. A study of police activities in the period following the liquidation of the ghettos reveals the growing importance of Polish police officers as well as other local volunteers in detecting Jews in hiding. Without Polish assistance, the Germans would have been unable to achieve their goals, and the occupation authorities were fully aware of the crucial importance of such local participation. Alongside Jewish testimonies, official declarations and documents produced by the German authorities testify to that effect. As long as the Jews remained in the ghettos, had to produce documents identifying them as Jews, and were branded as Jews, the Germans' task was simple. From the occupier's perspective, however, once the Jews had fled to the Aryan side, they became largely invisible. In order to detect them, one needed to use different tools, all of which necessitated the knowledge of cultural codes, accents, customs, everyday practice, and experience and all of which the Germans simply lacked. The Polish policemen and their helpers had all these tools at their disposal, and they used them with frightful efficiency.

From historical literature on the war and the occupation in Poland, one frequently learns that those who blackmailed and murdered the Jews were outcasts from the criminalized margins of society. Through these acts of collaboration, many historians argue that these evil people placed themselves outside the Polish national community. In other words, they should not be considered Poles. It is a very convenient line of reasoning that allows one to shed the heavy burden of tragic history. It is also a road to nowhere. Here, in this research, one can find villains among the people who, before the war, enjoyed enviable social respect and exercised important functions in public life. After the war, these people often returned to their important positions and enjoyed a high level of social recognition and support. When some of them had to face justice, their neighbors and friends signed letters for the courts by the hundreds in their defense. Meanwhile, under the occupation, these same people committed horrifying crimes against the Jews. What does this tell us about the policemen in question? What does it tell us about the people who later testified on their behalf? Is this a phenomenon that will allow us to better understand the moral condition of Polish society during and after the war?

These are considered to be some of the most disturbing aspects of wartime history, and this persuaded me to devote several years of research to the involvement of the Polish police in the "Final Solution to the Jewish Question" in Poland. For obvious reasons and much to the historians' chagrin, the policemen themselves were reluctant to talk about this part of their professional life. The wartime official police correspondence has been very poorly preserved, and the complete records of police stations amount to no more than a handful. There is no doubt that the police officers deliberately destroyed most of the records at the time of the German withdrawal at the end of the war. To fill in the gaps, one must look for the dispersed records of German and Polish institutions that interacted or overlapped with the Blue Police. The archival evidence is further corroborated by eyewitness accounts of both Poles and Jews. Finally, taking all these sources together, we face a palimpsest of memory constructed of different layers of descriptions, sometimes decades removed from one another.

The focus of this book is clearly defined and deals with the work of Polish policemen during the war, something that had a direct impact on the fate of the Jews under the occupation. A reader seeking an exhaustive overview of the wartime history of the Polish police will be disappointed. By the same token, the involvement of policemen in the resistance or their actions against the ethnically construed notion of Polish society shall receive little attention. These issues have been rather well-addressed—not by chance—in existing literature. Importantly, any discussion of the Polish police must entail more than a cursory look at their masters and minders, the German police. A particularly significant role in the extermination of the Polish Jews was played by the Polish Criminal Police and to a lesser extent by the voluntary firefighting brigades. The phenomenon of their involvement in the German genocidal policies has never been previously discussed in historical literature. Therefore, both organizations will find themselves at the focus of our analysis. At the same time, a study of the Polish police cannot overlook the Jüdischer Ordnungsdienst (the Jewish Order Service or the Jewish police), a force that was supervised directly by the Polish Blue Police.

This book is structured chronologically and follows the evolution of terror, which marked the successive stages of the Jewish tragedy. From this perspective, the German decisions regarding the policies of extermination—initially announced and then later implemented—will be of paramount importance. The initial thrust of German policies was an attempt to undermine, erode, and finally destroy the economic foundations of the Jewish community. This early attack on Jewish property started right after the conquest of Poland and gained momentum in early 1940. The Blue Police played a pivotal role in enforcing these German regulations.

The second period—the enslavement of the Jews—was closely associated with the establishment of the ghettos throughout the Generalgouvernement, and most of the larger ones were created between the fall of 1940 and early 1941. In the fall of 1941, the Germans issued the Third Regulation Concerning the Limitations of the Right of Residence in the Generalgouvernement, which introduced the death penalty for anyone who left the "closed Jewish quarter," as the ghettos were known in German bureaucratese. This time too, the Polish Blue Police was tasked with the enforcement of this law. In fact, the responsibilities of the Polish officers increased, and from November 1941, they began executing Jews who had been apprehended outside the ghettos, in accordance with this new law.

The third and final period of the destruction of the Polish Jews began with the liquidation of the ghettos in mid-1942. The liquidation of the ghettos—referred to by the Germans as

Aktionen—were bloody, public affairs, with the involvement of millions of Poles as spectators and, not infrequently, as active participants. Quite literally and without any poetic license, blood was running down the streets of Polish towns and villages during the *Aktionen*. According to recent studies, between 10 and 20 percent of Polish Jews were murdered during such *Aktionen*, and in some ghettos—in the Lublin district of the Generalgouvernement, for instance—the percentage of those killed in situ was as much as 50 percent.[4] The Blue Police, which in the meantime became an important cog in the German machinery of extermination, was involved in practically all the *Aktionen* in the Generalgouvernement.[5] They served in various capacities, from initially isolating the ghettos from the outside as well as hunting down Jews during the liquidations and driving the victims toward concentration points, to searching the empty ghettos for hidden survivors and pulling them out of bunkers and hideouts. But there were cases when the Blue policemen conducted liquidations on their own, without any major German involvement. All aspects of the participation of Polish policemen in the *Aktionen* will be included in the discussion about the *Judenjagd* (the hunt for Jews who sought refuge on the Aryan side).

Three issues will be discussed beyond the chronological order of this book: the role of the Blue Police in the extermination of Warsaw's Jews; the specific role of the Polish Criminal Police during this time; and the involvement of the voluntary firefighters in the Holocaust. The case of Warsaw requires a separate discussion due to the sheer number of Jews incarcerated in this ghetto as well as the significant police forces deployed in the area and tasked with the supervision of the largest closed quarter—to use the official

4 Jan Grabowski and Barbara Engelking, eds., *Night without End: The Fate of Jews in German-Occupied Poland* (Bloomington and Jerusalem: Indiana University Press and Yad Vashem, 2022). See in particular the following chapter: Alina Skibińska, "Biłgoraj County," pp. 55–108.

5 The situation was different in the district of Galicia—which was incorporated into the Generalgouvernement in August 1941 after the invasion of the Soviet Union—where the Germans established the Ukrainian Auxiliary Police (Ukrainische Hilfspolizei). Polish officers served here, however, in the ranks of the Criminal Police. This a topic will be discussed at length in chapter 7.

German nomenclature—in Europe. The importance of Warsaw is further exacerbated by the number of Jews who fled to the Aryan side of the city in July and August 1942. Thousands more fled during the liquidation of the ghetto in the so-called *Grossaktion Warschau* (the Great Action in Warsaw), a phenomenon that continued during and after the uprising in the ghetto in April 1943. Another thematic chapter looks at the Polish Criminal Police, an organization that is practically absent from historical literature but was nevertheless one of the most important elements of the German strategy of extermination. Finally, the thematic discussion will also include the role of both the Polish voluntary and professional firefighters in the implementation of the "Final Solution." This issue has not been studied at any length by historians, although, in reality, the firefighters often provided support to the police or even acted in their stead.

Note on Terminology

Throughout this book, certain terminology is used in an effort to remain historically accurate and because they are well-known terms in the field. In some cases, these terms may have been used by the Nazi regime to mask its true intentions. The use of such terms in this book are in no way indicative of the author's endorsement of such terminology.

Acknowledgements

There were many people who made this book possible. First, I would like to express gratitude to my mother, who was not only my first reader but also someone who lived in Warsaw under German occupation for five years and helped me to view the past from an eyewitness perspective.

My thanks go to Jarek Kurski, who came up with the title of this book somewhere midway between Kamloops and Hope in British Columbia, and to Kasia, who was relentless in ensuring the completion of this study. I am equally grateful to my graduate students from the University of Ottawa, whose questions forced me to rethink and revisit issues that I had long since considered solved.

As the former Ina Levine Invitational Scholar at the United States Holocaust Memorial Museum, I fondly recall the generosity of my friends Jürgen Matthäus, Elizabeth Anthony, Jacek Nowakowski, and Teresa Pollin. I am equally indebted to my friends at Yad Vashem: Yehuda Bauer, Havi Dreifuss, Robert Rozett, Dan Michman, and David Silberklang, who are always there to help.

I would like to recognize the contribution of my Polish colleagues, the historians Jan Tomasz Gross, Jerzy Kochanowski, Łukasz Krzyżanowski, Dariusz Libionka, Krzysztof Persak, Szymon Rudnicki, Anna Zapalec, and Marcin Zaremba, who agreed to read a draft of this work in the original Polish, and gave me their insightful comments. The remaining errors are, of course, the sole responsibility of the author.

My work would not have been possible without the wonderful assistance of so many archivists in Poland, Israel, the United States, Germany, and France, who went above and beyond their professional duties to steer me toward the pertinent collections and documents.

I would like to sincerely thank the entire staff of Yad Vashem Publications for their highly professional work and to acknowledge the extraordinary editorial effort of Adina Mendelsohn who skillfully transformed the English manuscript into a book.

I am deeply grateful to the Social Sciences and Humanities Research Council of Canada, which has generously supported my research over the years, and I also wish to express my gratitude to the University of Ottawa, which has recognized the value of historical research for over three decades. Finally, I would like to thank my friends and colleagues in the Department of History at the University of Ottawa, who offered their help and encouragement when the Polish memory wars arrived on our doorstep.

Map of the Generalgouvernement, September 1941

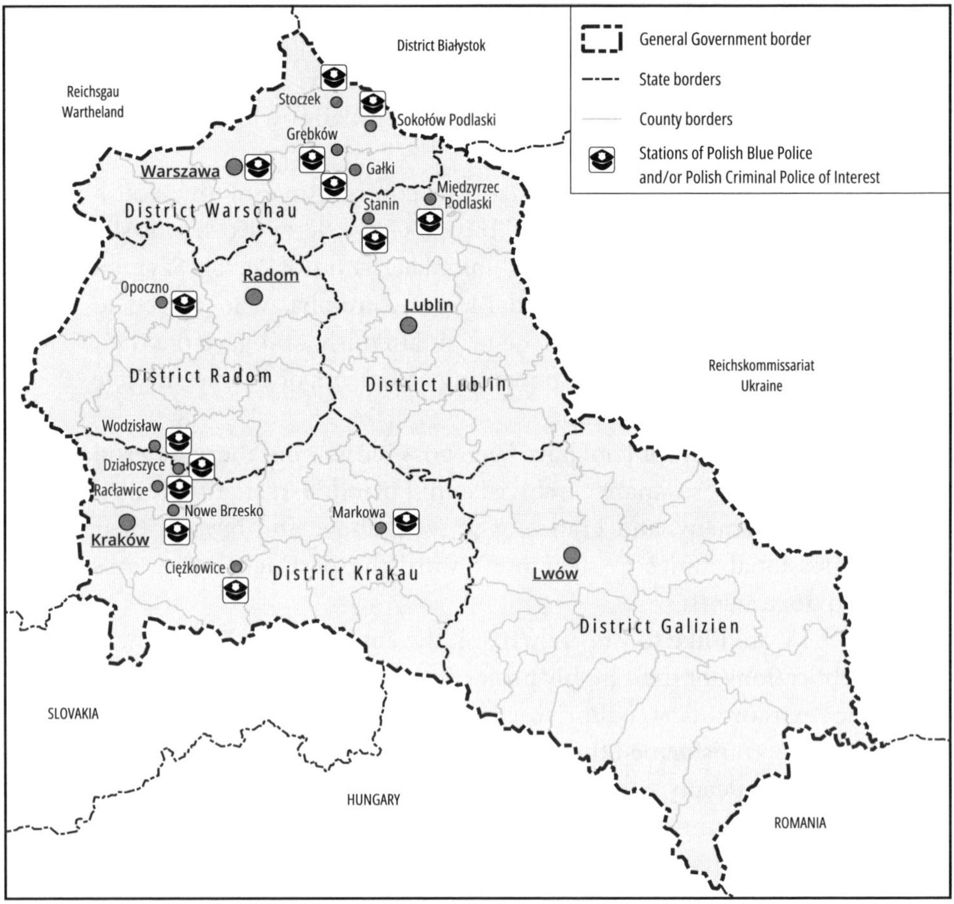

Map created by Zbigniew Gałęza.

Chapter One

The Beginning: September 1939

In the summer of 1939, the Polish State Police numbered 870 ranking officers and 28,000 constables, serving in more than 2,700 police stations across Poland.[1] The police force also included the Investigative Service, which was a specialized plainclothes division.[2] The ethnic makeup of the police corps—not an irrelevant issue in this study—was almost homogenous and entirely dominated by Poles. In 1923, 95 percent of the officer corps identified themselves as "Poles, Roman Catholics," and among the lower ranks, the ratio was as high as 97 percent. There was also a small number of Greek Catholics and Protestants. Among the over 1,000 police officers of rank, there were only twelve representatives of mosaic faith.[3] As far as the Jews were concerned, the only way to advance through the ranks was through assimilation and conversion. The rare neophytes who had managed to enter the police ranks—such as the Lublin-based Józef

1 Robert Litwiński, *Korpus policji w II Rzeczpospolitej: Służba i życie prywatne* (Lublin: UMCS, 2007), pp. 99, 104; Zbigniew Siemak, "Policja kryminalna II Rzeczypospolitej: Powstanie, organizacja, kadry i metody pracy," *Zagadnienia Społeczne*, 1 (2014), pp. 184–205; Adam Hempel, *Pogrobowcy klęski: Rzecz o policji "granatowej" w Generalnym Gubernatorstwie 1939–1945* (Warsaw: Państwowe Wydawnictwo Naukowe, 1990), p. 29.

2 For more on this topic, see Andrzej Misiuk, *Policja Państwowa 1919–1939: Powstanie, organizacja, kierunki działania* (Warsaw: Wydawnictwo Naukowe PWN, 1996), pp. 288–326.

3 Ibid., pp. 81–82.

Szeryński—often stressed their "Polishness" and demonstrated their distaste of the Jewish community from which they were estranged. Both in principle and in practice, the Polish police was made up along ethnic and religious lines, which essentially excluded minorities and placed "true" Poles first and foremost. Example came from the very top: Kordian Józef Zamorski, brigadier general of the Polish army and commander in chief of the Polish State Police, noted his thoughts in a diary. In one of many such comments made in his diary, he reported the following from the tourist destination of Zakopane on February 24, 1934:

> And everywhere Kikes, Kikes, and Kikes. This is a group, or a caste, or a race, that lives well in Poland. Fat, well-fed, smiling faces, deeply convinced about the power of their money —and this brazenness. One wants to cry out, "Heil Hitler!" In ten years' time these bastards will flood us, will strangle us, and we will be reduced to being Jewish slaves.[4]

The German invasion of Poland, which began on September 1, 1939, very quickly overwhelmed Polish defenses. In the first days of September, the police forces from western Poland started to withdraw eastward alongside the army units. Owing to the quickly deteriorating military situation and the rapid advancement of the German forces, chaos set in. In Warsaw and Pomerania, the policemen simply stayed put. Corporal Władysław Wesołowski from the Gosławice police station in Konin County recalled after the war that "due to the total mess, the police stations disbanded and each policeman [on his own] made his way east."[5] Officers from the northern parts of Poland were cut off by the rapid advance of the Wehrmacht, while their colleagues from Warsaw remained on duty, following the orders of Colonel Marian Kozielewski, commander of

4 Kordian Józef Zamorski, *Dzienniki (1930–1938)*, ed. by Robert Litwiński and Marek Sioma (Warsaw and Łomianki: Inst. Józefa Piłsudskiego and Wydawn LTW, 2011), p. 262. Zamorski was appointed commander of the Polish police in January 1935.

5 Deposition of Władysław Wesołowski, April 6, 1949, Archiwum Narodowe w Krakowie (ANKr), Sąd Apelacyjny w Krakowie (SAKr), 1014/IVK/116/50, p. 10.

the local police force.[6] On September 10, 1939, as the foundations of the Polish state were beginning to crumble, the police forces were militarized. However, the new order had little impact, since, for the most part, the central command had lost communication with the loose groups of policemen withdrawing eastward.

In certain areas, the police forces joined the military units and took part in the fighting against the Germans and, after September 17, 1939, also against the Red Army, which had attacked from the east. The September campaign cost the Polish police dearly: Between 2,500 to 3,000 officers were killed, and 10,000 were taken prisoner by the Soviets.[7] From among these prisoners, 6,000 were later taken to the infamous Ostaszków POW camp and murdered in the spring of 1940.[8] Some Polish policemen from the Soviet-occupied zone later made their way back through the cordon and into the Generalgouvernement. Therefore, some 10,000 Polish officers initially remained in the areas under German control.

The German Police in Poland

According to German war plans, the German police forces had a significant role to play in the attack on Poland.[9] Twenty-one

6 Piotr Majer and Andrzej Misiuk, eds., *Losy policjantów polskich po 1 września 1939* (Szczytno: Wydawnictwo Wyższa Szkoła Policji, 1996), pp. 53–70.

7 Jacek Dworzecki, "Policja w Polsce we wrześniu 1939 roku," *Zeszyt Naukowy*, 4 (2010), pp. 75–88.

8 The murder of the police officers was part of the largest mass murder of POWs in history, and it is known as the April 1940 Katyń massacre, during which the Soviets killed 22,000 Polish army officers who had been taken prisoner by the Red Army in September 1939.

9 For more information about the German police in the Generalgouvernement, see: Stanisław Biernacki and Jerzy Stoch, "Działania władz okupacyjnych (policji i administracji) w dystrykcie warszawskim przeciwko ruchowi oporu w latach 1939–1944," *Najnowsze dzieje Polski: Materiały i studia z okresu II wojny światowej*, 10 (1966), pp. 47–76; Lucjan Dobroszycki and Marek Getter, "Działanie urzędu komendanta policji i służby bezpieczeństwa w Radomiu w zakresie zwalczania ruchu oporu," *Najnowsze dzieje Polski*, 4 (1960), pp. 23–61; Włodzimierz Borodziej, *Terror i polityka: Policja niemiecka a polski ruch oporu w GG 1939–1944* (Warsaw: Instytut Wydawniczy Pax, 1985).

police battalions, which were attached to the various army groups and led by the commander of the Order Police (*Befehlshaber der Ordnungspolizei*) Kurt Daluege, were tasked with maintaining order behind the front lines. Another 8,000 policemen were drafted directly into the army in order to reinforce the military police.[10] On September 6, 1939, the first Einsatzgruppen (action groups) were deployed in occupied Polish territory in order to impose the "new German order" by way of terror. Einsatzgruppe IIB and Einsatzgruppe IV, composed of officers from the Gestapo (Geheime Staatspolizei, Secret Police), SD (Sicherheitsdienst, Security Service), and Kripo (Kriminalpolizei, Criminal Police), arrived in Warsaw on September 29, 1939.[11]

Within a few days and following the capitulation of the Polish capital, 120,000 German soldiers occupied the city and its environs.[12] The Berlin Kripo arrived in Warsaw on October 4, 1939, on the heels of the Wehrmacht and the Einsatzgruppen. Their task was to mobilize and control the local Polish police, who were deemed necessary to restore order and prevent the growing chaos in the occupied territory.[13] In November 1939, the Einsatzgruppen operating in Poland were transformed into the Commands of Security Police and Security Service (Kommandeur der Sicherheitspolizei und des SD, KdS). Each KdS was subdivided into several sections. Section IV included those in the Gestapo, and those in the Kripo were in Section V.[14]

10 Edward B. Westermann, "'Friend and Helper': German Uniformed Police Operations in Poland and the General Government," *The Journal of Military History*, 58:4 (1994), pp. 643–662.

11 Stanisław Biernacki, "Organizacja i metody działania policji hitlerowskiej w dystrykcie warszawskim," in *Stan i perspektywy badań w zakresie zbrodni hitlerowskich: Materiały z konferencji naukowej w dn. 27–28 kwietnia 1970*, vol. 1 (Warsaw, 1973), p. 194. See also Jochen Böhler, Klaus-Michael Mallmann, and Jürgen Matthäus, *Einsatzgruppen w Polsce* (Warsaw: Bellona, 2008).

12 Warsaw surrendered on September 28, 1939, after a three-week siege.

13 Report on the takeover of the police, September 6, 1939, Office of the Governor of the Warsaw District, The SS and Police Leader for the Warsaw District, 1939–1944, vol. 155, Archiwum Miasta Stołecznego Warszawy (AMSW), files 13–14.

14 The structure of the KdS was finally established after a major reorganization in May 1941. See Biernacki, "Organizacja i metody działania policji hitlerowskiej w dystrykcie warszawskim," p. 196.

At the same time, the Germans began to consolidate the administrative structures of the occupied areas. On October 26, 1939, by Hitler's decree, most of central Poland—excluding areas that had been incorporated directly into the Reich—was transformed into a new state-like entity known as the Generalgouvernement. Referred to by Governor General Hans Frank as *Nebenland des Reiches* (literally translated as "the land adjacent to the Reich"), the Generalgouvernement was a buffer state based on terror, and it was expected to be little more than a source of cheap labor, a supplier of agricultural staples for the hungry German population, and a source of raw natural resources necessary for German industry. The police structures that were developed and established in the Generalgouvernement mirrored those of the Reich but with some modifications. According to the German model, the police forces were divided into two sections: The Security Police (Sicherheitspolizei, Sipo) and the Order Police (Ordnungspolizei, Orpo). The latter included the Protective Police (Schutzpolizei, Schupo), which was deployed in the cities, and the Gendarmerie, which was stationed in rural areas and in smaller towns with a population under 5,000. This structure—copied from the Reich—was extended to the western parts of Poland that were annexed to Germany and known as Eingegliederte Ostgebiete.

Meanwhile in the Generalgouvernement, the German model underwent several changes that took into account the local situation. First of all, it was necessary for the occupiers to make use of the Polish police to rein in the exploding banditry and common criminality that had become a plague in the chaotic conditions following the collapse of the Polish state apparatus. The 5,000 Orpo officers who were initially deployed in the Generalgouvernement lacked the trust of the local population and were unable to communicate in Polish, and they were clearly unable to fulfill the tasks with which they had been charged.[15] Friedrich-Wilhelm Krüger, the Higher Leader of the

15 Peter Black, "Indigenous Collaboration in the Government General: The Case of the Sonderdienst," in Pieter M. Judson and Marsha L. Rozenblit, eds., *Constructing Nationalities in East Central Europe* (New York: Berghahn Books, 2005), pp. 243–266.

SS and Police (*Höherer SS- und Polizeiführer,* HSSPF) in the Generalgouvernement, admitted that much and informed Hans Frank that while the German police could maintain order in big cities, the situation in rural areas would deteriorate quickly without the deployment of the Polish police.

It was only in the summer of 1940 when the Orpo deployed thirteen Gendarmerie companies to the Generalgouvernement, sending one platoon to each county. These were the basic Gendarmerie units that, over time, assumed control over the rural stations of the Polish police. In May 1940, Hans Frank established the Special Service (Sonderdienst), a paramilitary organization for the *Volksdeutsche* (ethnic Germans and former Polish citizens). The Sonderdienst—whose ranks never rose above 2,500 men—failed to play a major role in the German terror apparatus. Owing to their excellent knowledge of the Polish language, many of its members were later transferred to the Blue Police or were the liaisons with the Polish officers.[16] While the Sonderdiensts spoke perfect Polish, their knowledge of German was, however, much more problematic. The German officials complained loudly that many *Volksdeutsche* were unable to cobble together a simple phrase in the official language of the Generalgouvernement. Julian Piwowarski, the former mayor of Miechów, a town north of Kraków, did not mince words when describing the members of the Sonderdienst: "On March 30, 1940, they established a German auxiliary police force, recruited from among the Polish Germans.... This police, other than getting drunk, performed no police duties and the only thing they knew how to do was to beat up the Jews whenever they encountered them."[17]

16 Friedrich Wilhelm Siebert, "Die Verwaltung im Generalgouvernement unter besonderer Berücksichtigung der Tätigkeit der Hauptabteilung Innere Velwaltung" in Josef Bühler, ed., *Das Generalgouvernement: Seine Verwaltung und seine Wirtschaft. Sammlung von Vorträgen der ersten wissenschaftlichen Vorträgsreihe der Verwaltungsakademie des Generagouvernements* (Krakow: Burgverl, 1943), pp. 75–88

17 Julian Piwowarski testimony, Archiwum Żydowski Instytut Historyczny (ŻIH), 301/6124.

The Polish Blue Police: The Polnische Polizei im Generalgouvernement

The decree concerning the establishment of the Generalgouvernement was signed by Hitler on October 12, 1939, and it was published twelve days later.[18] Soon after, Hans Frank issued executive orders regarding the "reconstruction of the administration."[19] On October 30, 1939, HSSPF Krüger issued a regulation ordering all Polish policemen to report for duty in the newly reorganized police force. Failure to comply carried harsh penalties.[20] The Polnische Polizei im Generalgouvernement (the Polish Police of the Generalgouvernement) was established on December 17, 1939, pursuant to the regulation issued by Governor General Hans Frank. HSSPF Krüger's directive brought about the desired effect, and as early as January 1940, the ranks of the Blue Police swelled to more than 10,000 officers, including 1,173 agents, or plainclothes policemen, who had belonged to the Investigative Service before the war.[21] The Germans purged senior ranks, kept most of the rank-and-file officers, and maintained the core prewar internal structures of the Polish police. Overall authority over the new organization was placed in the hands of the commander of the Order Police.

The Polish resistance and the government-in-exile—residing in Angers, France, at the time—authorized the Polish officers to

18 "Erlass des Führers und Reichskanzlers über die Verwaltung der besetzten polnischen Gebiete" (Führer and Reich's Chancellor's Decree concerning the Administration of the Occupied Polish Territories), *Reichsgesetzblatt*, part 1, October 24, 1939.

19 "Erste Verordnung über den Aufbau der Verwaltung der besetzten polnischen Gebiete" (First Decree on the Establishment of an Administration for the Occupied Polish Territories), *Verordnungsblatt des Generalgouverneurs für die Besetzten Polnischen Gebiete* (Official Gazette of the Governor General for the Occupied Polish Territories), October 26, 1939.

20 "Aufruf des Höheren SS- und Polizeiführers im Generalgouvernement für die besetzen polnischen Gebiete" (Announcement for [the residents of] the Occupied Polish Territories by the Higher SS- and Police Leader in the Generalgouvernement), *Verordnungsblatt des Generalgouverneurs für die Besetzten Polnischen Gebiete*, November 2, 1939.

21 Hempel, *Pogrobowcy klęski*, pp. 38–39.

report for duty with the Blue Police, without running the risk of being branded as traitors of the Polish nation. This policy shielded honest policemen from German reprisals, while it also gave the resistance insights into the evolving German strategy of terror. Moreover, the police was also crucial in providing the Polish population with a sense of security by fighting banditry and common crime that is always associated with the breakdown of social and political order. On top of this, the officers received instructions from the underground sources to do their best to shield the population from acts of reprisal planned by the occupying forces. All of these so-called reactivated policemen were also warned to always think of the "well-being of the Polish nation." While former policemen were thus authorized to join the "Blues," the resistance took a dim view of all the young recruits who wanted to start their police careers during the war and volunteered to join the service.[22]

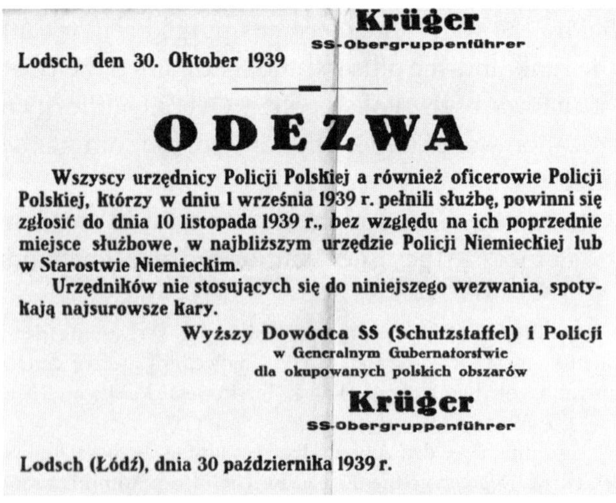

Krüger
SS-Obergruppenführer

Lodsch, den 30. Oktober 1939

ODEZWA

Wszyscy urzędnicy Policji Polskiej a również oficerowie Policji Polskiej, którzy w dniu 1 września 1939 r. pełnili służbę, powinni się zgłosić do dnia 10 listopada 1939 r., bez względu na ich poprzednie miejsce służbowe, w najbliższym urzędzie Policji Niemieckiej lub w Starostwie Niemieckim.

Urzędników nie stosujących się do niniejszego wezwania, spotykają najsurowsze kary.

Wyższy Dowódca SS (Schutzstaffel) i Policji
w Generalnym Gubernatorstwie
dla okupowanych polskich obszarów

Krüger
SS-Obergruppenführer

Lodsch (Łódź), dnia 30 października 1939 r.

The order of Friedrich-Wilhelm Krüger calling upon all former Polish policemen to report for duty in the Blue Police, October 30, 1939. Courtesy of Jerzy Kochanowski.

22 Robert Litwiński, "Policja granatowa w okupacyjnej Warszawie w obronie bezpieczeństwa i porządku publicznego: Od podległości wobec okupanta do współpracyz Polskim Państwem Podziemnym," in Robert Spałek, ed., *Porządek publiczny i bezpieczeństwo w okupacyjnej Warszawie* (Warsaw: IPN, 2018), p. 92.

The officers of the prewar Polish police joined the Blue Police in a variety of ways. Often, they would fill in a form in their local precinct or station and apply to their former commanding officer for reinstatement. Those others who found themselves in territories annexed to the Reich went through a longer administrative process.

Before the war, Captain Józef Wraubek served in the Kraków police. In November 1939, after several weeks of exile caused by the military campaign, he returned home. Right away, he established contact with his superiors, Colonel Wojciech Stano and Colonel Roman Sztaba, both of whom had been charged with the organization of the Blue Police in the Kraków district by the Germans. Despite initial doubts, Wraubek learned that serving the Germans was not tantamount to treason. He later noted the following in his memoir: "[Colonel] Sztaba pointed out to me that he organized the Blue Police on direct orders from the resistance and from the Polish government-in-exile."[23] The police, argued Sztaba, was to serve only the interests of Polish society and remain in close contact with the Union of Armed Struggle (Związek Walki Zbrojnej, ZWZ), the most important organization in the rapidly growing resistance movement.

Captain Alfons Piniecki, who served with the Poznań police until 1939, joined the "Blues" in a different manner. Right after the Germans entered the city, Piniecki was arrested by the Gestapo and held hostage.[24] When he was released in November 1939, he received a proposition that was hard to reject: to serve in the Blue Police or face an unlimited term in a concentration camp. At least this is the self-serving version given by Piniecki after the war, while he was trying to clear his name. However, there is no doubt that the Germans had a vested interest in beefing up the ranks of the Blue Police in the Generalgouvernement with policemen drafted from areas annexed to the Reich where the Polish police had been abolished. On the other hand, for many policemen—especially

23 Józef Wraubek, *Na Podhalu* (author's archive, undated manuscript).

24 Personnel files of the former employees of the Polish Police, prison guards and border guards, 1946–1952, Archiwum Akt Nowych (AAN), Ministerstwo Sprawiedliwości, 1656. The files have no individual archival classification, they have been arranged in alphabetical order.

the older and high-ranking officers—unemployment following the dissolution of the Polish police in the annexed territories was definitely a strong motivation for relocation. Piniecki completed the required application, and together with a large group of Poznań officers, he was transferred to Kraków. Initially, he took over the VI precinct in Podgórze, and later, as a fluent German speaker, he became a liaison officer between the Blue Police and their German overseers from the Schupo.

Captain Alfons Piniecki, 1947.
AAN, Ministerstwo
Sprawiedliwości, 1656.

Alfons Piniecki arrived in Kraków together with his son Henryk, who was to follow in his father's footsteps by choosing a career as a policeman. Four years later, the Home Army (AK) intelligence unit turned its attention to both Henryk and Alfons Piniecki. In a document titled "The List of PP [Polish police] Officers and Constables, Lackeys of the German Occupant," we read that "Piniecki, Alfons, police captain, Kraków, transportation unit, Franciszkańska Street. Takes bribes, blackmailer, notorious alcoholic. Accused by internal affairs of taking bribes and extortion. His twenty-year-old son shot eight Jews during the liquidation of the ghetto."[25] In order to understand the career path of this high-ranking officer of the Polish Blue Police and the life choices of his son, it is essential to know more about the realities of German occupation. Both Alfons and Henryk Piniecki will be discussed further in the section of this volume about the liquidation of the Kraków ghetto.

Czesław Zander was born in the Poznań area and began his career in the Polish police in 1920.[26] Before the war, he served without distinction in one of the precincts in Bydgoszcz. In September 1939, he and several other officers fled toward Warsaw, where he was soon taken prisoner by the Germans. Upon his release, he returned home, only to be re-arrested by the Gestapo under suspicion of cruelties against ethnic Germans allegedly committed during the so-called Bloody Sunday.[27]

Czesław Zander (left), prewar.
ANKr, SAKr, 979/IVK/230/4.

25 "The List of Polish Police Officers and Constables, Lackeys of the German Occupant," December 1, 1944, Archiwum Instytutu Pamięci Narodowej Oddział w Krakowie (AIPN Kr), 075/1, vol. 41, p. 284.

26 Interrogation of Czesław Zander, ANKr, SAKr, 979/IVK/230/49, pp. 5–9.

27 Bloody Sunday (*Bromberger Blutsonntag* in German). A term used in Nazi propaganda to describe the violent clashes between the Polish authorities and

Cleared of charges, Zander received an offer to resume his police career in the Generalgouvernement. In the fall of 1941, he arrived in Tarnów, where he reported to Major Ostrowski, the commander of the local Blue Police detachment. Zander took an oath, and upon receiving his new uniform, he went to Ciężkowice, a small town located halfway between Tarnów and Nowy Sącz in the south of the Generalgouvernement. Constable Zander will be encountered again in this volume on duty in Ciężkowice during the hunt for the Jews (*Judenjagd*), which started in his area in the fall of 1942.

Corporal Piotr Kulisz served in Łódź. When the Germans arrived and disbanded the Polish police, Kulisz found himself in a similar situation to that of Captain Piniecki in Poznań. He moved to the Generalgouvernement, and in January 1940, he reported to the Końskie police station. While he was filling in the admission form, he described his previous police career. Later, when he had received the required approval from the chief of the Końskie police, he was officially admitted into the ranks of the Polish Blue Police.

Over time, these admission forms became more elaborate. Starting in late 1940, each candidate had to provide proof of his Aryan descent. The declaration of racial purity included the following statement: "In compliance with the regulations, I attest and assure that there are no known circumstances which would indicate that: (a) my parents or grandparents on either side are of Jewish origin; (b) my (future) wife's parents or grandparents are of Jewish origin."[28] The oath—poorly translated at the time from German into Polish—that was taken by the candidates enlisting in the Blue Police reads: "I solemnly declare to loyally fulfill my duties, to display obedience to the German administration and its

members of the German minority who were suspected of shooting at the Polish soldiers as well as other acts of sabotage shortly before the German forces entered the city.

28 Application form, Personnel file of Piotr Kulisz, Archiwum Instytutu Pamięci Narodowej (Archive of the Institute of National Remembrance, AIPN), GK 656/6; Personnel file of Stanisław Banaś, Declaration, AIPN, GK 656/6; ANKr, Komenda Policji Polskiej w Krakowie, vol. 7, p. 20.

representatives. Furthermore, I declare that I am neither obligated to nor bound by any other oath of allegiance given to the former Polish state or its institutions or any political organization."[29] Indeed, as far as this obedience to the German administration was concerned, some Polish officers took their enthusiasm too far. In April 1940, the commander of the Miechów police warned his subordinates that the Nazi salute (*Hitlergruss*) was a distinct privilege of the Germans and that any Polish officers reported doing it would face serious consequences, including a prison sentence.[30]

In line with German design, the Blue Police became a community-based organization, which meant that the local commune and county authorities took charge of salaries and other costs associated with its operations. The posts, stations, and precincts of the Blue Police were usually located in public buildings, which meant that the local authorities were forced to pay their rent, too.[31] This transfer of financial responsibilities allowed the Germans to maximize profits while incurring little expense. The lack of ammunition, old equipment, badly torn uniforms, poor salaries, and—during the later period—the growing threat of reprisals from the resistance all conspired to complicate the lives of the officers. These difficulties were not only limited to rural detachments but also extended to the major cities, including Warsaw.

On March 16, 1942, the commander of the XIV precinct (Warsaw-Praga) complained to his superiors that his station was left without power for three weeks, his appeals to the power station had born no fruit, and his people had to work using flashlights and that, in these circumstances, escapes from the station's holding pens were inevitable.[32] In March 1942, Colonel Aleksander Reszczyński,

29 Service oath, File of Stanisław Banaś, AIPN, GK 656/6, ANKr, Komenda Policji Polskiej w Krakowie, vol. 7, p. 22.

30 County commander to police stations, ANKr, Posterunek Policji Polskiej w Brzesku Nowym (PPPBrzN), vol. 2, p. 12.

31 A letter by a clerk of the Financial Department, January 24, 1941, AMSW, Starostwo Powiatowe Warszawskie, 1136, pp. 3–4.

32 Letter from the commander of the XIV precinct, March 16, 1942, AMSW, II Komisariat PP, file 11, p. 9.

the commander of the Warsaw police forces, gave the chiefs of all the precincts a stern warning about vigilance and frugality, including saving every sheet of paper. He wrote, "Gentlemen who will forget about it risk very unpleasant consequences."[33] A special message was circulated by the commander of the Blue Police in the spring of 1942, which alerted station commanders to the fact that officers' shoes should be resoled no more than once every three months. It also reminded them that with the coming of spring, the constables would shed their heavy service overcoats, which would most likely reveal their shabby shirts and pants, and this, in turn, would expose the police to ridicule and lead to a loss of respect in society.[34] The police authorities tried to make do with the available resources. In May 1943, the Miechów County commander warned that given the shortage of uniforms, deceased policemen should not be buried in government-issued clothing.[35] Exceptions were made in the case of officers killed in the line of duty. Others were issued the recycled uniforms of their deceased comrades. The problems concerning basic equipment lasted until the end of the war.

In order to deal with some of these shortages, the police authorities had recourse to fines, levies, and extortion, which placed a disproportionate burden on the Jews, the most fragile and exposed segment of Polish society. The Judenrat (Jewish Council) in Otwock, a town southeast of Warsaw, received a suggestion to provide the Polish police with bicycles and high leather boots. At the same time, the local commander of the German Gendarmerie detachment requested an expensive fur coat.[36] Numerous other cases of similar extortions and blackmail will be addressed later in the book.

33 Letter from the commander Warsaw police forces, March 13, 1942, AMSW, II Komisariat PP, file 11, p. 12.

34 Minutes of the meeting of the police stations' chiefs, March 16, 1942, AMSW, II Komisariat PP, file 11, pp. 52, 54.

35 Daily orders of Miechów County police commissioner to the local police stations, May 7, 1943, ANKr, PPPBrzN, vol. 9.

36 Calel Perechodnik, *Am I a Murderer? Testament of a Jewish Ghetto Policeman*, ed. and trans. by Frank Fox (Boulder: Westview Press, 1996), p. 49.

Ranks and Salaries of the Blue Police Officers, November 28, 1939[37]

Rank (German)	Rank (Polish)	Monthly salary (zloty)	US/UK rank equivalent
Wachtmeister	Posterunkowy	190 zł.	Police officer/ Constable
Hauptwachtmeister	Starszy posterunkowy	215 zł.	Police officer/ Constable
Polizeimeister	Przodownik	240 zł.	Detective
Polizeiobermeister	Starszy Przodownik	260 zł.	Sergeant
Polizeileutnant	Aspirant	360 zł.	Lieutenant/ Inspector
Polizeioberleutnant	Podkomisarz	405 zł.	Lieutenant
Polizeihauptmann	Komisarz	495 zł.	Captain/Chief Inspector
Polizeimajor	Nadkomisarz	675 zł.	Commander
Polizeioberstleutnant	Podinspektor	750 zł.	Chief/ Superintendent

Given the high wartime prices, the policemen's salaries were unimpressive, to say the least. In order to better grasp the purchasing power of the policemen's pay—or the lack thereof—a look at the nonregulated or black-market prices of some of the basic commodities is necessary. The following amounts refer to the period of late 1941 and early 1942. In the later period of the occupation, the prices grew rapidly. Food at regulated prices, especially meat, was often hard to come by or not available at all:

37 List of officers' salaries, 1939, AMSW, Starostwo Powiatowe Warszawskie, 1137, pp. 11–12.

> Rye bread—6.25 zlotys/kilogram; sugar—32 zł/kilogram; beans—15 zł/kilogram; peas—16 zł/kilogram; boneless horse meat—14 zł/kilogram; beef with bones—20 zł/kilogram; pork—30–32 zł/kilogram; bacon—50–52 zł/kilogram; smoked bacon—50 zł/kilogram; butter—60 zł/kilogram; potatoes—2.80 zł/kilogram.[38]

Over time, the Germans raised the base salary of Blue Police officers, but their income continued to lag behind the galloping inflation, which further diminished their purchasing power. The police salaries were barely adequate enough to allow the purchase of rationed foods at regulated prices. Shopping on the bustling black market would bankrupt not only a rank-and-file constable but also a high-ranking officer. In these circumstances, it was altogether unsurprising that corruption was rampant in the ranks of the Blue Police. The temptation to pocket 200 or 300 zlotys per transport of foodstuffs arriving in the ghetto was just too much to resist. The associated risk was limited because the "Blues" would often split the bribes with their German colleagues—the Schupo or the gendarmes. When the Germans were not present, the Polish officers could take the whole bribe for themselves.

The process of the organization and consolidation of the Blue Police was complete by the fall of 1940. It was then that the institutional structures acquired their final shape, and the Germans established mechanisms of external and internal control over their Polish subordinates. According to a report filed in Kraków on September 20, 1940, there were 409 officers serving in six precincts. These numbers are very similar to the prewar number of officers: In August 1939, 430 officers were on duty in the city. The local Blue Police found itself under the command of the previously mentioned Colonel Roman Sztaba, who had been the district commander in Łuck (Lutsk) until 1939.[39] The situation in Warsaw was no different to Kraków: By mid-1940,

38 Franciszek Wyszyński, *Dzienniki z lat 1941–1944*, ed. by Jan Grabowski and Zbigniew Ryszard Grabowski (Warsaw: Mowią Wieki-Bellona, 2007), p. 60.

39 The police personnel in the Kraków district as of September 20, 1940, AIPN Kr, 075/1, vol. 47, pp. 1–3.

the ranks of the Polish police in the former capital of Poland had swelled to prewar levels.

In such a way, the Germans established close to 1,000 posts and stations of the Blue Police across the Generalgouvernement long before the end of 1940. It is difficult, however, to determine their exact number because some stations were consolidated, while other ones were occasionally shifted from one location to another. Other posts of the former Polish police located in the territories annexed to the Reich were simply closed. Later on, after the attack on the Soviet Union, the former Polish police stations on the eastern territories were either shuttered or transformed into posts of the Ukrainian Auxiliary Police. Overall, the research presented in this book deals with data concerning 124 posts of the Blue and Criminal Police from all five districts of the Generalgouvernement.

German and Polish police officers, Tarnów, undated.
Courtesy of Marek Tomaszewski.

The Polish Criminal Police

The wartime fates of the previously mentioned Investigative Service detectives developed along different organizational lines than those of their uniformed colleagues. First of all, historians have little to say about the Polnische Kriminalpolizei under the occupation and its activities as it is one of the many blind spots in the history of World War II in Poland. While comprehensive histories of the uniformed services such as the Blue Police and the voluntary and professional firefighters are yet to be written, the role and the actions of the Polish Criminal Police are virtually absent from the literature.[40] The role of the Polish detectives in the extermination of the Polish Jews therefore remains utterly unknown, although the theme is most definitely worthy of further study.

On the eve of Polish independence, when the young republic had started to organize its police forces, the Criminal Police—known as the Investigative Service—became a specialized unit of the State Police.[41] Created in 1919, it became an integral part of the State Police, although the process of integration was fraught with tensions and interdepartmental bickering. Regional and county-level units of the Investigative Service had initially served alongside regular police officers. In some cases, the detectives answered to the local police commanders, while elsewhere they reported to ranking officers of the Investigative Service. The Investigative Service assumed its final shape in 1927 with the establishment of the Central Investigative Service, which oversaw sixteen district offices and, in turn, supervised the county-level posts.

In principle, the chiefs of this Investigative Service were placed as deputy commanders of the district police headquarters (*komenda wojewódzka*). At the same time, the Investigative Service took over most of the powers of the Political Police, which had been disbanded shortly before. Consequently, the whole organization was divided into two parts: One part was tasked with common

40 The only book that offers some information about the Polish Criminal Police is Hempel, *Pogrobowcy klęski*, pp. 124–137.

41 Misiuk, *Policja Państwowa 1919–1939*, pp. 288–326.

criminality, and the other was responsible for political issues. A transfer from regular service to the Investigative Service was considered a promotion, and such offers were given to the most promising and better-educated officers. In Lublin, for instance, the local police district commander requested that the county police chiefs "select from among the more intellectually developed officers four candidates per county to serve in the Investigative Service."[42] Once admitted into the Investigative Service, new recruits had to take several specialized courses in various police techniques. In 1933, the Investigative Service ranks numbered 2,406 agents, including 138 higher officers and 2,268 constables.[43] On the eve of the war, the Polish Criminal Police had a well-educated staff, which allowed it to penetrate the criminalized margin of society as well as the political forces considered to be hostile toward the Polish state.[44] These characteristics were soon to become highly appreciated by the Germans.

While the regular Polish police retained its prewar structures and personnel—despite many changes—the Investigative Service underwent a more profound transformation. At the end of October 1939, Polish detectives were removed from regular police structures, and they were transferred to the Polnische Kriminalpolizei under the overall authority of the German Kripo. In Warsaw, the Polish Criminal Police and its hundreds of detectives came under the authority of *SS-Sturmbannführer* Harry Geisler.[45] The Kripo in the Generalgouvernement became part of the Commands of Security Police and Security Service (KdS), which was further divided into the following subsections: VA, Polish personnel; VB, criminal

42 See Siemak, "Policja kryminalna II Rzeczypospolitej," p. 194.

43 Misiuk, *Policja Państwowa 1919–1939*, p. 321.

44 Siemak, "Policja kryminalna II Rzeczypospolitej," p. 194. In 1938, there were 2,815 policemen serving in the Investigative Service.

45 Interrogation protocol of Wilhelm Tewes, questioned by the British occupation authorities in Germany, August 23, 1946, AIPN, GK 164/3754, pp. 3–4. The other commanders of the Warsaw Kripo included: *Kriminalrat* Strunz (*Inspektion*); *Kriminalkommissar* van Look *(Inspektion)*; *Kriminalkommissar* Dr. Rogensack *(Inspektion)*; *Kriminalkommissar* Georg Richter, *Kommissariatsleiter; Kriminalkommissar* Horst Corfei; *Kriminalinspektor* Friedrich Geisler. See AIPN, GK 164/3754, pp. 3–4.

executive service; VC, investigative branch; and VD, technical investigative support.[46] As a result of these changes, the Polish employees of the former Investigative Service—now known as the Polnische Kriminalpolizei or the Polish Criminal Police—became officers of the German Security Police (Sipo). In the early years of the war, the Polish Criminal Police had its Directorates in three major cities of the Generalgouvernement: Kraków, Lublin, and Warsaw. Later, after the attack on the Soviet Union, a fourth Directorate was established in Lwów (Lviv, Lemberg), the capital of the newly created district of Galicia (Galizien).[47]

All four Directorates were supervised by the Germans, but they also operated independently. The Polish detectives worked out of Investigative Bureaus (*Urzędy Sledcze*), which were often physically housed together with the posts of regular Blue Police, but they answered to their respective Directorates. In Warsaw, the Kripo headquarters were located at 7 Daniłowiczowska Street and at Ujazdowskie Avenue, while the External Investigative offices were established at Ostrów Mazowiecka, Garwolin, Skierniewice, Łowicz, Siedlce, Grójec, Mińsk Mazowiecki, Pruszków, and Sokołów.[48] On the eastern periphery of the Generalgouvernement, close to the demarcation line with the Soviet-occupied areas, the Investigative Offices of the Polish Criminal Police also doubled as the posts of the Border Police (Grenzpolizei).[49] In the absence of Gestapo posts, these Kripo stations often took on tasks usually associated with the Secret Police themselves. In any case, both

46 Stanisław Biernacki, *Okupant a polski ruch oporu: Władze hitlerowskie w walce z ruchem oporu w dystrykcie warszawskim 1939–1944* (Warsaw: Glowna Komisja, 1989), pp. 24–25.

47 Although there was no Directorate of the Polish Criminal Police in Radom (the capital of the district of Radom), there were several Polish Kripo stations located in the city and around the district.

48 An interesting exchange of correspondence between various Kripo stations can be located in AMSW, Deutsches Gericht, for instance, in files 1207/5185; 1207/5384;1207/5184; 1207/5151.

49 Investigation into the suicide of Ajzyk Szlezinger, Drohobycz–Borysław station, Derżawnyj Archiw Lwiwskoj Obłasti (DALO), Sondergericht Lemberg, file 450, p. 3.

organizations cooperated closely, and the Gestapo had unlimited access to the files of the Polish Criminal Police.

Although institutionally separate, both police organizations—the "Blues" and the Polish Kripo—worked hand in hand, sharing common space and conducting joint operations. In the area of the so-called measures directed at the Jews (*Judenpolitik*), their cooperation became particularly close, especially during the liquidation of the ghettos in 1942 and until the end of the war.

German Supervision

Some pictures require thought and comment. In the following photo, there are four uniformed men at the table, while two women serve them drinks and food. Three men are seated, and one is standing with visible respect—he is raising a glass and leaning toward one of the seated men, who has a slight smile on his face. The smiling man is leaning comfortably back with his legs crossed, and he is smoking a cigar. There is no doubt that he is the central figure in this photograph. What is the reason for the celebration? Is it his birthday? Or perhaps a promotion? We will never know. What we do know, however, is that while his comrades are in the dark-blue uniforms of the Polish Blue Police, the smiling man is an officer of the German Gendarmerie. In another undated photo, he is standing together with his German colleagues in front of the Gendarmerie station in Otfinów, near Tarnów in southeastern Generalgouvernement. This photo was taken in 1942 or 1943.

The Orpo, who had been tasked with the supervision of the Blue Police since the end of 1939, not only supervised the professional duties of the Polish officers but also ensured the political loyalty of the "non-German" personnel. HSSPF Krüger wrote that "in addition to the regular supervision we need to exercise all police means by which we can instill political loyalty [of the Blue Police] and obedience to the German administration and police."[50] The role of supervision of the Polish policemen went to the Gendarmerie in the rural areas

50 Oversight and control over the Polish police, AIPN, GK 656/2, pp. 3–5.

and to the Schupo in the cities. In practice, it meant that the "Blues" took orders from any uniformed German who decided to exercise his power. Meanwhile, the Polish detectives found themselves under much closer scrutiny.

Katarzyna Kozioł and her sister Józefa Chłoń serve food to policemen, Otfinów, 1942/1943. Third from the left is a German gendarme. Photo taken by Stanisław Chłoń. Courtesy of Renata Guzera.

The same German gendarme as the previous photo (fourth from the left), Otfinów, 1943. Photo Collection, Yad Vashem Archives (YVA), 4577/260.

In March 1940, the so-called reptile press (*prasa gadzinowa*)[51]—newspapers that had been licensed and censored by the Germans—stressed the relationship between the Polish and the German police in a flattering tone in one of its articles: "One Polish police captain told me: 'I can speak about it quite openly and everyone will agree with me. We work willingly and with enthusiasm because we see that our German superiors act with utmost integrity, and they really care about us.'"[52]

In line with the wishes of the Kraków police headquarters, the posts of the Polish police were to be located—circumstances permitting—either together with or in the vicinity of German police stations. This measure was taken to ensure tighter and more frequent control over the Polish officers.[53] Orders were given to employ the Polish personnel in joint operations with the Gendarmerie and the Schupo. In 1943, soon after the liquidation of the ghettos, the commander of the Starachowice Gendarmerie gave orders to transfer all unmarried Polish policemen to vacated Jewish houses located near the German police station.[54] At the same time, special instructions established the codes of conduct of non-German policemen toward the Germans, both those in uniform and civilians. Even when catching a German red-handed in the act of committing a crime, the Blue policemen were not authorized to use weapons.[55] From time to time, the county police commanders were summoned to meetings with the district commanders of the Gendarmerie. At the beginning of the occupation, such meetings were held every two months. Later, once routine had been established, the meetings were held on an annual basis. In Kraków, the capital of the Generalgouvernement,

51 The Polish term *gad* (reptile) is also a derogatory term to describe vile people.

52 "Współpraca policji niemieckiej z polską," *Dziennik Radomski*, March 13, 1940.

53 Instructions sent from the office of the HSSPF, October 30, 1942, AIPN, GK 656/2, pp. 60–61.

54 Letter from the commander of the Starachowice Gendarmerie to the Orpo commander in Radom, January 2, 1943, AIPN, GK 656/2, p. 62.

55 Instructions about how to act on duty when the Germans are involved, July 6, 1942, AAN, AK, 203-III-119, pp. 2–2a.

the first meeting of this sort was held on January 23, 1940.[56] During the meeting, the Gendarmerie chief personally reserved the approval of furloughs for his Polish subordinates, stressed the importance of maintaining discipline, and ordered increased vigilance in the face of mounting banditry and a growing black market.

From the beginning of the occupation, the German police authorities had little confidence in their Polish subordinates in Kraków. The commander of the local Schupo detachment filed biweekly reports with the *Stadthauptmann* (German-appointed mayor), in which he described the security situation in the city. In the spring of 1940, the tone of these reports was rather pessimistic: The Polish policemen shirked their duties; they failed to meet their quotas of fines and tickets; and they were completely unreliable in fighting the black market. Here, a historian might wonder about the extent of the Blue Police's agency, which allowed them to take bribes and keep their German superiors blissfully ignorant to the extent of their involvement in the struggle against the black market. A captain of Kraków's Schupo detachment complained to his superiors that the few *Volksdeutsche* on the force were more useful than all of their Polish colleagues put together. In May 1940, this lack of motivation translated into the dismissal of eight "Blues" from the Kraków police.[57]

According to the German ranking officers, the poor morale of Polish policemen was related mostly to the salary freeze that, when combined with the growing inflation, significantly lowered their standard of living. While the Germans took note of the grumbling of the troops, they paid particular attention to the attitudes and loyalty of the Polish commanders. In one of the reports, it says, "There are some who still believe in an Allied victory, but the majority has completely lost faith in the British, and the arrests and

56 Orders of the German Police Authorities, letter from the Miechów Blue Police commander to all chiefs of local stations in Miechów County, January 26, 1940, ANKr, PPPBrzN, vol. 37, pp. 2–3.

57 Report, May 11, 1940, ANKr, Starosta Miasta Krakowa (SMKr), vol. 346, pp. 7–8.

firings of disloyal officers achieved the desired dissuasive effect."[58] One year later, the mood of the Polish policemen seemingly improved. In the spring of 1941, one can read reports about the officers being "rather satisfied" with their lot, and the Germans surmised that this satisfaction was most likely related to important seizures of black-market merchandise, which was later distributed among the policemen.[59] This good mood apparently persisted until mid-1943, when the dramatic growth of banditry and the increased activity of the underground organizations began to threaten the policemen's personal security.

A mixed watch made up of Blue Police and the Schupo, 8 Chopina Street. The photo was most likely taken during the visit of Arthur Seyss-Inquart (Hans Frank's deputy) who visited the city on May 5, 1940. Courtesy of Marek Tomaszewski.

58 Report, 1940, ANKr, SMKr, vol. 346, p. 13.

59 Report, April 22, 1941, ANKr, SMKr, vol. 346, p. 83.

Training sessions, including the required German-language courses, added another layer to the occupation's supervision and control of the Polish officers. The lessons were obligatory, and policemen found in contempt of German requirements risked serious financial penalties and disciplinary action.[60] On the other hand, those officers who complied with the expectations of the Germans were adequately rewarded. Platoon leader Zdzisław Danielewicz, for instance, received a promotion to the rank of sergeant with the following justification: "He is devoted to the service, he is an exemplary policeman, he learns German well, and he works efficiently on behalf of the German administration."[61] In Warsaw, knowledge of German became a precondition for promotion, and skipping lessons was considered a negligence of duties.[62] From the authorities' standpoint, knowledge of German among the Poles was necessary to ensure direct coordination and cooperation and allowed for the better penetration and surveillance of the Polish police corps, which was not a trifling matter.

It is hard to say whether the upper echelons of the Blue Police tried to prevent direct contact between the subordinates and the Germans, but there is no doubt that, over time, the phenomenon of taking a complaint and going over the heads of the ranking officers must have raised some concern among the officers of the Blue Police. Finally, the situation became so serious that, on March 10, 1942, the Warsaw headquarters of the Blue Police issued a strict order that prevented the rank-and-file from taking "their service and private issues" to the Kommando der Schutzpolizei (the German Protective Police command) without

60 Letter from the commander of "Praga" area to the subordinate police stations, March 15, 1942, AMSW, II Komisariat PP, file 11, p. 95; and letter from the commander of the XV precinct, March 24, 1942, AMSW, II Komisariat PP, file 11, p. 116.

61 Officer Zdzisław Danielewicz's promotion letter drafted by Lieutenant Edward Czarski, the commander of the XVII station of the Blue Police, March 19, 1942, AMSW, II Komisariat PP, file 11, p. 24.

62 Letter from Schupo Captain Felsinger to the Polish Police headquarters, March 15, 1943, and Major Przymusiński's letter, April 6, 1943, AAN, AK, 203-III-214, pp. 29–29a.

proper authorization.[63] Indeed, in the preserved files of the Blue Police, one can find evidence of officers who took "their service and private issues" directly to the Germans. A report filed by the commander of Praga (Warsaw-East) police district on March 23, 1942, stated: "The Kommando der Schutzpolizei called the Polish police and requested that Constable Antoni Rzętycki be immediately returned to active service, transferred to a different unit, and sent elsewhere [rather] than to the Jewish quarter."[64] It is not known what Constable Rzętycki was doing in the ghetto, but a personal appeal to the Germans had immediately brought about the desired effect.

On top of everything, the gendarmes or the Schupo could simply mete out punishments to the Polish officers at their whim. They exploited that right frequently and usually without informing the superiors of the punished individuals. The monthly Warsaw police bulletin, "Orders of the Commander of Warsaw Police," included lists of Polish officers who had either been fired, suspended from the job, or placed under arrest.[65] The lists were divided into three sections: penalties imposed by the commander of the Orpo (*Kommandeur der Ordnungspolizei*); penalties imposed by the commander of the Schupo (*Kommandeur der Schutzpolizei*); or penalties imposed by the Polish chief of the Warsaw Blue Police.

Training and Recruitment

German-language lessons were offered in addition to specialized courses in police techniques. In smaller localities, the courses were given by the local chiefs of the Gendarmerie. In Opoczno in the Radom district, for instance, "Mr. Lieutenant" visited the post of the Blue Police once a month and, in the company of the Polish commander, conducted drills, taught German commands,

63 Minutes of the meeting of the police stations' chiefs, March 10, 1942, AMSW, II Komisariat PP, file 11, p. 52.

64 Letter from the Blue Police commander to the head of the "Praga" district, March 30, 1942, AMSW, II Komisariat PP, file 11, p. 166.

65 See Order no. 82, April 30, 1943, AMSW, II Komisariat PP, file 5, pp. 1–6.

inspected weapons, and gave lectures.[66] The young recruits received instruction in a special police school in Nowy Sącz—renamed by the Germans as Neu Sandez—and experienced officers had to attend special refresher courses from time to time. During the fall of 1943, the police course lasted for ten weeks, and the seventh preparatory course was held from October 4 to December 22, 1943, for 250 policemen from every district of the Generalgouvernement.[67] The officers learned drills, target shooting, and how to guard prisoners, and they attended specialized courses taught by higher officers and invited guests.[68] German lessons were among the most important topics, and this was clearly treated as a priority by the occupying authorities. Indeed, with time, knowledge of the German language among Polish officers markedly improved. In Starachowice in the central Generalgouvernement, the local Gendarmerie commander expressed his satisfaction with the young Polish recruits' progress in that particular area.[69]

A discussion of police recruitment and training cannot fail to mention—however briefly—the infamous Schutzmannschaft Battalion 202 (Auxiliary Police Battalion 202), which was formed by the Germans in the spring of 1942. According to initial planning, the Poles in the Schutzmannschaft Battalion 202 were to be deployed to the East to support German police units, and it took part in the operations against partisans in Belorussia and Ukraine.[70] Lacking volunteers due to the miserable failure of the first recruitment drive, the Blue Police started to delegate police officers for such operations instead. Some policemen who

66 Station register, Polish Police Post in Opoczno, April–October 1942, entry from August 6, 1942, Archiwum Państwowe w Kielcach (AP Kielce), Posterunek Policji Polskiej w Opocznie, 21/772.

67 Letter from the HSSPF office in Krakow to the Orpo district commanders, September 19, 1943, AIPN, GK 656/1, pp. 81–83.

68 The plan of lectures at the seventh course cycle of the police school in Nowy Sacz, AIPN, GK 656/1, pp. 74–78.

69 Report of the Gendarmerie commander in the Radom district, June 18, 1944, AIPN, GK 656/1, p. 68.

70 See Michał Wenklar, "Polacy w niemieckiej policji pomocniczej. Schutzmannschaftsbataillon 202 w świetle zeznań jego członków," *Studia nad Autorytaryzmem i Totalitaryzmem*, 34:4 (2012), pp. 35–50.

were sent to the training center in Dębica had been handpicked personally by Colonel Aleksander Reszczyński, the commander of the Warsaw police.[71] Starting in the summer and fall of 1942, some of the candidates who had volunteered for the Blue Police were automatically rerouted into the ranks of Schutzmannschaft Batallion 202, with no right of refusal.[72] In the training center in Kochanówka, the recruits took an oath of loyalty: "As a member of the Schutzmannschaft I pledge to be loyal, brave, and obedient, and I promise to duly fulfill my obligations in the struggle against nation-killing Bolshevism. So help me God!"[73]

Weapons and Discipline

Over time, the question of weapons—and specifically the lack thereof—became one of the most burning issues for the Germans who supervised the "Blues." In 1943, the number of occasions when the Blue Police officers "lost" their weapons or were disarmed by criminals or resistance fighters became so alarmingly high that the Germans decided to introduce draconian measures. Leon Skrzypek, a constable from a police post in Tarnobrzeg, was one of the first to experience the full force of the German wrath.[74] On January 21, 1943, while he was riding his bicycle to work in Dzikowo in Dębica County, Constable Skrzypek was overpowered by bandits who were fleeing from a break-in at the distillery nearby. Unable to resist, Skrzypek surrendered his service revolver to the bandits. His case was soon heard by the VI SS and Police

71 Report, July 7, 1942, AAN, AK, 203-III-119, pp. 4–4a.

72 Order of Generalgouvernement Orpo commander, April 22, 1942, AIPN, GK 695/2, p. 457. See for instance: "Following your application of September 14, 1942, asking for inclusion in the ranks of the Polish Police, I hereby order you to report for temporary duty in the Schutzmannschaft-Battalion 202"; Commander of the Orpo in the Generalgouvernement to Anton Baczor, September 29, 1942, AIPN, GK 658/1, p. 10.

73 Personnel file of Schutzman Anton Baczor, October 31, 1942, AIPN, GK 658/1, p. 13.

74 The Skrzypek case is discussed in: Disciplinary cases of Polish policemen, 1941–1944, AIPN, GK 656/3, p. 174–180.

Court (*SS- und Polizeigericht VI*) in Kraków, where the Polish constable stood accused of cowardly behavior and dereliction of duty. On March 8, 1943, the judges—officers of the Orpo and the SS—found Leon Skrzypek guilty and sentenced him to death. In a long justification, the judges underlined the fact that the weapon seized from Skrzypek could have been used by the bandits or it could have even fallen into the hands of the Polish underground and, consequently, be used to kill Germans. The judges wrote the following in justification of the sentence:

> The court came to the conclusion that the accused deserves the penalty of death. The German police authorities, in their struggle against the bandits operating in the Generalgouvernement, have to be able to rely on the cooperation and loyalty of the Polish police. If the Polish police fails, further struggle against the bandits becomes impossible.[75]

This was not, however, the end of Constable Skrzypek's case. On May 26, 1943, HSSPF Krüger waded in and commuted Skrzypek's sentence to five years in prison. Soon after, the commander of the Orpo decided to broadly publicize Krüger's leniency. The information about the case was placed on posters and plastered in every station and post of the Blue Police across the land, and it was published in internal police newsletters and bulletins. One can surmise that while the Germans sought to invoke fear in their Polish subordinates, they also wanted to place emphasis on the leniency and generosity of the authorities. Undoubtedly, the Polish police was an important element in the overall security strategy in the Generalgouvernement, and tightening the screws too tightly could lead to desertions and, consequently, to a loss of discipline. It was no coincidence, therefore, that from time to time, Governor Hans Frank also pardoned Blue policemen who had been sentenced to death by either martial or police court. In August 1943, the underground bulletin reported that four Blue

75 Court justification of sentence, AIPN, GK 656/3, p. 174–180.

policemen were tried by the VI SS and Police court in Kraków, the same court that had heard the case of Constable Skrzypek half a year earlier. The nature of their crime remains unknown, but all these policemen were also sentenced to death. The sentence was commuted to six years of imprisonment by Governor General Hans Frank, who exercised his right of pardon.[76]

Blue policemen at the police school in Nowy Sącz, 1941. Narodowe Archiwum Cyfrowe (NAC), 2-4669.

Toward the end of 1943, the situation on the Eastern Front quickly started to deteriorate, and the loyalty of the "Blues" toward their German masters grew increasingly dubious. Desertions, involvement with the underground, and lost weapons became so common that the Germans decided to apply more terror to punish disobedient and rebellious Poles. In the spring of 1944, the commander of the Orpo for the Warsaw district issued an order that authorized the German police to apply the principle of collective responsibility and arrest the families of delinquent Polish officers. According to the new directives, the police could arrest officers'

76 "Four Krakow Policemen Sentenced to Death," *Małopolska Agencja Prasowa*, August 1, 1943.

wives, parents, and siblings and send them to the Auschwitz concentration camp or to Germany as forced laborers. Children were to be transferred to orphanages.[77] This, however, was all in the distant future. For the time being, in the early months and years of the occupation, the Germans were able to organize the non-German police to staff most of the police stations and precincts in the Generalgouvernement. Staffing problems remained an issue, but over the course of 1940, the police ranks reached prewar levels with the help of officers transferred to the Generalgouvernement from territories annexed to the Reich.

Although the Germans threatened former Polish policemen who refused to join the Blue Police with harsh penalties, there is no record of any instance when an officer was punished for such an offense. There were, perhaps, very few officers who refused to follow the reinstatement order, so the Germans did not have to apply these strict measures to ensure proper police staffing in the Generalgouvernement. At the same time, the Polish resistance informed the officers who enlisted in the Blue Police—both individually and through numerous underground publications—that their foremost duty was to serve the best interests of the Polish nation. An assessment of the extent to which the officers of the Blue Police took this pledge to heart, and more specifically, the evolution of their attitude toward the most helpless and vulnerable segment of Polish society—the Polish-Jewish citizens—will be examined in the following chapters.

77 Report 993 (police intelligence), April 22, 1944, AAN, AK, 203-III-111, p. 58.

Chapter Two

The First Years of Occupation: Fall 1939–Fall 1941

Emanuel Ringelblum was the chronicler of life and death in the Warsaw ghetto. For every historian, and especially for historians of the Holocaust, Ringelblum sets unique moral and professional standards. A social activist and a man sensitive to human suffering and conscious of his responsibility to his own community, Ringelblum realized early on that his role was to document the suffering and the death of his own nation. Writing about the various threats facing the Jews, he could not fail to mention the Polish police. In his last book, he wrote the following:

> The Polish Police, commonly called the Blue or uniformed police in order to avoid using the term "Polish," has played a most lamentable role in the extermination of the Jews of Poland. The uniformed police has been an enthusiastic executor of all German directives regarding the Jews. The powers of the uniformed police in the sphere of collaborating with the Germans concerning the Jews were as follows: 1) guarding the exit gates of the Ghettos as well as the walls and fences enclosing the Ghettos or the Jewish districts; 2) participating in "resettlement actions" in the capacity of catchers, escorts, etc.; 3) participating in tracking down Jews who were in hiding after the "resettlement actions"; 4) shooting Jews sentenced to death by the Germans.[1]

1 Ringelblum, *Polish-Jewish Relations*, pp. 133–134.

On the second point—the role of the police in the liquidation actions, an issue to which this research will devote more space—Ringelblum wrote: "The blood of hundreds of thousands of Polish Jews, caught and driven to the 'death vans' will be on their heads."[2] The searches for hidden Jews—the *Judenjagd*—that were conducted by the Polish police and mentioned by Ringelblum in the third point of his account, resulted in the death of "tens of thousands of Jews" who had initially escaped the German killers.[3] These numbers should be kept in mind as there were few people who had a clearer vision of the extent of the Jewish catastrophe than Ringelblum. These questions will be addressed later in this research.

The Polish police started to enforce the German anti-Jewish regulations early on in the first months of the occupation, Ringelblum noted. According to some researchers, the role of the Polish police in the enforcement of "Jewish" regulations was limited until the ghettos were sealed.[4] An in-depth study of contemporary evidence leads, however, to different conclusions. Since its very inception in the late fall of 1939, the Blue Police enforced German regulations, including those aimed at the Jews. The process of removing Jews from the margins of Polish society began with the arrival of the Germans. Acts of terror struck the Jewish community with particular force and brutality, which clearly indicated that "racial differentiation" would be the cornerstone of the German new order. This violence, initially introduced by the Wehrmacht and implemented in the public sphere by the German police, paved the way for a more systematic regime of terror, built around special discriminatory laws and regulations.

Starting from December 1, 1939, all Polish Jews above the age of ten were required to comply with the *Judenkennzeichnungsgesetz*

2 Ibid., p. 135.

3 Ibid., p. 136.

4 Sylwia Szymańska-Smolkin, "Rola policji granatowej jako pośrednika w utrzymywaniu łączności między gettem a stroną aryjską," in August Grabski and Artur Markowski, eds., *Narody i polityka: Studia ofiarowane profesorowi Jerzemu Tomaszewskiemu* (Warsaw: Instytut Historyczny Uniwersytetu Warszawskiego, 2010), p. 217.

(the branding regulation) that forced Jews to wear white armbands with a blue Star of David.[5] Importantly, according to German legislation, confession had no bearing on the determination of one's racial identity. Race and only race—as construed by the Nazis—was the fundamental criterium, and those found defying the new order were to be severely punished. In March 1940, the *Nowy Kurjer Warszawski* (New Warsaw Courier, NKW), a tool of primitive German propaganda, warned that Jews apprehended on the streets without an armband would face fines, jail, or both.[6] On January 24, 1940, a new regulation forced the Jews not only to register their bank accounts with the authorities but also to declare all valuables, including personal items such as jewelry.[7] Furthermore, numerous restrictions barred Jews from using public transportation, and Jewish doctors, lawyers, and other members of liberal professions became unemployed. Within a few short weeks, Jewish retirees were stripped of their pensions, and the bank accounts of the non-Aryan population were frozen.

The Warsaw ghetto was established in October 1940, and on November 15, the ghetto was officially sealed. Along the ghetto boundary, the Germans erected high walls topped with broken glass and barbed wire. Crossing to the Aryan side of the city without proper authorization carried penalties that were meted out by the German courts, which had been established in occupied Poland in early spring 1940. Although in Warsaw the deadline for the population transfer into the ghetto was set for November 15, 1940, many people refused to believe that the Germans would dare to incarcerate hundreds of thousands of people in such a

5 "Verordnung über die Kennzeichnung der Juden und Jüdinnen im Generalgouvernement" (Decree about the Marking of Jews and Jewesses in the Generalgouvernement), *Verordnungsblatt des Generalgouverneurs für die Besetzten Polnischen Gebiete*, November 30, 1939. This regulation was signed by Hans Frank on November 23, 1939, and became law on December 1, 1939.

6 "Na nienoszących oznak żydów kary więzienia i grzywny nieograniczonej wysokości," *Nowy Kurier Warszawski*, March 15, 1940.

7 "Verordnung über die Pflicht zur Anmeldung jüdischen Vermögens im Generalgouvernement" (Decree on the Obligatory Duty to Register all Jewish Assets in the Generalgouvernement), *Verordnungsblatt des Generalgouverneurs für die Besetzten Polnischen Gebiete*, January 29, 1940.

way. True, construction of short sections of the walls was taking place here and there across downtown Warsaw already from the spring of 1940, but for many, the occupier's intent was still less than obvious. These doubts were, however, put to rest on November 16, when reinforced patrols of German, Polish, and Jewish police were deployed in and around the ghetto. At this point, the ghetto was permanently cut off from the Aryan side. Initially, inside this "closed Jewish quarter"—it was strongly forbidden to use the term "ghetto" as it might carry pejorative associations—close to 400,000 Jews tried to find shelter in desperately overcrowded conditions. In the following weeks, the Germans continued to resettle tens of thousands of additional Jews into the ghetto. Most of them had been driven out from smaller localities around Warsaw that had been successively "de-Judeized" (*entjudet*), to use the parlance of the times.

There were some, however, who refused to move into the ghetto. Thousands of Warsaw Jews, mainly converts and deeply assimilated people, decided to stay on the Aryan side. They did not remain there long. Between November 16 and 20, 1940, the Blue Police conducted a series of arrests of Jews found in contempt of the new regulations, and they were later delivered into the ghetto. As Emanuel Ringelblum noted in his diary, "On Friday night the Jews of Praga [the eastern part of Warsaw] have been arrested and brought in trucks to Muranów [a part of the ghetto] area; they sleep in the staircases and in the courtyards."[8] The rest were dumped into schools and other public buildings inside the ghetto. The estimates are imprecise, but the number of Jews intercepted during the November *razzia* (raid in German) was anywhere between 15,000 and 20,000 people. The victims of this huge manhunt were arrested with the help of special lists drawn up in advance.[9] In Warsaw, everyone had a good idea about the "racial origin" of one's neighbors, and this, in turn, greatly increased the efficiency of the

8 Emanuel Ringelblum, *Kronika getta warszawskiego: Wrzesień 1939–styczeń 1943* (Warsaw: Czytelnik, 1983), p. 199.

9 Tadeusz Obremski, *Wśród zatrutych noży: Zapiski z getta i okupowanej Warszawy*, ed. by Agnieszka Haska (Warsaw: Stowarzyszenie Centrum Badań nad Zagładą Żydów, 2017), p. 58.

Blue Police. In the subsequent days and weeks, the Polish police continued to track down the Jews living on the Aryan side and sent them to the ghetto. Denunciations, which flowed freely to police posts and to the German authorities, proved to be an essential tool of the police. The racially motivated denunciations, which are preserved in the archives in Warsaw, are second in number only to the politically motivated ones.[10]

The arrested Jews tried to explain their predicament to the authorities. Some argued that they considered themselves Poles, others that they had nothing to do with the Jews, and still others invoked their fervent Catholicism. This was all in vain. Many Jews were denounced to the authorities, whereas others—as we can read in the protocols of arrests—were delivered into the hands of the Blue Police by concerned citizens. One of the Jews who was denounced to the Gestapo was Arnold Szyfman, director of the Polish Theater, one of the most prestigious venues in the capital.[11] The same fate awaited Tadeusz Puder, a Catholic priest and one of the better-known converts, who was denounced to the Germans by a fellow priest, Dr. Stanisław Trzeciak, a vicious antisemite and a Gestapo agent.[12] The hunt for the Jews living outside the ghetto continued practically until the end of its existence, and once the ghetto had been liquidated, the hunt acquired an additional urgency. On January 13, 1942, the Blue Police headquarters in Warsaw once again sent a reminder to every precinct to arrest all converts living in their respective areas.[13]

10 Barbara Engelking, "*Szanowny panie gistapo!*": *Donosy do władz niemieckich w Warszawie i okolicach w latach 1940–1941* (Warsaw: IFiS PAN, 2003), p. 29.

11 Arnold Szyfman, *Moja tułaczka wojenna* (Warsaw: Ministerstwa Obrony Narodowej, 1960), p. 78. For the violation of the armband regulation, Szyfman was sentenced by the German Special Court to six months in prison.

12 For more on this issue, see Jan Grabowski and Dariusz Libionka, "Anatomia donosu księdza Stanisława Trzeciaka na księdza Tadeusza Pudra," *Zagłada Żydów, Studia i materiały*, 13 (2017), pp. 641–675.

13 There were times when mistakes happened: "One of the sergeants arrested one Baugarten, instead of a Jew Baugart. The German has been held for one night in a holding pen." Wrong actions of the Blue Police, January 27, 1942, AAN, AK, 203-III-123, p. 4.

Lumber merchant Henryk Hendler was one of the unfortunate converts who refused to move to the ghetto.[14] In October 1941, he was denounced to the Germans as a "full Jew" (*Volljude*) and was arrested by the Blue Police. Under investigation, Hendler defended himself by saying that he refused to move to the ghetto because "he could not stomach the idea of living among the Jews," whom he treated only with "hate and repulsion."[15] The judges of the German Special Court (*Sondergericht*) remained unmoved by Hendler's self-serving line of defense and sentenced him to three years in prison. The verdicts of the *Sondergericht* were usually tantamount to a death sentence, at least in the case of Jewish defendants. Many convicts died in these prisons, where there were special sections for Jews with conditions that were beyond appalling, and others, like Hendler, were shipped off to the Treblinka death camp in the summer of 1942.

The files of the German courts in Poland include special bilingual forms, the so-called *Strafanzeigen* (reports about crimes that were committed). Hundreds of preserved *Strafanzeigen* deal with those Jews who were apprehended outside the ghettos, and this allows historians today to treat these documents as quantifiable sources. It is striking that in nearly every known case, the Blue Police was either directly or indirectly involved in the arrests of Jews on the Aryan side of the city.[16] It seems that the civilian population only rarely reported the Jews to the German gendarmes, or, perhaps, the gendarmes were simply less present on the streets. In any case, from the standpoint of the Jews, the nationality of the arresting officers was of little importance: In both cases, the victims were delivered into the hands of the German prosecutors.

Zygmunt Łoszak, a platoon leader of the Blue Police, was on duty guarding the tramway cars that transited through the ghetto. In Warsaw, tramway line number 17 crossed from the Aryan side

14 Criminal proceedings against a Jew who resided in the Aryan quarter and pretended to be Pole, AMSW, Sondergericht Warschau, file 909.

15 Interrogation of Henryk Hendler, October 21, 1941, AMSW, Sondergericht Warschau, file 909, p. 9.

16 See Jan Grabowski, "*Ja tego Żyda znam!": Szantażowanie Żydów w Warszawie 1939–1943* (Warsaw: IFiS PAN, 2004), pp. 38–39.

and went through the ghetto. While in transit, the windows of the cars were closed, and there were no stops along the way. In September 1941, Łoszak filed a report with his superiors:

> In the aforementioned tramway car, already back on the Aryan side, on Bonifraterska Street, I saw a woman who looked to me like a Jewess. I asked her to show me her papers, to which she responded that she had no ID. Later on, being sure that she was Jewish, I delivered her to the IV police precinct.[17]

A tailor's apprentice, Szlama Kam, was arrested on April 14, 1941, when he "made an attempt to take tram number 3 from the Jewish quarter to the Aryan quarter without proper permission and without an armband," and according to the report of the Blue policeman, "He argued that he wanted to go to the Aryan side in order to buy bread...the explanations of the suspect are not credible."[18] A tram ride proved to be equally dangerous for thirteen-year-old Chana Helfmann, who testified the following after her arrest:

> I admit that, on February 12, 1941, I crossed [over] to the Aryan side without an armband and permission. I want to add that my father is unemployed, he has left us, my mother is also without work, so we have nothing to eat. That's the reason why I left the Jewish quarter on February 12, 1941, and went over, through the Żelazna/Leszno Street gate in order to beg for food. That same day, at 7:15 PM, when I took tram number 5 to get back to the Jewish quarter, I was stopped by the tram conductor, who delivered me into the hands of the Polish policeman, who, in turn, brought me to the I precinct of the Polish police. I have been released from custody after two weeks.[19]

17 Protocol of a crime being committed, September 15, 1941, AMSW, Prokuratura przy Sądzie Specjalnym w Warszawie (SSW), 1790, p. 3.

18 Report, April 14, 1941, AMSW, SSW, 1363, p. 5. For similar files, see: 1294, 1305. A particularly abundant collection of files concerning trials against the Jews residing on the Aryan side can be found in the AMSW, Deutsches Gericht.

19 Hearing, July 1, 1941, AMSW, SSW, 1498, p. 10.

In order to avoid arrest and deportation to the ghetto, Jews could change their place of residence—preferably by moving to another city—or, in rare cases, they were able to arrange good-quality identity papers that offered sufficient protection from police harassment. The documents produced by the Central Protective Council (Rada Główna Opiekuńcza, RGO—a charitable organization licensed and authorized by the Germans) were considered among the best. From time to time, they were given to "useful converts," who were authorized by the Germans to move around without Jewish armbands and could live outside the ghetto. Professor Ludwik Hirszfeld, an immunologist of world-class fame, was one such useful convert. In February 1941, despite the protection provided by the RGO, the agents of the Blue Police descended on Hirszfeld's house located in the leafy Saska Kępa quarter of Warsaw. As Hirszfeld noted in his memoir, the policemen were kind, and "they behaved with ideal kindness,"[20] which was not hard to understand, since some of their family members were former patients of Hirszfeld's wife, who was a pediatrician. But an order was an order, and that same day, Professor Hirszfeld together with his wife and daughter were escorted by policemen who "behaved with ideal kindness," and they were delivered straight into the ghetto. Henryk Makower was witness to the whole event:

> Had the professor not, for additional security, gotten involved with the whole RGO affair, he could have stayed quietly in his house. The story involved baptized Jews who applied, with RGO's support, to Governor Frank, stressing their sincere Catholic faith, complete lack of ties with the Jewish community, and they asked to be allowed to remain outside the ghetto. The RGO assured the professor that everything was going to be fine. The authorities studied the memorandum and sent the list of signatories together with their addresses straight to the Blue Police, requesting an immediate transfer

20 Ludwik Hirszfeld, *Historia jednego życia* (Warsaw: Czytelnik, 1946), p. 192.

> of these 100 percent pure (according to the regulations) Jews to the ghetto.[21]

The arrival of the converts raised huge interest among the inhabitants of the ghetto. Chaim Aron Kaplan, one of the most perceptive Warsaw diarists, noted the following on March 7, 1941: "The converts, arrested like common bums or convicts, were brought to the ghetto in front of everybody. Huge crowds accompanied them all the way to the door of the Judenrat headquarters."[22]

Professor Marceli Handelsman, one of the most eminent Polish historians, was another Jew who enjoyed the relative comforts of living on the Aryan side for a long time. Not unlike Hirszfeld, Handelsman also had permission to live outside the ghetto. In May 1942, a Blue policeman knocked on his door and delivered an order to appear in front of the Municipal Council office. The summons read: "To Mr. Professor Marceli Handelsman, Kielecka 42 apt. 4. In the matter regarding the letter of the Mayor-Commissioner of April 25, 1942, you are requested to appear in the office of the Mayor-Commissioner, Senatorska Street 14, during office hours, with proof of Aryan descent."[23] Unlike Hirszfeld, Professor Handelsman did not waste time looking for "proof of Aryan descent" and went into hiding. He remained in hiding until 1944, when he first became the target of the nationalist NSZ, and he was later delivered into the hands of the Gestapo.

Already at this early stage of the occupation, the Blue Police had proved its worth to the Germans. The examples are telling: On September 19, 1940, Józef Bożyk of the X precinct of the Warsaw police caught two Jewish boys walking without the required armbands on the Aryan side. He noted the following in his report:

21 Henryk Makower, *Pamiętnik z getta warszawskiego: Październik 1940–styczeń 1943* (Wrocław: Ossolineumm, 1987), p. 46.

22 Chaim A. Kaplan, *Scroll of Agony: The Warsaw Diary* (New York: Macmillan, 1965), p. 250. For more on the topic of assimilated Jews, see Katarzyna Person, *Assimilated Jews in the Warsaw Ghetto, 1940–1943* (New York: Syracuse University Press, 2014).

23 A request for Professor Marceli Handelsman to appear at the City Council, April 25, 1942, AMSW, Burmistrz Komisaryczny m. Warszawy, file 56, pp. 105–106.

> At noon, in front of the German store Juliusz Meinl I saw two Jewish-looking boys wearing no armbands. I asked one of them whether he was a Jew, and he replied that he was not and that I was wrong. When I asked him to show me his papers, he said that he had none. When I brought them to the precinct, they admitted that their names were: 1) Borensztein Mojżesz, son of Szmul-Josek and Mindla, born 18 May 1926; and 2) Borensztein Icek, son of Szmul-Josek and Mindla, born 11 September 1924, both of mosaic confession, living at Wołyńska Street 19 apt. 26. The abovementioned, moved around without armbands, tried to shop at Meinl, pretending to be Poles. While I escorted them to the police station, they continued to claim that they were Poles. It was only when I warned them that we would check their place of residence, they admitted to being Jews, and they put on the armbands, which they kept hidden in their pockets. It was not their first time, because I have seen them there before.[24]

The boys were fourteen and sixteen, respectively, so they were required to wear armbands, in line with the German regulation of December 1, 1939. One of the boys explained to Bożyk that their father was ill and their family had no means to survive, so that's why he "stood in front of the store and bought (for resale) the cigars from customers leaving the store. I took off the armband because no one would sell anything to a Jew," the boy concluded in his statement.[25] Their explanation did not sway the Polish policemen, and the Borensztein's case was transferred to the *Sondergericht*.

While the Borenszteins moved around Warsaw without their armbands, another group of Jews were arrested by Officer Edmund Wojciszewski in April 1941, having fallen victim to their own bravado and recklessness. These four Jews, armed with forged passes and armbands on their sleeves, took a drosky and told the driver to take them to the railway station. A Blue Police

24 The report of Józef Bożyk, September 19, 1940, AMSW, Deutsches Gericht, 1067 (1307), pp. 4–5.

25 Ibid.

officer, shocked to see Jews riding comfortably in a drosky, stopped them and checked their passes. The forged documents failed to stand up to the scrutiny of the watchful officer Wojciszewski, and all four Jews found themselves in front of the *Sondergericht*, which sentenced each of them to two and a half years in prison.[26] According to one of the Jewish survivors from Warsaw:

> Before the publication of the armband regulation, the Polish police oftentimes acted as hunters, because it was charged with delivering [to the Germans] a required quota of Jews slated for forced labor. Aware that the Jews were defenseless, that they cannot complain, some of the Polish policemen treated these people with utmost cruelty, beating them up with rubber truncheons. Once the Jews started to wear the armbands, the Polish police gained a new source of income: now they could track down Jews without armbands and extort from them ransom by threatening to deliver them to the Germans.[27]

German Control in Small Towns: The Case of Opoczno

Historians of the Holocaust have focused much of their attention on the largest ghettos, which were usually closed and surrounded by a wall. The everyday work of the Blue Police in these cities differed greatly, however, from what transpired in smaller towns and rural areas, where the vast majority of Polish Jews lived. Here, the Polish police not only had closer contact with the Jewish population—the officers usually recognized their Jewish neighbors from prewar times—but also dealt with a wider range of everyday pursuits. At this stage, one can also venture a hypothesis: The power that the blue-clad officers exerted over the Jews was directly related to

26 Verdict, March 20, 1942, AMSW, Sondergericht Warschau, 292, pp. 117–118.

27 Mieczysław Parker-Pokorny diary and memoirs, Yad Vashem Archives (YVA), O.25/105, p. 15.

the presence of the Germans. In smaller towns, where Germans showed up rarely or never, the Polish police officers had the final word. The Jewish drama played out on the periphery in small, semi-closed ghettos where the only physical obstacle between the Jews and non-Jews was a flimsy fence, or in open ghettos where there was nothing separating the Jews and non-Jews, and the borders existed only in people's minds. On top of this, in each district of the Generalgouvernement, there were some areas where entire Jewish communities avoided the German policy of concentration and ghettoization. These Jews were rounded up and resettled in the larger ghettos as late as spring and summer 1942, just moments before the liquidation *Aktionen* began.

Jews in Opoczno, c. 1941.
Photo Collection, YVA, 6835/7.

In order to better understand the role of the Blue Police in these remote areas within the context of the German strategy of terror, it is beneficial to examine the station register (*Księga stacyjna*) of the Blue Police post in Opoczno, a small town located in central Poland, halfway between Radom and Piotrków Trybunalski.[28] The register allowed the duty officer to note in appropriate columns the events that had occurred during the day, the names of the officers

28 Opoczno station register, March 1940–November 1943, AP Kielce, Posterunek Policji Polskiej w Opocznie, 21/772.

on patrol, a list of those absent, and other remarks that he saw fit to report.

According to prewar tallies, Opoczno had a population of 7,000 inhabitants, half of whom were Jews. At the end of 1940, the Germans established a ghetto, and they initially resettled 4,200 people there. Soon, however, more than 1,000 additional Jews were brought into the town from outlying areas. Over time, the living conditions badly deteriorated and insufficient food supplies combined with appalling sanitary conditions brought on a typhus epidemic and mass starvation. The Opoczno ghetto was liquidated in two phases: The first liquidation *Aktion* struck the Jews in the fall of 1942, and the second one took place in January 1943. The ghetto was liquidated with the usual brutality, and most of the Jews were sent to their deaths at the Treblinka extermination camp. The Opoczno ghetto was an open ghetto, and other than metal barriers, there was nothing standing between the local Jews and their fellow Polish citizens. In addition to the Polish police post, Opoczno also hosted a German Gendarmerie station with about ten officers on duty.[29]

The German commander and his deputy showed up once a month at the Polish Blue Police station, where they gave lectures, conducted drills, and inspected weapons. Given the insignificant German presence in Opoczno, how was it possible to maintain and enforce the invisible boundary of the ghetto? And for those who had plans to escape, what measures ensured that the Jews were unable to escape the deadly trap that the ghetto had become in order to seek assistance among their Polish neighbors? The Opoczno police station register gives us several—although fragmentary and not entirely satisfactory—answers to these questions. The register, which is one of the very few that have been preserved in the archives, is unfortunately incomplete. For instance, parts of the records spanning the period of September 1942–February 1943 are missing. Nevertheless, the register, which allows us to track the

29 Wolfgang Curilla, *Der Judenmord in Polen und die Deutsche Ordnungspolizei 1939–1945* (Paderborn: Schöningh, 2011), p. 519.

daily pursuits of the officers of the Blue Police, is an important and informative source.

In terms of general activity, the Polish officers in Opoczno and elsewhere throughout the Generalgouvernement were tasked with maintaining order, reinforcing public security, and fighting common criminality. Taking into account the unique challenges of the wartime situation, police activities did not initially differ much from the routine of earlier years. However, this situation changed in early 1940, when the Polish policemen were ordered to enforce the German strategy of mobilizing the Polish workforce for labor in Germany. In the first months of the occupation, voluntary recruitment was not a problem. Polish peasants from impoverished and overpopulated areas had a longstanding tradition of seeking a better future by working in Germany. In the Polish language, there is even a saying "*pojechać na saksy*" (to go to Saxony), which means to look for gainful employment abroad.

Later, however, when families back in the Generalgouvernement started to receive alarming news from their loved ones about the appalling working conditions in the Reich, the mood changed. Instead of volunteers, the village elders had to fulfill quotas of young people, who were later—often under duress—delivered to the processing stations by the Blue Police. Some of these appointed forced laborers simply went into hiding, and the Blue Police had to hunt them down. The *Kreishauptmann* of Krasnystaw wrote the following to his superiors in Kraków in the winter of 1940–1941: "There is much commotion and anxiety among the Poles regarding the draft of people to work in Germany. There are fewer and fewer volunteers."[30] At the same time, the Polish police started to enforce the German-imposed quotas of meat and grains, which the peasants were required to deliver to the state. The zeal—or rather the lack thereof—with which the officers tracked down the fugitive workers or offending peasants became one of the measures of their patriotism. However, for these policemen, the choices became starker, and the stakes were

30 Situation reports for February 1941, *Kreishauptmannschaft* Krasnystaw, Instytut Zachodni, I-21, p. 15.

higher when in 1942, the Germans started to send these groups of Polish offenders to concentration camps.[31] The struggle against the patriotic resistance movement became a major issue only in 1943, when acts of defiance and armed incidents became commonplace, triggering severe reprisals from the Germans.

But all this was still in the distant future. In the meantime, the actions of the Polish Blue Police directed against the Jews attracted only marginal attention from the underground organizations, which formed the so-called Polish Underground State. Nevertheless, with time, the various activities on the Jewish front—as some Polish diarists referred to it[32]—morphed into one of the most important assignments of the police, and the Polish officers emerged as an essential component in the German policies of terror directed at the Jews of Poland.

As already noted, the Blue Police had been enforcing the branding regulation since December 1939. As can be seen in the Opoczno police register, the officers took the regulations seriously. While Adam Weinberg and Rywka Rosenblum were simply stopped for failing to wear the required armband, Faja Furman, Ari Perec, and Chaim Mendelson were handed fines of 3 zlotys each for the same offense.[33] The fines were initially insignificant, but with time, they grew. An arrest and even a short stint in the local jail was much more of a threat to the Jewish offenders. In early 1941, Jews apprehended without armbands were punished with several months or even years of incarceration, as illustrated above. By late 1941, the absence of an armband had become a capital offense.

For the people of Opoczno—Jews and Poles alike—the actions of the Polish police clearly indicated that the rules of

31 Instruction to the voits (local officials) of Radom-Land *Kreishauptmannschaft* requesting that the local population be warned about the possible penalties for failing to deliver quotas, April 14, 1942, AIPN, GK 695/1, p. 109.

32 See for instance Wyszyński, *Dzienniki z lat 1941–1944*; Ludwik Landau, *Kronika lat wojny i okupacji*, vols. 1–3 (Warsaw: Państwowe Wydawnictwo Naukowe, 1962–1963).

33 Opoczno station register, March–July 1940, entries from April 25–26, 1940, AP Kielce, Posterunek Policji Polskiej w Opocznie, 21/772.

social interaction had changed profoundly and that the non-Aryan population was, henceforth, outside the boundaries of communal solidarity. From time to time, the register reported that the Jews were stopped for wearing dirty armbands. Interestingly, in these cases, the "Blues" demonstrated their own initiative, as the German regulations had nothing to say about the expected sanitary condition of an armband. As one can surmise, the issue was settled depending on the aesthetic sensitivities of the Polish officers, who could impose tickets and fines on the Jews at their whim. The violations of the armband regulation were often associated with the more serious charge of illegally leaving the ghetto.

Jews in Opoczno, c. 1941. Photo Collection, YVA, 6835/8.

In the summer of 1941, the station register noted that the Opoczno police were deployed to nearby Przysucha in order to conduct searches of Jewish houses and to arrest Jewish peddlers and itinerant merchants who had shown up in town without authorization.[34] The enforcement of restrictions on mobility was one of the initial activities of the Blue Police aimed at the Jewish population, but it was not the only one. In late 1940, the Polish officers started to enforce the German hygienic regulations and proceeded to control the sanitary conditions in the ghettos. Most of the time, they oversaw quarantines in houses that had reported cases of typhoid fever. These quarantines, which were often combined with the forced disinfection of clothing—the so-called steamer that ruined these garments—paved way for corruption. Perec (Peretz) Opoczyński, a writer and scholar, described these steamers in gruesome detail.[35] This issue shall be discussed further in the chapter devoted to the situation in Warsaw.

The quarantine caused additional fear, since it could also lead to the deportation of the sick together with their families. This happened, for instance, to more than 1,000 Jews in Kałuszyn, a town east of Mińsk Mazowiecki, who were first placed in quarantine and later resettled in the Warsaw ghetto.[36] Linking Jews and infectious diseases—mainly typhus—became one of the leading and constant preoccupations of the German propaganda apparatus in the

34 The German regulations made it impossible for Jews to leave their places of residence. In rare cases, Jews were able to obtain special passes with an authorization to travel. In the case when German officials issued too many passes, they were perceived to be "too lenient" and found themselves under the scrutiny of the Gestapo. See the case of Plonsk Landrat, May 12, 1942, AIPN, Gestapo-Zichenau, 148/3765. Similarly in February 1941, a German official working in the office of the *Kreishauptmannschaft* (county administration) in Skierniewice was fired for giving a local Jew authorization to travel to Warsaw. See *Kreishauptmannschaft* Skierniewice, February 24, 1941, Instytut Zachodni, I-21, p. 18.

35 Perec Opoczyński, "Księga parówki," in Monika Polit, ed., *Reportaże z warszawskiego getta* (Warsaw: Stowarzyszenie Centrum Badań nad Zagładą Żydów, 2009), pp. 59–85. In Warsaw, Emanuel Ringelblum organized a group of people who collected information about various aspects of Jewish life and death in the ghetto. They documented the German policies of terror and the ways in which Jewish society coped with the inhuman conditions. Finally, before the final liquidation of the ghetto, the documents were buried by Oneg Shabbat members. Dug up from the rubble of Warsaw after the war, they are one of the most important sources of information about the Holocaust.

36 Health protection issues, April 4, 1941, Instytut Zachodni, I-21, p. 28.

Generalgouvernement. Signs reading "Jews-Lice-Typhus" could be seen on countless posters, stamps, announcements, in film newsreels, and even in artistic performances as part of the traveling theater of the Generalgouvernement.[37] Once the liquidation of the ghettos began, the propaganda campaign conducted under the guise of "concern for the hygiene of the Aryan-Christian population" acquired an even more sinister meaning.

In a letter sent out by the Blue Police district commander to his county-level chiefs in the Radomsko area, his subordinates were told to increase vigilance on the hygienic front. Quoting the higher-level German official, the commander wrote: "I ask you to pay particular attention to vagrant Jews, moving around without armbands and with unkempt beards, because their shoddy clothes and long beards are a source of filth and germs, which cause contagious diseases."[38] The German propaganda department of the Miechów County administrative office acted along similar lines, and warned the voits and village elders "to use their influence on local priests so that the clergymen continue to encourage the Aryan-Christian population to maintain good hygiene."[39] On July 9, 1942, on the eve of the liquidations of the Miechów-area ghettos, German officials wrote: "The Polish urban and rural population needs to be reminded not to entertain any contact with the Jews! Jews are the carriers of all diseases!"[40]

Returning to Opoczno in the earlier period, the invisible but very efficient ring of vigilance and supervision established by the Polish police around the ghetto contributed to the dramatic increase in poverty, hunger, and starvation among the Jewish population. The Jewish peddlers and small-time itinerant merchants who smuggled foodstuffs from the surrounding villages into the city

37 Jan Grabowski, "German Anti-Jewish Propaganda in the Generalgouvernement, 1939–1945: Inciting Hate through Posters, Films, and Exhibitions," *Holocaust and Genocide Studies*, 23:3 (2009), pp. 381–412.

38 Blue Police commander to county Blue Police chiefs in Radomsko area, April 27, 1942, AIPN, GK 695/1, p. 137.

39 *Kreishauptmann* in Miechów to voits and village elders, July 9, 1942, ANKr, PPPBrzN, vol. 3, p. 13.

40 Ibid.

were stopped by the "Blues" with frightening frequency and accuracy. The Jewish testimonies and accounts are replete with evidence of graft, which was often included among the charges of those involved in smuggling and other forms of illegal trade. The station register provides us with many cases of fines meted out to Jewish merchants, but undoubtedly, most of the people fined were simply too poor to give the officers the expected bribe.[41]

The people of Opoczno were well aware of the "racial profile" of their neighbors, and this knowledge greatly facilitated the work of the Polish officers in their search for Jews breaking wartime regulations. In small towns, the ever-present phenomenon of denunciation became a particularly acute danger. One of the Jewish survivors recalled a Polish youth by the name of Zapolski who had intimate knowledge of the ghetto and its inhabitants, and whose reports, which were filed with the gendarmes, brought about large-scale human misery.[42] In the fall of 1941, the police register reported frequent visits of Polish officers to the ghetto, where they inspected the Jewish police. According to Alter Szymszonowicz, author of a dramatic testimony from Opoczno, for the most part, the Jewish policemen were recruited from among the "lowlifes" who had been resettled into the *shtetl* from Łódź. With time, the Jewish policemen became loyal sidekicks and useful tools for the German and Polish officers who issued their orders. In early 1941, the Opoczno Jewish police even established its own holding pen, a primitive jail to detain Jews who were found guilty of minor violations, such as unpaid fines. In mid-1941, the Germans authorized the Jewish policemen to carry rubber batons and wear hats decorated with an eagle and a Star of David. The direct supervision over the Jewish police lay in the hands of Polish officers, in accordance with German regulations.

This pattern of empowerment of the non-German organizations and institutions and their involvement in the enforcement of anti-Jewish regulations can be seen throughout

41 Opoczno station register, March–July 1940, AP Kielce, Posterunek Policji Polskiej w Opocznie, 21/772.

42 Alter Szymszonowicz testimony, *Walka państwa hitlerowskiego o Zagładę narodu żydowskiego w Polsce*, ŻIH, 302/5.

occupied Europe. In Warsaw, where the Jewish police were a force to be reckoned with, the rules of supervision were codified in a series of regulations, which clearly delineated the extent and range of the powers of the Blue Police. In smaller jurisdictions such as Opoczno, the orders of the Polish officers were the law. The Polish officers conducted drills for their Jewish subordinates and took part in joint patrols inside the ghetto. During these patrols, the officers searched Jewish dwellings, and they seized goods deemed illegal and fined their owners. Undoubtedly, the seizures reported in the station register are merely the tip of the iceberg, as most of the seized merchandise simply became the property of the policemen involved. Alter Szymszonowicz described the searches, the arrests, and the ever-growing fines in the following words:

> In the beginning they took away the merchandise for even the slightest violation, such as selling milk, or having [anything] in stock; later on they would give fines of 1,000–2,000 zlotys, or three months of imprisonment. Although a Jew could have no more than 150 zlotys, the fine could go all the way to 2,000 zlotys. This is why the Polish jail was always full.[43]

Later on, the Jewish police established its own jail, as previously stated. Finally, one should mention that the Polish police also enforced the curfew in the ghetto. In Opoczno, it meant that the Blue Police had to ensure that the Jews would be off the streets after 9:00 PM.[44]

On Duty in Miechów and Brzesko Nowe

On April 12, 1940, Hans Frank decided to remove Jews from Kraków, the capital of the Generalgouvernement. That same day, the Governor General noted the following in his diary:

43 Ibid.

44 Opoczno station register, April–October 1942, entry from April 24, 1942, AP Kielce, Posterunek Policji Polskiej w Opocznie, 21/772.

> In order to preserve and to uphold the authority of the National-Socialist state one cannot have the officials of this state encounter the Jews in the streets and thus be exposed to epidemics. That's why [the chief of the Kraków district] plans to cleanse Kraków of Jews as of November 1, 1940. He wants to conduct a great operation of removal of the Jews so that no more than 5,000 or 10,000 are left in the city. Those allowed to stay will include important artisans and all the others will be resettled elsewhere in the Generalgouvernement. Kraków will become the most Jew-free city in the entire Generalgouvernement.[45]

Hans Frank revisited this issue once again in August 1940 when he delivered a speech about the political structures of the NSDAP in the Generalgouvernement: "If, after midnight tomorrow, a Jew dares to show up here, in Kraków, without a permit, he will be sent off straight away to perform forced labor. The Jews have to disappear from all of Europe!"[46]

In mid-May 1940, the plan to remove Jews from the city acquired a legal framework. According to the regulations, the Jews had to leave Kraków within three months, taking with them no more than 25 kilograms of luggage per person. Before the end of spring 1940, anywhere between 30,000 and 40,000 of Kraków's Jews were removed from the city. Some of them moved to Miechów County, an area situated north of the city. The local German authorities in Miechów, however, were prepared to adequately unwelcome the newcomers. The local chief of the civil administration ordered the Polish police to extend strict control over the "non-resident" Jews who had migrated into the area.[47] Already by April 1940, the police had introduced an early curfew for the Jews residing in Miechów

45 Stanisław Piotrowski, ed., *Dziennik Hansa Franka* (Warsaw: Wydawnictwo prawnicze, 1956), p. 408.

46 Quoted from Max Weinreich, *Hitler's Professors: The Part of Scholarship in Germany's Crimes against the Jewish People* (New Haven: Yale University Press, 1999), p. 92.

47 Letter from the *Kreishauptmann* to all Jewish religious communities in the county; copies sent to all Blue Police stations in the county, August 7, 1940, ANKr, PPPBrzN, vol. 16, p. 1.

and the vicinity.[48] The supervision by the Blue Police included the seizure of goods deemed "excessive." Fiszel Szmajzer, an artisan from Kraków, learned this the hard way, when the policemen confiscated the few items that he had managed to salvage from Kraków.[49] After all, it was the police who decided what was and was not "excessive" property. In Miechów as well as in Opoczno, the resettled Jews soon learned that their humble belongings could be taken away from them. In the case of Szmajzer, the policemen seized a long list of objects, including "beds, chairs, wooden table and six packs of tea, 50 grams each," as can be read in the official report.[50] Many other Jews were stopped while they were attempting to smuggle foodstuffs in and out of Kraków.[51] The zeal of the Blue Police officers when impounding Jewish property sometimes forced the Germans to act. Chana Birnbaum, the owner of a bakery, saw her allotment of flour impounded by the Polish officers. The flour was needed, however, to bake the rationed bread for the Jewish population. It took a special order from the office of the *Kreishauptmann* to reverse the confiscation and to return the flour to the Jewish baker.[52] In January 1941, the "Blues" continued to arrest Jews trying to smuggle food to Kraków. A number of seizures, fines, and arrests were reported in the station registers.

In Brzesko Nowe, a town located around 32 kilometers northeast of Kraków, the fate of the Jews not only lay in the hands of the police and the German mayor but it also depended on the actions—or inaction—of many other people and institutions. In March 1940, the voit of the Gruszów Commune (*gmina*) requested that the commander of the Blue Police in Brzesko Nowe punish the voit of the Israelite community,[53] by which he meant the elder

48 Letter of the Blue Police county chief, April 15, 1940, ANKr, PPPBrzN, vol. 44, p. 9.

49 Protocol and report of seized items, March 20, 1941, ANKr, PPPBrzN, vol. 17, p. 8.

50 Ibid.

51 List of seized items, ANKr, PPPBrzN, vol. 45, pp. 104–109.

52 Letter from the office of Miechów *Kreishauptmann*, October 14, 1941, ANKr, PPPBrzN, vol. 17, pp. 17–17v.

53 See the letter from the voit Osika, March 11, 1941, ANKr, PPPBrzN, v. 17, unpaginated.

of the Jewish community, who had failed to deliver the requested number of Jews to perform forced labor removing snow. In March 1941, another voit asked the police to simply arrest those Jews who had refused to report for slave labor.[54] These letters had consequences. In the files of the Brzesko Nowe police, we find lists of wanted Jewish offenders who had been denounced to the authorities by local voits and village elders. With time, the tone of the official correspondence became increasingly threatening. In September 1941, an engineer leading a water-drainage project in the village of Grobla close to Brzesko Nowe complained to the chief of the Polish police: "We have to inform you that if our present appeal to the Local Authority produces no results, we will have no choice but to turn to the German Police Authorities."[55] Here, the concerned engineer attached a list of Jews who were absent from work. Engineer Gnoiński from Hebdów had similar concerns and also threatened the Polish police with reporting "missing Jews" directly to the "Higher Power" in Kraków.[56]

The fate of the Jews of Opoczno and Brzesko Nowe was, of course, not any different from the fate of the Jews elsewhere in the provinces. The control over the open ghettos—or Jews living outside the ghettos, as was the case in Brzesko Nowe—did not only lie in the hands of those people and institutions directly involved in the policies of terror and, later, of extermination. It was also the bystanders, or those simple people whose fear made an important contribution to the horrible efficiency of the German genocidal measures. At the same time, the realities of occupation empowered people of bad will, who could now use the German

54 Ibid.

55 Letter from Schmidt and Blachniak Construction to the Brzesko Nowe Blue Police commander, September 20, 1941, ANKr, PPPBrzN, vol. 17, p. 12. More letters on the same topic arrived at the police station in November 1941. Interestingly, the word "authorities" was consistently written with capital "A," which went against the rules of grammar, but certainly reflected well the spirit of the times.

56 Letter from Engineer Gnoiński, October 24, 1941, ANKr, PPPBrzN, vol. 17, p. 26. See also the letter from the chief of the *Arbeitsamt* (Employment office) in Kazimierza Wielka requesting that the Jewish Council send 100 Jews to land melioration work. September 18, 1941, ANKr, PPPBrzN, vol. 34, p. 34.

terror to gain power and wealth. They were the ones who allowed the German system to reach its full potential. Marczewski, a furrier from Sokołów Podlaski, seized this once-in-a-lifetime opportunity of advancement and became one of the top officials in the local administration. Marczewski strutted along the streets of the city, "telling the Jews that they could stay outside only until 8:00 PM and every person found [later in the] street would be put to death."[57] Not infrequently, the violence was not even motivated by greed; some young Poles in Sokołów quickly learned from the Germans that one could harm and humiliate the Jews with impunity, for instance, by cutting off their beards.[58] On May 6, 1941, the county mayor in Miechów went a step further and declared that "all sidewalks and paths in all towns and villages" of his county were off-limits to Jews.[59] Since then, the Jews could only walk in the streets or, to be more precise, along the sewers. A special order that was sent out to all precincts and stations of the Blue Police made the Polish officers responsible for the enforcement of this regulation too.[60]

In large part, what the Germans knew about Polish society—both about ethnic Poles and the Jews—depended on denunciations filed with the authorities or "confidential information" shared with the Blue policemen. The denunciations were essential to detect, among other things, Jews who had violated the ban on ritual slaughter, which became illegal on October 26, 1939. The Blue Police was tasked with the enforcement of this ban.[61] On April 29, 1941, the chief of the gendarmes from Miechów ordered the Blue Police to reinforce control over the Jews who were leaving

57 Josek Kopyto account, ŻIH, 301/4085.

58 Ibid.

59 To all Blue Police posts in the Miechów district, May 6, 1941, ANKr, PPPBrzN, vol. 16, p. 3. The letter is in poor condition, and the writing is barely legible.

60 Letter from the district police commander Major Stanisław Siwoń to police stations in the district, May 6, 1941, ANKr, PPPBrzN, vol. 16, p. 3. Siwoń was dismissed from service on March 31, 1943.

61 Letter from the head of the Veterinary Office of the Generalgouvernement to district heads, February 10, 1940, ANKr, PPPBrzN, vol. 30, p. 1. The letter began with the words: "Według informacji napływających od ludności miejscowej Żydzi w dalszym ciągu praktykują ubój [rytualny]" (According to information received from the local population, Jews still practice [ritual slaughter]).

their place of permanent residence "due to the [fear of] typhus epidemic."[62] In the official correspondence of the Polish police, Jews and homeless beggars were placed in the same category of high epidemic danger.[63] In Miechów County, the authorities established special disinfection units, which were to operate with the assistance of the Polish police. Over time, these units became a real threat to the Jews. At the end of June 1941, the chief of the Miechów Kripo issued an order to the Blue Police to arrest all Jews who were residing in the county without a valid permit and to transfer them into the custody of the Criminal Police.[64]

Indeed, from the beginning of the occupation, the Criminal Police demonstrated a great deal of interest in the "Jewish question." The Polish detectives, who were members of the prewar Investigative Service now serving within the structures of the Sipo, possessed an excellent knowledge of "Jewish affairs" due to an extensive network of informants. In 1940 and 1941, Sergeant Stanisław Kowalski, who headed the Polish Kripo in Miechów, called on the Polish Blue Police to extend stricter control over the Jews who had been resettled there from Kraków.[65] In July 1941, some Jews in the rural areas were forced to leave their farms, and the "Blues" escorted Poles to these places and allowed them to take over the vacated Jewish homesteads.[66] It is hard to establish the extent of these expropriations, but the first to go were the Jews from the Kozłów Commune: "The Jewish farmers shall be expropriated and removed," as stated in a short note signed by *Stadthauptmann*

62 Telegram from the Blue Police district headquarters in Miechów to all Blue Police posts in the district, April 29, 1941, ANKr, PPPBrzN, vol. 16, p. 2.

63 Letter from the district police headquarters in Miechów to posts in the Miechów district, April 10, 1941, ANKr, PPPBrzN, vol. 27, p. 6.

64 Letter from the Kriminalpolizei, Kriminalkomissariat Miechów to commanders of Blue Police posts in the district, June 24, 1941, ANKr, PPPBrzN, vol. 16, p. 24.

65 Letter from the Sicherheitspolizei, Kriminalkomissariat Miechów to commanders of Blue Police posts in the district, October 3, 1941, ANKr, PPPBrzN, vol. 17, p. 16.

66 Letter from the mayor of Miechów to the Gendarmerie in Miechów, July 8, 1941, ANKr, PPPBrzN, vol. 17, p. 10. The whole operation, conducted under the authority of the Kraków Real Estate Office, was coordinated by a certain Kluczniok, the chief of the Real Estate Office in Dziekanowice.

Schode of Miechów.[67] Schode's order was later sent to the appropriate posts of the Blue Police for further action. The identity of the Poles, described by the German mayor as "Polish Deportees,"[68] who were established—with police assistance—on the farms belonging to the deported and dispossessed Jews, is unclear. The takeover of Jewish property by the Aryan population also took place in other districts of the Generalgouvernement.

A few months earlier, in February and March 1941, in *Kreishauptmannschaft* (county administration) Skierniewice in the western reaches of the Warsaw district, the authorities removed the Jews from 140 houses and 2,134 apartments. Once the Jewish owners had been removed, their apartments were "disinfected," and Poles moved in.[69] The whole process of establishing ethnic Poles in houses that had been taken away from the Jews, a phenomenon that was occurring long before the beginning of the "Final Solution," has altogether escaped historical scrutiny. For the local peasants, the removal of Jews to the ghettos presented an unexpected, welcome, and previously unheard-of opportunity to improve their fortunes. The Germans were not pleased with this transfer of wealth. First, the takeover of Jewish property by the Polish peasants was associated with violence and chaos, something that the Germans frequently complained could damage the reputation of the authorities. Second, in line with the spirit of the German laws, it was the treasury of the Reich—and not the Polish peasants—that was to be the rightful and sole "heir" of the deported and murdered Jews. The fact that the Germans allowed the Poles to take part in this theft at all was directly related to the great volume of Jewish property "waiting" for new owners and a very limited number of Germans living in the Generalgouvernement who were prepared to participate in such robbery.[70] The Germans were quite obviously

67 Ibid.

68 Ibid.

69 The chief of Skierniewice County to the chief of the Office of the Governor General, April 3, 1942, Instytut Zachodni, I-21, pp. 42–43.

70 See Jan Grabowski, "Zarząd Powierniczy i nieruchomości żydowskie w Generalnym Gubernatorstwie: 'Co można skonfiskować? W zasadzie wszystko,'"

not interested in alleviating the fate of the impoverished Polish masses. The *Kreishauptmann* of Rzeszów noted this problem in the spring of 1941. According to the German official, the roundup and deportation of the Jews to the ghettos were fraught with logistical problems, and, most unfortunately, the Polish peasants immediately filled the spaces vacated by the deportees.[71]

Labor Camps

Any discussion of the role of the Blue Police in the implementation of the German *Judenpolitik* during the period of 1939–1942 cannot bypass the issue of labor camps, a poorly known aspect of the German attempt to impose total control over Jewish society. While we know little about the camps, we know even less about the guards who enforced iron discipline on the Jewish slaves, who worked in horrible conditions. According to Emanuel Ringelblum, the guards might have belonged to the "antisemitic riffraff" who had become particularly active since the first months of war. The historian of the Warsaw ghetto wrote the following:

> Later on, these individuals became the personnel of the various kinds of *Lagerschutz* [camp guards] whose task it was to keep watch over the Jewish labor camps. They tormented and tortured the Jewish prisoners with impunity, pitilessly wounding and killing anyone without sufficient money to buy off the torturers.[72]

This issue of the *Lagerschutze* falls within the focus of this study because, in many instances, it seems that the Blue Police had an important role to play in the recruitment and training of guards slated for the forced labor camps for Jews. The labor camps were one

in Jan Grabowski and Dariusz Libionka, eds., *Klucze i kasa: O mieniu żydowskim w Polsce pod okupacją niemiecką i we wczesnych latach powojennych 1939–1950* (Warsaw: Stowarzyszenie Centrum Badań nad Zagładą Żydów, 2014).

71 *Kreishauptmannschaft* Reichshof, April 9, 1941, Instytut Zachodni, I-21, p. 13v.

72 Ringelblum, *Polish-Jewish Relations*, pp. 41–42.

of the most conspicuous features in the landscape of terror of the Generalgouvernement. The only book that is devoted to this topic lists several hundred camps, some of which were for Poles, some for Jews (the so-called *Judenarbeitslager*, also known as *Julags*), and some held a mixed population of both Jews and Poles, although usually the two groups were barracked separately. Soon, however, the *Julags* became notorious due to particularly harsh conditions, which resulted in the high mortality of inmates. Not infrequently, labor was secondary to torture and humiliation, which made the camps an important element of the German genocidal policy.

Halina Krahelska was a prewar social activist and writer. During the occupation in Warsaw, she kept a diary in which she often described the plight of the Jews with concern, empathy, and, later on, with growing horror. In late 1941, she noted the following testimony of an inmate who was held in the Drewnica labor camp for Jews in the Warsaw area:

> They took me to the collection point in Leszno Street. There, in utter chaos, they proceeded with medical check-ups and registration. Around 9 AM they took us to the baths. Straight from there, they took us to Leszno Street, for a roll call. From there the "*Lagerschutz*[*e*]" (Poles and Ukrainians) armed with rifles marched us, hungry, through the city, more than 8 kilometers. Along the way they harassed us, they ordered us to run, they prevented women from giving us parcels [with food] and, to frighten away bystanders, they fired shots in Grzybowska Street. We arrived at the camp around 5 PM.... Our job was to drain the swamps; people had to stand in the water for up to ten hours per day. When we worked, they [the guards] whipped us, so that very many people died. They died of exhaustion, they fainted at work but the guards revived them and forced them back. They didn't beat those who kept working, but they whipped the sick and the weak until they dropped dead.[73]

73 Halina Krahelska, *Kronika* (unpublished manuscript), entry for July 9, 1942, AAN, 383/ II 1- 3.

The long description ends with the following words: "Nevertheless, this camp was hailed as one of the better ones. The people were starving, they worked very hard, so that no one would survive there for a longer period of time. During seven weeks 30 out of 400 inmates died."[74]

As stated previously, very little is known about the guards who enforced inhuman regulations and were responsible for thousands of Jewish deaths. In the scant literature, this question is usually dismissed with brief information about anonymous Germans or their Ukrainian helpers. We can learn some more from the scattered testimonies of those Jews who went through these camps and lived to tell the story.[75] In the only serious scholarly account of the issue, we read the following:

> Due to the number of these camps, during the early period the SS and police authorities were unable to provide enough of their own personnel to staff all the locations. Some camps were serviced by the Sonderdienst, by the Jewish police...or by Poles, trained by the authorities as guards.[76]

The forced labor camp in Mordy, a village located east of Siedlce, seems to have been one of these camps where "the SS and police authorities were unable to provide enough of their own personnel to staff all the locations." It was the Poles, recruited and trained by the Blue Police, who replaced them. In the spring of 1941, several hundred Jews from the Warsaw ghetto were shipped to Mordy. Their task was to drain the nearby swamps. Eighteen-year-old Izaak Jeruchemson was one of the Jewish forced laborers brought at that time to the camp, which, to be more precise, was located

74 Ibid.

75 See Mojsze Herdyk, *Obóz pracy*, YVA, M.10.AR1/409. Other accounts of Jewish prisoners can also be found in the Yad Vashem Archives: M.10.AR1/171; M.10.AR1/390; M.10.AR1/968; M10.AR1/373. As quoted in Havi Dreifuss (Ben-Sasson), *Relations between Jews and Poles during the Holocaust: The Jewish Perspective* (Jerusalem: Yad Vashem, 2017), pp. 93–95.

76 Józef Marszałek, *Obozy pracy w Generalnym Gubernatorstwie w latach 1939–1945* (Lublin: Państwowe Muzeum na Majdanku, 1998), p. 15.

in Stok Ruski, a hamlet close to Mordy. We know very little about Jeruchemson. In fact, practically all we know about him can be found in a thin police dossier titled "Prosecutor's file regarding the shooting of Izaak Jeruchemson."[77] As we learn from the file, Jeruchemson was killed on April 24, 1941, during a failed attempt to flee the camp. The Blue policeman who inspected the body found one photograph and two documents belonging to Jeruchemson in the pocket of the victim.

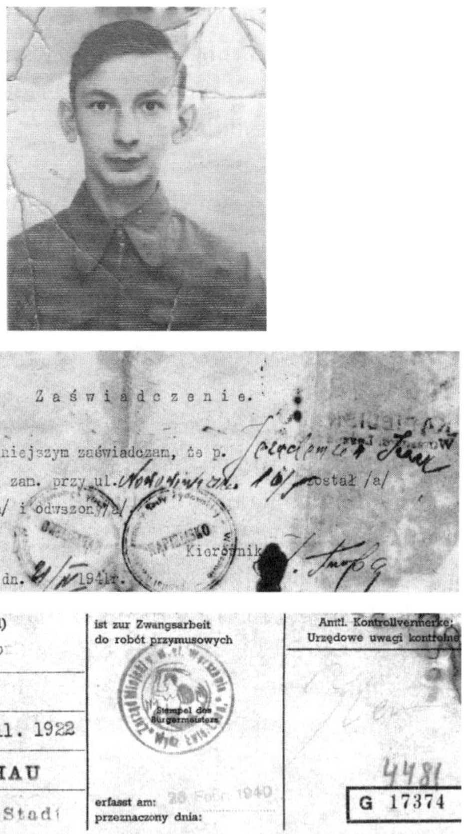

Personal documents of Izaak Jeruchemson, including a photo (top), a delousing certificate (middle), and orders to perform forced labor (bottom). From the collection of AMSW, SSW, 1379.

77 Prosecutor's files regarding the shooting of Izaak Jeruchemson, April–July 1941, AMSW, SSW, 1379.

The first document, issued by Leszno Baths in Warsaw, confirmed that Izaak Jeruchemson had been deloused and bathed on April 21, 1941. The second document, issued by the Municipality of Warsaw, stated that Jeruchemson was selected for forced labor. In the photo, there is a young, slender boy with protruding ears and a wave of dark hair combed to the side. If we discount the short and erroneous entry in the Yad Vashem Central Database of Shoah Victims' Names, this is all that is left of Izaak Jeruchemson. The investigation into Jeruchemson's death began on April 27, 1941, when Feliks Patkowski, a peasant from the village of Ciepielin, reported the finding of a young man's body next to his house. The police quickly established that the victim had fled from the nearby *Julag*. On the same day, the nearest station of the Blue Police took over the investigation, and they requested an autopsy and interrogated three *Lagerschutze* who were involved in the shooting. The police learned that Jeruchemson and two other Jews had escaped from the camp on the evening of April 24.

Three camp guards—Poles hailing from different areas of occupied Poland—were mobilized into action by Wacław Jabłoński, the commander of the guarding detail, and they went in pursuit of the fleeing Jews. According to one of the guards Witold Andruszkiewicz, eleven shots were fired during the chase. One Jew was killed, and two others were caught and brought back to the camp. The investigation ended here. On May 5, 1941, Sergeant Ekiert of the Mordy Blue Police station sent his report to the Polish Kripo headquarters in Siedlce. The last note in the file, written in German, was drafted by the Polish Kripo. Writing for his German overseers, the Polish detective concluded: "On April 24, 1941, three Jews escaped from the labor camp in Stok Ruski. Izaak Jeruchemson, one of the Jews, has been killed by the guards. The guards are Poles."[78] From the German standpoint, one can gather that the shooting was of no importance. Since the victim was a Jew and Poles were responsible for the shooting, the "interests of the German nation have not been hurt," to use the nomenclature of the court documents

78 Note, April 1941, Prosecutor's files regarding the shooting of Izaak Jeruchemson, April–July 1941, AMSW, SSW, 1379.

of the time. This officially ended the investigation into the death of the young Jew from the Warsaw ghetto.

This shooting in Stok Ruski was nothing out of the ordinary. During the spring and summer of 1941, the number of Jews murdered in the Generalgouvernement continued to grow. Krahelska, the previously quoted Warsaw-based author, noted the following in her diary:

> The Jewish labor camps are hell. In July 1941 there were 11 labor camps [in the Warsaw area] with a population of 3,000 workers or, to be more precise, slaves. Emaciated bodies, people driven to death by horrible conditions, by slave labor and the whips of their tormentors, some of them try to escape their hell. It is difficult to say how many managed to return to life. What is known, however, is that within a very short time ten people were executed for an escape attempt: two in the Ossowo camp, five in the Sajczyce camp and three who tried to flee the Sawina [Sawin] camp.[79]

Quite by chance, looking through the files of postwar courts, I came across the case of the murder of Izaak Jeruchemson once again. In 1946, five years after the above-described events, the case came to the attention of the authorities. This time, the investigation was triggered by an anonymous denunciation sent to the Citizens' Militia,[80] alerting the authorities to the fact that during the war, Witold Andruszkiewicz killed Jews in his role as a camp guard.[81] The postwar files do not mention Jeruchemson by name—he was just one more unidentified Jew—but there is no doubt that the denunciation concerns the events from Stok Ruski in April 1941. Andruszkiewicz's sister testified as follows:

> It was at the time when they put the Jews in a ghetto in Warsaw. My brother volunteered for the police and underwent training

79 Krahelska, *Kronika,* diary entry, August 25, 1941, AAN, 383/ II 1- 3.

80 The Citizens' Militia was the official name of the Polish police after 1944.

81 Dossier of Witold Andruszkiewicz (Blue policeman suspected of harming persons of Jewish origin), 1946–1947, AIPN, GK 453/465.

> in Mordy. Once his training was over, he kept guard over the working Jews. He told me himself that one time six Jews fled the camp, and all guards were sent in pursuit. He told me that he caught up with one jewboy [*sic*] and shot him.[82]

In another deposition, she gave more details:

> My brother received a summons to report to serve in the Polish uniformed police. Later, they took all of them to Mordy for a few days of training and then they sent them to Stoczek, to serve. He stayed there for a short time and, after a month, he came back home with a rifle.[83]

Elsewhere, in the same file, we learn more details about young Andruszkiewicz's service:

> Once he came back home, he told us that he was afraid, and that his colleagues mocked him. He told us that he had to keep watch over the Jews and once, when a few of them escaped, the Germans told them to shoot. My brother was running next to a German and when the German ordered him to shoot, my brother fired and killed the Jew.
>
> [Question]: From where do you know that your brother was in the police and that he killed a Jew?
>
> I know he was planning to join the police, we talked about it at home, and he received a summons to report to the police station in Warsaw. And he told me himself, at home, in the evening, that he shot the Jews.[84]

Interestingly, it is only at this late stage that the Germans make an appearance in the records, allegedly ordering the young Pole to shoot at the Jews. The wartime police files, contemporaneous

82 Deposition of Witold Andruszkiewicz's sister, Dossier of Witold Andruszkiewicz, 1946–1947, AIPN, GK 453/465.

83 Ibid.

84 Ibid.

to the shooting, make no mention of the Germans at all. In the postwar court records, the "sudden" appearance of the previously unnoted and absent Germans is a frequent phenomenon. Characteristically, it is not during the early stages of the investigation but later in court that the Germans appear on the scene, once the village community had had time to come together and defend its members and present a unified version of events. This pattern of self-serving and exculpating testimony will be noted in many instances in the later chapters.

Returning to the camp guard Witold Andruszkiewicz, a young man from the town of Rembertów close to Warsaw who was summoned in the spring of 1941 to the nearest station of the Blue Police. According to the available evidence, Andruszkiewicz had sought admission to the ranks of the Polish police sometime earlier. A few days later, his mother—concerned that her son had failed to return home—visited the police station "and brought bread, assuming that he was being detained."[85] Indeed, young Andruszkiewicz had been detained, although in a different way than what his mother had feared. She soon learned that her son was undergoing training in a special camp in Zacisze, close to Warsaw. Once she arrived in Zacisze, she saw her son and others "training, without rifles," and there were some barracks in the camp "with simple wooden bunkbeds and nothing more," recalled Andruszkiewicz's mother.[86] The young guard-in-training complained bitterly about the harsh conditions and lack of warm clothing. Together with him, there were 200 other young men who were being trained for labor camp duties. The camp operated under the authority of the Blue Police. One month later, at home during his first furlough, Andruszkiewicz spoke of how he and the other guards had to shoot the fleeing Jews, by order of the Germans.

The circumstances surrounding the death of Izaak Jeruchemson from Warsaw who was killed by the guards during an escape attempt from a labor camp raise a number

85 Deposition of Witold Andruszkiewicz's mother, Dossier of Witold Andruszkiewicz, 1946–1947, AIPN, GK 453/465.

86 Ibid.

of questions that may also indicate the scale of our ignorance. First, the guards in the camp near Mordy were recruited from among young Poles who had been brought from different parts of the country. At least some of them, as in the case of Andruszkiewicz, had previously applied to serve in the Blue Police and were redirected as guards to the labor camps. This was not an unknown practice. One year later, in 1942, hundreds of other volunteers for the police service were rerouted to the notorious Schutzmannschaft Battalion 202, which was eventually deployed against the partisans in the East.[87]

In 1941, the Polish resistance warned Poles against volunteering for the *Lagerschutz* formations that had been created by the occupying forces. It is most likely that this warning served as a strong deterrent and could have been at the root of the decision to send potential police recruits to carry out camp duties. Before assuming their duties in the camps, the young Poles would undergo special training. Despite the scale of this phenomenon—in the spring of 1941, there were 200 recruits trained in the Zacisze camp alone—we know nothing about these training camps. It goes without saying that this is an issue that begs for further study by historians of the Holocaust and the occupation. Those who are of a different opinion might want to reread the previously quoted paragraph from Ringelblum about "individuals who tormented and tortured the Jewish prisoners with impunity" in the *Julags*, the Jewish labor camps. After all, it is difficult to take issue with the Jewish historian who, day after day, week after week, and month after month collected evidence from inmates returning from various camps to the Warsaw ghetto.

In place of a conclusion and to allow for a comparative historical perspective, it is fitting to quote from the only book that deals with the history of the Blue Police. Discussing the period of time that has been the object of analysis in this chapter, Adam Hempel wrote as follows:

87 The personnel files of the volunteers reporting for duty in Schutzmannschaft Battalion 202 can be found in AIPN, GK 658/1–52.

> Until the beginning of 1941, the role of the Polish police institutions in the policies of the occupant was minimal. The Polish police was were to make sure that the Jews wore the prescribed armbands and, later on, whether they had permission to move outside the ghetto. In the first half of 1941, the Polnische Polizei's role grew and the officers were ordered to secure the borders of the ghettos. In principle, it was the responsibility of the Jewish police, and the Polish police was only deployed at the access gates.[88]

According to abundant historical evidence, Hempel is wrong. The Blue Police was deeply involved in the enforcement of German anti-Jewish regulations both inside and outside the ghettos and throughout the Generalgouvernement from the beginning of the occupation, and their role continued to grow together with the growth of German policies of terror.

88 Hempel, *Pogrobowcy klęski*, pp. 170–171.

Chapter Three

The Period of Transition: Fall 1941–Summer 1942

In July and August 1941, the plan for the extermination of European Jews had not yet been completely formulated. Even the order to prepare "the Final Solution to the Jewish Question" given by Hermann Göring to Heinrich Himmler on July 31, 1941, should be viewed as a general formula that still included several possible alternatives. The leaders of the Third Reich knew that something needed to be done with the Jews, but they still lacked a clear decision, an order. This order—later known as the *Führerbefehl* (Führer's order), the decision that condemned millions of European Jews to death—must have been given sometime between September and October 1941. It was in November 1941 when Reinhard Heydrich sent out the initial invitations to a conference—later known as the Wannsee Conference—which was to spell out the details and elaborate on the technical aspects of the planned extermination. Although we have no written proof since the decision was never committed to paper, it is obvious that during those few weeks, Hitler must have made up his mind. The decision made in Berlin quickly translated into concrete measures against the Jews, which were implemented in the Generalgouvernement and in other areas of Poland. This, in turn, further increased the participation of non-German forces—most of all, the Polish police—in the German *Judenpolitik*.

The decisions of the Nazi leadership, the growing brutality of the war in the East, and the mass murders that were being perpetrated by the Einsatzgruppen behind the front lines were not without impact on the measures adopted by the Germans in the Generalgouvernement. The terror directed against the Jews grew visibly in early fall 1941. The increased terror simultaneously struck Jews who lived in both the ghettos in large cities as well as those living in the smaller, usually open ghettos.

The Opoczno Blue Police Station: Fall 1941–Summer 1942

At the end of November 1941, in the previously mentioned town of Opoczno in the Radom district, Polish policemen started to arrest and fine any Jew, rather than only the so-called alien Jews, which had been done for quite some time. The time spent in police custody grew significantly. The arrested Jews most often hailed from the outlying villages and had been travelling to Opoczno in order to sell their produce. The station register also provides evidence of stepped-up control measures concerning the Jewish police. Such drills and checks occurred on each shift, although the register does not provide us with a more detailed description of the activities undertaken by the Polish officers in execution of their mandate inside the ghetto.

In the winter and spring of 1942, the authorities ordered that the rest of the Jews who were still living in the rural areas must be resettled in the nearest ghettos. Historians have paid little attention to this phenomenon, but it is worthwhile to note that until then, several hundred thousand Polish Jews still lived in their own homes, outside the ghettos. For the most part, they dwelled in villages far away from the large ghettos and far from German control and scrutiny. Once the decision to implement the "Final Solution" was reached, their fate changed dramatically. Throughout Poland, over the course of several winter weeks in early 1942, the Jews were forced to abandon their dwellings and move to the nearest ghetto. The Polish police became the primary institutional agent responsible for the ensuing move to the ghettos.

As we learn from the police station register, the concentration of the Jews in Opoczno was ordered in January 1942. The village elders and other local and commune-level authorities ordered individual Jews and Jewish households to leave their residence, and the Polish policemen escorted the victims to their destination. As mentioned earlier, the concentration of rural Jews was part of a general policy that paved the way for the liquidation *Aktionen*, which were soon to commence. The arrival of the new deportees substantially increased the population of the already overcrowded Opoczno ghetto to 4,230 people. The severe living conditions worsened even further.[1] The seizures of produce and other merchandise, often mentioned in the official correspondence of the local station of the Polish police, further added to the extreme misery of the Jewish population of the ghetto.

Excerpts from the Opoczno station register refer to the situation in the ghetto as follows:

> *January 28, 1942*: On patrol in Opoczno and control of the Jewish Order Service. Duration: 8 hours; Constables Franciszek Bieńko and Franciszek Matusiak. I fined Laja Gingold 5 zlotys for wearing a dirty armband on her sleeve. On patrol to the village Kraśnica in order to remove the Jews and bring them to Opoczno, for the duration.
>
> *January 29, 1942*: Control of the Jewish Order Service, issuing fines in the ghetto (sanitary regulations). On patrol in the Jewish quarter.
>
> *February 1, 1942*: In Opoczno, searching Jewish dwellings for illegal merchandise (the searches proved fruitful). Control of the Jewish Order Service, Constable Franciszek Bieńko.[2]

1 Alter Szymszonowicz testimony, *Walka państwa hitlerowskiego*, ŻIH, 302/5. See also "Opoczno," in Geoffrey P. Megargee, ed., *The United States Holocaust Memorial Museum Encyclopedia of Camps and Ghettos, 1933–1945, vol. 2: Ghettos in German-Occupied Eastern Europe* (Bloomington: Indiana University Press, 2012), pp. 266–267.

2 Opoczno station register, entries from January–February 1942, AP Kielce, Posterunek Policji Polskiej w Opocznie, 21/772.

In April 1942, the Germans carried out the so-called Communist *Aktion* (*Kommunistenaktion*), which saw the mass shooting of "leftist elements" in the ghettos throughout the Generalgouvernement. In fact, the police were not after the Communists, but they wanted to hunt down and kill anyone who could mobilize the Jews to carry out acts of defiance or struggle in the event of the liquidation of the ghetto. The *Kommunistenaktion* in Opoczno began on April 27, 1942. A few days earlier, the Jewish Council was ordered by the Germans to prepare a list of prominent community members. Armed with this list of names, the police arrested and later executed between twenty and thirty people in the Jewish cemetery. In the days preceding the *Kommunistenaktion*, the Blue Police received orders to tighten control over the ghetto. On the night of April 24, 1942, reinforced patrols appeared in the ghetto. In the station register, we read the following: "*April 24, 1942*: On patrol in the Jewish quarter in order to enforce the curfew." The patrol lasted two hours, from 9:00 to 11:00 PM, and Sergeant Marciniak made the following note: "Comments: Jews respect the curfew."[3] In July 1942, a few hundred Jews were taken from the ghetto and delivered to the *Julag* in Skarżysko-Kamienna.

On July 28, 1942, quite possibly in relation to this deportation, the station register reported the following comment by Sergeant Józef Smogala: "Special service in Opoczno—assisting an official from the Municipal Office in settling Polish families into the apartments vacated by Jews who have been removed."[4] On the same day that some Polish policemen helped new tenants move into "post-Jewish" apartments and houses,[5] their colleagues escorted a column of 100 Jews to forced labor in the Erystor factory nearby. In

3 Opoczno station register, entry from April 24, 1942, AP Kielce, Posterunek Policji Polskiej w Opocznie, 21/772.

4 Opoczno station register, entry from July 28, 1942, AP Kielce, Posterunek Policji Polskiej w Opocznie, 21/772.

5 The expression "post-Jewish property" (*własność pożydowska*), entered the Polish vocabulary during the war and, until today, remains a common way to describe property owned by the Jews until the Nazi-imposed robbery and dispossession.

August, the German gendarmes checked the state of preparedness of their Polish subordinates: "Mr. Lieutenant and Mr. Ensign gave lectures, conducted drills, and checked weapons," reported the station register.[6] The situation acquired additional importance and urgency in light of the looming liquidation of the Opoczno ghetto as well as other ghettos in the area, liquidations in which—as it was soon to become obvious—the Polish officers were to play a significant role.

In September, the "Blues" were ordered to guard the "post-Jewish" houses against thieves. On October 27, 1942, the liquidation unit (Liquidierungskommando), composed of German gendarmes and local Polish policemen with the help of the Jewish police, conducted a deadly deportation. Over the course of several hours during this bloody affair, up to 400 Jews—mostly the sick and the elderly—were shot in the ghetto, while the rest were herded onto a train destined for Treblinka. As was usually the case, some Jews were left behind in order to help clean the ghetto and gather more valuables. The day after the liquidation, the officer on duty noted in the comments section of the register: "*October 28, 1942*: Special duties in the former Jewish quarter in order to preserve order and to keep the civilian population away."[7]

Seizure of Furs

News about the impending attack against the Soviet Union had been circulating in the Generalgouvernement since at least the beginning of 1941. The Jews, who saw the possible arrival of the Soviets as deliverance, listened to these rumors and gossip with particular—and understandable—eagerness and hope. Unfortunately, the first weeks of war against the Soviet Union seemed to indicate that here too, the Germans would most likely repeat their earlier successes from the Polish and French blitz campaigns. Soon, however, the

6 Opoczno station register, entry from August 1942, AP Kielce, Posterunek Policji Polskiej w Opocznie, 21/772.

7 Opoczno station register, entry from October 28, 1942, AP Kielce, Posterunek Policji Polskiej w Opocznie, 21/772.

situation on the front became more complex. In November 1941, the German troops came close to Moscow, but it was obvious that the Blitzkrieg was over, and the resolution of the Russian campaign was not imminent, which forced the Wehrmacht soldiers to make closer acquaintance with Russian winter.

In order to support the troops and the economy of the Reich, the German authorities decided to further mobilize the populations of occupied Europe. The Jews, whose situation had deteriorated quicker than that of the German troops on the Eastern Front, were ordered to make particularly heavy sacrifices. While the ration cards for Jews diminished, the burden of forced labor continued to grow. In the last days of December 1941, in the midst of a particularly harsh winter, the authorities issued a special regulation requiring the Jews to surrender their warm clothing, particularly furs including coats, jackets, hats, and gloves, to the state.[8] The furs were to be sent to the German soldiers who were bogged down in the snow at the gates of Moscow in order to ensure the "final victory in the East." Those refusing to comply with the new law faced the death penalty, a punishment applied to Jewish offenders progressively more frequently and for increasingly trivial violations of wartime regulations. In this case too, the Blue Police was given the task of enforcing the new measure.

In Warsaw, the fur regulation was published on December 25, 1941. According to the announcement, the Jews were required to bring their furs to special collection points within a few days. In big cities, such as Warsaw, the Jewish community had a role to play in the collection of furs. In smaller, towns such as Brzesko Nowe, it was up to the Blue Police to take charge of the whole process.[9] Many Jews burned their clothing in acts of defiance,

8 The issue of the seizure of furs has been relatively well discussed in historical literature. The memoirs of Samuel Puterman are of particular importance here. See ŻIH, 302/27.

9 A regulation issued in Warsaw on December 25, 1941, by Heinz Auerswald, the German commissioner of the ghetto, ordered any furs to be surrendered to the authorities within three days. See the regulation regarding the surrender of furs and fur clothing under the penalty of death, December 25, 1941, in Marta Janczewska, ed., *Archiwum Ringelbluma: Konspiracyjne Archiwum Getta Warszawy, vol. 12, Rada Żydowska w Warszawie (1939–1943)* (Warsaw:

whereas others sold the furs for next to nothing to greedy Aryans who crowded the ghetto, drawn by the fire sale. One of the Warsaw Jews noted the following:

> We had to deliver the furs to the community offices. People had to queue in lines for days at a time, or you had to pay some smartass who would deposit the furs on your behalf. Imagine: not only [do] you have to wait in line to surrender your property to the murderers, but you even have to pay someone to do it for you! My parents—persuaded by me and my brother—let us burn all this that, one day before, was so precious, was the fruit of years of hard work. Others threw them out in the garbage or into the public toilets. One could find in the streets the most expensive mink, seal, and fox coats. These treasures were piling up in the streets, worthless. You could pick them up every few paces. Some enterprising individuals made money selling them on the other side of the wall. The clients from the Aryan side bought heaps of furs, paying for them a miserable few groschen—this is how some take advantage of other people's misfortune.[10]

A Polish diarist who was living on the Aryan side of Warsaw described these extraordinary transactions in the following words:

> Another of my friends, who paid 15 zlotys to get into the ghetto, bought a fur coat and started to go back, through the ruins. A Polish policeman stopped her and asked for 100 zlotys arguing that she must have paid so little for the coat, so now she can afford to compensate him. A Jewish policeman,

Wydawnictwa Uniwersytetu Warszawskiego and Żydowski Instytut Historyczny im. Emanuela Ringelbluma, 2014), pp. 26–27; Mietek Pachter, *Umierać też trzeba umieć…*, ed. by Barbara Engelking (Warsaw: Stowarzyszenie Centrum Badań nad Zagładą Żydów, 2015), p. 81; Natan Koninki testimony, "Oddajcie futra!" (after December, 1941), ŻIH, Oneg Shabbat Ringelblum Archive (Ring), I/484. In the Radom district, similar regulations dealing with the seizure of furs were issued on December 24, 1941, by Colonel Wurst, the Orpo commander. See YVA, JM 3499/10, p. 12.

10 Pachter, *Umierać też trzeba umieć…*, p. 81.

> fearful perhaps of losing a client, tried to convince the Polish officer to relent. The Pole finally agreed, but grudgingly, complaining that he took the risk for so little money and that the woman made such a good business.[11]

In smaller towns in the provinces, the Jews were ordered to bring their furs directly to the nearest Polish police station. It is altogether not surprising that these very valuable items presented a temptation that many officers were unable to resist. Some furs were simply stolen. The official documents of the Brzesko Nowe police station include nominative lists of Jews and the clothing that had been taken away from them. The seized clothing included not only furs but also woolen underpants, sweaters, children's clothing, bedcovers, woolen blankets, warm mittens, and even an old woolen scarf.[12] The zeal with which the local Polish police enforced the German regulations was, perhaps, linked to the poverty of the Jews of Brzesko Nowe. It is also indicative of the powers held by the Blue Police over the Jews. The police from Igłomie reported the "seizure of clothing from nine Jewish families working in the local estates" and that the chief of the local station had ordered his subordinates to "immediately seize from Jews residing in our area all furs, sheepskin coats, hats, and collars."[13]

In Warsaw, given the size and the relative wealth of the Jewish population, the thefts in the ghetto were particularly egregious. On May 1, 1942, the Gestapo arrested Józef Szeryński, the commander of the Jewish police in the ghetto. Szeryński stood accused of stealing furs in collusion with Lieutenant Michalski, the commander of the notorious Protective Guard Unit of the Polish Blue Police,[14] a special detachment of the Polish police deployed in and around the ghetto. According to one of the Jewish testimonies:

11 Krahelska, *Kronika,* diary entry, January 1, 1942, AAN, 383/ II 1- 3.

12 List of items deposited at the station on December 27, 1941, ANKr, PPPBrzN, vol. 17, pp. 39–46.

13 Ibid., p. 40.

14 In Polish: Oddział Wartowniczo-Konwojowy.

> Szeryński, accused of stockpiling the furs together with Lieutenant Michalski of the Polish police, was imprisoned in the Pawiak Prison. People mentioned a large number of stolen furs because both Szeryński and Czerniaków, the President of the Judenrat, were authorized to continue wearing their own fur coats.[15]

The issue of furs had wider ramifications. Havi Dreifuss, an Israeli scholar long involved in the study of the Warsaw ghetto, wrote in her book *Relations between Jews and Poles during the Holocaust*, that the fire sales of furs to Poles had a significant impact on Jewish public opinion and created a feeling of disappointment and a bitter aftertaste among the Jews. The crowds of Poles who swarmed into the ghetto in the quest for furs proved that those who claimed the German occupation would usher a new period of Polish–Jewish understanding and solidarity were incorrect. This was, actually, a very popular misconception in the Warsaw ghetto during the period of 1940–1941:

> This German order, coined the *Furs Aktion*, created a lively fur trade inside the ghetto, and hordes of Poles came in for commercial purposes. Interestingly, writers who described these events at the time or shortly thereafter did not ascribe this exploitation to the margins of Polish society.... Koniński described how Polish hordes (*tłum*), Polish policemen, and "ladies and gentlemen with no armbands" entered the ghetto; and even Chaim Aron Kaplan described the people who exploited the Jews as "Aryan speculators."[16]

The Polish police were judged extremely harshly by Jewish society in the second year of the war. By the end of 1941, the Polish officers were associated with the ever-present theft, blackmail, and merciless treatment of Jews who were being marched off in columns to forced labor or detained in police jails. Importantly, however,

15 Ber Warm testimony, ŻIH, 302/188.

16 Dreifuss, *Relations between Jews and Poles during the Holocaust*, p. 116.

the Jewish writers and diarists made clear distinctions between the Blue Police and the average Pole on the street. We learn the following from an anonymous testimony: "The Poles also detest their police and the attitude of the Polish police can in no way be indicative of relations between Jews and Poles. The Polish society rejects and condemns the police."[17] The already poor reputation of the Polish police was soon to deteriorate even further.

Prelude to the Holocaust: The Third Regulation Concerning the Limitations of the Right of Residence in the Generalgouvernement

One can track the development of German anti-Jewish measures through the prism of gradual restrictions regarding the right of Jews to reside in the Generalgouvernement, which, for all practical purposes, meant the increasing isolation of the ghettos. On September 13, 1940, the governor general issued the First Regulation Concerning the Limitations of the Right of Residence in the Generalgouvernement (*Verordnung über Aufenthaltsbeschränkungen im Generalgouvernement*), which announced the general policy of ghettoization.[18] During the next six months, the authorities proceeded with the establishment of the ghettos in Warsaw, Kraków, Siedlce, Częstochowa, Kielce, and in scores of other Polish towns and cities. The Second Regulation, which designated the ghettos as the only legal areas of residence for Jews, followed on April 29, 1941. Ludwig Fischer, the governor of the Warsaw district, was eager to please his superiors and issued further regulations, which rendered the situation of the Jews even more difficult. The decree (*Anordnung)* of June 17, 1941, was true

17 Anonymous testimony titled "Stosunki polsko-żydowskie," YVA, M10.AR1/92, as quoted in Dreifuss, *Relations between Jews and Poles*, p. 124.

18 All these regulations can be found in the official bulletin *Verordnungsblatt für das Generalgouvernement*. Digitized copies of *Verordnungsblatt* can be accessed at the Deutsche Digitale Bibliothek, in several Polish Digital Libraries, as well as in the major Holocaust-related depositories, such as Yad Vashem and the United States Holocaust Memorial Museum (USHMM).

to the spirit of the April regulation but provided a much more detailed list of areas in which the Jews had no right to stay.

Dr. Wilhelm Hagen, a Health Department official responsible for the sanitary conditions in Warsaw, also requested that further punitive measures be introduced against the Jews. On July 7, 1941, at the time when more than 5,000 people were dying each month in the Warsaw ghetto, Hagen wrote the following to Ludwig Fischer: "All individuals leaving the Jewish Quarter should be whipped, and if, when arrested, they will be in possession of any financial resources, they should receive severe fines. Jewish itinerant beggars should be executed."[19] Fine-tuned to the broad lines of the official policy, Dr. Hagen argued that these measures were necessary to protect the Aryan population against typhoid fever.

However, the most important measure, the one with the most far-reaching consequences, was the Third Regulation Concerning the Limitations of the Right of Residence in the Generalgouvernement, issued by Hans Frank on October 15, 1941. The chief provision of the Third Regulation was the introduction of the death penalty for every Jew who had been apprehended outside the ghetto without an armband and proper authorization. The same penalty was imposed on all those caught aiding Jewish refugees. This was one of the last "legal" measures introduced by the German authorities that was directed against the Jews. The Third Regulation became law by October, and its practical consequences soon followed.

These reinforced legal measures went hand in hand with the increased role and stepped-up activity of the Blue Police. On September 27, 1941, Ludwig Leist, the German governor of Warsaw, sent a letter to Ludwig Fischer, the governor of the Warsaw district and his direct superior. Leist was preoccupied with the fact that every day, groups of Jews were intercepted while trying to leave the ghetto. Leist warned Fischer that the resulting investigations and the ensuing judicial proceedings risked ensnaring and overwhelming

19 Wilhelm Hagen, "Krieg, Hunger und Pestilenz in Warschau 1939–1943," *Gesundheitswesen und Desinfektion*, 65 (1973), p. 122–125, as quoted in Raul Hilberg, *Sprawcy, ofiary, śiadkowie. Zagłda Żdó 1933–1945* (Warsaw: Centrum Badań nad Zagładą Żydów and Cyklady, 2007), p. 109.

the Warsaw *Sondergericht* (Special Court).[20] According to the governor of Warsaw, at least a few hundred Jews tried to flee the ghetto each day, and no less than 100 among them were caught. Many of them were subsequently released and sent home to await trial. They rarely showed up in court, and the police were wasting valuable time trying to locate the fugitives, complained Leist. The German administrator argued that a solution was to empower the Blue Police with investigative and judicial powers and establish a special Polish Police Court (*Polnische Polizeigericht*) that would deal with the Jews expeditiously and in a most severe fashion.

In the end, nothing came of Leist's plans, first, because police courts were unknown in Polish police practice, and second, because the German authorities feared that this would create a precedent and expand the powers of the Blue Police at the expense of the German police and the German judicial system.[21] Nevertheless, in the beginning of November 1941, in order to remedy the situation, the Germans started to transfer the arrested Jews directly into the custody of the Blue Police. The paperwork still went to the *Sondergericht* but the Jews were henceforth delivered by Polish officers to the Gęsia Prison, located inside the ghetto and run by the Jewish Order Service. On November 11, 1941, the Orpo instructed the Polish police to shoot on the spot Jewish women and children caught on the Aryan side, which followed a similar order issued a few days earlier regarding Jewish men.[22] Responding to the request of the German authorities, the Blue Police conducted two executions in the courtyard of Gęsia Prison.[23] The first execution took place on November 17, 1941,

20 Exchange of correspondence between Ludwig Leist and the chief of the Warsaw district, Zentrale Stelle Ludwigsburg, 211 AR-Z 77/66 BI/a, pp. 36–37.

21 Contrary to normal Polish practice, the Police Martial Courts (*Polizei Standegerichte*) were well known in Germany. Nevertheless, according to some Jewish testimonies, there were areas (for instance, in Radom) where such courts were, in fact, created. See Ichijela Leszcza testimony, ŻIH, 301/56.

22 Schupo Colonel Jarke to the Orpo commander in the Warsaw district, November 10, 1941, Zentrale Stelle Ludwigsburg, 211 AR-Z 77/66 BI/a, p. 31.

23 Barbara Engelking and Jacek Leociak, *The Warsaw Ghetto: A Guide to the Perished City* (New Haven: Yale University Press, 2008), p. 202. On the two occasions mentioned, twenty-four people were shot.

and this was followed by another on December 15. In both cases, the victims were selected from among the Jews found outside the ghetto without armbands. In such a way, these Jews became the first victims of the Third Regulation and of numerous conferences and meetings of the German police and justice officials. Below is a description of the execution in Gęsia Prison:

> The sentence has been carried out in the presence of [Heinz] Auerswald [the German commissioner of the ghetto], a prosecutor, a rabbi, and a priest (no one has been denied the right to last religious service). The Jewish police maintained order; Colonel Szeryński, cold as always, showed up, too. The Jewish policeman who told me this story fainted during the execution. The Blue Police provided the execution squad; a prison doctor was also on hand, he also gave us a firsthand account of this first mass execution in the ghetto.[24]

A report filed with the underground organization Union of Armed Struggle (ZWZ) provided even more details. According to the underground's informer, the execution was scheduled at 8:35 AM in the presence of Colonel Reszczyński, the commander-in-chief of the Warsaw Blue Police, his deputy, Major Przymusiński, and several other officers. Thirty-two policemen made up the execution squad. The German judiciary were represented by Neumann, a well-known and feared prosecutor attached to the Warsaw *Sondergericht*.[25]

According to the same informant:

> [They] were depressed, but Col. Reszczyński said to them: "Boys, heads up! Be strong!" The execution squad stood six meters from the poles to which the Jewish policemen tied the condemned with ropes. The glass-maker Pajkus cried

24 Makower, *Pamiętnik z getta warszawskiego*, p. 31. See also the poster announcing the execution ("Der Kommissar für den jüdischen Wohbezirk in Warschau, Heinz Auerswald"), November 17, 1941, ŻIH, Ring I/781/3. Eight Jews were found guilty by the Special Court of leaving the ghetto without authorization.

25 Israel Cymlich, *Moje przeżycia wojenne (1939–1943)*, ŻIH 302/324.

out: "That's what people do to people!" One could hear the desperate cries of the victims, one could see their frantic attempts to free themselves. The order was given, two salvos were fired followed by four additional, quite unnecessary, shots.[26]

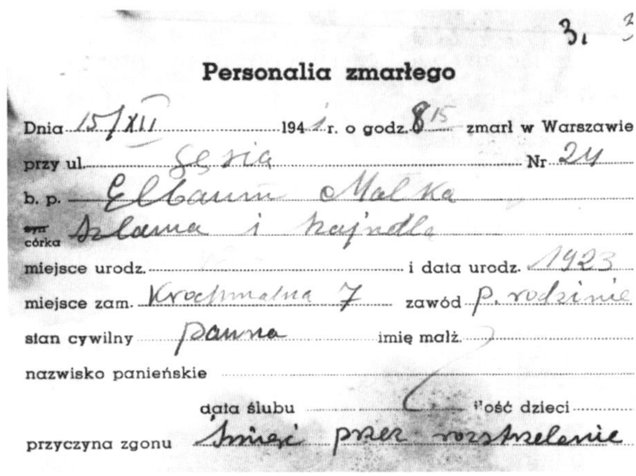
Personalia zmarłego

Dnia 15/XII 1941 r. o godz. 8 15 zmarł w Warszawie
przy ul. Gęsia Nr 24
b. p. Elbaum Malka
syn / córka Szlama i Rajzla
miejsce urodz. .... i data urodz. 1923
miejsce zam. Krochmalna 7 zawód p. rodzinie
stan cywilny panna imię małż. ....
nazwisko panieńskie ....
data ślubu .... ilość dzieci ....
przyczyna zgonu śmierć przez rozstrzelanie

Death certificate of a woman shot by the firing squad of the Blue Police. ŻIH, Ring I/224.

According to that report, Heinz Auerswald, German commissioner of the ghetto, showed up in his car right after the execution: "He jumped out of the car with a smile on his face and, having heard from the prosecutor that he was late, said: '*Schade. Sie haben es gut gemacht.* (Pity. You have done it well).'"[27] We have no eyewitness accounts from the second mass execution conducted on December 15, 1941, but in the Ringelblum Archive, one can find the death certificates of fifteen victims shot that day.[28]

The Gęsia Prison executions became major news not only in the ghetto but also on the Aryan side of Warsaw. It was not only

26 Report on the execution of eight people in the Warsaw ghetto, AAN, Delegatura Rządu na Kraj, 202-II-28, p. 67.

27 Ibid.

28 Dossiers titled "identity of the deceased," [Jewish Council in Warsaw, Central Jail?], fifteen Jews shot on December 15, 1941, in Gęsia prison, ŻIH, Ring I/224.

that mass shootings in the ghetto were out of the ordinary but it also seems that the Germans decided to circulate this information as widely as possible. The announcements and posters with the names of the victims plastered in public spaces were intended as a clear warning that the German *Judenpolitik* had changed and that the new regulations would be enforced without pity and to the extent of the law.

Henceforth, the Polish police, acting at the behest of and on orders from the Germans, conducted executions of Jews increasingly more often. There is no information about policemen refusing these orders. Quite the contrary. According to *Biuletyn Informacyjny*, a mainstream publication of Polish resistance, Constable Żelek from the XX Precinct in Warsaw even volunteered for one of the execution squads.[29] During that period, executions were a new element in the work routine of the Blue Police. Between late fall 1941 and early summer 1942, before the liquidation of the ghettos had begun, the Polish officers conducted executions in Warsaw, Klimontów, Kraków, Piotrków Trybunalski, Ostrów Mazowiecka, and Sokoły.[30] The full list of towns and cities where the "Blues" executed Jews is long, since the new regulations and the heightened level of terror applied to the whole Generalgouvernement.

Piotr Sałabun was the commander of a Blue Police detachment in Działoszyce, a small town located halfway between Kraków and Jędrzejów. In Działoszyce—like in so many other places—the Polish police increased its vigilance when dealing with the Jews in 1941. It was at that time when Sałabun and his people arrested a man called Nissenbaum and his daughter. Once in police custody, Nissenbaum was chained to the floor and "beaten nearly to death,"[31] as one of the Jewish survivors from Działoszyce recalled in his later testimony. Nissenbaum's daughter, "unable to stand the sight of her father's suffering," jumped out of the window of the police station.[32]

29 *Biuletyn Informacyjny*, December 4, 1941.

30 Szymon Datner testimony, ŻIH, 301/1998. See also Michał Majik testimony, ŻIH, 301/390.

31 Mosze Koteński declaration, February 18, 1949, Archiwum Instytutu Pamięci Narodowej Oddział w Kielcach (AIPN Ki), 128/209, p. 132.

32 Ibid.

Shortly before the liquidation of the ghetto, Sałabun's officers proceeded with several executions. In one case, they arrested everyone called Rafałowicz—and there were more than thirty such unfortunates. They led them outside the town and shot them all.[33] The reasons for this mass murder will probably remain unknown.

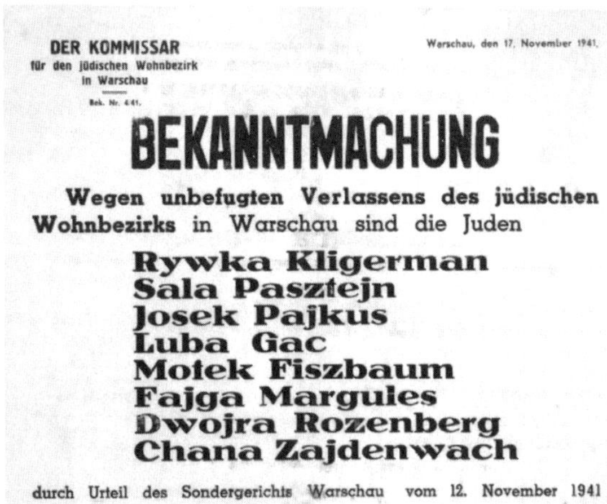

DER KOMMISSAR
für den jüdischen Wohnbezirk
in Warschau

Bek. Nr. 4/41.

Warschau, den 17. November 1941.

BEKANNTMACHUNG

Wegen unbefugten Verlassens des jüdischen Wohnbezirks in Warschau sind die Juden

Rywka Kligerman
Sala Pasztejn
Josek Pajkus
Luba Gac
Motek Fiszbaum
Fajga Margules
Dwojra Rozenberg
Chana Zajdenwach

durch Urteil des Sondergerichts Warschau vom 12. November 1941

Announcement of the execution of eight Jews found outside the Warsaw ghetto, November 17, 1941. ŻIH, Ring I/781/3.

Michal Majik, a Jew from Sokoły in the Podlasie area, gave the following account in his testimony right after the war:

> In the evening of the feast of Shavuot, they opened the gates of the prison and Janeczko, the chief of the Polish police with several other policemen, led Berl outside. They told him they would take him to the *Amtskommissar* [German administrator] who is waiting close to the building of the Jewish Council. Berl takes off and cleans his glasses and walks on. On both sides—the police. It is only close to the Judenrat that he sees the scaffold and the assembled Jews. The

33 Adam Langner testimony, February 13, 1949, AIPN Ki, 128/209, p. 130. The testimony was given in a DP camp in Germany.

> *Amtskommissar* orders Berl to be hanged, with his hands tied behind his back. He [the *Amtskommissar*] then says to get a few Jews from the Judenrat to help hang Berl. All members of the Judenrat had fled, so the Polish police dragged Berl to the scaffold, they tied the noose around his neck, and cranked him up to the very top. Berl's wife became hysterical and fainted, his children wailed.[34]

The small town of Klimontów, situated around 22 kilometers west of Sandomierz, was home to 3,100 Jews before the war, making up slightly more than three-quarters of the population. During the occupation, Klimontów found itself in the Radom district, in *Kreishauptmannschaft* Opatów. In 1940–1941, due to the arrival of deportees from other areas, the number of Jewish inhabitants grew to 4,000 people. The terror against the Jewish population intensified in the fall of 1941, especially after the publication of the Third Regulation and the introduction of the death penalty for leaving the ghetto. A ghetto as such was only established in Klimontów in May 1942, just a few months before the deportation of the local Jews to Treblinka. In practical terms, the application of the Third Regulation meant that Jews risked death when leaving the town limits. In August 1942, one of the Jews from Klimontów fled from the forced labor camp in Skarżysko-Kamienna. In retaliation, the Germans ordered the execution of several members of his family along with a score of hostages previously taken from the Jewish community. Here too, the Blue Police took part in the shooting of Jews. Lejb Zylberberg, one of the eyewitnesses, noted the following:

> In the evening, between 6 and 7 PM, when I was on my way back home, I saw the gendarmes and a company of Polish policemen leave the station with rifles on their shoulders. They went toward a square adjacent to the synagogue, close to the small house of prayer, now transformed into a jail where they held the poor people. They ordered them out. [The]

34 Michał Majka testimony, ŻIH, 301/390.

> Jewish policeman Putermilch went to get them, he tied their hands together forming groups of 6 to 7 people and he led them to the main synagogue. That's when the shooting began. That's how they killed all of them. Two sisters named Alert hid under a bench. Since they executed only 18 people, one Polish policeman shouted out that there were two other Jews in the Polish prison: Mendel Mark and Dawid Zilbersztajn. One could get them. The German gendarmes ordered to send them and to shoot them. In the meantime, one more woman slated for execution said that the two sisters were hidden under the bench. They pulled the girls out and they shot them too. A few minutes later a Polish policeman brought the two Jews from the Polish prison. One of them, Dawid Zilbersztajn, seeing what was going on, started to beg: "I am innocent, let me live!" It didn't help. He was killed too.[35]

The very first ghetto in Poland was established by the German authorities in Piotrków Trybunalski in October 1939. Initially, the ghetto had a population of 20,000, but soon, thousands of Jews from outlying communities were also herded into Piotrków. In the spring of 1942, on the eve of the liquidation, the local ghetto counted more than 25,000 Jews.[36] On April 1, 1942, the ghetto in Piotrków Trybunalski was declared a closed ghetto and each attempt to leave the Jewish quarter carried the death penalty. Here too, the Polish Blue officers, under the command of Jan Antczak—an officer with a long career in the prewar Polish police—had an important role to fulfill in the enforcement of German regulations.[37]

From the very beginning, the Polish officers secured the ghetto, prosecuted smugglers, kept guard around the ghetto, and—like their colleagues from Opoczno, Wodzisław, Warsaw, Kraków, and other cities and towns of the Generalgouvernement—supervised and drilled the Jewish police. In the period in question, there

35 Lejb Zylberberg testimony, ŻIH, 302/37.

36 "Piotrków Trybunalski," in Megargee, *The United States Holocaust Memorial Museum Encyclopedia* of *Camps and Ghettos*, pp. 280–282.

37 Protocols of interrogation of the detained, Łódź, 1952–1953, AIPN, BU 0330/236, vol. 9, pp. 3–64.

were sixty Polish policemen and between ten and twelve German Schupo policemen on duty in Piotrków. After the proclamation of the Third Regulation, Blue Police officers took part in several acts of terror initiated by the Germans. Constable Szczepan Pawlak, a prewar career policeman who was fluent in German, took part in all the *Aktionen* organized by the Schupo. Acting as an interpreter, Pawlak liaised with Muschala, the chief of the Piotrków police. It was Muschala who supervised Antczak and the rest of the Blue policemen and issued orders to his Polish subordinates.[38] In the beginning of August 1942, Muschala ordered Antczak to form an execution squad composed of Polish officers under his command. A local historian from Piotrków gave the following account of the executions that ensued:

> Between July and September 1942, sixty people were executed in the Rakowski Forest and on November 19, 1942, between 100 and 160 elderly Jews were taken out of the synagogue and shot, too. The very next day another group of prisoners, 560 people, was taken from the synagogue and executed in the forest. Between November and December 1942, 702 people were killed at the same spot.... Between July 1942 and 1944, the Gestapo, the Gendarmerie, and the Blue Police executed in the Rakowski Forest six hundred Poles and Jews from Piotrków and from the Moszczenica area.[39]

In Miechów, in early March 1942, the German *Kreishauptmann* and the chief of the local Blue Police tried to find practical solutions to the problems posed locally by the imprecise wording of the Third Regulation. In the Miechów area, where most of the Jews still lived in small communities and family groups outside the ghettos, the new regulation could have been understood and interpreted in a variety of ways. Therefore, one needed to make the vague law more explicit, precise, and better adjusted to the local conditions. On

38 Interrogation of Szczepan Pawlak, July 8, 1953, AIPN, BU 0330/236, vol. 9, pp. 4–8.

39 Anna Rzędowska and Dina Feldman, *Getto żydowskie w okupowanym Piotrkowie* (Piotrków Trybunalski: Biblioteki Piotrków 800, 2014), pp. 186–187.

March 5, 1942, Major Siwon, the commander of the Blue Police, finally instructed his officers that only those Jews who had left without permission the area of the commune in which their village or town was located could be treated as criminals in breach of the Third Regulation.[40]

Similar discussions about the interpretation of the new rules preoccupied German judicial authorities. The case of Zachariasz Goldberg, accused of having unlawfully left the ghetto, can be seen as an example of the legal challenges facing German lawmakers. In December 1941, Goldberg along with a column of other Jews and guarded by the police, left the ghetto in Częstochowa to go to a forced labor site nearby. On the way back, Goldberg left the marching column and knocked on the door of one of the houses nearby, and he begged for a piece of bread. After hearing the case, the Częstochowa *Sondergericht* declared Goldberg not guilty. In the justification of the verdict, the judges of the Special Court argued that "the Jew did not leave the ghetto but only separated for a moment from a guarded march column."[41] Prosecutor Wille, chief of the Kraków Department of Justice, filed an appeal in which he maintained that: "a closed group of Jews marching to work should be considered—while outside the closed Jewish Quarter—an extension of this quarter. Each Jew leaving such a group should be considered, therefore, as a Jew fleeing the ghetto."[42] According to Dr. Wille's interpretation of the law and from the standpoint of German jurisprudence, the Jews essentially carried the ghetto within themselves.

40 Orders of the Miechów County Blue Police commander to his subordinates, February 15–March 5, 1942, ANKr, PPPBrzN, vol. 16, p. 24.

41 Dr. Wille to the chiefs of the Departments of Justice in all districts, January 15, 1942, United States Holocaust Memorial Museum (USHMM), RG 15.026 M, roll 3.

42 Ibid. The importance of this document warrants its inclusion in original German: "*Die Zusammenziehung einer grösseren Anzahl jüdischer Arbeiter zu einem geschlossenem Trupp entspricht dem Gedanken der Bildung des jüdischen Wohnbezirks. Der geschlossene Arbeitertrupp ist für die Zeit seines Aufenthalts ausserhalb des jüdischen Wohnbezirks als eine Ausweitung desselben anzusehen; er nimmt gleichsam das Ghetto mit sich. Von einem Juden, der sich unbefugt von dem Arbeitstrupp entfernt, gehen dieselben Gefahren aus wie von einem Juden, der unbefugt das Ghetto verlasst.*"

In addition to the executions in prisons and murders authorized by the representatives of the lower ranks of the German administration, the Blue policemen, who were well-versed in the new realities of occupation, murdered the Jews on their own initiative with increasing frequency.[43] In Warsaw, the smugglers—children and youth, for the most part—were the first to feel the heat. On June 11, 1942, a Polish policeman who was targeting a smuggler took a shot and killed an innocent passerby. A few days later, another Blue policeman in pursuit of smugglers "reached out through the same hole through which the merchandise was being brought to the ghetto" and fired off a few shots. One of the smugglers was killed on the spot.[44]

The murders committed during this period of transition between the fall of 1941 and the summer of 1942 were the prelude to the bloody liquidation *Aktionen* that followed immediately after. It was during that period when the Polish policemen became familiar with—or rather accepted—the rapid depreciation in the value of Jewish life. The Ringelblum Archive recorded the words of Schultz, a member of the SS in charge of a Jewish working column in the Warsaw ghetto who addressed one of his charges as follows: "You are not a human being, you are not even an animal—you are a Jew!"[45] It is hard to say how many Polish policemen would have subscribed to Schultz's statement, but there is no doubt that Jewish life had progressively lost its value. This depreciation in the value of Jewish life extended beyond the members of the firing squads and spilled over to members of the voluntary firefighting brigades and simple bystanders or gawkers who started to take part in the German genocidal program in a variety of different ways.

43 Miriam Wecer Thau testimony, YVA, O.3/2716.

44 Daniel Fligelman diary, May 28–June 22, 1942, in Katarzyna Person, ed., *Archiwum Ringelbluma: Konspiracyjne Archiwum Getta Warszawy, vol. 5, Getto warszawskie: życie codzienne* (Warsaw: Żydowski Instytut Historyczny im. Emanuela Ringelbluma and DiG, 2011), p. 81.

45 Report titled "Gehenna Żydów polskich pod okupacją hitlerowską, czerwiec 1942" (unknown author), ŻIH, Ring I/144.

In the summer of 1942, still well before the liquidation *Aktionen* had begun, a fire broke out in Goraj, a small town in the northern part of Biłgoraj County:

> Someone cried out that it must have been the Jews who set the place on fire, so the citizens and the firefighters caught every Jew and Jewess they could find and—holding them by the hands—dragged them to the police station. Mrozik [the chief of the Blue Police] came out of his house and, without haste, shot the Jews. The locals took the wounded by their arms and legs, swung them and threw them into the flames. Many were thrown into the fire while still alive.[46]

The Blue policeman Andrzejczuk, who was serving in Janów Podlaski, took it upon himself to provide the chiefs of the Gendarmerie and Gestapo in Biała Podlaska with a nominative list of Jews who were suspected of harboring communist sympathies. There were twenty people on Andrzejczuk's list and the Germans shot ten of them.[47] Similar executions linked to the ongoing *Kommunistenaktion* occurred in Szczebrzeszyn, a district in Lublin in Biłgoraj County and the hometown of Zygmunt Klukowski, a doctor, director of a hospital, and author of an important diary. A scholar studying the fate of the local Jews there during the war wrote the following: "At the same time, the butchers took advantage of the situation because, as we read [in Klukowski's diary], 'After the end of the *Aktion*, they requested that the Judenrat provide them with 3 kilos of coffee and 2,000 zlotys as payment for the expended bullets.'"[48] But even this was not the last of the

46 Jan Mikulski, *Myśli, wspomnienia, uwagi, refleksje…* (Biłgoraj: n.p., 1970), typewritten manuscript available in the Biłgoraj Public Library. The deportations from the Biłgoraj area have been discussed in detail by Alina Skibinska, "Powiat biłgorajski," in Barbara Engelking and Jan Grabowski, eds., *Dalej jest noc: Losy Żydów w wybranych powiatach okupowanej Polski*, vol. 1 (Warsaw: Stowarzyszenie Centrum Badań nad Zagładą Żydów, 2018), pp. 204–358.

47 Testimony dealing with the fate of the Jewish inhabitants of Skarżysko-Kamienna, Chmielnik Kielecki, and Janow Podlaski, July 15, 1942 (unknown author), ŻIH, Ring I/1220/18.

48 Skibińska, "Powiat biłgorajski," p. 237. The passage quoted by Skibinska comes

"gains" associated with the *Aktion*. The local "gawkers"—a rather innocuous expression used by Klukowski to describe the bandits and robbers who preyed on other people's tragedy—penetrated the Jewish quarter in order to rob the emptied houses. The same scenario, where the locals took advantage of the German murders to enrich themselves, repeated itself over and over again, and not only in Biłgoraj.

Three days later, on May 11, 1942, in nearby Józefów Biłgorajski, the Germans committed another massacre. In the streets of the town and in the quarries nearby, they executed 120 people. We have no documents that shed more light on these events, but the scene must have, indeed, been terrible since even Becker, a German trustee of the local chemical plant Alwa, was shocked. "He told us later in the office," wrote Klukowski, "that it was something horrible, indescribable, and that he couldn't regain his composure, although he was someone who always rode herd on the Jews, saying that all of them ought to be exterminated."[49] Another witness, a Pole named Józef Skałuba, testified that the Polish police took part in the execution and that under orders from the Gestapo, they arrested 150 Jews and held them in custody. Some were released, whereas others were murdered by the Gestapo. In May and June, even more innocent people were killed. On the Rozłopska highway, gendarmes killed the two daughters of Lemer, the painter, and in the square in front of the Szczebrzeszyn Town Hall, they murdered the Jew, Gelernter; one month later, his brother was killed, and five days later, their father and a local shoemaker were also killed. At the end, Dr. Klukowski remarked, "People keep asking themselves: 'How many Jews were shot again? Whose house was robbed this time?' **These are quite unremarkable events nowadays and they no longer seem to excite people** [emphasis added, JG]."[50]

The violence, the murders, and the apparent inevitability of Jewish suffering became elements of the everyday psychological and moral landscape in the Generalgouvernement. This was

from the notes of Dr. Klukowski: Zygmunt Klukowski, *Zamojszczyzna 1918–1959* (Warsaw: Karta, 2017), entry for May 9, 1942.

49 Ibid., entry for May 13, 1942, as quoted in Skibińska, "Powiat biłgorajski," p. 239.

50 Ibid., entry for May 22, 1942, as quoted in Skibińska, "Powiat biłgorajski," p. 239.

especially true in the areas where the ghettos were not separated from the Aryan side. It was, however, precisely in these open or half-open ghettos where the vast majority of Polish Jews lived and died during this time. But even the liquidations of the largest, closed, and better-guarded ghettos did not occur in a social void: All of this took place in public, in full sight of millions of Polish bystanders.

Chapter Four

The Terrible Year of 1942: Liquidation *Aktionen*

The transformation of ordinary, ideologically moderate, and generally respected people into murderers, ready to follow the most inhuman orders of their superiors, is one of the issues historians of the Holocaust find hard to understand and even harder to explain. Unsurprisingly, the studies of perpetrators (in German, this area of research is called the *Tätergeschichte*) have focused on the Germans and, to be more precise, on the German policemen and members of the police reserve battalions, who murdered hundreds of thousands of Jewish women, men, and children between 1941 and 1942. This choice of research focus was not accidental. While the members of the Einsatzgruppen (mobile death units) were most often recruited from among motivated Nazis and people who were already prepared to murder the Jews, the members of these reserve battalions were a heterogenous group who belonged to various social and professional strata. According to historians, these middle-aged men—the younger ones had been drafted into the Wehrmacht—in principle should have been less inclined to listen to Nazi propaganda than the youth who had been molded and indoctrinated in German schools after 1933.

In West Germany in the 1960s, many of these reserve policemen stood trial, accused of wartime murders committed on Jews in the East. In his examination of the depositions and testimonies of former policemen who were members of the Reserve

Police Battalion 101 deployed in occupied Poland, Christopher R. Browning reached the conclusion that the decision to take part in the genocidal *Aktionen* was, in large part, related to peer pressure and was reflective of the need for collective belonging: In other words, the decision was based on the extent of each individual policeman's need for conformism.[1] Both the personal example of and pressure exerted by the commanding officer were also not without impact. The more fanatical a Nazi their leader was, the more likely their subordinates would follow his lead and take part in the murders.[2]

The case of *SS-Untersturmführer* Max Täubner, the commander of an auxiliary platoon of car repairmen whose task was to service the cars of the 1 SS Brigade, is illustrative of this phenomenon. Before he left for the front, Täubner, a fanatical Nazi, made a pledge to kill at least 20,000 Jews in the East. He remained true to his word. During one year in action behind the front lines, Täubner motivated the car mechanics, carpenters, and electricians serving under his command so successfully that they murdered close to 30,000 Jews on their own, without any orders from above. As indicated before, the personal zeal of the commanding officer might have had a significant impact on the decisions of his men. In this context, it is important to stress the word "decision," because everyone had a choice. One could simply refuse. As a matter of fact, participation in the execution squads was voluntary. Refusal to shoot did not carry any serious consequences. Harsh words from the commanding officer, ridicule and derision by their comrades in arms, sometimes a transfer to a less appealing duty—this is what awaited soldiers and policemen who broke ranks. Significantly, despite the lack of possible reprisal, there were so few men who opted out that the officers had no problem in finding a sufficient number of willing shooters.

It is important to note at this point that history is not a science—after all, Clio the Greek goddess of history was one of the Muses—

1 Christopher R. Browning, *Ordinary Men: Reserve Police Battalion 101 and the Final Solution in Poland* (New York: Harper Perennial, 2017).

2 Yehoshua R. Büchler, "'Unworthy Behavior': The Case of SS Officer Max Täubner," *Holocaust and Genocide Studies*, 17:3 (2003), pp. 409–429.

and that is why so much depends on the historians' interpretations of the collected historical evidence. Daniel Jonah Goldhagen, another scholar of the Holocaust, looked at the same files examined by Browning, which were discussed earlier. His conclusions, however, were very different. According to Goldhagen, it was not the sense of camaraderie, "front-line bonding" experience, peer pressure, or even the pressure exerted by the commanding officers that transformed ordinary Germans into mass murderers but, most of all, it was their deep-rooted, generational antisemitism. Following Goldhagen and using a colorful metaphor, one could say that the Germans "sucked antisemitism with their mothers' milk."[3] It gets worse. Goldhagen argues that German culture and the German national ethos were imbued not only with regular antisemitism but also with a particularly virulent strain, which the American historian referred to as "eliminationist antisemitism." While Browning's arguments were received favorably by most historians, Goldhagen's hypothesis was met with skepticism. Universal, one-key-opens-all-doors theories that promise to unlock the path to a better understanding of the past have one thing in common: They strive to explain some of the most complex historical issues in a very simple way. That is why, in most cases, they are also wrong.

In the case of Goldhagen, the problem was that his concept of "eliminationist antisemitism" lacked a credible explanatory value. Historians agree that German antisemitism was never a dominant ideology in German society. In fact, the majority of scholars believe quite the opposite and argue that antisemitism, in its most potent and deeply entrenched form, was rooted in Eastern Europe and the Balkans. In other words, such prejudice thrived in areas where millions of impoverished Jews—referred to as *Ostjuden* or Eastern Jews—called home. Therefore, could one say that the killers in German uniforms differed in some deep and distinctive way from the killers wearing Hungarian, Romanian, Slovak, or Croat uniforms? Were German policemen, who were the murderers of the Jews, any different from their colleagues,

3 Daniel Jonah Goldhagen, *Hitler's Willing Executioners: Ordinary Germans and the Holocaust* (New York: Vintage, 1997), p. 89.

the Latvian, Lithuanian, or Ukrainian policemen? Is the concept of "eliminationist antisemitism" really useful in helping people understand why thousands of Lithuanians, Poles, or Ukrainians—normal, ordinary people—took part in the robbery and murder of their Jewish neighbors?

If "eliminationist antisemitism" was purely and exclusively a German phenomenon, as Goldhagen argued, then the representatives of other nations should have been free of this dangerous bacillus. However, it is known that the policemen, soldiers, and civilians of all possible nationalities and ethnic backgrounds took part in the German genocidal project. Many did it with enthusiasm, and others participated without doubts or with little hesitation. Furthermore, unlike the German policemen, the Polish and Ukrainian officers murdered their own co-citizens, neighbors, and sometimes even childhood friends and classmates. In order to understand the mechanisms that transformed these Polish policemen—fathers of families and defenders of the public order—into mass murderers, we must turn our attention to some concrete examples and, more specifically, to the many concrete examples that reflect the evolution of the Polish officers' attitudes toward the Jews during the first months of *Aktion Reinhard* (Operation Reinhard).

Aktion Reinhard

In the late summer of 1941, after the establishment of the district of Galicia and its incorporation into the Generalgouvernement, Hans Frank's fiefdom boasted an area of 150,000 square kilometers (close to 58,000 square miles) with a population of more than 17 million people.[4] In early 1942, there were still 2 million Jews—

4 According to German counts, there were 2.7 million people living in the Radom district, 3.7 million people in the Krakow district, 3.5 million in the Warsaw district, 2.5 million in the Lublin district, and 4.7 million in the Galicia district. See Josef Bühler, ed., *Das Generalgouvernement: Seine Verwaltung und seine Wirtschaft. Sammlung von Vorträgen der ersten wissenschaftlichen Vorträgsreihe der Verwaltungsakademie des Generagouvernements* (Kraków: Burgverlag,

prewar Polish citizens—among them.[5] Close to 1 million Polish Jews lived in the territories incorporated into the Reich, in Bezirk Białystok (Białystok General District), and in the Eastern Territories under German administration. Although the fate of this last group was directly linked to the fate of Jews living in the Generalgouvernement, they will remain outside the scope of this study, due to the geographical limits of the presence of the Blue Police.[6] Between spring 1942 and spring 1943, the overwhelming majority of Polish Jews were murdered in the extermination camps, and any remaining refugees went into hiding. They either went underground or, in rare cases, attempted to survive "on the surface,"[7] using Aryan papers or doctored IDs. A significant number of Jews waited for death in the still-operating labor camps for the Jews (*Julags*) and in several secondary ghettos (*Restghettos*). However, the Germans gradually liquidated both the former and the latter over the course of spring, summer, and fall 1943. This part of the destruction of Polish Jewry is known in history as *Aktion Reinhard*.[8]

1943), p. 30. According to Czesław Madajczyk, the Generalgouvernement (including Bezirk Białystok) had a population of 18.183 million. See the section about population changes during the war and occupation in Czesław Madajczyk, *Polityka III Rzeszy w okupowanej Polsce*, 2 vols. (Warsaw: Państwowe Wydaw. Naukowe, 1970), specifically vol. 1, pp. 234–284, 533, 631; and vol. 2, pp. 165–176, 247, 259, 328.

5 According to Albert Stankowski and Piotr Weiser there were 1.99 million Jews in the Generalgouvernement. See Albert Stankowski and Piotr Weiser, "Demograficzne skutki Holokaustu," in Feliks Tych and Monika Adamczyk-Garbowska, eds., *Następstwa zagłady Żydów: Polska 1944–2010* (Lublin and Warsaw: Wydawn. Uniwersytet Marii Curie-Skłodowskiej and Żydowski Instytut Historyczny im. Emanuela Ringelbluma, 2011), p. 19

6 The exceptions here would be Jews from outside the Generalgouvernement who were resettled—on the eve of deportation to death camps—in ghettos within the Generalgouvernement (for example, German Jews resettled in the Warsaw ghetto or thousands of Slovak Jews were incarcerated in ghettos in the Lublin district), and those who escaped from death transports in the Generalgouvernement.

7 During this time, to live "on the surface" (in Polish: *żyć na powierzchni*) meant moving around freely, on the Aryan side, pretending to be a Pole.

8 The extermination of Jewish communities in the territories incorporated into the Reich, which, as I have already mentioned are outside the framework of this study, took a slightly different course.

It was the Germans who named this part of the Holocaust to commemorate Reinhard Heydrich, one of the architects of the "Final Solution to the Jewish Question," who was killed by members of the Czech resistance in June 1942. Many historians of the Holocaust maintain that until the liquidation of the ghettos in 1942, the local non-Jewish population as well as Polish institutions and organizations had nothing—or very little—to do with the existential choices facing the Jews. The description of the annihilation of the Jewish communities in Poland should not be, however, limited to the few largest and closed ghettos, such as those in Warsaw and Kraków, although, even in these cases, the ghettos were far from hermetically sealed. During the *Grossaktion Warschau*, which began on July 22, 1942, when some 300,000 Jews were shipped off from the Warsaw ghetto to the extermination camp of Treblinka, the Warsaw-based retired Polish engineer Franciszek Wyszyński noted the following in his diary:

> Horrible things are happening over there in the ghetto... people saw a Jew being thrown down from the fourth floor. The Germans will have a grave sin on their conscience, but after the war the power of our Jewry will be broken to a great extent and life will be easier.[9]

Even in Warsaw, with high walls surrounding the ghetto, the horrors of the liquidation *Aktion* unavoidably reached the Aryan side of the city.

The majority of Polish Jews, however, lived in open or half-open ghettos, such as the previously described Opoczno ghetto, where the physical separation from the Aryan side consisted of wooden fences and barbed wire and was much less of an obstacle than the psychological isolation from the outside world. Last but not least, one should bear in mind that several hundred thousand Polish Jews avoided ghettoization until the spring and summer of 1942, shortly before the deportations to the death camps. These Jews were very much members of their local communities right up until the 1942

9 Wyszyński, *Dzienniki z lat 1941–1944*, p. 172.

deportations. It must also be stressed that the liquidation *Aktionen*, as the Germans called the deportations to the extermination camps, which were conducted according to the same script in hundreds of locations became a horrible public spectacle of death watched by millions. It was during these *Aktionen* that the streets of hundreds of Polish towns and cities ran with blood—quite literally and without any poetic license. It was during these *Aktionen* that Polish neighbors took an active part in the destruction of the Jewish communities and contributed to the tragedy of their Jewish neighbors. Thousands of so-called gawkers followed and watched, while the Jews were herded to the trains for their last journeys. Thousands took part in the searches of the empty ghettos, stealing Jewish property and delivering into the hands of the police those Jews who had tried to avoid death by hiding in underground bunkers and hideouts.

Shraga Feivel Bielawski, who was hiding in the attic of his house, witnessed the liquidation of the ghetto in Węgrów, a small town northeast of Warsaw. He noted the following in his haunting memoir:

> I heard the screams of women and children from the town square just below our attic hideaway. The SS hurried their victims yelling: "Faster! Faster!" The screams of Jews mingled with the shouting of Germans and the laughter of Poles. Children wailed to their mothers: "Mama, I don't want to die! I don't want to die!" Everyone knew where they were going and what would happen when they got there. All day the SS with the enthusiastic help of the Poles loaded Jews onto open trucks that sped toward Treblinka.[10]

In addition to the gawkers, the bloody liquidation *Aktionen* included Polish voluntary firefighters, the *junaks*—young Poles from the Construction Service (Baudienst)[11]—and, most of all, the officers of the Blue Police.

10 Feivel Shraga Bielawski, *The Last Jew from Wegrow* (New York: Praeger, 1991), p. 68.

11 The Baudienst, or Construction Service, was an organization created by the occupiers in December 1940. Young Poles were forcibly drafted and later

In early 1942, Constable Lucjan Matusiak was promoted and assumed the duties of deputy chief of the Blue Police detachment in Łochów, a quaint little town located 56 kilometers northeast of Warsaw. During the next few months, Matusiak, who was a policeman with a long prewar career in the Polish state police, morphed into a vicious killer.[12] Matusiak's transformation was directly related to the liquidation of the small ghetto with 1,000 inhabitants in nearby Łochów-Baczki. During the first *Aktion*, the "Blues"—Matusiak among them—followed the gendarmes, who were their German colleagues and superiors. According to Polish witnesses, the transformation process of policemen into killers took some time, and it did not happen overnight. During the *Aktion*, the "Blues" initially pulled the Jews out of their houses and searched the attics and basements, looking for those who had tried to hide. Once the Jews had been found, the Polish policemen delivered them to the gendarmes for execution.[13] A few days later, during the final liquidation of Baczki, Matusiak and his colleagues, clad in their blue uniforms, began killing on their own, although still in the company of the German policemen. The Polish officers shot at random and often missed, so the gendarmes had to step in and finish off the wounded Jewish victims.[14]

Nevertheless, the Poles quite swiftly graduated from simple apprentices into murderers in their own right. It can be ventured that some of the Blue officers had learned their lessons so well that even before the end of 1942, they had surpassed and outpaced their German teachers. While Constable Matusiak was honing these new skills in Łochów, his counterparts in Opoczno were loading Jews onto trains destined for Treblinka. And when the trains left the station, the Blue officers—as we can read in the station register—

ordered to perform various kinds of labor tasks. The Baudienst was particularly active in the Krakow district. The *junaks* were often used by the Germans to take part in the liquidation of the ghettos.

12 The court files (August trial) of Lucjan Matusiak, AIPN, GK 317/28, vol. 3.

13 Józef Fedorczyk testimony, October 3, 1948, AIPN, GK 317/28, vol. 3, p. 29–29v.

14 Interrogation records of Wincenty Kołodziejczyk, April 24, 1945, AIPN, GK 209/57, p. 2. Kołodziejczyk was a Blue policeman in Łochow. See also Report, undated, and Bolesław Abczyński testimony, March 30, 1945, AIPN, GK 209/57, pp. 3, 25–25v.

entered the empty ghetto in order "to prevent the local population from robbing the abandoned Jewish property."[15] Not that they were very successful in enforcing the German orders. Scenes of plunder in the empty ghettos played out all across Poland, and the Polish police used this opportunity to their own advantage. Halina Krahelska, the Polish writer and social activist, noted the following in her diary:

> *October 1942*: In Radzymin [a town located around 25 kilometers northeast of Warsaw], after the deportation of the Jews, the Germans plundered Jewish apartments, leaving with several rings on each finger. Later [came] the Polish police. Local police wives hesitated, but wives of other policemen arrived from Wołomin and other towns nearby and took full loads of Jewish women's clothing: furs and robes. Once these "privileged" thieves were gone, it was the turn of the local population, who robbed and pillaged the apartments completely. In great majority, these were hungry, miserable, and poor people who stole various objects in order to quickly sell them. But other individuals showed up, too. People saw the wife of one of the village elders from the area as well as one lady whose husband owned a [large] thirty-five-hectare farm. The latter arrived in a cart, and when she found out that there was nothing left to steal, she started to holler and was furious. Finally, she loaded an old, dented basin on the cart and left. The sight of Poles stealing was plain awful.[16]

The following excerpts are from the Opoczno Blue Police station register about the activities of the policemen:

> *September 18, 1942*: In Opoczno, in Blonie, on the orders of the Gendarmerie, guarding the property of the deported Jews.

15 Opoczno station register, April–October 1942, entries from September 18 and 19, and October 28, 1942, AP Kielce, Posterunek Policji Polskiej w Opocznie, 21/772.

16 Krahelska, *Kronika*, October 1942, AAN, 383/ II 1-3.

> *October 28, 1942*: Special duties in the former Jewish quarter to maintain order and to prevent the local civilian population from wandering around.
>
> *October 30, 1942*: On guard in the former Jewish quarter.
>
> *November 1, 1942*: Four persons caught while stealing in the former Jewish quarter.
>
> *November 4, 1942*: Three persons detained in the Jewish quarter. Three officers from Bialaczow police station reported to guard the Jews.[17]

During the manhunts that followed the liquidations of the local ghettos, the Opoczno police station coordinated the activities of the hunters. In one of the rare entries in the station register—usually hunts for the Jews were simply not entered into the ledgers—the officer on duty noted the following: "*October 29, 1942*: At 10:30 PM, the village elder from Ogonowice called in that a Jew had been caught in the village. I ordered him to appoint guards and to send the Jew to the police jail in Opoczno."[18] As mentioned previously, only a handful of the entries in the police station registers have been preserved, and, as such, they offer only a fragmentary record of these areas of police activity, which are of primary interest for this study. As far as the operations against the Jews were concerned, the Blue Police officers preferred to commit as little as possible to paper. Indeed, in Sterdyn, a town located in the northern part of the Warsaw district close to Treblinka, the local routine was to never enter the anti-Jewish activities into the official records.[19] The local commander of the Blue Police had no qualms about it; he ordered his men to "arrange the matters" informally and in such a way that

17 Opoczno station register, April–October 1942, entries from September 18 and 19, and October 28, 1942, AP Kielce, Posterunek Policji Polskiej w Opocznie, 21/772.

18 Opoczno station register, April–October 1942, entry from October 29, 1942, AP Kielce, Posterunek Policji Polskiej w Opocznie, 21/772.

19 Trial proceedings, deposition of Franciszek Suchodolski, December 29, 1953, AIPN, GK 318/505, pp. 25–29.

the Germans would not ask any questions.[20] The ways in which the Polish officers on duty in Sterdyn informally "arranged the matters" concerning their Jewish problem will be closely examined in the next chapter.

The previously mentioned Alter Szymszonowicz from Opoczono started to write his testimony while in hiding at the end of 1943.[21] The Opoczno ghetto had been liquidated one year earlier. As Szymszonowicz noted, 6,000 Jews were driven to the deportation train, and hundreds of others were killed on the spot on that day of liquidation. Finally, according to this survivor from Opoczno, several hundred people—about 10 percent of the Jewish population—sought safety in bunkers and hideouts constructed inside the ghetto. They did not last long though, as Polish and Jewish policemen conducted searches and delivered their hapless victims to the Jewish cemetery where the Germans carried out mass executions. At this point, Szymszonowicz fled the ghetto and went into hiding on the Aryan side. After two months, in December 1942, a Polish Christian reported Szymszonowicz along with several other Jews to the Polish police, and they, in turn, informed the gendarmes. Szymszonowicz recalled:

> Moritz [chief of the Gendarmerie] ordered the Jewish police to deliver the Jews.... Finally, the Polish police delivered the two brothers Azriel. Moritz took them out in the street and, once they were in front of him, shot them in the back of the necks, right in front of the police building. Both brothers writhed in the street, fighting death for an hour. The murderer came back and, seeing them still alive, finished them off.[22]

For the few Jews of Opoczno who had managed to survive the first liquidation, their time came in January 1943. Szymszonowicz noted the following:

20 Opoczno station register, April–October 1942, AP Kielce, Posterunek Policji Polskiej w Opocznie, 21/772.

21 Alter Szymszonowicz testimony, *Walka państwa hitlerowskiego*, ŻIH, 302/5.

22 Ibid.

> Monday, January 2, [1943], at 6 AM, when I woke up and went out into the street, I saw a Polish policeman standing next to my house, on guard. I look to the other side [of the street] and see Polish policemen everywhere, with their pistols drawn. It was still dark. I pretended not to see anything, and I approached one of the policemen. I see that they are not the local officers. I go back home and tell Fiszl Horowicz, my brother-in-law, that we are done for. That we are surrounded on all sides by the Polish police. Some time later, I went once again outside and saw gendarmes who were also there to make sure that we wouldn't run. That same day, the Polish policemen quietly removed things from Jewish houses and carried them back to their own homes. Through a peephole in the attic, I saw a policeman carrying a sewing machine from the apartment which belonged to one of my neighbors, a Jewish tailor.[23]

Szymszonowicz, who was hidden "in the attic, at one Christian's place,"[24] survived until liberation. The last entries in his diary are dated 1944. After the war, he made a considerable effort to recover his house. No further information has been found about his fate.

On Duty in Brzesko Nowe, Miechów, and Działoszyce

In the official police documentation, there are but a few traces directly describing the participation of the Blue policemen in the liquidation *Aktionen*. In the case of the Brzesko Nowe police detachment, the first document that alludes to the upcoming *Aktionen* is dated August 22, 1942. In a firm tone, the local authorities requested that the elder of the local Jewish community immediately remove all the Jews who had flocked into the city during the previous days. One can read in the letter that failure to comply would force the authorities to alert the German

23 Ibid.
24 Ibid.

Gendarmerie. These so-called undesirables were probably Jewish refugees from towns and ghettos nearby, which had been liquidated earlier that month. Ten days later, the deportations from Działoszyce, Miechów, Słomniki, and from smaller locations began. By mid-August, the Germans created a transit camp close to Słomniki, on damp meadows adjacent to the Szreniawa River. It was there where close to 8,000 Jews who had been deported from Miechów, Koszyce, Proszowice, Skalbmierz, Skała, and Słomniki were to await their fate.[25] The conditions in the camp were brutal, and hundreds of Jews fell victim to hunger and exhaustion. Some were later sent to forced labor camps, and the rest were transferred straight to the Bełżec extermination camp.

On September 2–3, 1942, the Germans liquidated the Działoszyce ghetto, the largest ghetto in the area, with the help of auxiliary troops as well as the Blue Police and the *junaks* from the Baudienst. Not unlike Słomniki, the Działoszyce Jews were first driven outside the city into the open fields where 15,000 people were held in catastrophic conditions. In addition to the Działoszyce Jews, the transit camp also held people from Miechów and Książ Wielki. Tasked with the destruction of Działoszyce, the Liquiedierungskommando arrived from Miechów on a narrow-gauge train. According to one Polish eyewitness, "The arrivals included a number of German gendarmes, Blue policemen, as well as the *junaks* brought from all over the place."[26]

Abraham Langner, one of the Jewish survivors, described the liquidation of Działoszyce in the following words:

> Polish policemen stood on both sides, and we were in the middle. I could also see four Germans in brown uniforms: Schmidt [the deputy *Kreishauptmann*], the chief of the Gestapo, and two others, mounted on horses. The chief of

25 A detailed account of the liquidations of the ghettos in Miechów County can be found in Dariusz Libionka, "Powiat miechowski," in Engelking and Grabowski, *Dalej jest noc*, vol. 2, pp. 64–108.

26 Deposition of witness Kazimierz Woźniakowski in the Municipal Court in Kazimierza Wielka, January 26, 1948, AIPN, GK 196/336, p. 90. See also USHMM, RG 15.174 M.

> the district's name was Beyerlein.[27] We marched in rows, and the policemen continued to rush us along. Whoever lagged behind was shot. All the time we heard screams and shots. The streets were running with blood. This time it was not the Germans, it was the Polish police. I heard with my own ears when a German officer ordered them not to shoot people within the town's boundaries. But Całowan, the commander of the Polish police, a dangerous murderer with crooked legs, continued to shout in Polish: "Continue shooting!!" I heard him several times...that's how, before the evening, 2,000 people have been killed during the deportation.[28]

The chief of the local Blue Police, mentioned here as Całowan by Langner, was none other than Piotr Sałabun, mentioned previously in this study.[29] Jan Łach, a Polish farmer from nearby Jakubowice, received an order from his village elder to prepare his cart and horses to transport the Jews. He was able to confirm Langner's testimony practically word for word. From his perch above the cart, Łach observed the liquidation of Działoszyce. According to him, the *Aktion* was driven "by the Gendarmerie with the help of Polish Blue Police and the *junaks* from the Baudienst."[30] The Polish policemen and the *junaks*, supervised by the Germans, hunted the Jews down in the squares, streets, and houses. Jan Łach's cart was one of sixteen commandeered for the purpose of removing the Jews from the ghetto. The Jews were loaded in batches, twelve people to a cart each time. Once the victims had been loaded, the whole convoy—escorted by Polish policemen and the *junaks*—drove to the nearby Jewish cemetery, where the German gendarmes

27 Friedrich Beyerlein was the chief of the Sipo and SD post in Miechów. See Jerzy Michał Żelaśkiewicz, *Społeczność żydowska w Książu Wielkim do 1942 r.* (Warsaw: Jerzy Żelaśkiewicz, 2010), p. 65.

28 "Abraham Langner," in *Działoszyce Memorial Book*, tr. and ed. by Fay and Julian Bussgang (New York: Jewishgen.Inc, 2012), pp. 332–333. After his escape from Poland on February 13, 1949, Langner filed a similar testimony in a DP camp in Germany. See Abraham Langner testimony, AIPN Ki, 128/209, p. 130.

29 Lists of policemen, undated, ANKr, PPPBrzN, vol. 15, p. 64.

30 Deposition of witness Jan Łach in the Municipal Court in Kazimierza Wielka, January 26, 1948, AIPN, GK 196/336, p. 90. See also USHMM, RG 15.174 M.

executed the Jews. Afterward, the *junaks* pushed the dead and the wounded into pits that had been prepared in advance.

In terms of the activities of the Baudienst in Działoszyce, one of the Jewish survivors noted the following after the war:

> Germans entered the city like a hurricane, riding on motorbikes with sidecars. Chaim-Lezer went to the attic, to see what was afoot. From his vantage point, he saw the *junaks* who surrounded the city. The *junaks*, armed with spades, shovels, and crowbars, stood 3–4 meters apart, forming a cordon, a real solid wall. We were not at all surprised that the *junaks* agreed to perform the dirty work for the Germans. Sometime later, they herded the Jews from Działoszyce toward Miechów, where they left them on a damp meadow. The *junaks* guarded the entire area, preventing the Jews from escaping.[31]

Together with the Blue Police and the Sonderdienst, the *junaks* were equally active in nearby Książ Wielki. The liquidation started on August 29, 1942. There were no Germans in this town, and according to Chaim Ehrlich, a survivor from Książ Wielki, the chief of the local Blue Police detachment was a "relatively decent fellow" and his subordinates were easily bribed.[32] On the eve of the liquidation, however, everything changed. The members of the Jewish Council were summoned to Miechów where they were told that the entire Jewish community were to be resettled to Słomniki. In the meantime, the Polish police in Książ Wielki, "without any reason shot dead sixteen Jews, including the brother of the testifying [Ehrlich]."[33] Ehrlich clearly remembered the name of the Blue policeman who was the most active shooter: "Emil Suchar strolled the city in the company of Krasiński, our village

31 Joseph E. Tenenbaum, *Legacy and Redemption: A Life Renewed* (Washington, DC: United States Holocaust Memorial Museum and Holocaust Survivors' Memoirs Project, 2005), pp. 105, 110.

32 Chaim Ehrlich testimony, AZIH, 301/788.

33 Ibid.

elder (*sołtys*), and shot the Jews at random."[34] The next day, the deportation began. There were reports of widespread robbery and wanton violence committed in Książ Wielki and Słomniki by the *junaks* together with the Polish police and the Sonderdienst. While writing his "Additional Report for September 1942," the chief of the Baudienst in the Kraków area stressed the important role played by Polish youth in the liquidation of the ghettos in the Miechów area.[35]

Mordechaj Canin, a Jewish journalist and writer, visited Miechów in 1947. At the time, there were ten Jewish survivors of the Holocaust who still lived in the city. Some of them shared their stories with Canin as follows:

> Already one day before the "resettlement," the Jews knew that a Sonderkommando was on the way to liquidate the town but all escape routes have been cut off by the *junaks* who were summoned to play a role in this historic spectacle. The *junaks* have been organized by the Germans in troops known as the Baudienst. That very day, they surrounded the town. Jews, who learned by chance about the deportation, scattered in all directions. But the *junaks* caught them in the fields and brought them back to town. Those who resisted were killed with spades. All round, in the fields, Jewish bodies littered the area. Polish youths had a sporting competition: who had murdered more Jews. This first slaughter claimed hundreds of victims.[36]

It is important to look back at the liquidation *Aktionen* in the area from a general perspective, however. The officers of the Blue Police on duty in Miechów County were placed on alert on June 30, 1942.

34 Ibid.

35 Additional report for September 1942, AAN, Rząd GG, 111, vol. 490, p. 221. "One has to stress and to praise the actions of 4 troops of Section 102 of the Baudienst from Miechów during the Jewish Action." The *junaks* from the same section also took part in liquidation actions in Wachock on October 23 and 24, 1942. See AAN, Rząd GG, 111, vol. 490, p. 239.

36 Mordechaj Canin, *Przez ruiny i zgliszcza: Podróż po stu zgładzonych gminach żydowskich w Polsce* (Warsaw: Nisza, 2019), p. 355.

On that day, *Kreishauptmann* Alfons Kelpers sent out a memo ordering the concentration of Jews in nine selected locations: Jewish quarters.[37] The concentration was to be completed by July 13, 1942. The German administrators reminded the Polish police about the Third Regulation of October 15, 1941, which introduced the death penalty for any Jew who resisted "resettlement" as well as for all Poles who gave them shelter. At the same time, the Polish mayors and village elders received additional information and warnings about the "Jewish threat." In the aforementioned memo about the concentration of the Jews in selected *Sammelghettos* (combined ghettos), Kelpers made the Polish officials aware of the threat of typhus epidemics associated with the presence of Jews.[38]

The Polish village elders received another document, threatening communities with collective responsibility: Their fate would be execution by the German police. Henceforth, the elders were told that the principle of collective responsibility would apply to all villages with reported "acts of violence directed against the German Power."[39] Severe penalties would be applied in the case of "villages harboring hobos and homeless people, those without fixed addresses and otherwise having no right of residence in the area."[40] During this time, all of these categories of people functioned as codewords for Jews, and the elders were fully aware of the real meaning of these German instructions. In order to reinforce control over the population and to further isolate the Jews, the authorities ordered the Polish peasants to form special night watches. These roving patrols of peasants—usually armed with pitchforks and axes, with an occasional rifle thrown in—were to intercept the undesirables and escort them to the nearest police station. However, threats were only one of the ways in which the

37 Instructions of the Commissar *Kreishauptmann* of Miechów, Office of Internal Affairs, Department of Police, June 30, 1942, ANKr, PPPBrzN, vol. 3, pp. 12–13.

38 Letter from the Department of Propaganda of the Office of Miechów *Kreishauptmann* to voits and village elders, July 9, 1942, ANKr, PPPBrzN, vol. 3, p. 13.

39 Document titled "To Mr. Elder of the Village," undated, ANKr, PPPBrzN, vol. 11.

40 Ibid.

Germans mobilized the Poles into action. From time to time, the authorities would publish an amnesty for those who reported the Jews whom they had been previously hiding to the police.[41]

Some Jews refused to follow the German regulations, and despite the presence of the Blue Police, they started to seek shelter in various locations better known from prewar times, even if these locations were off limits to the Jews, hence why a significant number of Jews showed up in Brzesko Nowe and the vicinity. The commander of the local detachment of the Polish police expressed his concern and called in the elder of the still-existing Jewish Council to give him a stern warning. He wrote, "I order you to remove the non-resident [Jewish] population from Brzesko Nowe no later than by 8 AM on August 24, 1942.... Should you fail to comply with this order, I will inform the Gendarmerie in Miechów."[42] In light of the new policies of terror, most of all the notorious Third Regulation regarding residency restrictions of the Jews, informing the Gendarmerie about the "illegal" Jews was tantamount to signing their death warrant. Stanisław Cęckiewicz, one of the Polish witnesses, described the liquidation of Brzesko Nowe as follows:

> In many places, all across the town, they put up announcements ordering all Jews to report at a given time and day to the New Market Square. One could bring only one piece of hand luggage. All voluntary firefighters have been placed on alert. The voit received orders to supply a number of horse-driven carts, which lined up on the side of Lubelska Street, all the way to the hills in the direction of the Hebdów

41 "Who gave assistance to a Jew, or who still assists a Jew and who will declare it to the nearest Gendarmerie station no later than 4 PM, on September 9, 1942, shall avoid criminal charges. Those who will send the items purchased from a Jew to the following address: Warsaw, 20 Niska Street, before September 9, 1942, or who will report it to the nearest station of police or Gendarmerie, shall also avoid criminal charges." [signed] The Chief of SS and Police for the Warsaw Area. Announcement of September 5, 1942, regarding the death penalty for hiding the Jews, AAN, Delegatura Rządu na Kraj, 202-II-31, p. 63.

42 Letter from Blue Police commander in Brzesko Nowe to the president of the Jewish Council, August 22, 1942, ANKr, PPPBrzN, vol. 11, p. 122.

> colony. And the *Aktion* began. The miserable victims (entire families), carrying their bundles, set off from New Market Square, toward the waiting carts. At the same time, the Blue policemen, together with the Wehrmacht, the Gestapo, and the firefighters, started to search the Jewish apartments. The Gestapo pointed to the furniture and other items that they wanted loaded on their truck and delivered to the depot, which had been created for the day in a storage area in the former Orthodox church. It was the firefighters who were charged with loading and unloading this stuff.[43]

The *Aktion* in the Miechów area posed unforeseen logistical challenges for the Germans. Their own forces were inadequate for the task at hand, and the concentration and deportation of such a large number of Jews required the mobilization of all available Blue Police officers. On August 31, 1942, the officer on duty in the Brzesko Nowe station of the Blue Police received a telegram from the Blue Police county headquarters in Miechów requesting all detachments to send reinforcements to Słomniki. The "Blues" were to report in full uniform and with weapons within five hours and no later than 10:00 PM.[44]

Two days later, the same orders were given to the detachments in Igołomie, Wawrzeńczyce, Gruszów, and Kowale. The Polish officers of these detachments had to report to the Gendarmerie post in Kazimierza Wielka, where a "resettlement" *Aktion* was to begin as well.[45] In both cases, the orders were issued without prior warning and executed forthwith. In the first days of November, once the liquidation in Brzesko Nowe was over, the Blue Police officers began their hunt for the hidden Jews. On November

43 Stanisław Cęckiewicz, "Prześladowania nowobrzeskich Żydów," *Internetowy Kurier Proszowicki*, https://www.24ikp.pl/skarby/felietony/wydarzenia/20120421zydzi_nb/art.php (accessed July 2016).

44 Message from Blue Police headquarters in Miechów to Blue Police station in Brzesko Nowe, August 31, 1942, ANKr, PPPBrzN, vol. 11, p. 126.

45 Telephone messages from Miechów PP HQ to police stations in Igołomie, Wawrzeńczyce, Gruszów, and Kowale, September 2, 1942, ANKr, PPPBrzN, vol. 11, p. 126.

12–13, the "Blues" caught seventy Jews hiding in the town and the vicinity. Having drafted a nominative list of their victims—a rare occurrence during the liquidation of the ghettos—the Polish officers delivered the Jews into the hands of the Germans, either for execution or transportation to the Bełżec extermination camp.[46] The nominative list, which has been preserved in the Kraków archives, seems to confirm the often-noted observation that the majority of people who were caught during these liquidations were women, children, and the elderly. Young men had a somewhat better chance of survival, at least for the moment.

On November 16 and once again on November 27, 1942, a few days after the conclusion of the hunt for local Jews, the Brzesko Nowe police station received a visit from Sergeant Major Mikołaj Wojdyła from the Proszowice detachment of the Blue Police. The sergeant major checked everything; the weapons, the uniforms, and, of course, the effectiveness of the police work.[47] The inspection revealed that there was still much room for improvement: The crime detection rate left a lot to be desired, the officers were overworked "due to special actions" all around the county, half of the men were constantly dispatched "to protective details" away from home,[48] and the chief of the Brzesko Nowe station Sergeant Wójcik was swamped with paperwork. Ending on a more positive note, Sergeant Major Wojdyła concluded that "The officers' living conditions have improved, especially now, after the deportation of the Jews."[49] The improvement of the Polish officers' "living conditions" was also due to the theft of Jewish property, which had been deposited at police stations earlier. The commander of the Miechów County Blue Police berated his subordinates as follows:

46 List of names titled "Delivered, 13 XI," November 13, 1942, ANKr, PPPBrzN, vol. 17, pp. 70–71.

47 Reports of audits/controls of Blue Police stations in November and December 1942, ANKr, PPPBrzN, vol. 21, pp. 26–28. See also report of an audit of the Brzesko Nowe station conducted on December 27, 1942, ANKr, PPPBrzN, vol. 21.

48 Ibid.

49 Ibid.

> Recently, and in relation to the liquidation of Jewish property, many precincts and stations received office equipment and furniture. I have learned that some policemen took away, exchanged, or stole the furniture intended for sole use of their police stations. In order to redress the situation, I require that a detailed inventory of the abovementioned equipment be drawn up by every detachment.[50]

It was during the phase right after the liquidation *Aktionen* when the authorities started to hunt down the Jewish refugees who had fled to the Aryan side, and official German correspondence started to use the term *Judenjagd* (the hunt for Jews). In order to find the "missing" Jews, the authorities created a special mixed detachment, the so-called Jagdkommando (hunting unit), which was composed of gendarmes and Polish Blue Police officers.[51]

On Duty in Markowa

The earlier examples of the role of the Blue Police in liquidation *Aktionen* have dealt with cases in which the Jews were concentrated in the ghettos prior to deportation. The *Aktionen* involved the German police and other auxiliary troops, such as the so-called Trawniki men (Trawniki-Männer), mostly Ukrainian volunteers who had been drilled at a training facility in Trawniki, a village close to Lublin. In addition to taking part in the liquidations of the ghettos, the latter were also deployed to guard the death camps in the Generalgouvernement. During these *Aktionen*, the Polish Blue Police usually played second fiddle to the Germans and their Ukrainian helpers.[52] Usually, the "Blues" had to cordon off the

50 Miechów Blue Police County Commander to local Blue Police commanders in all Miechów country area stations, December 1, 1942, ANKr, PPPBrzN, vol. 54, p. 178.

51 More attention will be given to these Jagdkommandos in chapter 5.

52 Ethnic Ukrainians predominated among the so-called Trawniki men but there were also many representatives of other nations, recruited by the Germans from among Soviet prisoners of war.

ghetto in order to prevent the Jews from fleeing the deportation, and some had to force the Jews into the concentration area, which was usually the largest square in the ghetto. Moreover, the Polish officers escorted the old and infirm as well as the children to the execution sites—the shootings were usually carried out by the gendarmes in the local Jewish cemetery. They were also required to herd their victims toward the railway stations and load them onto the cattle cars. During the *Aktion*, the "Blues" conducted searches of Jewish houses and apartments, pulling out those who had attempted to hide. Once the *Aktion* was over, the Polish officers were left in charge of the former ghetto in order to prevent the locals from looting it. From the German standpoint, it was not only the issue of public security but also an attempt to prevent their own financial losses. After all, according to the letter of the law, the "post-Jewish property" belonged to the treasury of the Reich.

At this stage, one can venture a hypothesis: The degree of involvement of the Blue Police in the liquidation *Aktionen* was inversely proportional to the availability of the German forces. In the case of the liquidations of the ghettos, when the Germans had no more than a few gendarmes or Gestapo men close at hand, the role of the Polish officers in the "evacuation" of the Jews grew accordingly. This is what one could see, for instance, in Działoszyce and Brzesko Nowe. This greater role went hand in hand with increased agency and initiative. There were also cases in which the liquidation of Jewish communities, although ordered by the Germans, were conducted without their direct involvement, for instance, in Markowa and in other villages located near Łańcut, Przeworsk, and Jarosław.[53]

There were a few hundred Jews who lived in Markowa and some other villages nearby—Sietesz, Husów, Lipnik, Tarnawka, Handzlówka, Albigowa, and Kańczuga—and the majority of them were rather well integrated in the local Polish population. More importantly, until the very end, these Jews avoided concentration

53 See Jan Grabowski and Dariusz Libionka, "Distorting and Re-writing the History of the Holocaust in Poland: The Case of the Ulma Family Museum of Poles Saving Jews During World War II in Markowa," *Yad Vashem Studies*, 45 (2017), pp. 29–61.

in ghettos. In 1942, they were still living in their own houses and were trying to lead a normal life under the circumstances. This situation changed when the local detachments of the Blue Police received orders from the Gendarmerie to deliver "their" Jews to the concentration point in Łańcut. Given the absence of any Germans in these villages and the inadequate number of Blue Police in the area, it was up to the voluntary firefighters to step in. The participation of Polish firefighters in the Holocaust has left practically no trace in Polish historical literature, which is unfortunate because the issue is of significant importance and archival evidence is readily available.

In the fall of 1942, Jakub Einhorn lived in Husów, a village nearly 5 kilometers away from Markowa. One day, he learned from the chief of the local voluntary firefighters that all the Jews were to report to a selected location in the village, and from there, they would be escorted to Łańcut. Einhorn paid the firefighter for the tip, and as a result, he decided to flee the area with his wife and child. Other local Jews must have come to the same conclusion, since the next day only a handful showed up at the meeting point. Those who did were transported on carts to Łańcut and delivered to the Gestapo in the town, where they joined other Jews who had been brought to Łańcut from other villages. Their final destination was the extermination camp of Bełżec.

Once the carts left Markowa for Łańcut, the Polish firefighters and the Blue Police started to hunt down the Jews who had fled the deportation. The searches involved many local people and lasted for months. Notably, they were conducted without any Germans present. It needs to be stressed once again that these liquidation *Aktionen* clearly demonstrate the direct link between the lack of German presence and the parallel growth of the importance and involvement of the Blue Police and the Polish firefighters. There is more to the story. The gendarmes' nationality and their place of origin also played a role. From the perspective of the hunted Jewish refugees, the gendarmes from Silesia, for instance, who spoke fluent Polish—it was no coincidence that many of them served in the Generalgouvernement—were much more dangerous than their colleagues who hailed from Germany. The German policemen from *Altreich* (old Germany) had fewer contacts with both the local population and the Blue Police and were thus less of a threat to the hidden Jews.

The *Aktion* in Adamów (close to Łuków in the Lublin district) in October 1942 initially resembled the independent liquidation of the Jewish communities in Markowa and the vicinity. But here, the events took a different, surprising turn. Having received orders to conduct an *Aktion*, the "Blues" herded the Jews of Adamów to the main market square from where they planned to march them to the nearby railway station. Instead of following orders, the Jews "attacked the Polish police, seized their weapons, and fled into the forest."[54] As one can gather from the survivors' testimonies, the whole event brought dishonor to the Polish police, which started to investigate the remaining survivors of Adamów.[55] According to other sources, however, after the liquidation, a few dozen Jews were held in the local police lockup. A unit of Jewish partisans from the nearby forests descended on the town, liberated the prisoners, and killed any Pole who had taken part in the earlier bloody liquidation of the ghetto. Some Blue policemen might have been killed during this incident, which would explain the later investigations of Adamów survivors by Polish officers.

The list of executions conducted by the Blue Police—with minimal German presence, or simply in their absence—is extensive. Therefore, the discussed cases are presented here to depict a modus operandi, a pattern of action, rather than to provide an exhaustive description of the topic.

Noach Lasman, a Jewish survivor from the Lublin district, lived in the Łosice ghetto until November 1942. Łosice was liquidated in two phases. The gendarmes, working together with the Liquidierungskommando, were responsible for the original—

54 Mosze Józef Feigenbaum, *Slaughter in Podlasie: Notes from the Holocaust*, tr. by L. M. Zell (unpublished manuscript) p. 106. This is the English translation of his memoirs, originally written in Yiddish in 1948. I am grateful to Amir Feigenbaum for lending me a copy of his father's memoirs.

55 For more about Adamów, see Jean-Charles Szurek, "Powiat łukowski," in Engelking and Grabowski, *Dalej jest noc*, vol. 1, pp. 595–596.

and largest—*Aktion*, which took place on August 22, 1942. On that day, 100 Jews were murdered in the town during the *Aktion*, and several thousand were deported to Treblinka.[56] Several hundred Jews were left behind in the secondary ghetto to clean up the deserted houses and remove furniture and other items to which the Germans took a fancy or that could later be sold to the Polish public at auctions. The reprieve for the Jews of the *Restghetto* in Łosice did not last long. Noach Lasman noted the following in his memoir:

> On November 22, we went into hiding in our dugout. Five days later, the Germans surrounded the secondary ghetto, and the Polish policemen marched the few hundred surviving Jews to the Niemojki railway station. Someone who managed to flee this marching column later told me that on the way, well-dressed Jews were being murdered and robbed. Close to [the village of] Zakrze, he saw one of the Blue policemen "sell" one Jew to a peasant who liked the elegant high-heel boots of the victim. All the policeman had to do [to conclude the transaction] was to shoot the Jew in such a way so as not to stain the clothes and the boots with blood.[57]

According to Lasman, the gendarmes were involved in the liquidation of the ghetto, but it was up to the Polish policemen to deliver the Jews to the trains destined for the extermination camp of Treblinka. The killings performed on the way from Łosice to Zakrze, which were not ordered by the Germans but upon the request of a local Polish bystander, went clearly beyond the professional obligations of the officers of the Blue Police.

56 "Łosice," in Megargee, *The United States Holocaust Memorial Museum Encyclopedia of Camps and Ghettos, 1933–1945*, pp. 645–647.

57 Noach Lasman, *Wspomnienia z trzech światów*, ed. by Andrzej Niziołek (Poznań: Wydawnictwo Miejskie Posnania, 2018), p. 329.

The Painful Issue of Bullets: The Liquidation of Wodzisław

The files of the Blue Police station in Jędrzejów are undoubtedly one of the most interesting sets of documents of the Polnische Polizei im Generalgouvernement preserved in the Polish archives.[58] The Jędrzejów police post located in the Radom district oversaw a score of smaller police stations scattered across the territory of prewar Jędrzejów County. This is why the commander of the Jędrzejów post received a steady stream of reports, accounts, and other paperwork from Blue Police stations in Sędziszów, Wodzisław, Szczekociny, Secemin, Włoszczowa, Moskorzew, and Lelów.

Among these documents, one can find detailed accounts of weapons and ammunition filed by the commanders in the field with their superiors at the county level. In the eyes of the German police authorities, the issue of weapons in the hands of the Blue Police presented a challenge and a problem. More precisely, the Orpo officers tasked with the supervision of the Blue Police treated all reports about "stolen rifles" and "missing ammunition" with considerable skepticism. The commander of the Blue Police in Nowy Targ, a town south of Kraków close to the Slovak border, noted: "The Nazis, not trusting our people, allocated no more than a few old rifles with a handful of bullets to each detachment."[59]

With time, more rifles, pistols, grenades, and ammunition found their way into the hands of the Polish policemen, but the Germans remained very vigilant and concerned about the proper accounting of weapons. Later, control of weapons became an issue of life and death, both for the Germans, who feared that the "lost" rifles might be used against them, and for the Poles, who faced severe penalties—including death—for the loss of a firearm. Beginning in the second half of 1943, once the resistance fighters had started to disarm policemen, reports about missing weapons became more and more frequent. Until the end of 1942, however, the reports about lost weapons were rare. Missing ammunition

58 Police files, Blue Police headquarters in Jędrzejów, Internal Affairs Department (*Innere Verwaltung*), *Kreishauptmann* Office Kielce, AIPN, GK 652/48, vol. 1.

59 Wraubek, *Na Podhalu*.

was an altogether different problem. The "Blues" needed bullets for their own purposes, most likely for hunting but, quite conceivably, for sale as well.

Order no. 6, dispatched by the chief of the Miechów police to the commanders of local detachments on April 9, 1942, made reference precisely to this problem: "The available ammunition has to be duly reported in the station register before the end of each shift. The commander of each post and each officer are responsible for each and every bullet."[60] It was with regard to such procedures and concerns that Lieutenant Grenda, commander of the Polish police in Radomsko County, wrote to his subordinate, the chief of the Blue Police post in Szydłowiec, requesting further information about three bullets left unaccounted for by Constable Andrzej Owczarek on duty at the local station.[61] As mentioned earlier, the Germans treated each and every unaccounted bullet with utmost seriousness.

At this point, it is necessary to closely inspect the reports that were flowing from the field to the Jędrzejów headquarters of the Blue Police during the spring and summer of 1942. On March 17, 1942, platoon leader Wacław Szczęśniewski from the Lelów detachment fired several shots while in pursuit of a supposedly suspect individual. Staff Sergeant Józef Karyś of the Polish Criminal Police, who also took part in the chase, witnessed the shooting. Both officers later presented their accounts to the commander of the Lelów police station, who, in turn, wrote a report in Polish and sent it to the headquarters in Jędrzejów. In Jędrzejów, the Lelów report was translated into German and submitted to the commander of the Gendarmerie in *Kreishauptmannschaft* Jędrzejów. On March 23, 1942, less than one week after the shooting, the Germans accepted the report and authorized a shipment of ten bullets to the Lelów station of the Blue Police.[62] In a similar way, the Polish police had to report bullets fired against dogs. In rural areas, the policemen

60 Order of the Miechów Blue Police commander to local station chiefs, April 9, 1942, ANKr, PPPBrzN, vol. 1, p. 28.

61 Letter from the Radomsko county Blue Police commander to the Blue Police chief in Szydłowiec, April 9, 1942, AIPN, GK 695/1, p. 97.

62 Report of a weapon fired, March 19, 1942, AIPN, GK 652/48, vol. 1, pp. 22–28.

were expected to shoot dogs if they had grounds to believe that the animals were either wild or sick with rabies. In order to make the reports more credible, the Polish policemen were told to send the shell casings or keep them on hand for later inspection.[63]

POLNISCHER POLIZEIPOSTEN
in SZCZEKOCINY
Posterunek Polskiej Policji
w Szczekocinach

Police report about the shooting of a wild dog. AIPN, GK 652/48, vol. 1.

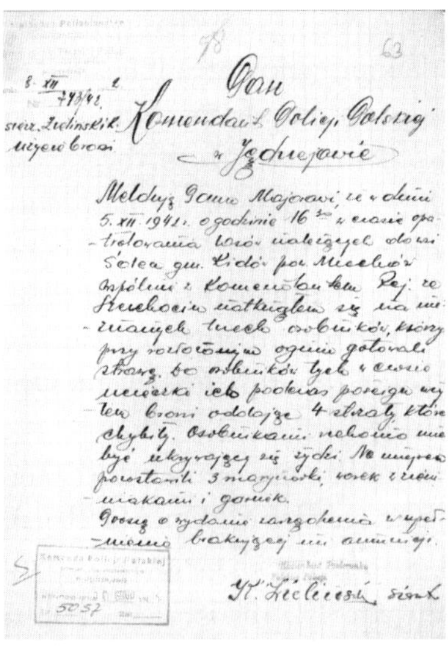

"I report...that I encountered three unknown individuals who were cooking food over the fire. I chased after them and I fired four shots which missed. These individuals are said to have been Jews." Report about missing bullets from the Jędrzejow Blue Police station. AIPN, GK 652/48, vol. 1.

The report of the commander of the Szczekociny detachment, filed on March 29, 1942, and reproduced above, is a typical

63 If shell casings could not be produced for whatever reason, one had to attach a special explanatory note to the report. See report from the Moskorzewo police post, November 24, 1942, AIPN, GK 652/48, vol. 1, p. 35.

example of such a document. It is worthwhile to note that in cases involving so-called suspicious individuals and rabid dogs, Polish policemen usually expended—and reported—single bullets. In late summer and the fall of 1942, during the German liquidation of the ghettos in the Jędrzejów area, the Blue policemen started to shoot people, not dogs, and the number of expended bullets grew rapidly. That is why the reports dealing with the bullets shot at the Jews look different. Since few of these documents have been preserved, they require significant attention. On November 21, 1942, the commander of the Wodzisław station of the Blue Police informed his superiors in Jędrzejów of the following: "I report that during the liquidation of Jews in Wodzisław, I received from the Gendarmerie in Jędrzejów 300 rifle bullets. In order to compensate the officers for shots fired, I distributed ammunition among the men listed below."[64]

The nominative list, provided by the commander from Wodzisław Sergeant Władysław Buczek, contained the names of fourteen Polish officers who had received bullets necessary to replenish their stocks that had been exhausted by the shooting of Jews. Along with the report, the commander from Wodzisław expedited ninety-one shell casings and seventeen bandoliers, which are thin strips of metal that tie several bullets together. More was to come. Ten days later, Sergenant Buczek sent another ammunition request to Jędrzejów. In his letter dated December 1, 1942, Buczek wrote the following to his superior: "I need an allocation of rifle bullets in order to restock our supplies of ammunition, which have been used while shooting the Jews during the last deportation from Wodzisław."[65] This was followed by a detailed list of the shooters—and Sergeant Buczek proved to be an active participant himself:

64 Wodzisław station Blue Police commander to the Jędrzejów County Blue Police commander, November 21, 1941, AIPN, GK 652/48, vol. 1, pp. 37–38 (Polish original and a German translation of the report).

65 The original Polish letter reads as follows: "*Proszę o przydzielenie uzupełniającej amunicji karabinowej dla tut. posterunku P. P., która została wystrzelana przez szereg[owych] tut[ejszego] posterunku do żydów w czasie ostatniego wysiedlania ich z Wodzisławia.*"

1. For Sergeant Buczek Władysław—20 bullets
2. For Constable Klepka Józef—10 bullets
3. For Constable Wójcikiewicz Władysław—5 bullets
4. For Constable Szczukocki Ludwik—20 bullets
5. For police candidate Węckowski Zdzisław—16 bullets

Total: 71 bullets[66]

Polnischer Polizeiposten
in WODZISŁAW
Posterunek Polskiej Policji
powiatu Jędrzejowskiego
w Wodzisławiu

dnia 21.XI. 1942

Nr. 1068/42.

Amunicja do karabinów-
rozliczenie.-

Pan Komendant Powiatowy P.P.

w Jędrzejowie.

Melduję Panu Komendantowi, że w czasie likwidacji żydów w Wodzisławiu otrzymałem od Żandarmerji z Jędrzejowa 300 sztuk amunicji do karabinów z której do uzupełnienia wystrzelanej amunicji przydzieliłem niżej wymienionym szeregowym jak następuję.

L. P.	Data przydziału.	Nazwisko i imię policjanta.	Stopień służbowy.	Przydział służbowy	Ilość wydanej amunicji.-	Uwagi.
1.	5.X.942.	Buczek Władysław	sierż.	Poster.P.P. w Wodzisławiu	20	
2.	5.X.942.	Wieczorek Kom.Rej.	St.sierż.	Sędziszów	25.	
3.	5.X.942.	Klepka Józef	plut.	Wodzisław	20.	
4.	5.X./42.	Szczukocki Ludwik	.".	.".	20.	
5.	5.X.942 .	Machowski Józef	.-.	-"-	36.	
6.	5.X.942 .	Wójcikiewicz Władysław	-"-	-"-	15.	
7.	5.X.942.	Węckowski Zdzisław	kandyd.	-"-	20.	
8.	5.X.942.	Niedziela Franciszek	plut.	Nawarzyce	5.	
9.	5.X.942.	Gorgis Jan	kand.	-"-	20.	
10.	5.X.942.	Jabłoński Józef	kpr.	Oksa	20.	
11.	5.X.942.	Machnik Józef	-"-	Słupia	5.	
12.	5.X.942.	Żelichowski Stan.	kand.	Prząsław	11.	
13.	6.X.942.	Włodarczyk Mikołaj	plut.	-"-	5.	
14.	5.X.942.	Chaja Wojciech	-"-	Nawarzyce	5.	
15.	6.X.942.	Gorgis Jan	kand.	-"-	10.	
16.	14.X.942	Węckowski Zdzisław	-"-	Wodzisław	17.	
17.	14.X.942.	Szczukocki Ludwik	plut.	-"-	20.	
18.	15.XI.42	Klepka Józef	-"-	-"-	10.	
19.	15.XI.42	Węckowski Zdzisław	kand.	-"-	16	
				Razem	300 szt.	

Wystrzelonych łusek 91 i 17 łudek przyniniejszym przesyłam.

Komendant Posterunku
Polskiej Policji

Report about the number of bullets shot at the local Jews by Blue policemen in Wodzisław. AIPN, GK 652/48, vol. 1.

66 Blue Police station chief in Wodzisław to his superior in Jędrzejów, December 1, 1942, AIPN, GK 652/48, vol. 1., p. 61.

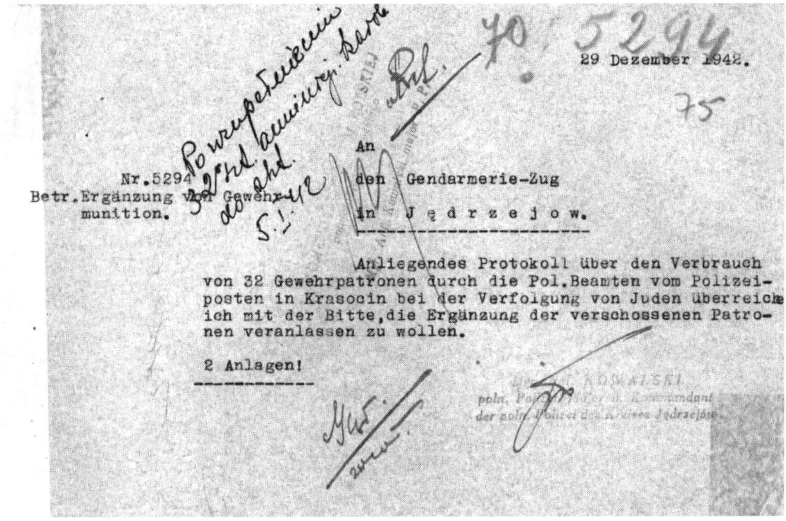

29 Dezember 1942.

Nr.5294
Betr.Ergänzung von Gewehr-
munition.

An
den Gendarmerie-Zug
in Jędrzejow.

Anliegendes Protokoll über den Verbrauch von 32 Gewehrpatronen durch die Pol.Beamten vom Polizeiposten in Krasocin bei der Verfolgung von Juden überreiche ich mit der Bitte, die Ergänzung der verschossenen Patronen veranlassen zu wollen.

2 Anlagen!

Thirty-two bullets fired against Jews by the members of the Krasocin post of the Polish police. AIPN, GK 652/48, v. 1.

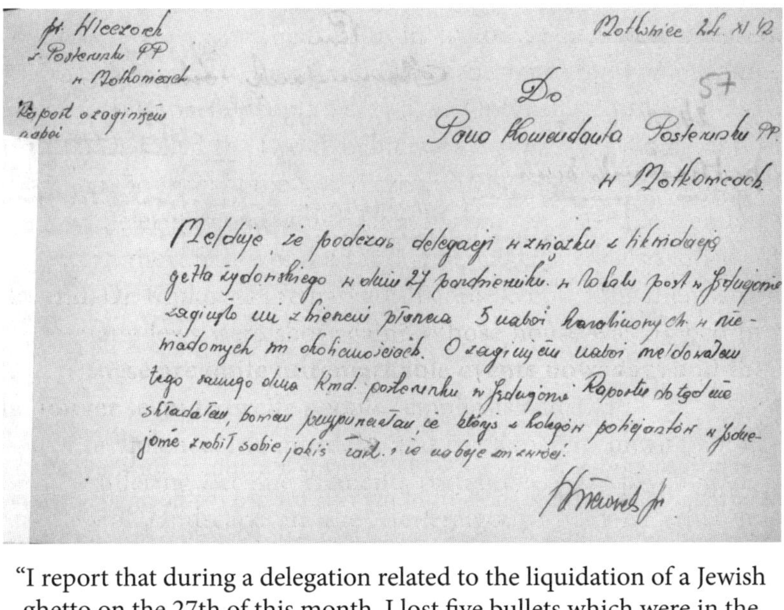

st. Wieczorek
z Posterunku PP
w Motkowicach

Raport o zaginięciu naboi

Motkowice 24.XI.42

Do
Pana Komendanta Posterunku PP
w Motkowicach

Melduję, że podczas delegacji w związku z likwidacją getta żydowskiego w dniu 27 października w [illegible] post. w Jędrzejowie zaginęło mi z kieszeni płaszcza 5 naboi karabinowych w niewiadomych mi okolicznościach. O zaginięciu naboi meldowałem tego samego dnia Kmd. posterunku w Jędrzejowie. Raportu do tej pory nie składałem, bowiem przypuszczałem, że ktoś z kolegów policjantów w Jędrzejowie zrobił sobie jakiś [illegible], i że naboje mi zwróci.

Wieczorek st.

"I report that during a delegation related to the liquidation of a Jewish ghetto on the 27th of this month, I lost five bullets which were in the pocket of my service coat." AIPN, GK 652/48, v. 1.

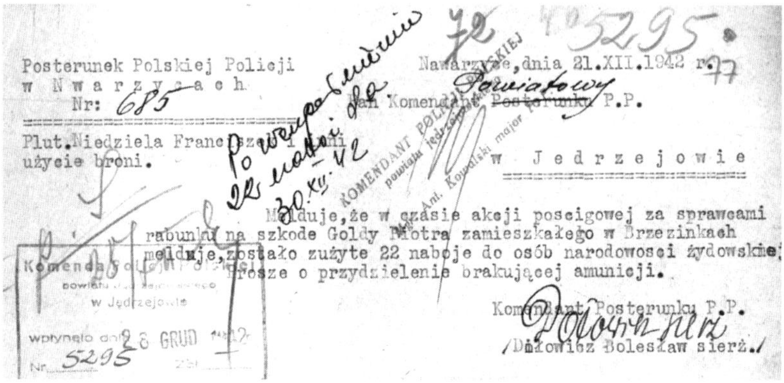

Posterunek Polskiej Policji
w N w a r z y c a c h.
Nr: 685

Nawarzyce, dnia 21.XII.1942 r.

Pan Komendant Posterunku P.P.
w J e d r z e j o w i e

Plut. Niedziela Franciszek i [illegible] użycie broni.

Melduje, że w czasie akcji poscigowej za sprawcami rabunku na szkode Goldy Piotra zamieszkałego w Brzezinkach melduje, zostało zużyte 22 naboje do osób narodowosci żydowskiej. Prosze o przydzielenie brakującej amunicji.

Komendant Posterunku P.P.
/Dżłowicz Bolesław sierż./

Komenda Policji Polskiej powiatu w Jędrzejowie
wpłynęło dnia 28 GRUD 1942
Nr 5295

“I report that during the chase...we used 22 bullets against persons of Jewish nationality. Please, send us the missing ammunition.” Commander of Nawarzyce Blue Police station.” AIPN, GK 652/48, v. 1.

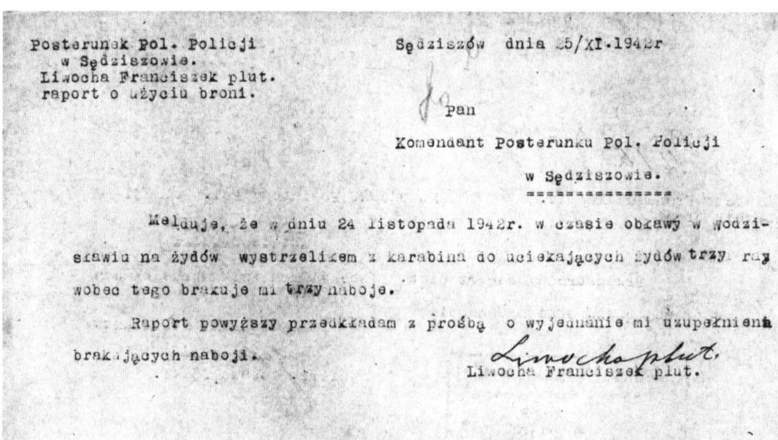

Posterunek Pol. Policji
w Sędziszowie.
Liwocha Franciszek plut.
raport o użyciu broni.

Sędziszów dnia 25/XI.1942r

Pan
Komendant Posterunku Pol. Policji
w Sędziszowie.

Melduję, że w dniu 24 listopada 1942r. w czasie obławy w Wodzisławiu na żydów wystrzeliłem z karabinu do uciekających żydów trzy razy wobec tego brakuje mi trzy naboje.

Raport powyższy przedkładam z prośbą o wyjednanie mi uzupełnienia brakujących naboji.

Liwocha Franciszek plut.

“I report that on November 24, 1942, during a manhunt for the Jews in Wodzisław, I fired three shots from my rifle toward the fleeing Jews, so I need three bullets now...” AIPN, GK 652/48, v. 1.

The Włodzisław ghetto was small, and it had a population of 3,000–4,000 people. Unsurprisingly, historians have little to say about its liquidation. The German scholar Wolfgang Curilla summarized the end of Wodzisław in one short paragraph:

> On September 23 or 24, 1942, the entire Jewish population of Wodzisław was deported to the Treblinka extermination camp. One platoon of Gendarmerie from Jędrzejów took part in the *Aktion*. One unit of SS, Gestapo, and the Polish police also participated. Three thousand Jews were deported and about seventy others were killed during the *Aktion*.[67]

The *USHMM Encyclopedia of Camps and Ghettos* provides some more information:

> The town had a small Polish (Blue) Police force, consisting at first of three and then two policemen, named Szczukocki and Machowski. The latter participated in the shooting of local Jews; after the war, he was sentenced to death by a Polish court in Kielce and executed.... The Germans liquidated the Wodzisław ghetto on or around September 20, 1942.... Following the liquidation Aktion, the German authorities established a remnant ghetto in Wodzisław. At the beginning of November 1942, 90 Jews lived there, but this number reportedly grew to 300 before its liquidation that same month. On November 20, the remaining Jews were resettled to the Sandomierz ghetto.[68]

The official correspondence of the Blue Police broadens our knowledge of the fate of the Jews of Wodzisław and adds some more depth to the entry in the USHMM encyclopedia. From the report filed by Sergeant Buczek, which dealt with two *Aktionen* that led to the liquidation of the ghetto, we learn that Polish officers

67 Curilla, *Der Judenmord in Polen*, p. 494.

68 "Wodzisław," in Megargee, *The United States Holocaust Memorial Museum Encyclopedia of Camps and Ghettos, 1933–1945*, pp. 344–345.

shot 300 bullets at the Jews. As we read in the encyclopedia, not just one but all the Blue policemen from the local detachment took part in the murders. The local Blue Police contingent was six—and not two—men strong, and further reinforcements were called in from nearby detachments in Nawarzyce, Oksa, Słupia, and Prząsław. There is little doubt that Constable Józef Machowski, the policeman mentioned in the entry, fired most often at the Jews, but his colleagues were not far behind him and fulfilled their duties with similar zeal. While Machowski used thirty-six bullets during a single day of the *Aktion*, other Polish officers fired between five and twenty times. According to the few survivors of this *Aktion*, close to 200 Jews lost their lives that day on the streets of the liquidated ghetto. Finally, the police reports make no mention of the transfer of any surviving Wodzisław Jews to the ghetto in Sandomierz. Indeed, even if such a transfer took place, it must have involved the small number of Jews who had survived the massacre. One of the Polish witnesses wrote the following:

> A few days after the Sunday killings, they started to sell off post-Jewish property at auctions. A special commission went from house to house, and they placed a table on which they put everything that was to be auctioned in front of the door. New tenants started to move into the dwellings left behind by the Jews, but many houses remained abandoned and fell into disrepair and ruin.... Machowski, a Blue policeman who after the war was tried and executed in Kielce, acted with particular cruelty. People said that one should avoid wandering off into the woods, because so many Jews were hiding there and, when scared, they could shoot.[69]

A few years after the war, Machowski together with one other former Blue Police officer from Wodzisław stood trial for their crimes against Jews and Poles.[70] According to witness accounts,

69 Wojciech Skrodzki, "Żydzi z Wodzisławia," *Tygodnik Powszechny*, 28 (2006).

70 The description of this case is based on documents and depositions. See Trial files of Józef Machowski and Józef Klepka, USHMM, RG 15.180 M, roll. 20. The originals can be found in AIPN, Ki 013/1127.

Machowski boasted in 1942 that during a day-long *Aktion*, "he had killed about thirty Jews."[71] Kałm Fajrajzen survived the liquidation and later testified at Machowski's trial: "I saw Józef Machowski beating Jews up and killing the Zalcman and Klienmann families (5–7 people) just because they failed to report on time to the concentration area."[72] Machowski himself said in his defense that he "shot when the Germans forced him to shoot," but even then, "he fired into the ground, and not toward the Jews."[73] Machowski's mistreatment of ethnic Poles did not help his case. "He executed the persons of Jewish nationality, and he treated brutally the Polish population striking them with a rubber baton, beating them with his fists and kicking them," testified one of Machowski's Polish neighbors.[74] In Kielce in 1950, Machowski was sentenced to death. The case was appealed all the way to the Supreme Court, which, however, confirmed the sentence that had been meted out by the lower courts. Bolesław Bierut, the president of Poland, refused to pardon the convict, and on May 21, 1951, the former platoon leader Machowski was executed in Kielce Prison. To the best of my knowledge, this was the only death sentence that was carried out after the war of a Blue policeman who had been found guilty of murdering the Jews.[75]

71 Witness testimony, trial files of Józef Machowski and Józef Klepka, USHMM, RG 15.180 M, roll. 20.

72 Kałm Fajrajzen testimony, trial files of Józef Machowski and Józef Klepka, USHMM, RG 15.180 M, roll. 20.

73 Machowski testimony, trial files of Józef Machowski and Józef Klepka, USHMM, RG 15.180 M, roll. 20.

74 Deposition of the witness Mieczysław Barański, September 22, 1948, AIPN, Ki 013/1127, p. 27.

75 Piotr Szowkalo—the officer serving in the Pilica and Wolbrom Blue Police posts and a member of a notorious Jagdkommando—was another policeman who was sentenced to death and executed after the war. Unlike Machowski, the reason for Szowkalo's sentence was related to his execution of Poles rather than Jews. See the dossiers of Piotr Szowkala, District Court in Sosnowiec, Archiwum Instytutu Pamięci Narodowej Oddział w Katowicach (AIPN Ka), 566/10. This case is discussed in detail in Libionka, "Powiat miechowski," pp. 166–168. Another death sentence was announced against Michał Wiesiołowski, the Blue Police commander in Biłgoraj. He is said to have been executed in Zamosc after the war, but I was unable to locate court documents related to this case.

Police officer Józef Machowski, one of the very few Polish policemen sentenced to death and executed for having murdered the Jews. Undated photo taken shortly after the war. AIPN Ki, 013/1127.

It is difficult to follow the successive phases of Machowski's police career that transformed this average, otherwise unremarkable officer with a long prewar career in the Polish police into a ruthless killer of his fellow citizens—the Jews. It is troubling that the murders of the Jews did not prevent Machowski from being considered by his peers "a good Pole and a patriot."[76] During the trial, one of the witnesses—a member of the local unit of the Home Army (AK)—confirmed that on several occasions, Machowski supplied him with bullets for the resistance.[77] Władysław Buczek, the commander of the Wodzisław detachment, testified against his former subordinate and accused him of having murdered the Rajzman family at the end of 1942. Buczek learned about the hidden Jews from someone called Stawinoga from the village of Piotrkowice. Stawinoga kept the Jews on his farm for some time but grew tired of his unwanted guests. Finally, he asked Buczek to

76 Trial files of Józef Machowski and Józef Klepka, USHMM, RG 15.180 M, roll. 20. See also the 1948 trial of both policemen: AIPN, Ki 013/1127.

77 According to AK member Wacław Pawełczyk, Machowski delivered him ammunition on several occasions, although he knew that Pawelczyk was active in the resistance.

solve the problem and "liquidate these Jews."[78] Stawinoga offered the commander of the Blue Police 10,000 zlotys—a respectable amount of money at the time—for the killings. Buczek claimed to have refused the offer, but Machowski readily agreed to act in his stead. Looking at Buczek's credibility, however, it might be good to keep in mind that this is the same man who shot twenty bullets against the Jews during the first liquidation of Wodzisław, as attested by the nominative list shown above. It was difficult, if not impossible, to establish the precise number of Jews killed by the Polish constable. Some witnesses talked about ten, others about twenty victims. Machowski himself, as indicated earlier, boasted about thirty executed Jews. Abram Romankiewicz, a Jewish survivor from Wodzisław, put it succinctly: "We were not paying attention [to numbers] because, at the time, Jews were being killed all around, in many cities."[79]

Indeed, in late fall 1942, killings of the Jews became so commonplace that Jewish death simply became natural and, in a way, something to be expected. Emanuel Ringelblum, the historian of the Warsaw ghetto, made a reference to this phenomenon, writing that the Jews were henceforth considered "the deceased on leave," and that killing someone who was already condemned to death was neither a sin nor a crime.[80] This kind of logic might well have informed the actions of both the Blue Police officers and the many civilians who decided to take part in the hunt for the Jews.

The issue of expended ammunition—and these accounts often raised suspicions among the German police officials—was also at the center of a report filed with the gendarmes by Lieutenant Urbański, the commander of the Polish police in Krasnystaw County in the Lublin district:

78 Deposition of Władysław Buczek, October 8, 1948, trial files of Józef Machowski and Józef Klepka, AIPN, Ki 013/1127, p. 28. See also: USHMM, RG 15.180 M, roll 20.

79 Deposition of Abram Romankiewicz, August 7, 1950, USHMM, RG 15.180 M, roll. 20, pp. 32-32v.

80 Ringelblum, *Polish-Jewish Relations*, p. 77.

> On June 28, 1943, at 14:00 hours, in [the] village [of] Felin, Rybczewice Commune [24 kilometers northeast of Krasnystaw], the officers from the Rybczewice detachment, while on patrol, caught seven Jews. They had earlier fled the camp in Lublin.[81] To wit: 1) Jakub Szapiro from Lublin, age 43; 2) Handelman Mordko, age 39; 3) Majer Berko-Hersz, age 40 from Piaski; 4) Necman Herszek, age 30; 5) Necman Sara, age 32; 6) Necman Chana, age 4; and 7) Bereschling Chaja, all of them from Piaski, Lublin County. Herszek Necman had been shot by the officers from Rybczewice during an escape attempt. The policemen used seventeen bullets and the Jew had been buried at the scene. The remaining six Jews, together with their money and clothes, were delivered to the Piaski Gendarmerie post.[82]

The surviving documentation does not provide any evidence of how the German gendarmes reacted to the news of so many shots fired at one fleeing Jew.

The problem with the ammunition, however, went beyond a simple bullet count, as can be seen from the report filed by Polish policemen in Stanin, which is quoted on the opening pages of this volume. Stanin is a village situated around 14 kilometers east of Łuków in the Podlasie area of eastern Poland. In January 1943, the locals delivered twenty-two Jews to the station of the Blue Police. The next day, the Polish officers executed eleven of these Jews, but they had to cease shooting "due to the poor quality of the ammunition," as can be read in the report filed by Sergeant Mazur with his superiors in the county police headquarters in Łuków.[83]

Before moving on from the issue of weapons and ammunition used by the Polish officers toward the Jews, it is not irrelevant to

81 The Jews had most likely fled from the Piaski ghetto, which was liquidated at the same time. See USHMM, RG 15.207 M, roll. 11.

82 Report, Urbański files, USHMM, RG 15.207 M, r. 11. For the originals, see AIPN, GK 418/991, p. 4.

83 Report of Sergeant Mazur to the county commander in Łuków, Stanin Police Post, January 13, 1943, AP Lublin, Posterunki Policji Polskiej w Dystrykcie Lubelskim, file 1035.

mention Węgrów, a small town northeast of Warsaw. Wacław Grabowski moved to Węgrów in 1941, where he worked for a local agricultural business. On September 22, 1942, during a bloody *Aktion*, the Germans along with their Ukrainian and Polish helpers liquidated the ghetto. Soon after, once most of the Germans and Ukrainians had left, the Polish firefighters and policemen began the "mopping up" operation: hunting down and killing the Jews who had survived the *Aktion*. In his memoir, Grabowski wrote the following:

> In the fall of 1942, I witnessed the following scene: Walking with my wife on Gdańska (Starowiejska Street), we saw on the other side of the street, close to Szpilman's house, a few Polish Blue policemen, standing in a field of potatoes. In the middle of the field, paralyzed with fear, cowered a group of Jews. I heard one of the policemen talking to the others, asking which one of them had not yet cleaned his rifle. That's when one of them pointed his weapon at the potato field and, firing off several shots, killed all the Jews who sought shelter.[84]

It can be gathered that the officers had already used and cleaned their weapons earlier that day and were not eager to unnecessarily trouble themselves to clean their rifles again, as mandated by the regulations.

Among other official documents that give us insight into the role of Polish officers in the liquidation *Aktionen*, the per diem zloty amounts allocated to individual policemen should not be forgotten. The files of the local administration in Radomsko County in central Poland contain numerous forms filled in by policemen on "ghetto liquidation duties." Seeking reimbursement, the officers had to indicate the distance traveled, the means of transportation used, as well as any time spent away from their home post. Ewa Wiatr was the first—and, so far, the only—researcher to have looked at these intriguing documents:

84 Tadeusz Wacław Grabowski, *Wspomnienia* (manuscript in the author's possession). I am grateful to Dr. Michał Grabowski for making his father's manuscript available to me for my research.

> Platoon Leader Stanisław Kawa from Kobiela used full sentences in his description of his duties: "On 6 October at 2 o'clock I went by truck to Żarki with the gendarmerie from Radomsko in order to deport Jews. On the same day, after the deportation of Jews from Żarki I went to Koniecpol with the gendarmerie to deport Jews from Koniecpol. On 7 October 1942 in the afternoon I went with the gendarmerie to Radomsko, where I served in the Jewish quarter until 6 PM on 21 November 1942." His remuneration was 425 zlotys, with 7 per diem allowances in the amount of 9 zlotys and 40 per diem allowances in the amount of 8 zlotys. Kawa was also reimbursed for accommodation for the first 7 days of his mission. Another policeman, Corporal Piotr Kipigroch from the station in Stobieck Miejski, stuck to facts: "6 o'clock on 6 October 1942 arrival at the Polish Police station in Żarki; assistance at the deportation of Jews. Departure at 5 PM on 6 October 1942, Polish Police station in Koniecpol – arrival at 7 PM on 6 October 1942; assistance at the deportation of Jews. Departure at 12 o'clock on 7 October 1942.[85]

Similar daily accounts can be found in the reports produced by the Baudienst. The time spent by the young Polish *junaks* of the Construction Service liquidating the ghettos is listed hour by hour, day by day.

The requests for ammunition from Wodzisław were by no means unique. Similar reports arrived in the Jędrzejów County headquarters from other detachments. On December 29, 1942, the commander of the Krasocin station asked the chief of the county police to send him thirty-two bullets as a replacement for those used against the fleeing Jews.[86] On December 21, 1942, in their hot pursuit of the fleeing Jews, the Polish policemen used twenty-two bullets, and on December 8, 1942, Sergeant Zieliński from the

85 See Ewa Wiatr, "'Turning Jews Over': The Participation of 'Blue' Policemen in Deportations of Jews Illustrated with the Example of the Radomsko County" (English edition), *Zagłada Żydów, Studia i materiały*, 10 (2014), p. 311.

86 Krasocin Blue Police commander to his superior in Jędrzejów, December 29, 1942, AIPN, GK 652/48, vol. 1, p. 75.

Irządze Blue Police station requested four bullets from Jędrzejów to compensate the local officers who had shot at the Jews detected in their area.[87] The last two reports deal with the period immediately following the liquidation of the ghettos, when the Polish police combed the areas adjacent to the liquidated Jewish communities, looking for Jews on the run.

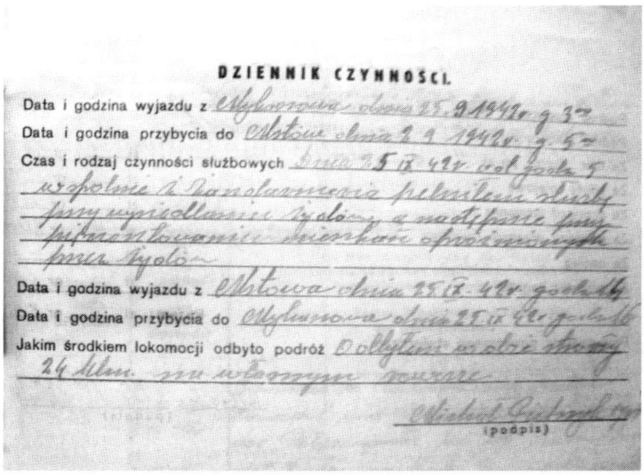

DZIENNIK CZYNNOŚCI.

Data i godzina wyjazdu z Mykanowa dnia 25.9.1942 r. g. 3
Data i godzina przybycia do Mstowa dnia 25.9.1942 r. g. 5
Czas i rodzaj czynności służbowych dnia 25 IX 42 r. od godz. 5 wspólnie z żandarmerią pełniłem służbę przy wysiedlaniu Żydów, a następnie przy pilnowaniu mienia opróżnionych przez Żydów
Data i godzina wyjazdu z Mstowa dnia 25.IX.42 r. godz. 16
Data i godzina przybycia do Mykanowa dnia 25.IX.42 r.
Jakim środkiem lokomocji odbyto podróż rowerem w obie strony 24 klm. na własnym rowerze

(podpis)

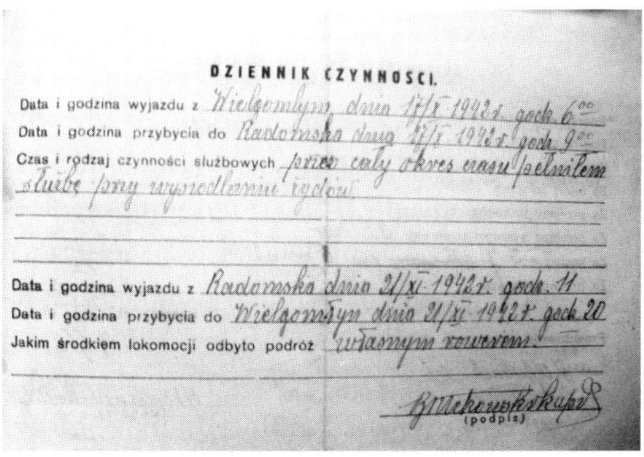

DZIENNIK CZYNNOŚCI.

Data i godzina wyjazdu z Wielgomłyny dnia 17/X 1942 r. godz. 6⁰⁰
Data i godzina przybycia do Radomsko dnia 17/X 1942 r. godz. 9⁰⁰
Czas i rodzaj czynności służbowych przez cały okres czasu pełniłem służbę przy wysiedlaniu żydów.
Data i godzina wyjazdu z Radomsko dnia 21/XI 1942 r. godz. 11
Data i godzina przybycia do Wielgomłyny dnia 21/XI 1942 r. godz. 20
Jakim środkiem lokomocji odbyto podróż własnym rowerem.

(podpis)

Travel expenses and documents of Constable Michał Pietrzyk, September 25, 1942 (top), and Corporal Bolesław Klekowski, October 17, 1942 (bottom). State Archive in Piotrków Trybunalski, collection 949, Gemeinderverband in Radomsko. Courtesy of Ewa Wiatr.

87 Nawarzyce Blue Police post commander to his superior in Jędrzejów, December 21, 1942, AIPN, GK 652/48, vol. 1, p. 63; and Irządze Blue Police post commander to his superior in Jędrzejów, December 8, 1942, AIPN, GK 652/48, vol. 1, p. 77.

Liquidation *Aktion* in the Kraków Ghetto

Sergeant Franciszek Banaś had served in the Kraków police since the early 1920s. He continued his service as a Blue policeman until the fall of 1943 when he deserted and went into hiding following the mass arrests of the local Polish officers by the Germans. Immediately after the war, Banaś presented himself to the Kraków Jewish Historical Commission and gave an exhaustive testimony in which he described everything he knew about the fate of the Jews of Kraków during the Holocaust.[88] Indeed, Sergeant Banaś knew a lot about the issue since he was quite often on duty guarding the borders of the ghetto. Being a prudent man—he had extensive police experience and was a former member of the underground Home Army—Franciszek Banaś decided to withhold his true identity, and in 1945, he gave his account under the alias "Stefan." Twenty-five years after the war, he wrote his memoir, which was published in 2009.[89] Comparing Banaś's testimony given in 1945 with his much later memoir is a revealing and interesting exercise in itself. According to the Kraków policeman, it was the wartime recruits to the Polish police—young people open to German propaganda—who proved themselves to be the most dangerous for the Jews. Banaś wrote:

> From the very beginning, the Germans started to drive a wedge between Poles and Jews, some shadowy characters bought into it, became informers or followed [German] orders blindly and with zeal. When I write these words, I think of individual officers, especially those recruited during the war. It was they who brought shame to the police corps.[90]

88 "Stefan" testimony, ŻIH, 301/2058.

89 Franciszek Banaś, *Moje wspomnienia*, ed. by Michał Kalisz and Elżbieta Rączy (Rzeszów: Instytut Pamięci Narodowej, Komisja Ścigania Zbrodni przeciwko Narodowi Polskiemu, Oddział w Rzeszowie, 2009). It is a pity that the publishers of Banaś's memoirs overlooked the fact that in the collections of the Jewish Historical Institute in Warsaw, one can find the earlier testimony of the Kraków policeman.

90 "Stefan" testimony, ŻIH, 301/2058.

It is worth stressing that both in his early testimony and in his later memoir, Banaś tried to defend the honor of the uniform he wore.

The main gate of the Kraków ghetto was near the main market square Rynek Podgórski, and the others were located at Zgody Square and Lwowska Street. There were also two other gates on Limanowski Street. Each gate was guarded by the Blue Police. Banaś wrote the following:

> There is a Polish policeman standing by the gate of the ghetto. His orders are to take away the food from Jews who are returning to the ghetto from work. I need to add here that among the Polish officers there were some understanding people, people who took pity. But there were also officers who eagerly took the food away from the Jews and who pocketed the profits.... Many tears have been shed at these gates because of the zeal of some officers who, inspired by greed and their own stupidity, harmed the people.[91]

This greed was built on solid foundations. Allowing a food wagon into the ghetto could fetch the "Blues" anywhere between 200 and 300 zlotys or the equivalent of a monthly salary of a rank-and-file officer. Banaś wrote that these "corrupt individuals" within the force were known to have threatened officers who demonstrated leniency and turned a blind eye to the Jews smuggling food into the ghetto.[92] Officer Kaczynski was one of these "corrupt individuals," who denounced Banaś to the Germans. According to Banaś's testimony to the Kraków Jewish Historical Commission, he said, "I barely avoided getting shot." In his later memoir, however, he expanded on his experience:

> One time, in the guard house, I said to the young policemen, these shitheads, that they should not add to human misery. I added that a Polish policeman had no right to shoot the Jews. If the Germans want to do destroy the Jews, then that's their

91 Ibid.

92 Ibid.

> problem. But we Poles cannot have anything to do with it. So, one of these punks says: "Mr. Banaś, I had no idea that you are a Jewish uncle, and that you want to defend them!"[93]

The terms "Jewish uncle" (*żydowski wujek*) and "Jewish aunt" (*żydowska ciotka*) were used during the war to describe people who were sympathetic to the plight of the Jews. Both terms were used with derision and were intended to embarrass or threaten the people in question. If we are to trust Banaś, more experienced policemen turned a blind eye to smuggling in the ghetto and sometimes even tried to help the Jews. With time, however, the police corps became increasingly demoralized, according to Banaś.[94] Then, the liquidation *Aktionen* began. Unlike the smaller ghettos where the Jews were murdered or deported over the course of one day, the populations of the larger ghettos were "resettled" in stages. In Warsaw, there were three liquidation *Aktionen*,[95] and the same situation occurred in Tarnów. The first *Aktion* in Kraków, during which more than 150 people were murdered on the streets of the city and a further 7,000 were deported to the Bełżec extermination camp, lasted from June 1–7, 1942. "Stefan" wrote the following:

> The German soldiers, various kinds of SS-men and Gestapo officers kept shooting at the Jews. The sanitation trucks and Polish youths drafted into the Baudienst followed the [marching] column of Jews, collected the bodies, and placed them on the trucks. The trucks delivered the bodies to the cemetery and dumped them into [mass] graves which had been prepared in advance.[96]

The second *Aktion* took place on October 28, 1942. According to "Stefan," some of the trustworthy policemen saved a score of Jews from certain death over the course of the second *Aktion*.

93 Banaś, *Moje wspomnienia*, p. 131.

94 "Stefan" testimony, ŻIH, 301/2058.

95 For more information about Warsaw, see chapter 6.

96 "Stefan" testimony, ŻIH, 301/2058.

Interestingly, the rescue efforts were led by Oswald Bousko,[97] a German–Austrian policeman from Vienna. His courageous deeds will be described in more detail later in this volume.

On December 6, 1942, the Germans divided the Kraków ghetto into two parts: ghetto "A" and ghetto "B". Those who were still able to work were herded into ghetto "A", while all the others were placed in ghetto "B". The final liquidation of the ghetto began on March 13, 1943. Eight thousand of the *Arbeitsfähige Juden* (Jews able to work) were taken to a labor camp in nearby Płaszów, and the rest were either murdered in the ghetto or deported to Auschwitz.[98] Sergeant Banaś witnessed that *Aktion* too:

> In Wita Stwosza Street, I saw five huge lorries filled with dead bodies. How many people can fit into these sanitation trucks? There was a gate in Węgierska Street, a gate through which they transported the cadavers. I could see blood literally oozing out of the trucks so that puddles of mud formed on the street. Blood mixed with dirt remains damp for quite some time, so one could smell the stench of blood hanging in the air for a long time.[99]

Edward Kubalski, a proud citizen of Kraków and the author of a fascinating diary written during the occupation, noted the following on March 20, 1943:

> During the liquidation of the ghetto, there was an orgy of violence, and Jews were treated in an inhuman way. People who watched all of this from their windows told unheard-of stories. One is filled with disgust when one thinks about the sadistic bloodsucking that occurred, for instance—as I heard from a medical doctor whom I know—during the mass killing of the sick in the Jewish hospital.[100]

97 Also spelled Bosko.

98 "Kraków," in Megargee, *The United States Holocaust Memorial Museum Encyclopedia of Camps and Ghettos, 1933–1945*, pp. 527–530.

99 "Stefan" testimony, ŻIH, 301/2058.

100 Edward Kubalski, *Niemcy w Krakowie: Dziennik 1 IX 1939–18 I 1945*, ed. by

However, even after the liquidation, hundreds of Jews still remained hidden in the Kraków ghetto. Day after day, German and Polish policemen combed the area of the former ghetto and pulled the Jews out of their hideouts and bunkers. It was only a matter of time before other Jews, who were lacking water and food, had to flee to the Aryan side. Unfortunately, the road to "freedom"—in the eyes of the dying Jews, due to the horrible realities of the German occupation in Poland, the Aryan side seemed like a zone of incredible liberty where one could still live—was blocked by the Blue policemen who guarded the borders of the liquidated ghetto. In line with German orders, the Polish police were required to shoot each and every Jew they encountered. Polish policemen who failed to comply had to contend with dire consequences, including death. "So, there were policemen," wrote Banaś, "who dared to shoot, but there were only three or four of them. They certainly regret their deeds, and it weighs heavy on their conscience."[101] In fact, as Banaś wrote in his previously quoted testimony, the Polish policemen did not fear the Germans. When stopped and interrogated, they could easily come up with an excuse for why they had failed to open fire on the Jewish refugees. Even if the Germans threatened the Polish officers with death, noted Banaś, practically all of them "with the exception of three or four" seem to have ignored the orders without suffering any visible consequences.[102]

It is hard to say how many of these shooting Polish policemen served in and around the Kraków ghetto, but the aforementioned Henryk Piniecki—the son of Alfons who was the liaison officer in the Kraków police headquarters—was certainly one of them.[103] At the time of the final liquidation of the ghetto, Piniecki was not quite twenty-one years of age and had been on the force for barely a few weeks. In March 1942, he was transferred from the III precinct to the guardhouse at Zgoda Square, whose men controlled the access to the ghetto. In a deposition given a few years after the war, Karol

Jan Grabowski and Zbigniew R. Grabowski (Kraków and Budapest: Austeria, 2010), p. 266.

101 "Stefan" testimony, ŻIH, 301/2058.

102 Ibid.

103 Investigation of Henryk Piniecki, ANK, SAKr, 1015/IVK/125/50.

Gawronski, the commander of the Zgoda guardhouse, described the sequence of events as follows:

> Early in the spring of 1943, during the liquidation of the ghetto, we received orders to shoot any person trying to leave the area. Officers found in contempt [of that order] were threatened with arrest. Polish police guarded the ghetto from the outside, while the Jewish police kept guard on the inside. I remember that early one morning, while on duty in guardhouse number 2, I heard a shot. When I ran out of the guardhouse, I saw Officer Piniecki shooting for the second time a woman lying on the ground, from a distance of no more than 3 meters. The woman had tried to bypass the gate and crawl under the barbed wire. She was with a child of five years or so. Piniecki fired off the second shot at the moment when I came out of the guardhouse, and all of this happened while I was no more than 10 meters away. Piniecki wanted to kill the child too, but I ordered him to stand down. Right away, I informed the Jewish police, and they took away the child and the body of the woman. Because of this, Piniecki got a lot of heat from his fellow officers.[104]

And so concluded the deposition of the commander of the ghetto guardhouse. According to Piniecki himself, he learned how to shoot Jews from other policemen: "On the first day of duty, I saw a Jew and a Jewess slip out of the ghetto. The Jewess ran near me, and I let her pass; the Jew ran toward Nadwiślańska Street, and there he was shot by another officer."[105]

While Sergeant Gawronski insisted that shooting a woman lying on the ground was an immoral thing and something disgraceful for a policeman to do, his superiors held a different opinion. For his vigilance, young Piniecki received a financial reward and a pair of shoes, all of which was made public in an internal communiqué published by the Kraków Blue Police headquarters.[106]

104 Deposition of Karol Gawronski, ANK, SAKr, 1015/IVK/125/50.
105 Investigation of Henryk Piniecki, ANK, SAKr, 1015/IVK/125/50.
106 Ibid.

Henryk Piniecki, 1947. AAN, Ministerstwo Sprawiedliwości, 1656.

Piniecki maintained that he was just following orders. He also claimed that he had no previous police experience and had only completed his police training course in Nowy Sącz several weeks after the liquidation of the ghetto.[107] After the war, Henryk Piniecki worked for the Railway Protection Service, and, as such, he had to undergo a vetting process by a special Rehabilitation Commission, created in 1946.[108] On his resume, Piniecki mentioned his service in the Kraków police but modestly withheld the information about "suppressing the Jewish nationality"[109] in the ghetto in March 1943. The commission also received an affidavit from his alleged commanders from the Polish resistance. It is a revealing document and worth a longer citation:

> In the field, January 23, 1943. Sergeant Henryk Piniecki, aka "Spokojny" (Moderate), deputy chief of the Operational

107 For the murder of the Jewish woman, Piniecki was sentenced to twelve years in prison by the Kraków Court of Appeals.

108 The documents relating to the rehabilitation procedure of Piniecki can be found in Akta byłych funkcjonariuszy Policji Państwowej, Straży Więziennej, Korpusu Ochrony Pogranicza i Straży Granicznej (Dossiers of Former Officers of Blue Police, Prison Guards, Border Protective Corps and Border Patrol), 1946–1952, AAN, 1656.

109 The expression in the original Polish is: "*Tłumienie narodowości żydowskiej.*"

> Group of Special Tasks, fought with heroism for the salvation of the Polish State and of the Polish Nation. The Polish National Council of State, serving as an underground Polish Government, acting on behalf of the Polish Organization of National Defense (POON), taking into consideration that Sergeant "Moderate" has already received a silver Cross of Merit, owing to his continued struggle against the enemy, awarded him today the Cross of Valor [*Krzyż Walecznych*] as per regulations. He was promoted at the same time to the rank of lieutenant. Signed: Constitutional Dictator John Without Mercy (Jan Bezwzględny) general of POON. The duplicate has been issued for the purpose of submission to the Military Recruitment Center. Signed: Marcin Stanisławski, under the occupation known as John Without Mercy, currently living in Poznań, 16 Skarbek Street, apt. 1.[110]

If one were to trust the affidavit produced by the "Constitutional Dictator John Without Mercy," young Piniecki joined the Blue Police for patriotic reasons, driven by a sense of civic duty and following the orders of his organization in the resistance. Historians of the occupation know little about this mysterious organization POON. One can even risk saying that we know so little about the wartime accomplishments of POON because it most likely did not exist at the time. It is certain, however, that the organization thrived after the war, and Alfons Piniecki, the former captain of the Blue Police and the father of the accused Henryk, began to issue various forms and declarations that were intended for official use and meant to help people boost their "patriotic" credentials. In 1950, Alfons Piniecki was already signing the forms as "general-brigadier and the chief of staff of POON."[111] There was the "Constitutional Dictator John Without Mercy," promotions to the ranks of colonel and general, and people were awarded the

110 The materials about the alleged activities of POON can be found in the file of Renata G. Hamerska in the Archive of General Elżbieta Zawacka (Archiwum i Muzeum Pomorskie Armii Krajowej oraz Wojskowej Służby Polek). I am grateful to Anna Zapalec for drawing my attention to this file.

111 Ibid.

highest Polish distinctions, such as the Cross of Merit, Polonia Restituta, and Virtuti Militari. "John Without Mercy's" activities finally caught the attention of the Citizens' Militia, who, in 1955, started to look for people issuing false declarations. One can safely assume that POON and "John Without Mercy" are nothing more than products of the rich fantasy of Piniecki, both father and son. In this case, the POON affidavit did little to help the accused. The Rehabilitation Commission tasked with studying the case of Henryk Piniecki received additional information about his service in the Blue Police and the ongoing criminal proceedings into the murder of the Jewish woman in Kraków.

Returning to Sergeant Banaś from the Kraków police force, it is highly unlikely that in 1970, when the former Blue policeman decided to sit down and write his memoir, he still remembered his testimony delivered to the Jewish Historical Commission in Kraków twenty-five years earlier. It was during these years that the recollections of Franciszek Banaś underwent an important transformation, and the image of the Jews—seen through the prism of his memoir—has little in common with the narrative offered to the Jewish Commission immediately after the war. Reflecting in his memoir on the early years of his police career, Banaś wrote about his transfer from the regular beat to the river patrol in 1925: "Thank God! I was so fed up with Kazimierz [the Jewish part of Kraków], with these thieves, scoundrels and Jews, and most of all with the bums and beggars!"[112]

The memoir is replete with antisemitic clichés and stinging remarks about the Jews, which leave little doubt as to the depth of Banaś's prejudice. According to the Polish officer, Jews were scoundrels, exploiters, Freemasons, and bloodsuckers who corrupted innocent Polish girls working in Jewish factories.[113] Despite all of this, during the war, Banaś rescued several Jews and offered temporary assistance to many others.[114] Concluding his description of the liquidation of the Kraków ghetto, Banaś

112 Banaś, *Moje wspomnienia*, p. 83.
113 Ibid., p. 84.
114 See Banaś's file in YVA, M.31.2/1824.

wrote: "Thanks to commerce and various swindles, Jews acquired huge fortunes in Poland. They left it all and left this world."[115] In 1980, Yad Vashem, the World Holocaust Remembrance Center in Israel, awarded Franciszek Banaś the title of Righteous Among the Nations.[116] One of the reasons given by Yad Vashem for awarding him this honor centered around the rescue of the Hoffman family. The Polish policeman knew the Hoffmans before the war. In his memoir, Banaś wrote: "I provided the Hoffmans with food. I liked this man. He was not like a Jew. He was a righteous man, so I tried—as much as I could—to save this family."[117] The antisemitism of the righteous policeman Banaś does not take away from his wartime deeds. In fact, quite the opposite, because his attitude and worldview illustrate the complexity of the moral choices that existed under the occupation and demonstrates that cases of antisemites rescuing Jews were not as infrequent as one would think.

In Kałuszyn, Siedlce, and Biłgoraj

Adam Kamienny hailed from Kałuszyn, a small *shtetl* sitting on the Warsaw-Siedlce highway, 16 kilometers east of Mińsk Mazowiecki. Today, the most visible symbol of the town is a tacky gold statue of a Polish *ulan* (a mounted cavalryman), which blinds drivers using the Terespol–Warsaw route with reflected sunlight. During the war, however, Kałuszyn's main feature was its ghetto, which had a population of close to 4,000 people. Practically until the very end, the ghetto in Kałuszyn was an open one. In the winter of 1941–1942, after many Jews from the outlying areas had been resettled in Kałuszyn, the living conditions in the Jewish ghetto became unbearable. Each and every month, close to forty people starved

115 Banaś, *Moje wspomnienia*, p. 134.

116 The term "Righteous Among the Nations" describes non-Jews who have been honored by Yad Vashem, the World Holocaust Remembrance Center in Israel, for risking their lives to aid and save Jews during the Holocaust.

117 Banaś, *Moje wspomnienia*, p. 111.

to death or died of hunger-related diseases.[118] In August 1942, the inhabitants of the ghetto heard rumors about an imminent deportation. Kamienny along with many other Jews believed that the labor camps in the vicinity offered them the best chance of survival. Flight to the Aryan side was definitively considered the more dangerous option: Long-term chances of survival living among the Poles were considered slim.

The closest labor camp was located next to Mrozy, south of Kałuszyn. In order to secure a place there, one had to pay a hefty bribe. Similar "payments" were offered for admission to other forced-labor camps.[119] Shortly after Kamienny's arrival in Mrozy, many other refugees from Kałuszyn came too:

> One of them told us what was going on in the city, about gendarmes organizing auctions of Jewish houses and possessions, others said that one could buy our houses, with everything that was inside, for 500, 200, or even for 50 zlotys. They told us about Polish firefighters who (together with the gendarmes, or on their own) walk around with axes and crowbars, smashing apartments to pieces, looking for hidden Jews, and stealing whatever they can. The peasants from all over the area arrived in town, as if they participated in some kind of festivity, and took part in these auctions in order to quickly enrich themselves. Sometimes, having bought for a few zlotys an apartment, they found the lifelong possessions of several families, or even hidden money and precious objects. Like vultures feeding off carcasses, they converged

118 Dariusz Libionka, ed., *Akcja Reinhardt: Zagłada Żydów w Generalnym Gubernatorstwie* (Warsaw: Instytut Pamięci Narodowej, 2004), p. 65.

119 See the memoir of Chaja Rosenblatt in Jan Grabowski, ed., *Szczęście posiadać dom pod ziemią… Losy kobietocalałych z Zagłady w okolicach Dąbrowy Tarnowskiej* (Warsaw: Stowarzyszenie Centrum Badań nad Zagładą Żydów, 2016), p. 107. For a more detailed discussion of this kind of survival strategy, see Martin Dean, "Jewish Survival in Forced Labor Camps for Jews: The Agricultural Camps in Czortków County of Eastern Galicia, 1942–1944," in Alexandra Garbarini and Paul B. Jaskot, eds., *Lessons and Legacies, vol. XIII: New Approaches to an Integrated History of the Holocaust. Social History, Representation, Theory* (Evanston: Northwestern University Press, 2018).

> on this battlefield soaked in the blood of 1,200 innocent people, women, children, and the elderly.[120]

In October 1942, the Germans established a secondary ghetto in Kałuszyn, one of several ghettos created at the time in the Warsaw district. In line with the decision of the Warsaw governor Ludwig Fischer, only six such Jewish quarters were allowed to continue operation in the district: Warsaw, Sobolew, Kosów Lacki, Rembertów, Siedlce, and Kałuszyn.[121] These *Restghettos* had a dual purpose: On the one hand, they allowed the authorities to continue to take advantage of the remaining Jewish slave labor, while on the other hand, such ghettos promised "legal status," and they attracted some of the hidden Jews who had found survival on the Aryan side impossible. Around December 1, 1942, several hundred Jews—Adam Kamienny among them—arrived from Mrozy to Kałuszyn. The scene they found was nothing short of horrific: The town had been plundered, and the houses from which the Polish neighbors had even stolen the doors and window frames were in ruins. This secondary ghetto was not to last. The final liquidation started soon after the arrival of the Jews from Mrozy. "Out of the door," wrote Kamienny, "we see all around us Ukrainians, the 'Blacks,'[122] the gendarmes, the Gestapo, Polish police, and Polish firefighters. They drive large groups of people toward the main square, where they force us to sit down in the dirt."[123]

In Kałuszyn, like in so many other places, the Polish police were not only guarding the perimeter around the liquidated ghetto but were also involved in the operations taking place inside the Jewish quarter herding the Jews to the concentration areas. Later, they guarded the marching columns of Jews to the railway station

120 Adam Kamienny testimony, YVA, O.3/843. Kamienny's diary has been published (along with the diaries of three others) in Barbara Engelking, ed., *Sny chociaż mamy wspaniałe...Okupacyjne dzienniki Żydów z okolic Mińska Mazowieckiego* (Warsaw: Stowarzyszenie Centrum Badań nad Zagładą Żydów, 2016).

121 Regulation issued by Governor Ludwig Fischer on November 16, 1942. See Curilla, *Der Judenmord in Polen*, p. 68.

122 The term "Blacks" was used to describe the auxiliary Ukrainian units.

123 Engelking, *Sny chociaż mamy wspaniałe*, p. 71.

in Mrozy and stood guard over the victims until the trains of death destined for Treblinka arrived. In nearby Sokołów Podlaski, the situation was no different: It was the Polish police who loaded the Jews onto the cattle cars. Simche Polakiewicz noted the following in his poignant testimony:

> At the station, they chased us off the lorries, and we were surrounded by armed murderers. Some of them checked the wagons, trying to find room to squeeze in an additional few Jews. A Polish policeman asked me whether I knew where I was going. I said that yes, I did. I told him that "those who now send me there will share my fate one day." The policeman answered by striking my head with a rifle butt. Then, the murderers led us to the wagon, where they found some space for us.[124]

In the dossiers of the underground Government Delegation for Poland, a civilian arm of the Polish resistance, one can find a letter sent from Piotrków Trybunalski, the same city described in the previous chapter where the local Polish police had executed Jews trying to leave the ghetto a short time earlier. Now, during the liquidation of Piotrków Trybunalski on October 12, 1942, and in the period that followed, the local civilians joined in: "The behavior of our people is simply appalling," reads the underground report, "They steal, rob, break into the empty houses and carry away whatever they can."[125] A score of Polish looters died at the hands of the Polish and German policemen.[126] The situation was no different in Mińsk Mazowiecki, where the liquidation impacted 6,000 Jews who were later deported to the extermination camp of

124 Simche Polakiewicz, *W cieniu Treblinki: Zagłada Sokołowa Podlaskiego*, ed. by Katarzyna Markusz (Kraków: Austeria, 2023), p. 253.

125 Report on Jewish matters, October 27, 1942, AAN, Delegatura Rządu na Kraj, 202-II-29, p. 16.

126 "Wyrzutki społeczeństwa polskiego," *Biuletyn Informacyjny*, October 16, 1942, as quoted in Joshua D. Zimmerman, *Polskie Państwo Podziemne i Żydzi w czasie II wojny śiatowej* (Warsaw: Wydawnictwo Naukowe PWN, 2018), p. 236.

Treblinka. Maria Chróścik, a Polish woman, gave her account to a Jewish survivor right after the war:

> She [Maria Chróścik] told me [the Jewish survivor] that the whole city looted whatever was left of the Jewish property. "Germans took the cream," she said. "Poles took the buttermilk." She told me how the locals delivered the Jews into the hands of the Germans. She told me how greedy the people were and without pity for the Jews.[127]

Both Siedlce and Biłgoraj, cities in eastern Poland, have not been mentioned until now. Constable Kokot served in one of the Blue Police detachments in Siedlce, 80 kilometers east of Warsaw. Jakub Handlarski, who survived the liquidation of the local ghetto, wrote the following after the war:

> I knew the policeman Kokot well during the occupation. I know that before the liquidation, he used to take meat from the Jewish butchers and refused to pay. He also took bribes from people involved in illicit trade. On August 23, 1942, in a square adjacent to Piłsudski Street [and] in broad daylight, Kokot started shooting Jews, firing into the crowd. This also continued the next day. I think that he could have killed 30–50 people this way. He killed my brother Herszek and my sister Mona right in front of me. It was right after they chased us out into the square. Kokot's behavior was worse than that of the Germans and the Ukrainians.[128]

Jan Mikulski, a Polish forest ranger, came to Biłgoraj in the Lublin district on November 2, 1942, in order to pick up cash from the bank to pay his men who were working in the forest. On that very day, he learned that the local ghetto was being liquidated:

127 Chil Kirszenbaum testimony, *Bezkarny mord na Żydach w Mińsku Mazowieckim*, YVA, O.3/842.

128 Deposition of witness Jakub Handlarski, April 9, 1945, AIPN, GK 209/250, pp. 181–182.

On the streets, in the squares and gardens, I see dead bodies of women and children. Wiesiołowski, the commander of the Polish police, surrounded by scores of kids aged 6–12, is searching the attics, backyards, cellars, and sheds. For each Jewish child brought to him, he gives the Polish children bonbons. He takes small Jewish children by the neck and shoots them in the head with a small caliber revolver.[129]

A group of gendarmes and Blue policemen at the Biłgoraj police station. In the first row, a man is wearing a grotesque mask with a hat sliding off his head. A police dog is at his feet. Has he been caught by the German and Polish policemen proudly standing for the picture? The photograph was removed from the burning Biłgoraj police station a few moments after the Germans pulled out from the city in the summer of 1944. Courtesy of Mirosław Tryczyk.

129 Mikulski, *Myśli, wspomnienia, uwagi, refleksje....*

The Role of Polish Firefighters

In an attempt to identify the reasons for the tragedy of Polish Jewry, Emanuel Ringelblum reflected at length not only about the Polish police but also about the role of the voluntary and professional firefighters:

> Besides the Blue Police, the fire brigades also played an active part in "resettlement actions" in the country by cordoning off Jewish blocks of flats, hunting down the Jews hiding in the attics, cellars, etc. We have specific knowledge of the fire brigades' participation in "liquidation actions" in Kałuszyn and Biała Podlaska. It must be said in favour of the fire brigades that they did save some few Jews during the so-called "kettle" at Niska Street in Warsaw. They hid them in the firemen's cars and drove them away from the danger spot.[130]

By using the pronoun "we"—as in "we have specific knowledge"—Ringelblum is not trying to impress his readers with the usage of the rhetorical form known as *pluralis maiestatis*. It is also not a reference to the accumulated knowledge of the dying Polish Jewish community. Instead, Ringelblum is referring to the concrete knowledge that had been acquired by the members of the Oneg Shabbat group, which was responsible for the growing archive in the Warsaw ghetto. Their knowledge was based on hundreds of reports that were flowing into Warsaw from the provinces, the liquidated ghettos scattered across the Generalgouvernement, and the incorporated territories during the summer of 1942.[131] In the quoted passage above, Ringelblum touches upon a matter that has

130 Ringelblum, *Polish-Jewish Relations*, pp. 136–137. Oneg Shabbat was a group of people who worked with Ringelblum to collect evidence of Jewish life and death during the occupation. The collection of documents (today known as the Ringelblum Archive) was buried shortly before the liquidation of the Warsaw ghetto. The archive was recovered from the ruins of Warsaw after the war.

131 The incorporated territories (Eingegliederte Ostgebiete) were areas of western and northern Poland such as Pomerania, the Poznań area, and Silesia that were directly attached to the Reich.

already been repeatedly mentioned in this study: The role of the Polish firefighters in the liquidation *Aktionen*.

Given the questions that stand at the center of this study, this is an issue of significant importance. While the role of the police is to enforce rules and to regulate social behavior—using coercion, if necessary—the firefighters' professional code of conduct is based on one simple obligation: to save human lives. A brief overview of the issue of the firefighters' role during the liquidation *Aktionen* can bring us one step closer to understanding the reasons behind the transformation of normal people into murderers. Although the presence of Polish firefighters during the liquidations of Brzesko Nowe, Klimontów, Kałuszyn, Markowa, Opatów, and many other locations has been previously mentioned in this volume, one would certainly look in vain for any mentions of this phenomenon in existing historical literature.[132] However, the abundance of available archival data leaves no doubt that this is an area in need of further study. The sources include not only memoirs, diaries, and the underground press but also correspondence generated by the German institutions involved in the supervision of Polish firefighters and the files of Polish local municipal and village authorities. After all, it was the latter institution that paid the firefighters' salaries and kept an eye on their expenses. Last but not least, a historian can take a look at the voluminous files of the German and Polish courts, which add a wealth of pertinent information. This evidence allows us to assert that the Polish firefighters played a non-negligible role in the German plan of the "Final Solution to the Jewish Question" in the Generalgouvernement.

For the Polish firefighters—both the volunteers and the professionals—the German occupation meant significant changes

132 The first book which tackled the issue of the Polish firefighters' involvement in the Holocaust was a study by Tadeusz Markiel and Alina Skibińska, *"Jakie to ma znaczenie, czy zrobili to z chciwości?": Zagłada domu Trynczerów* (Warsaw: Stowarzyszenie Centrum Badań nad Zagładą Żydów, 2011). The same issue has been discussed further in Jan Grabowski and Dariusz Libionka, "Distorting and Rewriting the History of the Holocaust in Poland: The Case of the Ulma Family Museum of Poles Saving Jews During World War II in Markowa," *Yad Vashem Studies*, 45:1 (2017), pp. 29–60.

to their daily routine. In order to maintain social order after the occupation of Poland, the Germans decided to keep two uniformed Polish organizations. One was the police, and the second was the firefighters. Just as with the Polish police, the structure of the firefighting organizations was significantly altered, although the lowest rungs—the firefighting sections—were the least affected by the changes. Not unlike the police, the firefighters resumed their duties in October 1939, but this time under the overall control of the German Fire Protection Police (Feuerschutzpolizei).[133] More importantly, the Germans decided to dissolve the horizontal links between the various firefighting detachments in different counties and to abolish the professional institution of the Union of Polish Firefighters (Straż Pożarna, SP) and its equivalent among the voluntary firefighters (Ochotnicza Straż Pożarna, OSP).[134] The occupiers purged the organization of Jews and other individuals deemed "politically suspect."[135] Both the voluntary and professional firefighting sections were placed under the authority of the Office of Fire Protection of the Generalgouvernement (Feuerschutzamt des Generalgouvernements), which, in turn, answered to the commander of the Orpo. In this way, both of the Polish uniformed organizations—the police and the firefighters—were placed under the authority of the Orpo. In theory, it meant that the gendarmes issued orders to firefighters in the rural areas, while the Schupo issued them in the cities. In practice, Polish firefighters, like the Blue policemen, simply had to obey orders issued by any German in uniform.

Regardless of the period, the work of firefighters carries dangers that are inherently linked to the very nature of this profession. In our period of interest, however, threats specific to

133 Piotr Matusak, *Straż pożarna* (Warsaw: Fundacja "Warszawa Walczy 1939–1945," 2014), pp. 76–77.

134 The status of voluntary firefighters was officially established based on a regulation issued by Hans Frank on April 22, 1941. See "Verordnung über den Feuerschutz im Generalgouvernement" (Decree on Fire Protection in the Generalgouvernement), *Verordnungsblatt für das Generalgouvernement*, April 29, 1941.

135 In the larger cities, there were always a few Jewish members of the OSP—usually sponsors, wealthy donors. In rural areas, Jews—with rare exceptions—were not allowed to become members.

time of war and occupation added to the traditional challenges of the firefighters. War, sabotage, the prevalence of banditry, and acts of terror all conspired to complicate the firefighters' duties and significantly increased the risks associated with their everyday tasks. It needs to be stressed, however, that at the same time, the firefighters received certain perks and privileges that might have persuaded some young men to join its ranks. Many new recruits joined the firefighting units after the initial purge, which was completed before the end of 1939 when all Jews were removed from the service. The process was partially linked to the authorities' decision to boost each firefighting section from six to nine men, and it was also due to the aquamarine-colored ID cards that were issued by the German police to Polish firefighters. This card offered its owner protection against deportations to Germany for forced labor, shielded them in case of a sudden manhunt for hostages in the streets—the so-called *łapanki*, which was a daily horror in Polish cities from 1943 onward—and allowed one to disregard the curfews. Firefighters also received additional quotas of coal, sometimes food, and a modest stipend of 50–60 zlotys per month.

The Polish firefighters took part in the German policies of extermination in a variety of ways. From simply loaning a mechanical pump that would allow the Germans to pour water on quicklime under the feet of those Jews who were transported in cattle cars (as it happened in Nowy Targ),[136] sealing the borders of the ghettos during the liquidations (as in scores of towns across Poland), guarding Jews during the loading of the death trains (as in, for instance, Miechów),[137] to outright active participation in the liquidation *Aktionen* (in several ghettos mentioned previously as well as many others that have not) as well as in the burial of victims

136 Henryk Stefański to the Main Commission for the Study of Nazi Crimes, March 31, 1965, AIPN, OK Kr, Ds. 6/70/29, p. 165, as quoted in Karolina Panz, "Powiat nowotarski," in Engelking and Grabowski, *Dalej jest noc*, vol. 2, p. 273. Quicklime would burn the bodies of the victims, preventing people from sitting or lying down on the floors of the wagons.

137 Samuel Salzberg testimony, YVA, M.9/508, as quoted in Libionka, "Powiat miechowski," p. 80.

of mass shootings and even organizing manhunts for fleeing Jews without any direct German involvement.

Firefighters and Blue policemen putting out the fire in Fischl's mill, Tarnów, 1941. Photo taken by Mr. Augustyn Dagnan. Courtesy of Marek Tomaszewski.

The efficiency of the OSP and the threat they presented to the Jews were related to the paramilitary discipline within each firefighting section as well as the social trust and respect commanded by the firefighters. The individual units coordinated their activities, and they expected—and usually received—full cooperation from the locals. In the winter of 1941–1942, when the Germans had begun to put their plans for *Aktion Reinhard* in the Generalgouvernement into motion, they also turned their attention to the lower rungs of the Polish village authorities, especially in the rural areas. It was at that point when the authorities decided to establish various types of night guards or village guards, which, according to official justification, were intended to provide inhabitants with additional security and to reinforce the firefighters in case of major calamities. The real reason for the establishment of these night guards, however, was to hunt down the Jews fleeing from the ghettos as well as the escaped "Soviet slaves," to which Soviet POWs were often referred.[138]

138 See Andrzej Żbikowski, "'Night Guard': Holocaust Mechanisms in the

After the war, one of the leaders of a local night guard unit testified that "the guards, in addition to fire protection and fighting banditry, had to catch the Jews."[139] Some of the village guardsmen were also appointed—on a rotating schedule and for a limited time—as so-called hostages or people who were personally responsible for the security conditions in their village. The introduction of this paramilitary discipline into the rural communities would greatly facilitate the detection of Jews in hiding in the months to come. The efficiency of the night guard units was further enhanced by the frequent involvement of sections of the firefighting brigades. The village guards received logistical and administrative support from the voluntary firefighting organizations of the OSP, a phenomenon that was particularly visible in southeastern Poland.

Stanisław Żemis was a Polish teacher and a social activist who lived in Łuków. He closely observed the liquidation of the local Jewish communities and noted his impressions in a diary. He could not overlook the role of the village guards:

> In Trzebieszów, on Monday, some kind of citizens' watch, local peasants guarding the village against bandits during the night, received orders to catch all the local Jews and to deliver them to Łuków. They surrounded the whole village and the manhunt started. They dragged the Jews from their houses, they caught them in the fields, in the meadows, they brought them in front of the school, which nowadays houses the offices of the commune (*Urząd gminy*) and they held them there the whole night. Whatever was not stolen of the Jewish possessions, they also brought to the same place. All the

Polish Rural Areas, 1942–1945, Preliminary Introduction into Research," in Jan T. Gross, ed., *The Holocaust in Occupied Poland: New Findings and New Interpretations* (Frankfurt am Main: P. Lang, 2012); Jan Grabowski, *Judenjagd: Polowanie na Żydów 1942–1945: Studium dziejów pewnego powiatu* (Warsaw: Stowarzyszenie Centrum Badań nad Zagładą Żydów, 2011); Jan Grabowski, "Rural Society and the Jews in Hiding: Elders, Night Watches, Firefighters, Hostages and Manhunts," *Yad Vashem Studies*, 40 (2012), pp. 49–74.

139 See the case of Adolf Zygmunt, commander of a night watch in Zwierzyniec, Archiwum Instytutu Pamięci Narodowej Oddział w Lublinie (AIPN Lu), 326/161, as quoted in Skibińska, "Powiat biłgorajski," p. 232.

> furniture was either robbed or burned in front of the watching Jews. [Later] the carts assigned by the commune delivered the Jews to Łuków. On top of this, the poor passengers had to, of course, pay eighty zlotys for each of these carts (again shots are being fired outside!).[140]

In the districts of Lublin, Warsaw, and Kraków, the firehouses often doubled up as provisional holding pens for Jews caught outside the ghetto. This is what happened in places such as Kraśnik, Węgrów, Stoczek Węgrowski, and the villages close to Dąbrowa Tarnowska and Miechów. In many areas, firefighters and the Blue Police made up a numerically significant uniformed contingent that reinforced the German liquidation commandos. One can venture that the Germans established this system of control and enforcement mainly—if not solely—in preparation for the upcoming "Final Solution." This hypothesis is even more likely since the system described above was only known in the Generalgouvernement. It had no parallel in the occupied East, not to mention in the occupied countries of Western Europe.

The preparations for the physical destruction of Polish Jews were finalized in the spring of 1942. The plans, which were expanded in Lublin by the chief of SS and Police (SSPF) Odilo Globocnik and his staff—the so-called headquarters of *Aktion Reinhard*, or *Einsatzstab Reinhard*—involved individual liquidation *Aktionen*, but they left the details to the initiative and creativity of the local commanders.[141] Decisions were therefore made to include the Polish firefighters in the planned *Aktionen* by local commanding officers. Sometimes, for instance during the *Grossaktion Warschau* in July–September 1942 or during the uprising in the Warsaw ghetto in April–May 1943, the firefighters' main duty was to

140 Stanisław Żemis diary, AZIH, 302/30. For a long time, the diary was erroneously assigned to Stanisław Żemiński. It was only recently established that the author's real name was Stanisław Żemis. See Krzysztof Czubaszek, "Stanisław Żemis—świadek zagłady Żydów w Łukowie," *Zagłada Żydów, Studia i Materiały*, 14 (2018), pp. 279–311.

141 Dieter Pohl, "Znaczenie dystryktu lubelskiego w 'ostatecznym rozwiązaniu kwestii żydowskiej,'" in Libionka, *Akcja Reinhardt*, pp. 48–51.

prevent any fires burning in the liquidated ghetto from spreading to the Aryan side of the city. In other cases, the firefighters were involved in a lot more than their protective duties and joined the ranks of the perpetrators and their enablers.

Returning to the previously quoted passage from Ringelblum, it is important to ascertain whether the accusations formulated by the historian of the Warsaw ghetto against the Polish firefighters are, indeed, based on firm historical evidence. Ringelblum made specific reference to the areas of Kałuszyn and Biała Podlaska, where firefighters were said to have participated in the liquidation of the local ghettos. This does not mean that the Polish firefighters only liquidated these ghettos. Rather, it is an indication of Ringelblum's cautiousness. The Jewish historian, writing in hiding in an underground bunker with no access to the exhaustive documentary evidence that had been collected earlier by the Oneg Shabbat group, was relying solely on his own memory.

The ghetto in Kałuszyn, the aforementioned small town located east of Mińsk Mazowiecki, was liquidated in the fall of 1942. Adam Kamienny, who witnessed the destruction of his town, made specific reference to the cruelty of the local voluntary firefighters. According to Kamienny, the Polish firefighters worked hand in hand with the gendarmes, looking for hideouts and valuables, and smashing the walls of Jewish houses with crowbars and axes. The OSP members acted the same way a few weeks later during the liquidation of the secondary ghetto when, together with the gendarmes and the Blue policemen, they herded the Jews toward the concentration point in the central square.[142] In the event that Kamienny's testimony is deemed insufficiently persuasive, one might want to look at the notes made by Chil Kirszenbaum, another survivor from Kałuszyn, who described the liquidation in the following words:

> There were still some 2,000 Jews in the ghetto. Many people went into hiding in the attics. Polish firefighters conducted

142 Adam Kamienny testimony, YVA, O.3/843.

> searches in these attics, and whenever they found the Jews, they delivered them to the gendarmes, who killed them. In this way, they dragged out about 400 people from the attics.[143]

What about Biała Podlaska? Can one find a corroboration of Ringelblum's statements here too? Biała Podlaska was liquidated on September 30, 1942, at which point 3,600 local Jews were murdered in the streets of the *shtetl* or in the nearby Jewish cemetery. Everyone else was deported to the extermination camps of Sobibór and Treblinka.[144] In Biała Podlaska too, hundreds of Jews went into hiding inside the liquidated ghetto. Mosze Józef Feigenbaum, one of the survivors of this liquidation, wrote the following:

> For some time we had enough water and food but how long can you stay put in these conditions? The Polish firefighting brigades were of particular use to the Germans in finding the hideouts. They worked with such zeal that whenever they thought a hideout was in the attic, they would even tear down the roofs.[145]

At this stage of inquiry, a historian must ask questions about the scale of the discussed phenomenon. Was the participation of Polish firefighters in the brutal liquidations widespread or exceedingly rare? Can one describe the OSP members from Kałuszyn and Biała Podlaska as black sheep who tarnished the image of other firefighters? Unfortunately, the copious historical evidence leaves us with little doubt that the Polish firefighting brigades took part in the German genocidal program in all districts of the Generalgouvernement. Furthermore, as will be shown, the smaller the police forces—both German and Polish—in the area, the greater the role of the firefighting brigades. Much was riding on the role of the local leadership, something very visible in the

143 Chil Kirszenbaum testimony, YVA, O.3/842.

144 "Biała Podlaska," in Megargee, *The United States Holocaust Memorial Museum Encyclopedia of Camps and Ghettos, 1933–1945*, pp. 615–617.

145 Feigenbaum, *Slaughter in Podlasie*, p. 38.

cases of Gniewczyna and Węgrów, but the firefighters' paramilitary training and hierarchical structures helped to transform the OSP units into a dangerous tool in the hands of the Germans.

The firefighters mobilized for action, nevertheless, had a broad scope to decide how much they could exercise their own will. Incidentally, Ringelblum mentioned this degree of agency while writing about the Warsaw firefighters who saved some Jews from the German guns and delivered them to relative safety outside the liquidated ghetto. Unfortunately, there were very different expressions of such agency. We have another description of the firefighters' behavior—also from Warsaw—from the time of the ghetto uprising:

> One of the firefighters ordered to fight fires on this side of the wall told me how they chased the Jews, who wanted to jump out of balconies and windows, with streams of water, back into the burning houses. Later, they robbed the goods left behind. They used to say: "Jews. They don't care one way or the other, and it is better if we, rather than the Germans, take their things."[146]

Both the police and the firefighters acted according to the same script, the latter often accompanying the former in hunting down the Jews and, in some instances, acting in their stead.

The Blue Police detachment in Mszana Dolna illustrates this phenomenon. In the summer of 1943, the police received information about two Jews hiding in a farm in the nearby village of Skrzydlna. The Jews in question, Jumek and Josek Grybel, were locals and well known to their Polish neighbors.[147] The information arrived while the detachment was in a state of alert

146 Adam Kamienny diary, as quoted in Engelking, *Sny chociaż mamy wspaniałe…*, p. 104.

147 Interrogation of Jan Gąsior, January 20, 1950, ANKr, SAKr, 1020/IVK/147/50, pp. 6–8. In 1943, the Blue Police post in Mszana Dolna was under the command of Jozef Pospieski, who was branded in the underground leaflets as a Gestapo agent. See "Dalszy wykaz współpracowników gestapo!!!" *Małopolska Agencja Prasowa*, June 4, 1943.

during a lockdown, with officers confined to the building. The task of apprehending the Jews was delegated, therefore, to the firefighters. The firemen in Mszana Dolna had no firearms, but the seizure of both unarmed Jews was seen, as one can surmise, as a simple and safe operation. Having received the orders, the OSP members left the fire station, surrounded the house in question, arrested the Jews, and delivered them into the hands of the police for execution. In Zagorzyce, around 21 kilometers west of Rzeszów, the chief of the OSP Paweł Nogieć, caught an unknown man "who was most likely of Jewish origin," and later surrendered him to the gendarmes who happened to be passing through the village.[148] It was soon established that the unknown man's name was Jan Byczek, a traveling thread salesman, and that he was not a Jew but a Pole. Disregarding his supplications and pleas, the Germans took Byczek away and—just to err on the side of caution, or as the German saying goes, *auf der sicheren Seite bleiben*—executed him the next day.

Władysław Okulus, the mayor of Węgrów, looked on in horror and disbelief when the local ghetto was liquidated. Over the course of one day, in full view of the Polish inhabitants of the city, between 1,000 and 2,000 Jews were put to death. Mayor Okulus was horrified not only about the murders perpetrated by the Germans and Ukrainians from the visiting Liquidierungskommando but also with the actions of the local Blue policemen, firefighters, and ordinary inhabitants who, in a variety of ways, contributed to the tragedy of their Jewish neighbors. The Polish mayor had no illusions about the Germans' enthusiasm for murdering the Jews, but the willingness with which the Węgrów voluntary firefighters joined the *Aktion* shocked him. His shock reverberates throughout his testimony given immediately after the war to the Jewish Historical Commission.[149] Mayor Okulus wrote that the firefighters from Węgrów showed up in the ghetto and joined the liquidation *Aktion* on their own accord, without any need for German orders nor with

148 Deposition of Paweł Nogiec, APKr, SAKr, 1041/IVK/244/50, pp. 5–6.

149 Władysław Okulus testimony, ŻIH, 301/6043.

their encouragement.[150] Sevek Fishman, a tailor in Węgrów, also witnessed many crimes committed by his Polish neighbors, who were part of the OSP.[151] Fishman noted that the firefighters, acting together with bands of civilians, were most conspicuous, searching the ghetto and hunting down the hidden Jews. At one point, they caught Fishman's wife, and when the woman was unable to hand over her earrings quickly enough, they tried to cut her ears off. According to Fishman's testimony, when they fled, they both could hear the laughter of bystanders who were amused by the scene that had unfolded.[152] Mayor Okulus wrote: "For the Jewish population, it was a biological tragedy. For the Polish population, it was a moral one. The size of this moral tragedy is impossible to determine, but its results are frightening."[153] The firefighters, led by their commander Wincenty Ajchel, showed up in the ghetto wearing uniforms, and "they threw themselves [on the Jews] like a pack of hunting dogs on their prey. From this moment on and until the end of the *Aktion,* they worked hand in hand with the Germans, and as locals and firefighters, they operated more efficiently than the Germans," wrote Okulus. Throughout the day, Commander Ajchel carried with him a heavy briefcase into which his subordinates deposited valuables that had been taken away from the Jews. In the evening, after "work," they would share the loot.

Voluntary firefighters in Pilica, a small town close to Miechów, behaved no differently. The aforementioned Mordechaj Canin wrote as follows after the war: "Here, the whole life of the town was Jewish. But all the firefighters were Poles. And these firefighters later helped to extinguish the Jewish life in the city."[154] The "later" that Canin is referring to happened in early September 1942 during the brutal pacification of the *shtetl*:

> The Pilica firefighters, with brass helmets on their heads and with axes in [their] hands, jumped right into the middle of the

150 Ibid.

151 Sevek Fishman interview, USC Visual History Archive (VHA), 18608.

152 Ibid.

153 Władysław Okulus testimony, ŻIH, 301/6043.

154 Canin, *Przez ruiny i zgliszcza*, p. 359.

> panic and started to murder the Jews in the streets. They went as far as dragging the Jews away from Ukrainians, just so they could kill them themselves. The German bandits saved bullets and simply watched how enslaved nations execute orders no worse than they themselves. The streets of Pilica ran red with Jewish blood. More than half the Jews were killed in the pogrom by Ukrainians and the Polish firefighters. Once the Jews had been deported, the firemen destroyed both Jewish cemeteries.[155]

Chaim Gradel managed to flee from Treblinka. Soon, he ventured back to his native Ratoszyn southwest of Lublin, where he found refuge in a hideout that had been dug out under the house of Zygmunt Chlebicki, a Polish farmer. However, he did not enjoy this safety for long:

> The next day our house had been surrounded by several men of the local firefighting unit, who had discovered our hideout. They wanted to deliver us to the gendarmes, but our host got them drunk and gave them supper. They also took leather goods worth a few thousand zlotys, which they found with us. And then, in our host's barn, they found several other hidden Jews about whom we had no idea at all. They proposed that they themselves would hide them. A few days later, the peasants Heniek (firefighters' commander), Tomek Koper, Bronek Boczkowski, having robbed them, led them to the forest, and killed them.[156]

The examples are plentiful, and what happened in Mszana Dolna, Zagorzyce, Kałuszyn, Węgrów, Pilica, Ratoszyn, and Biała Podlaska was definitely no exception. In practically all the locations slated for liquidation *Aktionen,* the Germans placed the Blue Police and the firefighters on alert. It is unclear how much warning had been given to the Polish uniformed groups about the upcoming operations. In the Biłgoraj area, some members of the civil and

155 Ibid., p. 362.

156 Chaim Gradel testimony, YVA, O.33.161.

self-government institutions knew about the liquidations weeks in advance. In Jordanów, a town close to the Slovak border, the first to know about the liquidations was the local instructor of the firefighting brigade, who was delivering from Nowy Targ the posters announcing the imminent *Aktion*. The same morning, he handed the posters—signed by the Germans—to the secretary of the Polish mayor's office for further distribution.[157]

The news traveled fast. The local peasants quickly learned about the imminent liquidations and, sensing economic opportunity, flocked to the boundaries of the neighboring ghettos. Stanisław Żemis from Łuków, Dr. Klukowski from Szczebrzeszyn, and numerous Jewish survivors noted this troubling phenomenon.[158] Lejb Zylberberg from Klimontów was one of these Jewish witnesses: "That same day, on October 16 [1942], Poles, anticipating the deportation and smelling the loot, arrived in the city with carts. There were peasants who arrived from villages nearby and Jews gave them valuable things for nothing, for a piece of butter."[159] Sometimes, the Jews learned about the impending "resettlement" at the last possible moment and without warning, when the Judenrat announced the number of people required to fill the daily quota indicated by the authorities. At this stage, some Jews decided to flee, and it was up to the firefighters along with other locals to catch the fugitives.

Brzesko Nowe, already mentioned here on several occasions, lies 32 kilometers east of Kraków, and the role of the local firemen has already been mentioned in this study too.[160] Skała is not far away from Brzesko Nowe. Here too, the Polish policemen together with intoxicated Polish youths from the Baudienst and in the company of firefighters acted with particular cruelty toward the Jews.[161] The firemen searched for hideouts, and whenever they

157 Declaration of Stanisław Karas, August 24, 1973, AIPN, OK Kr, Ds. 6/70/22, p. 63, as quoted in Panz, "Powiat nowotarski," p. 268.

158 Klukowski, *Zamojszczyzna 1918–1959*; Stanisław Żemis testimony, ŻIH, 302/30.

159 Lejb Zylberberg testimony, ŻIH, 302/37.

160 Cęckiewicz, "Prześladowania nowobrzeskich Żydów."

161 Dawid Nassan testimony, ŻIH, 301/3262.

found the hidden Jews, they herded them to the Jewish cemetery, where the German gendarmes executed the hapless victims.

The voluminous, and therefore unique, collection of police documents from Brzesko Nowe, preserved in the Kraków archives, has already been put to use on several earlier occasions in this study. Thanks to this official correspondence, we learn that the firefighters' involvement in the liquidation *Aktion* was neither limited to the ghetto nor to the cemetery nearby; it extended well beyond the city limits, including to the banks of the nearby Wisla (Vistula) River and to all the areas where the Jews tried to hide.[162] Aron Sztarkman witnessed the liquidation of the town of Opatów located midway between Kielce and Sandomierz in central Poland. He wrote: "The gendarmes, the auxiliary police, the Blue Police, the firefighters, all of them took part."[163]

The Polish underground press also noted the firefighters' involvement in German crimes. *Biuletyn Informacyjny*, the most important newspaper published by the resistance, published a short note regarding the liquidation of the Warsaw-area ghettos on October 22, 1942:

> The murdered and deported Jews of Wołomin, Stoczek, Węgrów, Radzymin, Jadów, Siedlce...We hear from many places about mass killings of Jews but nowhere is the news so horrible as from Wołomin and Stoczek. The firefighters in Wołomin and the riffraff of Stoczek took an active part in the liquidation *Aktion* and will go down in history as those who searched for Jews in hiding, helping to murder and to rob them.[164]

162 Minutes of interrogations, depositions of witnesses, notes from the investigation, November 23, 1942, ANK, PPPBrzN, vol. 39, pp. 32–36.

163 Arele (Aron) Sztarkman testimony, ŻIH, 302/108.

164 "Liquidation of the Ghettos in Wolomin and Stoczek," *Biuletyn Informacyjny*, October 22, 1942, quoted in Dariusz Libionka, "Polska konspiracja wobec eksterminacji Żdó w dystrykcie warszawskim," in Barbara Engelking, Jacek Leociak, and Dariusz Libionka, *Prowincja noc: Życie i zagłada Żydów w dystrykcie warszawskim* (Warsaw: IFiS PAN, 2007), p. 453.

Informacja Bieżąca, another underground bulletin, reported on the events in Stoczek:

> On September 24 [1942], during the deportation, the Polish firefighters covered themselves with infamy, dragging Jews out of their houses and stealing their possessions. The henchmen's lackeys received praise from the German officials.[165]

The files of postwar investigations and court proceedings provide further evidence of the crimes of the Stoczek firefighters. This time, however, the witnesses were unable to say whether the people "who covered themselves in infamy" were the firefighters wearing brass helmets or members of the firefighters' orchestra who wore shakos. One of the Polish witnesses told the following to the court: "During the occupation I lived in Stoczek. There was no closed Jewish quarter in our town. I was there at the time when the Germans deported the Jews—with the assistance of firefighters in shakos."[166] Others reported seeing the Blue Police in addition to the Germans and the Polish firefighters.[167] In Stoczek, like in so many other places, some of the Jews tried to flee and went into hiding in nearby villages. However, the catchers were waiting there. Anastazja Karapata saw the local firefighters in action:

> I stood on the roadside and saw the members of the Stoczek Voluntary Firefighting Brigade who delivered Polish citizens of Jewish nationality to Stoczek. I saw among them Fajga with her son and daughter. When they were close to us, the Jewess cried out to my sister: "My dear Ms. Witkowska, save me!!" To which my sister replied: "But how can I save you?!" The firefighters took these Jews to Stoczek and surrendered them to the gendarmes, who promptly shot these Jews in the Jewish cemetery.[168]

165 *Informacja Bieżąca*, October 23, 1942, as quoted in Libionka, "Polska konspiracja wobec eksterminacji Żdó w dystrykcie warszawskim," p. 454.
166 Józef Burczak testimony, June 21, 1951, AIPN, GK 318/134, p. 8.
167 See Anastazja Karapata testimony, April 11, 1950, AIPN, GK 318/134, p. 102.
168 Ibid.

At the time of the liquidation of Stoczek, Chaim Kwiatek was seventeen years old. On September 22, 1942, his hometown was surrounded by Germans, Ukrainians, and the Polish Blue Police. According to Kwiatek, Germans and Ukrainians "stopped at the gates," while "the Poles searched the hideouts."[169] It was the Poles who gave the Germans a list of all the Jews living in Stoczek. Given the fact that there was no ghetto in Stoczek and that the Poles and Jews lived side by side, a nominative list was of particular importance. Chaim Kwiatek's testimony is the only Jewish account of what happened in this small town on the day of the liquidation. Kwiatek not only saw the unfolding tragedy from up close but was also familiar with all the Poles who, over the course of a few hours, mutated from neighbors, classmates, and friends into murderers and the accomplices of murderers. Indeed, when drawing up a list of people who took part in the murder of the Jews, Kwiatek often used diminutive forms, which implies a familiarity between the victims and their butchers. In addition to Czesław Grudziądz and Kazimierz Postek, we can see on the list: "Lutek"; "Tommy" Figler; "Czesiek" Jasiński; "Johnny" Kalinowski; or "Danny" Pigul. As Kwiatek wrote, the chief responsibility lay with Łaszyński, the local voit and "seventy other murderers."[170] Chaim Kwiatek knew that the Germans were murderers—that much was obvious to everyone. It was much less obvious and completely unacceptable, however, that one's own neighbors and former friends would become killers too. In his short testimony, Kwiatek wrote the following:

> Konszar, our rabbi from Stoczek, gave a speech in which he offered people consolation and called upon everyone to die a martyrs' death. At the time I was hidden in a peasant's barn, but I could see the suffering of these people. Łaszyński, the voit, went around with a stick and struck people with it. From my hideout, I could hear how Tommy Figler and Czesław Grudziądz searched our house and talked among themselves: "We have already caught the old Kwiatek woman (my

169 Chaim Kwiatek testimony, ŻIH, 301/668.

170 Ibid.

> mother) and her daughter and took them away. But where is the old one and his sons?" I then saw Tommy Figler and Pigul catching the Jew Mendel Motel Oszceg—they beat him up, they took his watch and rings, and brought him to the collection area. Dawid Sukiennik, a small child, escaped from a hideout. He was caught by old Dzieciątek who then gave him to Kazimierz Postek. Postek tortured the child in order to force him to reveal where the others were. The child brought him to a place where three Jewish families were hiding. Five people arrived at the location, armed with sticks and whips, and they beat the captives without a pause. When all the Jews were gathered together, the Germans loaded them onto carts and delivered them to Sadowne railway station from where they were taken to Treblinka. All in all, 500 people were taken from our town. Only the Poles were left. Many firefighters crisscrossed the town looking for Jews, and whenever successful, they arrested and robbed them. In the meantime, my brother, father, and my brother's wife fled to the forest.[171]

Władysław Janiszewski and Wacław Zasłonka, two firefighters from Stoczek, were among the gravediggers involved in burying the victims of the liquidation *Aktion*.[172] In the Jewish cemetery, Janiszewski saw the dead body of a Jewish woman: "I took off the earrings and a ring from the body and I gave them to the commander [of the Blue Police] Pawłowski. In return, he allowed me to take the shoes taken off the dead Jewess. It was my wife who later wore these shoes," added the firefighter Janiszewski.[173] On another occasion, the firemen used a spade to strike down a Jew who had managed to dig himself out of a mass grave. In both Stoczek and Węgrów, some people turned to selling teeth with

171 Ibid.

172 Stanisław Trajan, at the time deputy mayor of Stoczek, testified that "Łazanka was ordered to bury the dead **because he was a fireman** [emphasis added, JG]." Trial testimony of Stanisław Trajan, November 30, 1948, AIPN, GK 317/100, p. 40.

173 Władysław Janiszewski testimony, trial proceedings, November 30, 1948, AIPN, GK 317/100, pp. 38–38v.

gold fillings that had been pulled from the mouths of dead Jews. Soon, people called these enterprising individuals "the dentists." Janiszewski, the previously mentioned fireman, observed that "Next to the body, I saw a rubber jaw[174] with a golden crown, so I cut off the gold crown with a spade, and I put it in my pocket."[175] According to his postwar testimony, the "dentist" lost the crown, because there was a hole in his pocket.

In a memoir written by the previously mentioned forester from Biłgoraj Mikulski, we find the following description:

> It happened sometime in the beginning of December 1942. A former career sergeant in the Polish army from Dyle[176] together with the local firefighters organized a manhunt to catch Jewish children, especially boys aged 10–14, who have been hiding in the nearby forests. The manhunt proved to be a success. They loaded fifteen children on a huge carriage drawn by several horses. Four firefighters in shining helmets stood guard in each corner of the cart, axes dangling from their belts. The children, with madness in their eyes, looked somewhere far in the sky. They might have even been oblivious to the world outside; lost in thought, they knew that their last hour has come, that death was inevitable. I stood at the gate of my forest ranger's house and all four firefighters saluted me with expressions of satisfaction on their faces. I said to myself: "O, tempora!"[177]

Mikulski's account concerns the actions undertaken by the firefighters from Dyle, but the Jewish children, the targets of the manhunt, most likely hailed from the nearby *shtetls*, which had been liquidated in November 1942. Dyle is located in the middle of a triangle with Frampol to the northwest, Biłgoraj to the southwest,

174 This is most likely referring to a dental bridge.

175 Władysław Janiszewski testimony, trial proceedings, November 30, 1948, AIPN, GK 317/100, pp. 38–38v.

176 Dyle is a village situated 10 kilometers northeast of Biłgoraj.

177 Mikulski, *Myśli, wspomnienia, uwagi, refleksje....* "*O tempora, o mores*" (Oh, times, oh, manners) is a Latin expression indicating the downfall of civilized behavior.

and Zwierzyniec to the east. Frampol was liquidated on November 2, 1942, and Zwierzyniec two days later. According to Polish witnesses, the hunt for the Jewish refugees lasted several days:

> The Germans were afraid to enter the forests, that's why they sent the firefighters in their stead. Some firefighters took part under duress, others [took part] willingly, even with joy.... They drove thirty Jews from the woods and [kept them] in a local school. People said that the Frampol rabbi was among those caught.[178]

It is worth stressing that according to Mikulski, at least some of the firefighters joined the hunt on their own prerogative, without coercion or pressure. In addition to hunting down the fugitives, the firefighters also took part in the organized robbery of Jewish property.[179] According to Alina Skibińska:

> Both the oral testimonies and the trial proceedings provide a wealth of information about the involvement of the OSP [in the Biłgoraj area during the liquidation *Aktionen*]. The same thing happened in each and every location where actions have taken place, but the firefighters from Frampol and Krzeszow must have been particularly "active." Władysław Bełżek, one of the accused, provided the names of fifteen members of the OSP from Krzeszow who hunted down the Jews, but even that was not enough to start an investigation against them. Similar cases were reported all over the place.[180]

In Węgrów, the liquidation of the secondary ghetto did not go according to German plans. With nothing more to lose, no more illusions as to their fate, and well aware of the bloody suppression of

178 Marianny Wąsek testimony, "Zagłada Żydów we Frampolu," and Stanisław Oszust testimony, andrzejburlewicz.blog.onet.pl/2015/11 (accessed October 18, 2016), as quoted in Skibińska, "Powiat biłgorajski," p. 288.

179 The case of Tomasz Jamiński, 1951–1954, AIPN Lu, 326/60, as quoted in Skibińska, "Powiat biłgorajski," p. 259.

180 Ibid.

the uprising in the not-too-distant Warsaw ghetto, the Jews decided to resist. Most often it was passive resistance. The defenseless Jews barricaded themselves in their houses, surrounded by the police and various gawkers and bystanders. Just like in the Warsaw ghetto, the Germans decided to burn down the Jewish houses in order to force the Jews out into the open. The Germans set houses on fire, and the firefighters dragged the Jews out of the burning houses with grappling hooks. Later, the Węgrów firefighters guarded the Jews and led them to the Jewish cemetery, where the Germans conducted mass executions.

Brzesko Nowe, Stoczek, Węgrów, Skała, and Biłgoraj were located across the Kraków, Warsaw, and Lublin districts of the Generalgouvernement. This does not mean, however, that firefighters in other regions behaved in a different way. In the Radom district, the situation resembled that seen elsewhere. The Jewish community of Klimontów, a small town situated 24 kilometers west of Sandomierz, was destroyed on Friday, October 30, 1942. The *Aktion* started early in the morning when the liquidation commando—the SS, German police, Ukrainians from Trawniki, and the Schupo—surrounded the ghetto. According to a Jewish witness, other people and organizations were also involved: "Polish police from nearby towns showed up too, the firefighters led by Lasota, their commander; the Jewish police and the Judenrat."[181]

The brutal pacification of Klimontów resembled many other *Aktionen* that had struck Jewish communities in the area. During the liquidation of the ghetto, the Blue Police officers from Klimontów took part in the execution of twenty-two Jews and killed thirteen others in the forest nearby.[182] The deportations went

181 Lejb Zylberberg testimony, ŻIH, 302/37.

182 Charges against Feliks W., Edward S., Marian M., Zygmunt O., and Genowefa L., July 29, 1948, Archiwum Państwowe w Radomiu, PSSK, 1102, as quoted in Sebastian Piątkowski, "Oprawcy, prześladowcy, ratownicy: Problematyka Zagłady w aktach radomskiej ekspozytury Prokuratora Specjalnego Sądu Karnego w Lublinie," *Zagłada Żydów, Studia i materiały*, 4 (2008), pp. 484–498. See also Sebastian Piątkowski, "Między obowiązkiem a kolaboracją Policja 'granatowa' w dystrykcie radomskim w latach 1939–1945," in Edyta Majcher-Ociesa, ed., *Z dziejów policji polskiej w latach 1919–1945* (Kielce: KTN, 2010), p. 178.

hand in hand with the murders. For the most part, the victims were women, children, and the elderly, who could not keep up with the pace of the marching columns that were being herded toward concentration points. Murders were often associated with theft. Lejb Zylberberg wrote the following:

> Peasants flocked from the villages and started looting. The Germans shot one Pole who had been found in a Jewish house. After half an hour, a fireman showed up in the cemetery, leading an older woman. The woman took him aside, rolled up her dress, and put something in his hand. Then, she wanted to take off, she thought he would release her, but he held her tight. In the meantime, Teiser [a gendarme], that bandit, showed up and shot the woman. Saturday, October 31, 1942, there was one who had fled the transport. Two Poles brought him to Klimontów and delivered him into the hands of the firefighters.[183]

Similar scenes were also reported in Wolbrom, not far from Kraków.[184] The majority of ghettos in the Generalgouvernement were liquidated between the spring and winter of 1942. In some cases, in place of the destroyed ghettos, the Germans decided to establish so-called *Restghettos*. As mentioned previously, that is what happened in Warsaw, among other places. A secondary ghetto was also created in Węgrów, however these *Restghettos* were not to last; they were liquidated one after the other between the winter and summer of 1943. The final destruction of the Węgrów ghetto, which housed around 300 Jews, took place on April 30, 1943. Again, as during the previous *Aktion* in September 1942, the local OSP was to play an important role in the killings of their last Jewish neighbors. The firefighters' assistance was even more necessary because, contrary to the first *Aktion*, the German forces now only consisted of the local gendarmes and the Schupo. It was in these cases when the Germans were at a numerical disadvantage that

183 Libionka, "Powiat miechowski," pp. 81–82.

184 Ibid.

the role of the locals—mostly the Blue Police and the firefighters—grew accordingly.

In extreme cases such as in villages in the sub-Carpathian region, for example, Markowa, where today the Museum of Poles Saving Jews in World War II stands, the Polish firefighters took it upon themselves to search for and arrest the local Jews. In some cases, they also murdered the captured victims. The firefighters were also known to voluntarily join the liquidation *Aktionen* without any specific German order. It is of little consequence whether they acted out of religious or ideological reasons, motivated by fear or loyalty toward the firefighting collective or by simple visions of "Jewish gold." From the standpoint of the dying Jews, it made no difference whatsoever. In some cases, the Polish firefighters not only joined the liquidation *Aktionen* but also conducted them on behalf of the Germans in their stead.

In cities and smaller towns where German or Polish police forces were stationed, the firefighters usually fulfilled an auxiliary role. In the rural areas, however, the role of the OSP units—the only uniformed and well-organized force in such places—grew accordingly. More importantly, with the Germans' blessing, the firefighters were able to gain a degree of control over the rural communities. This process of consolidation of power, which can also be referred to as a gradual criminalization of the OSP members, can best be seen in Gniewczyna, a village located near Łańcut in the sub-Carpathian region of the Kraków district. According to one Polish witness:

> In May 1942, the locals, a coalition, or better said, a cooperative of the village "elite": the chief of the OSP (also the chief inspector of the OSP, appointed by the Germans), the more active members of the firefighting unit, village elders from two parts of the village together with their helpers, and several members of the resistance (sort of a wild, unorganized armed movement) initiated a roundup of local Jewish families. They caught most of the members of all eight Jewish families living in the village, both adults and children. They placed the poor wretches on carts, like pigs or calves brought

> to a market, and drove them to Leiba and Szangla Trynczer's house, right in the center of the village, close to the church, presbytery, and the school.[185]

Over the course of the next few days, the members of this new "elite" raped the Jewish women and tortured the men, trying to extract information about the location of furniture, cutlery, clothing, and other valuable items that the Jews had previously left with trusted Polish neighbors for safekeeping. Finally, once the victims had nothing more to offer, the firefighters called the gendarmes in Jarosław. The Germans arrived, took the Jews out, and shot them all in a public execution, with crowds of Polish villagers watching the scene. This formation of a criminal elite made up of OSP firefighters can similarly be seen in the cases of the Markowa, Husów, and Sietesz OSP.[186] Not unlike in Gniewczyna, here too the leaders of the new elite were recruited from among the firefighters, sons of local peasants, neither poor nor rich, average members of rural society. Here too, the members of the firefighting posse managed to impose their will on the rest of their community, at least as far as the fate of the local Jews was concerned. The liquidation *Aktion* in Sietesz started on August 3, 1942.[187] Kreidla Frieder, who lived in the village, fled into the nearby fields with her family. According to her testimony given shortly after the war, other Jews chose to seek shelter in the nearby forest. All of them were soon apprehended by the roving OSP units from Markowa, Sietesz, and Kańczuga. The Jews were soon rendered to the Germans for execution. Kreidla Frieder's testimony concludes as follows: "The only one to survive was Natan Goldman, a small boy, who now lives in [Mandatory]

185 Markiel and Skibińska, *"Jakie to ma znaczenie, czy zrobili to z chciwości?"* p. 70.

186 The passages dealing with the activities of the OSP from Markowa have been discussed in Jan Grabowski and Dariusz Libionka, "Bezdroża polityki historycznej: Wokół Markowej, czyli o czym nie mówi Muzeum Polaków Ratujących Żydów podczas II Wojny Światowej im. Rodziny Ulmów," *Zagłada Żydów, Studia i materiały*, 12 (2016), pp. 619–642.

187 There are several dates given by the witnesses. According to Jakub Einhorn, the liquidation in Markowa, Husów, and the surrounding area started on September 2, 1942.

Palestine, who managed to flee the bullets and hid in the forest."[188] The investigating prosecutor in Przemyśl wrote the following to the court:

> As soon as the policemen arrived, Teofil Ryznar, the village elder, summoned the members of the firefighting brigade and some of the night watchmen from Sietesz and ordered them to catch the Jews. Once the Jews were apprehended, they were viciously tortured, and one of the firefighters struck Aron Silberman so hard with a wooden bat on the head, that he crushed his skull and one of Silberman's eyes popped out.[189]

Things looked no different in Markowa, located close to Sietesz. There too, the plan was to force the Jews to a collection point in the village from where they would be delivered to the Germans in Łańcut. The orders to concentrate the Jews most likely reached the village elder through the officers of the Blue Police. In any case, there were no Germans reported in the immediate area at that time. The Markowa Jews—just like their counterparts from Sietesz—refused to comply and fled to the local forests. The same day, well before sunset, a posse of Polish firefighters rushed into the forests to look for the fugitives. According to Jewish witnesses and survivors, thirty-eight firefighters—their Polish neighbors—took part in the manhunt. The firefighters' mission proved to be a success with thirty-five out of approximately forty Jews caught within a few hours. The captives were badly beaten, and they were later placed in the village lockup, guarded by members of the Markowa voluntary firefighting brigade.[190] It is altogether plausible that the liquidations and deportations in smaller locations such as Sietesz or Markowa, where the Jews were able to avoid prior concentration in the ghettos, were conducted solely by Poles in uniforms, and in this case, in the uniforms of the voluntary firefighters.

188 Kreidla Frieder testimony, August 11, 1949, Archiwum Instytutu Pamięci Narodowej Oddział w Rzeszowie (AIPN Rz), 353/113, pp. 46–48.

189 Trial proceedings, AIPN Rz, 353/113, p. 206.

190 For a more detailed discussion of the Markowa situation, see Grabowski and Libionka, "Bezdroża polityki historycznej."

In December 1942, Ferdinand von Sammern-Frankenegg, the chief of police and SS for the Warsaw district, issued an order, which, in a way, concluded the wave of liquidation *Aktionen* in the Generalgouvernement that had been taking place since mid-March. In his letter, von Sammern-Frankenegg ordered that all Jews encountered outside of the few previously mentioned secondary ghettos be shot forthwith and without any further procedure. The order, issued to both the Gendarmerie and the Schupo, applied equally to the Polish Blue Police. The order reads as follows:

> The Leader of SS and the Police
> Warsaw, December 10, 1942
> Warsaw Area
> Ia 3218. L.dz. 6383/42
>
> Re: Regulation regarding Jews encountered living without permission outside the Jewish residential areas in the Warsaw district
>
> To the Chief of the Orpo in the Warsaw area, Warsaw
>
> The resettlement of Jews into Jewish residential areas in Warsaw and Lublin districts, as per police regulation of October 28, 1942, should have been completed by November 30, 1942. In line with paragraph 2 of that regulation, under no circumstances can Jews remain outside of, or leave, the aforementioned Jewish residential areas. Jews who work in munition factories or other production establishments and who are being placed in closed camps do not have to move to the new residential areas. According to § [section] 3 of the same Regulation, Jews found in noncompliance with § 2 will be punished by death. Consequently, all Jews encountered outside the Jewish residential areas without permission will be shot on the spot, without any further investigation. The same applies to Jews apprehended during the actions against the bandits. The Gendarmerie officers will receive

> precise instructions on how to execute this order. I wish to be informed, on the 30th of each month, how many Jews have been killed pursuant to this order.
> The Leader of SS and Police for the Warsaw area.
> [—] Sammern[191]

Von Sammern-Frankenegg's order marked the beginning of a new and final phase of the Jewish tragedy: the hunt for the Jews in hiding, a phase that would last until the end of the German occupation. *Aktion Reinhard* also indicated a new level of involvement of the Blue Police in German genocidal policies. The enforcement of various regulations paved the way for the direct involvement of the Polish police officers in the killings. During these few short months, thousands of Blue policemen—fathers of families, pillars of local communities, not infrequently heroes of armed resistance, officers with many years of service in the prewar police force—morphed into killers' apprentices and, very soon, into murderers in their own right. Historians, however, are unable or unwilling to offer reasons for such a transformation. The German orders alone are not enough to explain the genocidal criminalization of normal people.

The all-present antisemitic propaganda, the rapidly advancing dehumanization of the victims, the encouragement by the Germans to commit crimes, the feeling of impunity, as well as the deep and widespread hatred of Jews so visible in Poland before the war must have all played a role in the fostering of genocidal actions by the Polish officers. During the liquidation *Aktionen*, the Blue policemen took part in mass murder both inside and outside the ghettos, helped to load their victims onto the trains of death, and they searched the liquidated ghettos for Jews who had decided to go into hiding.

191 This document was published for the first time in Jan Grabowski and Dariusz Libionka, "Meldunki Obwodu 'Praga' Policji Polskiej o zatrzymaniach Żydów w Warszawie w okresie maj–lipiec 1943 r.," *Zagłada Żydów, Studia i materiały*, 10 (2014), pp. 592–621. The original document is held in AMSW, Komenda Policji Polskiej "Obwód Praga" 1939–1944, 1710, file 10.

The last logical step on the road to their involvement in the genocide was to deliver the Jews directly to the death camps. This is precisely what the Polish policemen from Włodawa did: In the summer of 1943, they brought their Jewish neighbors on carts straight to the gates of *Vernichtungslager* Sobibór.[192]

192 Hearing of Erich Bauer from Sobibór, sentenced to death in Berlin on May 8, 1950. His sentence was later commuted to life in prison. See initial interrogation of Nietsche and others, January 16, 1963, Bundesarchiv Ludwigsburg (BAL), B162/3749, p. 4. I am grateful to Jason Tingler for drawing my attention to this document.

Chapter Five

Judenjagd: 1942–1945

Polish Fascism and its ally, anti-Semitism, have conquered the majority of the Polish people...The blind folly of Poland's anti-Semites who have learnt nothing, has been responsible for the death of hundreds of thousands of Jews who could have been saved despite the Germans.[1]

Emanuel Ringelblum, Warsaw, 1944

The history of the Holocaust in Poland can be divided into three main phases, which provide the chronological framework for this book: the beginning of the occupation and the establishment of the ghettos; the liquidation *Aktionen*; and finally, the hunt for the Jews who had survived the deportations to the death camps. This third and final phase, codenamed by the Germans *Judenjagd* (the hunt for the Jews) and which lasted until the end of the war, can be further subdivided into two distinct stages: the hunt for victims who sought rescue within the liquidated ghettos; and the search outside the ghettos on the Aryan side, which was carried out both during an *Aktion* and after it was over. From the point of view of German strategy, the actions of the Polish police were of fundamental and essential significance during both stages. If it had not been for the assistance of the local population, and particularly the information that an entire

1 Emanuel Ringelblum, *Polish-Jewish Relations*, p. 247.

network of informers had provided the Polish police, the chances of discovering the hidden Jews would have been rather slim.

This problem has been fairly well discussed in a number of publications, and there is no reason to elaborate here beyond the necessary minimum. The moment the Jews cast off their armbands, the moment they went underground, they essentially disappeared and were out of sight of the Germans and the German institutions. In turn, this widened the operational field of the Polish policemen. As far as Jews were concerned, the Germans were not physiognomists. In colloquial terms, they did not know how to recognize a Jew from afar. This was mainly because only a small number of Jews had lived in the Reich before the war. In 1939, they made up less than half a percent of the country's population. Equally important was the far-reaching assimilation of the German Jews, who—with few exceptions—spoke excellent German, whose dress and manner were no different from those of ordinary Germans, who usually lived among Germans, and very often married them.

Although the situation in the East—including Poland—was vastly different, some things made the identification of the "racial enemy" considerably easier for the Germans, namely armbands with the Star of David that the Jews had to wear as well as the walls and fences of the ghettos. When the ghettos were liquidated, the situation changed dramatically: Jews who decided to seek help on the Aryan side became extremely difficult to capture from the Germans' point of view. In order to catch them, the Germans had to resort to other means and different techniques, and they devised new approaches. In this endeavor, they were aided by the Blue policemen and undercover agents for whom the lack of an armband was hardly a major obstacle. The primary reason for the arrest of Jews in hiding were denunciations or "confidential information," which abound in reports by the Polish policemen. In their hunt for Jews, both informers and policemen used many proven methods, which evolved and improved over the course of the occupation. It might be worth devoting some attention to these methods, as they were the reason why the chances of survival for Jews hiding in Poland were so slight.

Poor Command of the Polish Language

For poorly assimilated Jews, their inability to speak Polish was one of the most difficult barriers to overcome. The father of Samuel Willenberg, a fugitive from Treblinka and the author of a deeply shocking account about the extermination camp, spoke in a very heavily accented vernacular (known as *żydłaczenie*) and therefore had to pretend to be mute for most of the German occupation.[2] In his struggle for life, Willenberg the elder was aided by his talent as a painter. He painted pictures of the Blessed Virgin Mary and Child, which helped him earn a living and, at the same time, authenticate himself in the eyes of the ever-vigilant Christians of Warsaw. However, the *żydłaczenie* and a bad accent were only the beginning of any potential problems; the syntax and construction of sentences was also important. As every "expert" knew, Jews liked to ask questions during a conversation, or at least that was a commonly held belief. Perhaps such a view originated from the approach to the teaching and exegesis of Talmud in the *heder* (Hebrew school for children), or maybe it was just a stereotype and cliché derived from antisemitic superstitions. Regardless of the reason, in order to avoid the carefully set traps, knowledge of every stereotype and superstition became absolutely necessary for Jews in hiding.

Appearance

If one had a swarthy complexion, an elongated face, a long nose, or protruding ears, they were doomed to death. Tadeusz Obremski summed the situation up as follows:

> The Jews who behaved the calmest were those with a typical Jewish appearance. They realized that they had no chance of surviving on the Aryan side, because they would be exposed as soon as they ventured out. So, they were resigned to their

2 Samuel Willenberg, *Bunt w Treblince* (Warsaw: Res Publica, 1991), pp. 127–128.

> fate. They felt like poultry in a henhouse, awaiting their turn to go under the knife.[3]

Those who decided to escape from the ghetto despite their physical "handicap" could never go out onto the streets during the day. They were the ones said to be "unable to walk." Those with dark, curly hair "could walk," as long as they dyed and straightened it. That was neither easy nor safe, as a skilled policeman or *szmalcownik* (blackmailer) could easily spot their dark roots, which in turn could lead to a further and more detailed examination. Speaking of physical attributes, in the case of men suspected of "wrong" racial descent, the main problem was circumcision. In such situations, the matter was simple to resolve, as it was enough to pull down the suspect's pants. In some partisan units, special periodic *schwanzparades*, or inspections of manhood, were carried out for that very purpose, namely to seize any "racially suspect" man who had managed to sneak into the partisan ranks. In Polish cities, the hunt for Jews assumed such proportions that when one of those captured, a man of impeccably Aryan appearance, was dragged inside some building, he would ask his tormentors, "Gentlemen, how did you know I'm a Jew?" to which he heard in reply: "We grab everyone as they go." For wealthier Jews and those with the necessary contacts, they pinned their hopes on the medical underground. For a good deal of money, a man could undergo surgery to disguise his circumcision. However, few had access to doctors who were willing to take such a risk, and the operation itself often ended in failure.[4]

From the perspective of an observant policeman, the way one moved was as important as one's appearance. After years of living in the ghetto and years of increasing terror, many Jews

3 Obremski, *Wśród zatrutych noży*, p. 167.

4 Maria Ciesielska, "Lekarze wykonujący operacje plastyczne i zabiegi likwidujące skutki obrzezania w Warszawie w czasie II wojny światowej," in Alicja Bartuś and Piotr Trojański, eds., *Cena odwagi: Między ocaleniem życia a ocaleniem człowieczeństwa* (Oświęcim: Fundacja na Rzecz MDSM, Wydawnictwo Naukowe Uniwersytetu Pedagogicznego im. Komisji Edukacji Narodowej, 2019), pp. 209–223.

were almost radiating with palpable fear. The potential victim was characterized by an unsteady gait, a hunched posture, and shifty, frightened eyes. Any lingering doubts could be easily dispelled by a brief examination of one's knowledge of Catholic prayers. A Hail Mary or an Our Father usually sufficed when racially profiling a detainee. A variation of such a line of questioning was an exam on liturgy: "What do we say during confession? What does the priest say at the end of Mass? What are the forms of penance?" A more advanced repertoire included questions on Polish cuisine: "Tell us, please, what we do serve on Christmas Eve?" A seemingly innocent question about the date of a name day or a patron saint could prove fatal for the Jews. One's mind had to be sharp even when lighting a match, as according to racial "experts," Jews are cowards and therefore afraid of fire, so they would light a match by striking it away from themselves, while real Poles would light it boldly, pulling the sulphur head toward themselves. While today it all may seem ridiculous—even absurd—not so long ago, it determined who lived and who died.

In the struggle for survival, Aryan papers and the correct appearance were helpful, but bravado, feistiness, and the ability to think on one's feet were no less important. Alfred Górny, the author of the following account that was submitted to the USC Shoah Foundation Visual History Archive (VHA) in 1996, was hiding with Aryan papers near Kraków:

> I gave rides to policemen along the way, along with the commander of the Dobczyce police station and so on. "And what was that?" "They caught Jews, we caught Jews." I said, "And what are some Jews to me?" They said, "Go, because they're talking about you." So, I went with that Szafran. I looked and they were all surrounded by policemen with rifles. There's a horse-drawn cart, and those policemen are shouting: "Jews, get on!" One comes up to my wife and says: "Not this one! She's not Jewish. Get in the ditch!" There was that Ukrainian, he put up the most fight, he pulled out his Ukrainian identity card, he wanted to take off his pants, show them, but they slapped him and put him on the cart with this wife. They say

to engineer Budzyński: "You too, get in the ditch!" like, he's not Jewish. And Szafran and me neither, of course. So, we sit in that ditch. They put Budzyński's wife, that brunette, onto the cart, and those Ukrainians. Then Budzyński says to me: "Mr. Górny, my wife is in mortal danger, and you know them all. Go there."

[Question:] So she was Jewish?

"Go there." So, there I was, thinking I'll go there, the German police, they took the Jews. But I couldn't lose my face and that woman had to be saved. "All right," I said to the platoon sergeant, "I'll go with you." Because Budzyński's wife was screaming, saying that she was invited to dinner with [the] director of the Rezner company that evening, that they would be punished for everything. But they didn't care! The alarm was raised, it is written in the book that the peasants send word that there were Jews walking on the Raba River. Because we were walking along the river, the Raba. And they had to do their duty. We went from Winiary to Dobczyce. It was Pentecost in the afternoon. The police station was located in the market square, in a little two-story house. The whole market was packed with people! Crammed! "Jews! They are bringing Jews! They are bringing Jews!" So we went inside the station, up the stairs, and here they come: "Will there be a shooting? Will there be a shooting? By the Raba, like usual?"

[Question:] They were waiting for that?

The station commander is away. He's with his mistress. His name was Piotrowski. The platoon sergeant had a field telephone with a crank handle and he called the German police in Myślenice, because that was his duty. But it was afternoon, and luckily there was no policeman on the phone at that station. No one answered. So, I say: "It's going to be a scandal. He really is Ukrainian, and so's his wife. Come on, I know them. This is Engineer Budzyński's wife, whom I know very well. She is invited to that Rezner fellow." They were afraid of that Rezner. "Come on, let them go." "I can't.

At most, Sergeant Piekarski can let them go." "Where is he?" "At his mistress's place." "And where is the mistress?" "Over there, around the corner." I go to that Piekarski. I bang on the door. Finally, after some time, a dark-haired wench in an unbuttoned shirt opens the door. She says, "What?" I say, "I need to see Commander Piekarski." "Who are you?" He's undressed, only wearing his boots and pants, the rest is off already. "Oh, the driver! Come on in, have a drink!" He poured. We drank. "Come on, let's have some fun. She's a very nice lass." I said, "Sure, but later. Right now, we have a difficult situation on our hands. There was some alarm. The peasants sent word that there were some Jews, but those were no Jews, not at all," I explain to him. He says, "Well, what can I do?" "Let them go." "Well, let's have another drink." We had another drink. "Damn those peasants! I'll kick their asses tomorrow! I'll show them!" He got dressed. We walk out. There's a crowd, again. "Oh, here he comes! Where's the shooting gonna be? Where's the shooting gonna be?" We go upstairs. The Ukrainian pulls out that *Kennkarte* [identity card] again, the commander looks at it and rings with that crank. No one answers in Myślenice, at that German police station. He thinks for a moment and says, "All right!" To the platoon sergeant, "Write down that they're not Jews. We know this driver here. He can vouch for them." All right, so he wrote down in the book that it wasn't the Jews and that the alarm was false. And we went downstairs. And just imagine, there's that crowd standing there, the platoon sergeant shouts through the window from above: "There will be no shooting, these are not Jews!" The crowd slowly disperses, and Mrs. Budzyńska says: "What, are we supposed to go on foot? Give me some horses right away!" I thought to myself, is this woman crazy? What if they reach the Germans on that phone? So, I say to her: "Ma'am, let's go!" "No! There must be some horses here!" So, that platoon sergeant actually went and grabbed some peasant, told him to harness up, we got on the cart, and went on. We came back to that spot, and there they were, sitting in the ditch the whole time. They were waiting for us. Well, they

> could see from a distance that we were coming alone, without the police, so everyone was relieved.[5]

A slip-up and subsequent death could be caused by ostensibly insignificant things that eluded even those most experienced in the art of hiding. An example is the story of Łucja Jurczak, a Polish woman who hid Jews near Międzyrzec Podlaski. According to her account, the most dangerous people for Jews were the local Polish policemen:

> I am thinking about those policemen in Międzyrzec. That some of them even collaborated with the Germans later on. And that was a danger, because they knew Poles, after all.
>
> [Question:] Did they know everybody?
>
> They also knew the Jews. I remember, in the first year I was captured as a Jew. Do you know what it was about? Because I had my *Kennkarte* [identity card] on me, and I went to the forest to pick berries. And at that time a lot of Jews were escaping from the ghetto. And they [the police] took me, along with others. And that's when the Polish policeman was so unpleasant. Even the gendarmes wouldn't grill me like he did. "If you live in the village, why are you wearing stockings?" You know, he even paid attention to such details. Even the accent, I made a mistake and said something like… I accented some half-Jewish word.... He even took that into consideration for me. And he said later: "Oh, then at most," he says, "you'll go to Germany for labor if you're really not Jewish." You see? Well, I managed to save myself then. But those were, you know, difficult moments. It always bothered me that it was a Pole.[6]

Evidently, even such things as wearing stockings, something associated with posh city living, could prove potentially dangerous.

5 Alfred Górny interview, VHA, 22077.

6 Łucja Jurczak interview, VHA, 36453.

Another habit typical of the intelligentsia that aroused the vigilance of the Blue policeman was the sight of a country dweller holding a newspaper. In such a situation, a justified suspicion arose. The farmer was carrying the reading material home for someone who was well educated but had the so-called wrong racial profile.

Włodzimierz Wyszyński, an agent of the Polish Criminal Police in Lwów, recognized a Jewish woman who was hiding with Aryan papers by the fact that she lived alone. By 1943, one of the characteristics of Jews was that they no longer had families. This distinguished them from the rest of society. This is why the more foresighted among those in hiding sent postcards to themselves, supposedly from their relatives. Others would go out for days on end, having previously informed their coworkers or roommates about upcoming family gatherings. Another Polish Kripo agent warned an arrested Jewish woman not to admit, God forbid, that she spoke German, "because it was the Jews who almost always spoke German."[7] Many Jews tried to move out of their homes for fear of a chance meeting with those who had known them before the war and thus a potential denunciation, which could be the direct consequence of such an encounter. On the other hand, it was easier to find help in one's native area—or at least that is how it seemed to many Jews at first. Very often, a person's fate hinged on the decision whether to stay in their hometown or leave for parts unknown.

However, knowledge of the many traps did not warrant safety. Moreover, Jews in hiding had to be lucky—very lucky indeed—and luck could be neither bought nor guaranteed. One of those who learned that lesson was Ludwik Kon, who left his hometown of Dąbrowa Górnicza and moved to Warsaw in search of rescue. Kon "could walk," had great appearance, and had perfectly forged papers under the name of Andrzej Brzeziński.[8] Nevertheless, he could not have predicted that one day, while he was strolling down the street, he would bump into a schoolmate who knew very well that

7 Court session of October 31, 1953, AIPN, GK 317/616, pp. 85–88.

8 The case of Ludwik Andrzej Kon aka Ludwik Andrzej Brzeziński, April 1941, AMSW, Sondergericht Warschau, 378.

the blond man in front of him was not named Brzeziński. He also could not have predicted that his former schoolmate had made a career in the Kripo during the occupation and would immediately hand him over to the gendarmes.

Identity card of Ludwik Kon. The name on the card reads Andrzej Brzeziński. AMSW, Sondergericht Warschau, 378.

But it also happened that a Jew who had been denounced, arrested, and interrogated in the notorious Gestapo headquarters in Warsaw would look into the face of the Gestapo officer and recognize a fellow soldier from the Austro-Hungarian army, a brother-in-arms from the trenches of World War I. The Gestapo officer, whose soldierly ethos was apparently stronger than his racial vigilance, would let the Jew go and offered to help him if he was ever arrested again.[9] A stroke of luck was apparently just as important as best-laid plans.

9 Zbigniew Ryszard Grabowski, *W skorodowanym zwierciadle pamięci* (Warsaw: Żydowski Instytut Historyczny im. Emanuela Ringelbluma, 2018), p. 62.

All those tests and traps—the list could go on—created a dense network in which thousands of Polish Jews perished. It was one of the reasons why the Holocaust in Poland was so complete, so total. The hunting method described above, based on knowledge of the codes of culture, language, and religion, was completely inaccessible to the Germans. Polish policemen and their informants, however, used the cultural codes as their basic tools for effective identification of Jews in hiding.

This chapter will analyze many examples of wrongdoings carried out by the Polish police against the Jews, with minimal or indirect German involvement. The aim is to emphasize the efficiency and initiative of the Blue policemen, who, while operating within the system created by the Germans, undoubtedly imbued it with their own new and original features. Examples of this agency can be found in every district of the Generalgouvernement as the arrest, robbery, and murder of the Jews became an integral part of the strategy of Polish policemen from 1942 onward, regardless of the area where they happened to be serving.

In the winter of 1943–1944, Emanuel Ringelblum was hiding in the Krysia bunker on Grójecka Street in the suburbs of Warsaw. Ringelblum—the chronicler of the life and extermination of the Jews in the Warsaw ghetto—was not idle. On the contrary, he spent whole days writing his last work, *Polish-Jewish Relations During the Second World War.* When it came to evaluating wartime relations between Jews and Poles, the author had no illusions. In his earlier notes from the ghetto from 1940–1941, he expressed some hope for the future of relations between the two nations. Poles and Jews, Ringelblum thought at the time, would survive the hell of the occupation together, and this painful lesson should make it possible to start a new chapter and change the treatment toward minorities in the Polish Republic. But then came the liquidation of the ghetto and the hell of hiding. By the end of 1943, the historian of the Warsaw ghetto assessed the Poles' attitudes toward Jews from the perspective of the months he had spent on the Aryan side—in hiding, in the bunker, in the camps. Ringelblum became a witness to the Holocaust, a time when Polish Jews were murdered before his very eyes, when he and a handful of other survivors resembled, as he put it, someone waiting for inevitable death. In his reflections on the cause of the Jewish tragedy, Ringelblum described the criminal perfidy of the Germans, but at the same time, he did not spare bitter words about the Polish Jews. He blamed their leaders, the members of the Jewish Councils, and the Jewish police officers. He also partly blamed Polish society, which had failed to extend civic solidarity to the dying Jews. Ringelblum put his reflections in the form of rhetorical questions:

> We ask further, why was it possible to considerably reduce the evil of denunciations, spying and collaboration with the Germans within one's own community, while nothing was done to check the giant wave of blackmail and denunciation of the handful of Polish Jews that had survived the slaughter of a whole people?...Will it not be forever a disgrace that in a town like Czestochowa, for example, practically none of the Jewish inhabitants were saved, only because before the war hostile feelings towards the Jews were current in this town? Why has the Polish antisemitic press not stopped its incitement against the Jews even for a moment.... Why do the few idealists who defend the Jews and give them refuge so rarely meet with cooperation from the community or the great majority of the community?[10]

Ringelblum continued that for the Jews perishing in the gas chambers of Bełżec, Treblinka, Majdanek, and Sobibór, the attitudes of Polish society were essentially indifferent:

> But to those few who are still alive in some underground cave, in a secret hide-out in some suburb, or living as "Aryans" "on the surface," these questions are not purely theoretical. Whether this small remaining handful of Jews will be able to hold out against the tide of German hatred and the Polish community's passive indifference will depend to a large extent upon the attitude of the Polish community.[11]

10 Ringelblum, *Polish-Jewish Relations*, pp. 8–9.
11 Ibid., p. 9

Ringelblum was killed several months after he wrote these words, and it was his Polish fellow citizens who played a significant role in his death.[12] While Ringelblum's comments refer to Polish society as a whole, the persecution of the Jews during the third phase of the Holocaust—the *Judenjagd*—can be best explored by examining the behavior of the Polish policemen. An examination of the attitudes of the officers of the Blue Police and the Polish Kripo agents provides a useful framework for the analysis of the evolution of the *Aktionen* directed against the Jews. The police had the means, the permission, the motivation, and the opportunity to operate on so-called Jewish territory in a particularly ruthless and murderously effective manner. In addition, after the liquidation of the ghettos, operations against Jews were often carried out by the Polish police alone, without any direct German supervision. According to Ringelblum, the number of victims of the Blue Police during that period—that is, Jews who had managed to escape from the Germans earlier—was estimated at tens of thousands.[13]

Holocaust statistics are always subject to a large margin of error. Much effort was made to conceal the scale of the extermination, so our estimates reflect the scope of our ignorance. In the study of the third phase of the Holocaust, the margin of error is particularly wide, even though the number of victims here was smaller than in the two preceding stages. This does not mean, however, that we should not attempt to establish the most reliable data possible. In the case of the activities of the Polish police after the liquidation of the ghettos, we can rely on local research carried out in recent years concerning the activities of the Blue Police at county level.[14] It turns out that in the county of Węgrów, the Polish police at that time was virtually always involved in capturing Jews. The Blue policemen murdered Jews on their own or took part in executions together with German gendarmes. What is particularly important is that the Germans themselves never set out in search of Jews without the assistance of the Blue policemen, and in most

12 For more information about Ringelblum's fate, see chapter 7.

13 Ringelblum, *Polish-Jewish Relations*, p. 136.

14 See Engelking and Grabowski, *Night Without End*.

recorded cases, they were accompanied by Polish officers.[15] The hunt for Jews in the counties of Miechów, Nowy Targ, Bochnia, Dąbrowa, and Dębica was similar. Polish policemen—either acting alongside the German gendarmes or alone—were responsible for the majority of murders committed against Jews in hiding.

As discussed in the previous chapter, no one will ever be able to accurately determine the scale of the Blue Police's complicity during the period of the liquidation of the ghettos, as unavoidably, the incomplete data defy quantification. We can, however, agree with Ringelblum, who stated that the Polish policemen were responsible—to a greater or lesser degree—for the deaths of hundreds of thousands of Jews, and in the final stage (the *Judenjagd*) for the deaths of tens of thousands of people who would have otherwise had a significant chance of surviving the war.

Searches in the Liquidated Ghettos

The previous chapter discussed in some detail the participation and role of the Blue Police in ghetto liquidations. An extension of that topic was the behavior of the Polish police as well as the firefighters in the days immediately following the liquidation. After the German liquidation units had already left the emptied ghettos, it was the Polish police and the gawkers who were given the task of searching abandoned houses and dragging from their bunkers and hiding places any Jew who had decided to wait out the *Aktion*. This is what happened in Tarnów and also in Węgrów,[16] mentioned herein several times. The journalist Mordechaj Canin, born in the town of Sokołów Podlaski, spent the war away from Poland. Shortly after the war, he visited Węgrów, where he listened to the accounts of the few Holocaust survivors still in the area:

15 See "Tabele i statystyki," Engelking and Grabowski, *Dalej jest noc*, vol. 1, pp. 369, 485, 588.

16 William Kornbluth, *Sentenced to Remember: My Legacy of Life in Pre-1939 Poland and Sixty-Eight Months of Nazi Occupation* (Bethlehem, PA: Lehigh University Press, 1994), p. 82.

> After the Jews were driven out of Węgrów, Polish police went through the Jewish houses looking for hiding Jews. Many people hid underground.... Gitl Góra told me that she hid in a bunker at the Węgrów butcher's house. There were sixty Jews in that bunker under the floor of his apartment. When all the inhabitants left the apartment, the butcher's dog hid under the bed. Looking for the Jews, Polish policemen saw the dog and shot it. The bullet that killed the dog went through the floor into the bunker and punctured a bucket with water prepared for days. Fifty Jews hid between the layers of the double ceiling. They lay there for eight long days without food or water. Out of thirst, they drank their own urine, out of thirst, they licked the sweat off each other's foreheads. Two weeks later, all the bunkers were empty. Some of the Jews escaped into the forest, the rest were shot by Polish policemen.[17]

The involvement of the Polish police and firefighters in the murder of the Jews of Węgrów has been discussed before, so there is no doubt that the accounts collected by Canin in 1947 are fully confirmed by other documents that are contemporaneous with the events and the testimonies of Poles and Jews from postwar years.[18]

What deserves special emphasis is the extraordinary resourcefulness of the Blue Police. We can judge from the surviving accounts that from the point of view of the Germans, this resourcefulness was exceptionally useful in those first days and weeks after the liquidation. In August 1942, after the residents of Wiśnicz Nowy (today Nowy Wiśnicz) were driven out, many Jews fled the town and went into hiding in the vicinity. One of the survivors gave the following testimony after the war:

> For several months, there were hunts for Jews. German police from Kraków would arrive, from dozens up to a hundred men

17 Canin, *Przez ruiny i zgliszcza*, p. 230.

18 Jan Grabowski, "Powiat węgrowski," in Engelking and Grabowski, *Dalej jest noc*, vol. 1, pp. 447–463.

with dogs, and search in the woods. Often unsuccessfully. The searching Germans were not as dangerous as the "Blue" Police, who had informers everywhere. Adolf Ackerman's family were hiding in Borowina—with considerable help from neighbors. All of them were killed by the "Blue" Police. On September 1, 1942, lawyer Izajasz Fragner, his wife, and her sister Maria Wiedelman were shot. They were captured in a hiding place in Rajbrom; they were shot in Lipnica Murowana. The execution was carried out by the "Blue" Police accompanied by an ethnic German, a *Volksdeutsch*. One of the policemen was Musiał, a resident of Lipnica Górna. In every village there was an *Ortschutz* [village guard]—a dozen or so men whose duty was to keep order. They cooperated with the "Blue" Police during their actions.[19]

Liquidation of the Węgrów ghetto. Photo Collection, YVA, 503/3333.

19 Antoni Łucki testimony, ŻIH, 301/1388.

The Hunt for Jews on the Aryan Side: The City

Before the war, Mark Verstandig was a prosperous lawyer in Mielec. In 1942, he and his wife went into hiding near Połaniec and Sandomierz. In 1943, fearing exposure, Verstandig sent his wife to Warsaw in the company of a kindhearted Pole, Czesław Kubik. Trouble for Frieda Verstandig and her companion began immediately after they left the train station. The rickshaw driver, with barely a glance at the woman, changed the route and dropped the two passengers off right in front of the nearby police station, where Blue policemen were already waiting. Some cabdrivers and rickshaw drivers, as Mrs. Verstandig soon learned, had an "understanding" with the police and would bring all persons bearing the stigma of "wrong descent" to the station.[20]

At the police station, several officers began questioning Kubik, while the station head interrogated the woman personally. From other sources, we know that at the time it was the Blue Police captain, Czesław Ciesielski.[21] Verstandig wrote: "The policemen soon realized that Kubik was not a Jew. They even feared that he might be a member of the Polish underground (perhaps on a mission to hide an important Jewish woman)."[22] At the same time, upon searching Verstandig's wife, the station commander found treasure that she was carrying on her: "Jewelry, several thousand dollars in American gold coins, old Austrian gold coins, etc. The policeman was ready to take everything and let the woman go in exchange."[23] Eventually, after a brief negotiation, the head of the police station agreed to release Mrs. Verstandig for half the loot. As her husband suspected, the Polish police chief was not sure if he was really dealing with a Jewish woman—she had excellent papers, the correct appearance, and spoke Polish without a trace of an accent—or whether he was

20 Mark Verstandig, *I Rest My Case* (Evanston: Northwestern University Press, 2002), p. 166.

21 See AMSW, II Komisariat PP, file 16.

22 Verstandig, *I Rest My Case*, p. 166.

23 Mark and Frieda Verstandig's letter, Czesław Kubik's file, August 10, 1987, YVA, M.31.2/4094.

robbing an important underground courier. In such cases, extreme caution was always advised.

Frieda Verstandig's experience at the Blue Police station in Warsaw also gives us some idea of the fortunes that were collected by the policemen who hunted Jews. In the above-quoted letter to Yad Vashem, the Verstandigs write about a pile of gold coins and jewelry resting on the desk of the station's commanding officer. There is no doubt that such a sight must have had an extremely mobilizing effect on the officers of that station. Underground reports of the time mention the scale of blackmail operations that were carried out by the Warsaw police: "Jews are constantly blackmailed. Agents in civilian clothes come, often accompanied by a Blue policeman...the demands vary. I know about a demand of 20,000 zlotys, but I have heard of some who were satisfied with 1,000 zlotys."[24]

Henryk Lewandowski was brought to the same police station several months earlier, even before the final liquidation of the Warsaw ghetto. Together with a group of other Jews, he was "grabbed" in front of the train station:

> There must have been ten of us then. There was a police station on Aleje Jerozolimskie [Jerozolimskie Avenue] opposite Śródmieście Train Station, near the Polonia Hotel. And they grabbed us all there.
>
> [Question:] You were captured by the Blue policemen?
>
> Yes. Well, it started with, right, you had to show what you had. So, father had some, right, money stuffed into his shoes. Anyway, they took everything. They were going to take us to the Warsaw ghetto, but we asked them not to and they let us go the next day.
>
> [Question:] Did they take the money?
>
> Yes.[25]

24 Underground report about blackmailing, December 1942, AAN, Delegatura Rządu na Kraj, 202-II-28, p. 70.

25 Henryk Lewandowski account, December 1942, AAN, Delegatura Rządu na Kraj, 202-II-28.

It should be added that the railway police station preyed on those visitors seeking help in Warsaw, who usually began their "adventure" in the capital city at Warsaw Central station. For many newcomers, that adventure not only began but also ended there, thanks to the Polish police officers.[26]

It might also be worthwhile to return to the question of deference and fear that the punishing hand of the Polish Underground State had sparked in the Blue officers' souls, something that may have led the policeman who interrogated Mrs. Verstandig to be more cautious than usual. For many captured Jews, alleged contact with the underground was a last resort, as no other argument made as much of an impression on the police. Mark Verstandig left his hiding place near Sandomierz in mid-1943 and also came to Warsaw. It was a time of a particularly ruthless hunt for Jews, shortly after the suppression of the ghetto uprising. In his engaging memoir, he writes the following:

> A second later, there was a hand on my shoulder and a corpulent Polish policeman ordering me to come with him to the railway police station because I was a Jew. I looked him up and down and, removing his hand from my shoulder, said icily: "Why so familiar? Did we feed pigs together on the farm? When you address me, kindly use the polite forms. And I am not a Jew, so get lost."
>
> "We'll soon see about that at the police station. I've certainly never met a Jew as impudent as you."
>
> "Listen, my friend," I said with a smile, "if I come with you, you may be sure that you will not reach the police station alive. Feel my briefcase; see how heavy it is. Under the books there are hand grenades. I'm not alone. There are others behind me

26 The Blue Police post at the railway station also had its own small remand prison with cells for both men and women. One of the women sent to such a cell was a ŻOB liaison officer captured by the police. See Hela Rufeisen-Schüpper, *Pożegnanie Miłej 18: Wspomnienia łączniczki Żydowskiej Organizacji Bojowej* (Kraków: Beseder, 1996), pp. 55–59.

and in front of me. We don't like carrying out executions on the street. But if you insist, let's go."

The fat policeman was as white as a ghost.[27]

In both cases, the Jews were handed over to the police by informers. Frieda Verstandig was taken to the station by a rickshaw driver, while her husband was pointed out to the "fat policeman" by a catcher who was lurking in the street. There is no doubt that the Warsaw railway Blue Police station was the last link in the chain of blackmail operations. Adolf Berman, one of the leaders of Żegota, learned this in January 1944, and this matter will be discussed later.[28]

In mid-January 1943, another person who was brought to the police station on Jerozolimskie Avenue was fourteen-year-old Józef Sroka. He had come to Warsaw from Jarosław via Kraków with his mother, Mrs. Mila Sroka. Two undercover officers approached them right after their arrival at Warsaw Central station, showed them their identity cards, and ordered the mother and son to go with them to the police station. Józef and his mother were arrested along with a group of both male and female smugglers who were carrying bags. As Józef Sroka remembers, when they were at the police station, the smugglers were sent elsewhere, while the undercover policemen led the Srokas to the third floor, where a ruddy-faced policeman of about fifty years old, tall in stature, was waiting for them. In the room there was a desk, and the policeman ordered Sroka's mother to empty her bag onto the desktop. At the same time, he pointed his finger at one of the undercover policemen in the next room. At that signal, the undercover policeman ordered the young Sroka into the indicated empty room, where there were two desks. "Show me your cock," he said to the terrified boy as they entered, and immediately added, "Come on, show me your *shmock*" (a vulgar term for penis in Yiddish). With barely a glance, the officer muttered, "All right," and pushed the boy into

27 Verstandig, *I Rest My Case*, pp. 164–165.

28 See section "The Stifling Year of 1944: Special Units of the Polish Kripo" in chapter 7 of this volume. Żegota was an underground organization to aid Jews in Poland.

the main interrogation room. "He's a Jew, checked!" he declared to his superior. The man picked up Józef's mother's prewar passport and said, "Well, and this passport is also forged! How dare you still claim to be Polish!" Sroka's mother replied: "When we had to fight for Poland in September, my husband went to war, so I guess we can say that we are Poles!" The ruddy-faced policeman turned pale and asked, "What unit did your husband serve in?" "In the 1st Podhale Rifle Regiment," Sroka's mother replied. After a moment's consideration, the senior policeman returned the documents to the woman and said: "You may leave."[29]

Identity card of Józef Sroka as a worker in the Bosch factory in Kraków, 1943. Courtesy of the family of Józef Sroka.

It is hard to say whether the policeman was a veteran of the 1st Podhale Rifle Regiment or if someone close to him had served in that unit. Maybe he realized that one day, in the not too distant future, Poland would regain independence and the time of reckoning would come. The important thing was that he released the two Jews from custody and saved them from certain death. However, the story did not end there. When Józef Sroka and his mother left the railway station, three young Poles were already waiting for them in front of the building. After a while, there was a brief exchange: The young men declared to Mrs. Sroka that they knew she was Jewish. Faced with blackmail and with no other way

29 Author's interview with Józef Sroka (b. 1928, residing in Haifa), November 19–20, 2019.

out, Mrs. Sroka decided to return to the police station. So, they both climbed to the third floor, and once again came face to face with the ruddy Kripo agent who had let them go several minutes earlier. Upon seeing the two Jews, the policeman exclaimed: "What are you still doing here?" To which Sroka's mother replied, "There are blackmailers waiting for us downstairs, they know that we are Jews." Then the policeman ordered one of the undercover officers to arrest the three resourceful Poles, who were standing patiently in front of the police station, while he accompanied the Jewish woman and her child to the nearest streetcar.[30]

No one will ever be able to estimate how many Jews came out of an interrogation at the railway station free from harm. What can be stated beyond any doubt is the importance of "a stroke of luck," which, combined with determination and the will to fight for survival, was very often a vital element for the survival of Jews in hiding.

In the described case, the Jews went free without any payment. An example of the many different forms of payment is the story of Maria Wanda Gadomska, who had to flee from a burned-down hideout in the spring of 1943. In her account given years later, she recalled the following:

> I still had dark hair back then. And on a cloudy day, I got dressed, and because they told me I had eyes that betrayed me, that they were Jewish eyes, I put on dark glasses. And I put on an overcoat and then another overcoat, one over the other. And wearing these dark glasses, with my dark hair, with a kerchief over my head, I sat on a rickshaw with my bundles and tried to take them [things stored in the hideout] home. Well, that must have attracted attention. Today, after all those underground dealings, I know exactly what attracted attention, but then I didn't know, apparently. Because it must have attracted attention to wear dark glasses on a cloudy day. Whatever for? So, I was stopped by a policeman.

30 Ibid.

> [Question:] A Polish policeman?
>
> Yes. A Polish Blue policeman. He got in and sat next to the rickshaw driver and told him to take us to a hotel, I didn't know where, he muttered something. I was sure we were going to some police station, but he took me to a hotel on Chmielna Street. It was a street where there were always many prostitutes and hotels with rooms to rent by the hour. So, he took me to this hotel, told me to undress, told the rickshaw driver to wait, so it was clear what he wanted from me, but I still didn't know how it would end, whether he would take me to the Gestapo or to the police station, whether he would let me go wherever I wanted. But then he said that he was a decent man, and he didn't want to hurt me.[31]

For the Blue policeman, the rape of the defenseless woman was apparently a gesture of goodwill. He could have simply killed her or handed her over to the Germans. As one can judge from the cited account, in his own mind, the policeman remained a decent man. After all, by 1943, the usual norms of behavior no longer applied to the Jews, something that is easy to forget. By continuing to rationalize his own behavior, the policeman—whose last name is unknown—could have concluded that by keeping the woman alive, he was putting himself in danger. After all, the Third Regulation Concerning the Limitations of the Right of Residence in the Generalgouvernement of October 15, 1941, obliged all Poles to inform the authorities about the whereabouts of Jews in hiding. Those who refused to do so were threatened with the most severe penalties. Arguments of such a kind were often cited by the defense during the postwar August trials held in Poland against people suspected of collaboration with the Germans.

In Maria Wanda Gadomska's account, there are also several other elements worth noting: The Jewish woman looking for a hiding place had supposedly Jewish eyes, which betrayed her identity, and which she covered with dark-tinted glasses; she also had dark

31 Maria Wanda Gadomska interview, VHA, 26215.

hair, which she hid under a kerchief. Both must have aroused the suspicions of the observant policeman. Any remaining doubts were dispelled by the two overcoats the woman was wearing. It was common knowledge that escaping Jews put on everything they owned, and each piece of clothing had a measurable value, which could mean an extra day or week of life. During the occupation, the sight of a person wearing several sweaters or a couple of overcoats could, therefore, have very dangerous consequences for Jews on the run.

Adam Gelbard was hiding in Warsaw and came into close contact with the Blue Police during his first run-in with them. As in the case of Maria Wanda Gadomska, here too the policemen were satisfied with extortion and let their victims go:

> In the evening, the middleman came to see if we had already moved in. "Yes. That's good." And he left. A moment later, two Blue policemen arrived in his wake. One was in uniform, the other was in civilian clothes. He hit me at once. "You, Jews!" and so on. They searched everything we had and took everything. The watches I had, four or five of them, five-ruble coins, all I had. He got me there, because he carried out a personal search with great skill. He made me drop my pants. He took all the money. I remember my mother saying to them then, "Is this what you do? You policemen? And my husband, an army officer, fought in that war, and that doesn't convince you? And you are serving the Germans?" "Why are you saying such things?" And my mother showed them a photo of my father. The one that's standing over here. It was taken in 1939. The man looked at that picture, and there was another picture she had, where I'm sitting with my father on a bench, taken two weeks before the war, right after my father came back to get a better uniform. "Let's go. We're going to the Gestapo." My sister had this coat made from foal fur, it was hanging in the hallway. We grabbed everything we had. He took one suitcase and left the other one, the worse one. We also grabbed a briefcase and some other small things and went

> down the stairs. While going down the stairs, he pressed some money into my hand, which, as it later turned out, was not much. He says, "There you go, c'mon, there you go, right," or so he said. He gave us some coins and said, "When we go down to the street, you go left, we go right." So, we went down. Terror. It was our first run-in in Warsaw. We were on the street. They actually went one way, and we went the other. And then my sister remembered that she hadn't taken that fur coat. We were destitute, all we had left was a handful of coins and that foal fur. So, I went back to get the coat, and that woman immediately came at me, yelling, our landlady, saying, "So you're still here? I'm going to get the Germans right away." I said, "My sister left it here." She said, "What are you, so-and-so." She didn't let me take that coat, that fur coat. She chased me away. She yelled after me, loud, in that staircase.[32]

Another survivor described his encounter with a Blue policeman as follows:

> So, as I came out, and there's a cart driving by with a police foreman, and he said, he called me, so I saw him take out a revolver and held it like this. I came to him. He said, "Sit down." He said, "What nationality are you?" I said, "There you go, I'm Koprowski." I had changed my name, I had a different ID. He said, "No, I believe your name is Koprowski, but we'll go to the doctor, and the doctor will check if you are not a Jew, if you are a Pole, a Catholic." "I can say Pater Noster for you." I knew it. "That's not enough that you can say it. You could have learned it," he said to me. And I got in. He moved away from me and held that revolver out to me, and said, "If you so much as move your hand, you'll get two bullets in one go." I said, "Sir, why don't we get out of the carriage and talk a bit?" And he said, "All right." He got off the cart with me. He stood. "Sir, I'm of Jewish descent," I said. "What good will it do you

32 Władysław Iwaszczukiewicz (born Adam Gelbard) interview, VHA, 43591.

> if you take me away, put me in German hands? What's in it for you? I have a good gift that I got from my mother, after my father, I can give it [to] you." "What have you got?" "I have a gold cigarette case with numbers, I can give it to you. And I'll give you twenty dollars and a hundred dollars in paper to go with it." He said, "All right. Where do you want me to take you now?" I said, "Nowhere."[33]

The handful of above-cited examples that illustrates the activities of the Blue Police in a city—in this case, Warsaw—shows how police interventions ended with the looting and rape of Jewish victims. But not murder. A hypothesis can be made at this point about the specific nature of a policeman's work under urban conditions. The fundamental difference between the countryside and the city was whether or how easily the policemen could dispose of the bodies of their victims. In rural areas, in so many known cases, victims were buried without informing the Germans. In the city, this situation posed a serious problem that clearly limited the officers' freedom of action, thus increasing the victims' chances of survival. In the city, blackmail, rape, and robbery may or may not have marked the end of police intervention. In the countryside, it was usually just the beginning of the horror. Unlike police officers in the villages, their colleagues at the city police stations were much closer to the German authorities. After all, in every town there were outposts of the Schupo as well as other German secret and uniformed services, and every Polish police station was staffed by German liaison officers. Jews could be arrested and taken to the police station, but this entailed the risk of potential complications if they mentioned the robbery that almost always accompanied the arrest. Jews could be killed, but that involved more cumbersome bureaucratic duties in the city. Preparing reports and filling out *Strafanzeige* forms (bilingual reports of a crime that had been committed) was certainly a time- and labor-intensive endeavor.

It is undoubtedly true that Jews in occupied Poland were excluded from civic solidarity. It is arguable whether or to what

33 Paweł Koper interview, VHA, 12706.

extent the concept of solidarity based on citizenship had developed in Poland during the interwar period, but there is no doubt that the years of economic boycott, the growing antisemitism of the late 1930s, and the German propaganda and terror of the period in question had removed Jews from the sphere of mutual social obligation. The exclusion of Jews took place not only among less educated people, who were more susceptible to populist arguments, but also among the Polish intelligentsia. Aurelia Wyleżyńska, a writer, feminist, and author of one of the most interesting diaries from occupied Warsaw,[34] wrote about it as did the ethnographer, scholar, and social activist Adam Chętnik. During the war, Chętnik lived in Warsaw and kept a diary. In the spring of 1942, he recorded an increase in terror directed against the Jews. Although Chętnik did not know it at the time, the murders and executions in the ghettos were just a prelude to the Holocaust, which would begin within days. He wrote the following:

> [The] Polish nation, brought up in the Christian spirit, would not know how to persecute the Jews in a similarly cruel way, even if it wanted to do so. We did boycott Jewish trade, in defense of trade and the national good, but in our country, Jews were treated as people, not victimized. The Germans approach the matter in accordance with the broken swastika—heathenishly. As for the Jews, the matter in general is still complicated. What would happen to them after the war? Somehow, we do not hear anything about selecting some island or a country for the Jews where they could settle. And cultural societies may not accept their parasitic life and preying on other nations. After what happened in Poland occupied by the Bolsheviks (or rather the Judeocommune), it is difficult to trust them, much less consider them fellow citizens.[35]

34 Aurelia Wyleżyńska, *Kroniki wojenne, 1939–1944*, 2 vols. (Warsaw: Państwowy Instytut Wydawniczy, 2022).

35 Adam Chętnik, *Wspomnienia z lat okupacji* (Warsaw: Muzeum Historii Polskiego Ruchu Ludowego, 2014), pp. 97–98.

Patriotic Policemen

A report by cell 993 of the AK counterintelligence states that on April 16, 1944, four German soldiers, deserters from the eastern front, appeared at the Warsaw-East railway station. The deserters approached the Blue policemen on duty at the station and began asking how they could join the Polish partisans. "The policemen directed them to the Świetokrzyskie Mountains," the author of the report commented.[36] *Se non è vero, è ben trovato.* It is difficult to say whether the event described actually took place, but the sabotage of German orders by the Blue policemen went hand in hand with their commitment to the work of the underground. According to various estimates, a significant percentage of Blue policemen were involved in the underground movement. German liaison officers estimated that group of officers with underground links at about 30 percent of the entire force, and Commander Aleksander Reszczyński claimed in 1942 that almost half of his subordinates were involved in the resistance.

The situation of the Blue policemen who found themselves between the rock of German terror and the hard place of increasing pressure from the Polish Underground State is particularly evident when we take a closer look at the police station in Żarnowiec in Miechów County. In January and May of 1943, the outpost faced two attacks by the partisan units of the People's Guard (Gwardia Ludowa). In January, the post was seized, and in May, the Germans had managed to bring reinforcements. As Marek Getter writes, "Most of the local police force [serving in Miechów County] were deeply involved with the underground. The crew of the Żarnowiec post was executed to the last man for offering no resistance to the People's Guard partisans who had attacked the post."[37] Dariusz

36 Report by cell 993, April 17, 1944, AAN, AK, 203-III-111, p. 43. The codename "993" refers to a police section in the Security and Counterintelligence Department within Branch II of the Information and Intelligence Division of the Home Army headquarters. There was also a section called 993/W, which was a separate liquidation branch in charge of carrying out death sentences.

37 Marek Getter, "Policja polska w Generalnym Gubernatorstwie 1939–1945," *Przegląd Policyjny*, 1–2 (1999), pp. 74–91.

Libionka adds that after the attack on the Żarnowiec station, the Germans shot six policemen.[38] Perhaps the scale of the repression shocked the officers, and the lesson was learned, because a year later, on May 5, 1944, the Directorate of Underground Resistance (Kierownictwo Walki Podziemnej, KWK) issued a statement saying that two policemen from the same Żarnowiec police station—Jan Blaszka and Franciszek Sochacki—were sentenced to death by the Special Civil Court (*Specjalny Sąd Cywilny*) of the Kielce-Radom district for denouncing Poles who were members of independence organizations. Both sentences were carried out.[39]

Evidence of the increasing involvement of the Blue policemen in underground work as well as the growing repressions of the occupying authorities can be seen with the arrest of Kraków Blue Police commanders, Majors Franciszek Erhardt and Ludwik Drożański, in November 1943.[40] At that time, several dozen Blue policemen were also arrested, and after torture during the investigation in Montelupich Prison, many of them were shot at the Płaszów camp. More detailed information on this subject can be found in the archives of the Health Office in Kraków, where several protocols on the examination of the bodies of executed policemen have been preserved.[41]

There is no doubt that the years 1943–1944 were a time of increased involvement of the Blue Police officers in underground activities. From the point of view of this study, however, the most important question is the connection between the patriotic activity of the Polish officers and their attitude toward both the hidden Jews and those who hid them. As the surviving sources suggest, that connection was neither simple nor obvious. The chapter on ghetto liquidations in this volume mentioned the commander of the Polish police in Działoszyce. Abraham Langner, the previously mentioned Jewish survivor from Działoszyce, recalled a certain

38 Libionka, "Powiat miechowski," p. 145.

39 Clippings from the Polish underground press 1943–1944, KWK, May 5, 1944, Ghetto Fighters's House Archive (GFH), Adolf Berman collection, 5853, p. 199.

40 Banaś, *Moje wspomnienia*, pp. 141–143.

41 Records of the deceased, Health Office in Kraków, ANKr, 29/83/345. I am grateful to Dagmara Swałtek-Niewińska for providing this information.

Całowan, "a fellow with crooked legs, a dangerous murderer,"[42] who, against the orders of the Germans, called for the murder of Jews during the liquidation of the town. Całowan—as mentioned by Langner above—has already been discussed in this volume because this man was, in fact, Piotr Sałabun, a Polish police sergeant with over twenty years of experience who had joined the police force in 1919, a well-liked man, and quite respected.[43]

With the outbreak of war, Sałabun was found in Radziechów, 70 kilometers northeast of his native Lwów. Soon after the September defeat, Sałabun escaped behind the border to the area under German occupation, where in 1941, he made contact with Lieutenant Colonel Roman Sztaba, one of the commanders of the Blue Police in the Kraków district and also the head of the underground Security Corps of the Union of Armed Struggle (ZWZ) in Kraków. If Sałabun is to be believed, it was Lieutenant Colonel Sztaba who nominated him for the rank of second lieutenant of the police and gave him the conspiratorial codename "Wiktor." In the following years, Sałabun served as the commander of the police station in Sancygniów (during the occupation, *Kreishauptmannschaft* Miechów), in Działoszyce itself, and in 1943, he was promoted to deputy county commander in Miechów, where he served until the end of the war. As far as the murders of the Jews were concerned, after the war he claimed that it was a blatant lie: Not only did the commander never murder any Jews, but he rescued and protected them. Initially, the case was supposed to be examined by the court in Kielce, but in the aftermath of the Kielce pogrom in 1946, it was taken over by the Regional Court in Kraków. On February 22, 1949, a hearing was held there.

The flattering portrayal of Piotr Sałabun's service was not shared by Chaim Jakubowicz, a cobbler who was born near Pińczów and testified several years after the war:

42 "Abraham Langner," in *Działoszyce Memorial Book*, pp. 332–333. See also his testimony from February 13, 1949, AIPN Ki, 128/209, p. 130.

43 Suspect interrogation report, February 4, 1948, AIPN Ki, 128/206, pp. 4–6.

On March 21, 1943, I saw with my own eyes how Sałabun shot Saul Rafałowicz from Działoszyce, who was wounded during the manhunt. During this *Aktion* seventeen people were killed. On May 17, 1943, during a hunt for Jews organized by Sałabun (he himself led the manhunt on horseback), three of my sisters, Fajgla, Salka, and Ruchla, as well as my two brothers, Abram and Zelman, Dawid, who was four years old, and my cousin Hanka, were captured near the village of Podrózie and shot in the field of Mr. Ciesielski.[44]

Piotr Sałabun identity card issued on September 21, 1940.
AIPN Ki, 128/206.

Jakubowicz, who joined a Jewish partisan unit, provided several other examples of cruel murders committed by the deputy commander of the Miechów Blue Police. Jewish partisans and their families were killed one by one:

44 Chaim Jakubowicz testimony, Piotr Sałabun trial, 1948–1963, AIPN Ki, 128/206–212.

> Rywel Federman with his family and others. After shooting them, Sałabun forced Polish civilians to bury the murdered, and Federman's wife, who was still alive, was also buried. During the next manhunt, during the battle in the Królewskie Forests, Citizen Izrael Łaźniarz (a partisan) was captured, chained to a wagon, tortured, and murdered. On Sałabun's orders, the captured partisan, Citizen Kirchenbaum, was murdered. During Sałabun's activity, our Jewish population was killed. On November 9, 1943, Sałabun and his police force captured the former commander of a group of Jewish partisans, Herman Paliwoda (whom Sałabun knew personally because he used to sew fur for him), his fiancée Różycka, and his brother Dawid Szmul. Różycka and Dawid Szmul were shot in the presence of Sałabun, and Paliwoda was taken to the police station, where under torture he had to hand over the money we had (dollars and gold), and then he was shot by Sałabun in the Grabina Forest.[45]

Jakub Stróż, who hid near Działoszyce after the liquidation of the ghetto, had similar things to say about Sałabun. "People warned me more than once that Sałabun rides through the fields on horseback with policemen and takes farmers to help and they shoot the Jews."[46] In February 1949, Estera Federman, who survived the Holocaust in Poland, was in a DP camp in Germany. In 1942–1943, she and her two brothers had been hiding in the village of Chałupki in Pińczów County. Upon hearing of Sałabun's impending trial, she gave a brief testimony before a German notary, in which she described some of the actions of the Działoszyce policeman. In February 1943, Sałabun knocked on the door of Woźniak's house, where Estera Federman was hiding, demanding that the Jews be handed over: "Hand over all the Jews and no harm will come to you," he assured Woźniak. The farmer refused and the search yielded no results. Soon, Sałabun appeared in the neighboring village of Lipówka and personally shot eleven Jews found there. Four weeks later, he found

45 Ibid.

46 Jakub Stróż testimony, Piotr Sałabun trial, 1948–1963, AIPN Ki, 128/206–212.

six Jews in the village of Zielona, whom he also shot.[47] Juda Sarna, who was also in the Działoszyce ghetto during the war, saw "at the corner of Krakówska Street that [Sałabun] pulled Aron Chabe, a crippled man who could not keep up with the rest, out of a column marching to the train station and shot him." He then ordered Juda Sarna's brother to pull the corpse aside.[48]

In 1943, Franciszka Stróżka was twenty-five years old. After the liquidation of the Warsaw ghetto, she escaped from the city and took refuge in the vicinity of Działoszyce. Blessed with the correct appearance and armed with decent Aryan papers, the young woman successfully passed for a Pole. In the spring of 1943, Commander Sałabun, followed by four or five Blue policemen, arrived on horseback in Świerczyna, where she was living at the time. Sałabun dragged the Jewish Grześ family out of a nearby barn. Franciszka Stróżka testifies that after a thorough search of their hiding place, Sałabun ordered the Jews to line up over a previously dug grave:

> [He] ordered the Grześ family to undress, and when one of the women refused, he hit her over the head with the butt of a revolver, and then ordered one of the policemen to shoot them, and the policeman shot everyone in turn. There was a man killed then, two women and a child of two or maybe four years old...I saw the killing of the Grześ family from a distance of a few steps, even though I was Jewish, in the village I was believed to be Musiał's sister...no one in the village knew that I was Jewish.[49]

On January 4, 1949, the Regional Court in Kraków received a letter from Norbert Michta, a member of the Armia Ludowa (AL) during the war, who reported that in February 1944, the AL sentenced Sałabun to death for the murder of Jews and Poles. However, some influential members of the Działoszyce

47 Estera Federman testimony, Piotr Sałabun trial, 1948–1963, AIPN Ki, 128/206–212.

48 Juda Sarna testimony, Piotr Sałabun trial, 1948–1963, AIPN Ki, 128/206–212.

49 Franciszka Stróżka, Piotr Sałabun trial, 1948–1963, AIPN Ki, 128/206–212.

intelligentsia viewed Sałabun's wartime activities from a completely different perspective. A document presented at the trial reads as follows:

> We certify that Citizen Sałabun Piotr, whose patriotic attitude towards all Polish citizens and whose police activity during the entire German occupation we know and remember well, has always been a good Pole...in the eyes of all Polish citizens of the town of Działoszyce and in almost the entire county, he has always been considered a patriot and a good Pole.[50]

Fourteen citizens of Działoszyce signed the statement, including the local parish priest Franciszek Madej, two pharmacists, a stationmaster, a doctor, and two clerks. In short, the entire elite of Działoszyce.

As time passed—the case went on for many years and passed through various courts—the voices of the Jewish witnesses who spoke about the murders committed by Sałabun quieted down. Most of the survivors fled Poland. The only one who persistently appeared in court—even as late as 1951—and testified against Sałabun was Chaim Jakubowicz. However, his voice was becoming more and more isolated. At the same time, the merits of Commander Sałabun, who "did no harm to anyone," were emphasized more and more emphatically.[51] In September 1950, the Presidium of the National Council in Skalbmierz issued a certificate of civic morality to Sałabun in which we read: "In the years 1941 and 1942 [the defendant] was a good Pole, he warned citizens of impending searches, he cooperated with the underground movement in supplying underground press, weapons, and ammunition."[52] During the trial in 1951, Polish witnesses unanimously claimed that Sałabun had no part in the murder of Jews and that the Polish policemen did not have to shoot anyone during the liquidation of Działoszyce, "because the

50 Trial document, Piotr Sałabun trial, 1948–1963, AIPN Ki, 128/206–212.

51 Trial testimonies, Piotr Sałabun trial, 1948–1963, AIPN, Ki, 128/206-212.

52 Certificate of civic morality, Piotr Sałabun trial, 1948–1963, AIPN, Ki, 128/206-212.

Jews voluntarily reported to the town hall, from where they were taken to a camp."[53]

However, it was not only ethnic Poles who came out in defense of commander Sałabun. Dr. Andrzej Zieliński, who had to hide due to his non-Aryan ancestry, as he testified after the war, was referred to Sałabun by Lieutenant Colonel Roman Sztaba himself. According to Zieliński, Sałabun not only took care of him but he even had false papers prepared for him and his wife.[54] The most important witness to the defense of the Blue policeman, however, was probably Dr. Fabian Szlang, a journalist from Kraków, who was also "racially handicapped," as they used to say during the occupation. Szlang spent over two years under Sałabun's roof, helping the commander with official correspondence in German.[55] On the other hand, Stanisław Brodziński, the secretary of the Polish Workers' Party in Miechów during the war, testified against Sałabun. He confirmed that the defendant had participated in capturing Jews in hiding,[56] while Ludomir Wróbel, a farmer from Pińczów, described Sałabun as "a tormentor of Poles and Jews."[57]

In 1951, the Provincial Court (*Sąd Wojewódzki*) in Kielce sentenced Sałabun to twelve years in prison. The sentence was upheld by the Supreme Court in 1952. Five years later, as a result of an extraordinary appeal by the attorney general of the Polish People's Republic, the Supreme Court ordered a retrial. The statement reads as follows:

> The defendant selflessly provided considerable help to Jews, namely to the Zieliński family, and above all to Szlang. Also to others, as evidenced by the testimonies of Lis, Zawiert, Czekaj, Ordyński, Kaczmarczyk, and Winierski. As a member

53 Trial testimonies, Piotr Sałabun trial, 1948–1963, AIPN, Ki, 128/206-212.

54 Andrzej Zieliński testimony, April 14, 1948, Piotr Sałabun trial, 1948–1963, AIPN, Ki, 128/206-212, p. 133.

55 Dr. Fabian Szlang testimony, Piotr Sałabun trial, 1948–1963, AIPN Ki, 128/206–212.

56 Stanisław Brodziński testimony, Piotr Sałabun trial, 1948–1963, AIPN Ki, 128/206–212.

57 Ludomir Wróbel testimony, Piotr Sałabun trial, 1948–1963, AIPN Ki, 128/206–212.

> of the ZWZ and the AK during the occupation, the defendant helped these organizations by engaging in activities that were extremely damaging to the occupier. In the house of the defendant, clandestine classes were held, and he provided weapons and ammunition.[58]

In 1958, the Provincial Court in Kielce sentenced Sałabun to five and a half years' imprisonment, stating that while the defendant had helped some Jews, he had committed vast injustice against others. This was not the end of the Miechów policeman's court battles. Two years later, a higher court rejected the testimony of the Jewish witnesses as unreliable—in the meantime, as mentioned above, the Jews who had given testimony incriminating Sałabun had left Poland—and the former Blue policeman was acquitted, clearing him of the charges. As evidenced by Piotr Sałabun's case, murder and rescue did not have to occur separately. One could be a patriot, a member of the underground, and a cruel murderer of Jews simultaneously. The documents and testimonies abound with examples of the evolution of such attitudes—from rescuer to murderer, from murderer to rescuer—or, indeed, of their coexistence, as in the case of Sałabun.

Sergeant Władysław Królik was on duty at the station of Grębków, a small village situated north of the Warsaw-Siedlce Road. The commander of the Grębków post was the then-Sergeant Adolf Bielecki, and his subordinates included Antoni Iwanek, Jan Grajewski, Piotr Grochal (deputy commander), the aforementioned Królik, Sałek, and Babulewicz (first names unknown), Lucjan Marciniak, and several other officers.[59] At the end of 1943—the exact date has not been established—Commander Bielecki was "confidentially" informed that in the village of Gałki, there were Jews hiding in the house of

58 Supreme Court statement, Piotr Sałabun trial, 1948–1963, AIPN Ki, 128/206–212.

59 Antoni Iwanek indictment, November 18, 1949, AIPN, GK 317/133, pp. 4–4v, 36–38. Iwanek had served in the police force before the war from 1920 in Węgrów County. A more extensive discussion of this case can be found in Engelking and Grabowski, *Dalej jest noc,* vol. 1, pp. 501–508.

Aleksandra Janusz. Having arrived there, Deputy Commander Grochal looked under the floor and dragged out nine Jews, who had previously lived in nearby Kałuszyn: the Rubins and their child, Mrs. Kajzer, Gurszyn (whose name is barely legible on the interrogation protocol), and others whose names cannot be determined today.[60] If his own explanations given later during the investigation are to be believed, Officer Iwanek advised Commander Bielecki to let the Jews go, but the latter ordered the killing of the captives.[61] Aleksandra Janusz, in whose house the Jews were hiding, recalled the search somewhat differently. She testified about what took place after entering the house:

> [Królik and Iwanek] asked me where the "poodles" were. I asked them what "poodles" they meant, because I didn't know what they were talking about, so they said, "They're here, they're here," and then Królik took a pitchfork and went to an adjacent empty apartment, where there was a cellar covered with manure and where nine Jews were hidden.[62]

Upon seeing the Jews coming out of their hiding place, Królik laughed, "Well, well, Mr. Rubin, I know you, you're from Kałuszyn, you made shoes for me; I won't do anything to you, I'll just take you out there, near the forest, and there we'll fire a few shots and you'll run away, I won't shoot you!"[63] After a while, four more policemen appeared in Mrs. Janusz's house, and the smiling Królik was seen by Janusz's daughter taking a wad of banknotes from his acquaintance Mr. Rubin, the shoemaker. Then, three

60 Minutes of the main hearing against Grochal, Babulewicz, and others, April 17, 1952, AIPN, GK 318/460, vol. 1, pp. 147–165. Piotr Grochal was a police officer with prewar experience who had served since 1934.

61 Iwanek defended himself somewhat unconvincingly: "I discussed with the commander what to do with them, because if the Germans found out, they would have killed us too." He did not really explain why the Germans should kill Polish policemen simply because Jews were discovered. See minutes of the main hearing against Antoni Iwanek, January 17, 1950, AIPN, GK 317/133, p. 37v.

62 Aleksandra Janusz testimony, April 22, 1949, AIPN, GK 317/134, pp. 5–6.

63 Ibid.

policemen led the Jews toward the forest from where a series of shots soon reached the ears of the Gałki residents. Some time later, the policemen returned to the village, and Królik asked the landlady to give them water, because they needed to wash blood from their hands. Finally, Iwanek tried to extort 3,000 zlotys from Mrs. Janusz, "for having harbored the Jews."[64] However, it did not end there. Two weeks later, bandits claiming to be police officers showed up at Mrs. Janusz's house. "Some bogus policemen came to my apartment, ransacked all the bedding, trunks and everything that was upstairs, looking for gold. I was in the fields with my children at the time."[65]

What conclusions, albeit very preliminary, can one come to after learning about the fate of the Rubins from Kałuszyn? What first draws attention is the omnipresent denunciation that was dangerous for both the Jews and the Poles who were hiding them. Second, the greed of so-called Jewish riches or the mythical Jewish gold is seen as a motive, even if it was ostensibly secreted in the pockets of a poor shoemaker from Kałuszyn. The desire for "Jewish riches" was derivative of antisemitic clichés that were ubiquitous in Polish society on many levels. Third, it sheds light on the considerable degree of agency that characterized the actions of Polish officers, who in so-called Jewish-related matters could make their own decisions to detain, rob, and shoot their victims without any order from their German superiors or without the latter learning about the murders. Finally, it is clear that Polish policemen did not kill strangers: Very often, as in the discussed case, they murdered their own neighbors whom they had known well and for some years.

Władysław Królik himself is an unusual character: His personal file, which luckily survived in the decimated archives of the *SS- und Polizei Gericht* (SS and Police Court), includes accolades from his German superiors. They wrote, for example, that "Królik is an efficient, energetic, and brave policeman."[66] Królik, a murderer of Jews, was also praised by his superiors from the underground

64 Ibid.

65 Ibid.

66 Personal file of Władysław Królik from Grębków, Bundesarchiv Berlin-Lichterfelde, SS- und Polizei Gericht VI, Krakau, NS/7, file 1185, p. 8.

because, aside from his service in the Blue Police, he was a patriot and a soldier of the II Department (codename "Smoła" [Tar]) of the Home Army (AK)—intelligence and counterintelligence.[67] Królik, alongside Grochal who accompanied him during the murder of the Jews, was even described by the chronicler of the Węgrów underground movement as a man who represented "the best and most idealistic human element of all walks of life."[68] No wonder that Officer Królik enjoyed the widespread respect of his Polish neighbors, as evidenced by letters in his defense sent at the end of the 1940s to the Court of Appeals in Warsaw.[69]

The Banality of Evil in Ciężkowice

Hannah Arendt titled her famous essay on the Eichmann trial, *Eichmann in Jerusalem: A Report on the Banality of Evil.*[70] With such a title, even those who have never held the book in their hands know more or less what the author is proposing. If Arendt is to be believed, Eichmann—one of the architects of the "Final Solution to the Jewish Question" and Heydrich's right-hand man in Jewish

67 Tadeusz Wangrat, *Polska i powiat węgrowski w przededniu i w czasie II wojny światowej* (Węgrów: Światowy Związek Żolnierzy AK Obwód "Smoła," 2010), pp. 56–57. In the AK, Królik served together with Józef Dominiak and Edward Podgórniak. He was also highly praised as a patriot who fought banditry.

68 Jan Gozdawa-Gołębiowski, "Powiat Węgrowski w latach okupacji hitlerowskiej 1939–1944," in Arkadiusz Kołodziejczyk and Tadeusz Swat, eds., *Węgrów: Dzieje miasta i okolic w latach 1441–1944* (Węgrów: Towarzystwo Miłośników Ziemi Węgrowskiej, 1991), p. 347. It should be added, however, that opinions about Królik were divided. Another witness wrote the following to the authorities after the war: "The favorite and inseparable trio of Królik, Grochal, and Marciniak, whose most favorite activity was hunting for hiding people." Report prepared by Stanisław Michałowski from the village of Gałki, Grębków Commune, January 17, 1945, AIPN, BU 0255/327, pp. 5–6.

69 Władysław Królik was found guilty by the court on various counts of murder committed against Jews, Poles, and Soviet POWs, and he received a death sentence that was later commuted to life imprisonment. He was released from prison in 1959. See Judgment, October 27, 1952, AIPN, GK 318/126, pp. 850–870.

70 Hannah Arendt, *Eichmann in Jerusalem: A Report on the Banality of Evil* (London: Penguin, 2022).

affairs—was a well-trained bureaucrat, who had been given a task and did his best to fulfill it. Unsurprisingly, this was the version of events that Eichmann himself presented when he was tried in Jerusalem in 1961, and this interpretation was creatively developed by Hannah Arendt. Unfortunately, however, as tempting as such an interpretation may seem, in the case of Eichmann, it is simply false. Adolf Eichmann was a devout antisemite all his adult life, and his hatred of Jews went far beyond what his official duties required.

After the war, in exile in Argentina, Eichmann recorded his memories for posterity. In one of the surviving tapes, the *SS-Obersturmbannführer* says that his greatest achievement, his greatest triumph in life, was the deportation of almost half a million Hungarian Jews to the Auschwitz death camp before the end of the war, in the spring and summer of 1944. His most painful defeat, he said, was in Belgium, when the trains had already been prepared for the deportation of the Jews but departed even though they "weren't full," as Eichmann put it.[71] If one were to search for an example of a true case of banality of evil, a closer look at Corporal Czesław Zander who served at the Blue Police station in Ciężkowice would be in order.

Already mentioned earlier in this work, Zander was born near Poznań and started his career in the police in 1920. Until 1939, he served at the police station in Bydgoszcz. After Bydgoszcz was annexed to the Reich, he lost his position and was unemployed, like all Polish policemen in the incorporated territories. He saw a return to his profession in the fall of 1941, when he was sent by the Germans to the Generalgouvernement, where he began his service in the Blue Police. To be more precise, he was sent to Ciężkowice, halfway between Tarnów and Nowy Sącz. Thus, Zander was not a volunteer from the wartime enlistment but an officer with almost twenty years experience in the police force of the Second Polish Republic. As evidenced by documents attached to the postwar trial, he was also a man in his fifties who had settled down and was a married father of three children.

71 For more on Eichmann's Argentine confessions, see Bettina Stangneth, *Eichmann Before Jerusalem* (New York: Vintage Books, 2014).

In 1942, Zander and other local policemen started to deal with the "Jewish question" increasingly more often in their work. Although there were very few Jews in Ciężkowice, nearby Bobowa—also part of Zander's domain—had almost 700 Jewish residents before the war. In both towns, the Polish police were the sole authority: German gendarmes appeared there only rarely, coming from the posts in Gorlice or Jasło on "special errands." Between the fall of 1941 and the summer of 1942, another 700 Jews from neighboring localities were sent to the Bobowa ghetto, so that on the eve of the liquidation, almost 1,400 people were living there in appalling conditions.[72] The ghetto in Bobowa was liquidated on August 14, 1942. Several dozens of people were murdered in the streets, and another 700 were killed in a mass execution in a nearby forest. The rest were sent to the labor camp of Szebnie and to the death camp of Bełżec. The few who managed to survive escaped to the Aryan side. It was at that point when the skills of Zander and his companions from the police post in Ciężkowice proved especially valuable from the point of view of the occupying authorities but particularly dangerous from the perspective of the Jewish victims. And there could have been many Jewish victims, as the local Jews were joined by those escaping from the large ghetto in Tarnów, which had been liquidated over the course of three operations from June 1942 to September 1943.

Some years after the war, several inhabitants of Ciężkowice spoke about Officer Zander's attitude to the "Final Solution to the Jewish Question." The best approach when examining the process of radicalization and brutalization of the Bydgoszcz policeman is to listen to the eyewitnesses of those events. One day, at the time when the Germans were liquidating local ghettos, Bronisława Piskorska was on her way home from work:

> As I was walking to the bridge on the Biała River, on that bridge I saw a Blue policeman who served at the station in Ciężkowice,

72 Among the displaced were 160 Jews from Gorlice and sixty Jews from Oświęcim. See "Bobowa," in Megargee, *The United States Holocaust Memorial Museum Encyclopedia of Camps and Ghettos, 1933–1945*, pp. 487–488.

a certain Czesław Zander, who, during my encounter with him, was leading an unknown Jew along that bridge. As I was walking past this Jew led by the "Blue" policeman Zander, I saw that the Jew had his hands clasped around the neck and the escorting policeman Zander was walking in close proximity to the Jew. After crossing the bridge, [as I was] passing this escorted Jew, at that moment, the Jew started to run away in the direction of the marketplace in Ciężkowice, where at that time, I did not want to look. I was shocked when I heard shots after this Jew and during those shots there was a great rush, where again some policeman ran in [two illegible words] in the same direction of those shots toward the marketplace, and at that time, out of fear, I did not stop but went home. When I came home, a moment later I found out that the Jew led by Zander had been shot at the marketplace.[73]

Czesław Zander (left), Ciężkowice, April 12, 1942.
ANKr, SAKr, 979/IVK/230/4.

73 Bronisława Piskorska testimony, criminal proceedings in the case of Czesław Zander, ANKr, SAKr, 979/IV/230/49.

Marian Chołowczyc, a young railroad worker, was also on his way home from work, walking on the same road, at the same time, and on the same bridge:

> When I was on the bridge over the Biała River, I noticed that an unknown man was running away through the marketplace, chased by [Officer] Zander, who served at the Ciężkowice post. The escaping man was running in the direction of nearby bushes that grow by the Biała River, and he took off his jacket to make it easier for him to run. Policeman Zander crouched on his knee several times shooting after the fleeing man with a handgun. The fleeing man was gravely wounded, and he fell to the ground just as he reached the bushes. Policeman Zander ran toward the prone man, who was lying by the bushes, and as soon as he reached him, one shot was heard with which he probably killed the man. I observed the abovementioned incident from a distance of about 50 meters.[74]

"The abovementioned incident" was observed by many other people, whose names Chołowczyc did not recall, but who were residents of nearby houses, according to the witness. After shooting the man, Zander headed slowly to the police station, and a man named Sosenkowski appeared by the murdered Jew. He was another Blue policeman and Zander's colleague, who had rushed over at the sound of the shots. Chołowczyc continues his testimony as follows:

> People started coming slowly to the spot where the dead man was lying, and I also went there. There, lying in a pool of blood, I saw a man who had been killed. This man could have been about thirty years old, and from his facial features, it was obvious that he was of Jewish nationality, which was also confirmed by the stories told by that policeman Zander and the locals who said that this Jew had escaped from the

74 Marian Chołowczyc, criminal proceedings in the case of Czesław Zander, ANKr, SAKr, 979/IV/230/49.

> ghetto in Tarnów. A local gravedigger named Charazy buried the dead man on the spot where he had been shot by order of the police.[75]

One of the many people on the bridge over the Biała River that day was Genowefa Czernek, who was there at that time "on some errand" and was also a witness to the same scene. She testified as follows:

> When I reached the bridge over the Biała River, coming from the other side I saw a policeman named Zander Czesław, who was leading another man, whom I recognized as a Jew. But this Jew was walking at a distance of three paces from Zander and had his hands clasped behind his neck. Behind him was Zander, the policeman, holding his rifle forward ready to fire. When they got closer to the marketplace, while still on the bridge, Zander ordered an unknown man (the Jew) to go faster, telling him: "Run!" After that order, the man moved quickly, going toward the marketplace. At that moment, I suddenly heard gunshots, and when I looked back, I saw only fire after the gunshot…there were three such shots. The man was shot by Zander. It was a Jew who was lying by the bushes. I didn't go any further because I couldn't bear it. I stopped on the road and saw people undressing the killed Jew.[76]

Another execution took place in the cemetery in Ciężkowice. This time, Zander drove five people to the shooting. One of the victims was a woman:

> [The officer] ordered [her] to kneel over the grave. The woman pleaded with Zander that she had children and that she was not guilty at all. At that point Zander paid no attention to her,

75 Ibid.

76 Genowefa Czernek, criminal proceedings in the case of Czesław Zander, ANKr, SAKr, 979/IV/230/49.

> ordered her to take off her sheepskin, and turn the other way. At that time, when the woman turned around, Zander shot her with a shotgun.[77]

Quite obviously by the fall of 1942, killing Jews had become part of the routine of the Polish police officers in Ciężkowice, Bobowa, and the surrounding areas. According to the Poles who lived there, executions occurred frequently. Sometimes they were carried out by Germans, sometimes by mixed Polish-German patrols, and sometimes as independent activities of the Ciężkowice Blue Police, an example of which is the capturing and shooting of two Jews hiding in the buildings belonging to the farmer Władysław Śliwa. According to his neighbors, it was the farmer himself who betrayed the Jews:

> It is presumed that it [the betrayal] was done by Śliwa, because people feared that he had been harboring the Jews, and in addition it happened in his yard, and Czesław Zander often visited him, i.e., Śliwa. However, it is clear that it was Zander who shot them together with Topor [another policeman], because on that day there were no Germans or Polnische Polizei [officers] in the village of Bruśnik.[78] After shooting them, Ludwik Wójcik drove the Jews from Bruśnik to Bobowa.[79]

Referring to yet another murder, one of the local Poles noted, "After carrying out such executions, Zander was very happy and immediately went for a beer."[80] After the war and following a long trial, Zander was sentenced to eight years in prison. He was released under amnesty in 1956. According to the assessments by various

77 Bronisława Iskańska testimony, September 30, 1949, criminal proceedings in the case of Czesław Zander, ANKr, SAKr, 979/IV/230/49, pp. 205-205v.

78 Bruśnik is a village 6 kilometers from Ciężkowice.

79 Władysław Śliwa neighbor's testimony, criminal proceedings in the case of Czesław Zander, ANKr, SAKr, 979/IV/230/49.

80 Witness testimony, criminal proceedings in the case of Czesław Zander, ANKr, SAKr, 979/IV/230/49.

authorities attached to the case file, he was a widely respected man with a reputation of a "good Pole."[81]

How can we understand this rapid transformation of an ordinary Polish policeman like Czesław Zander into an unscrupulous and merciless murderer of innocent people? Let us return to the scene on the bridge in Ciężkowice as previously described. It is an autumn afternoon, a lot of people are heading home after work, others are minding their own business. On the other side of the river, there is a market square with many passersby and onlookers. A Jew, unknown to anyone, walks along the middle of the bridge, and three steps behind him walks Officer Zander with a loaded gun. The locals do not know the Jew, but one glance is enough for them to determine his racial identity—probably by his facial features. At one point, Zander tells the Jew to run. Apparently, this is some kind of a lethal game: to kill the fleeing Jew. Many such scenes have been described in wartime literature, and there is no point in citing them here now. The Jew, obeying the order, drops his hands, takes off the jacket that restricts his movement, and starts to run away. Ignoring the passersby, Officer Zander kneels, bends down to shoot, and severely wounds the fleeing Jew. Then, he goes up to the man lying there on the ground and kills him with one shot. A moment later, he walks away slowly, in no hurry, not trying to hide, and heads to the police station. The locals gather around after the shots, some are bent over the corpse, others are helping themselves to the clothes of the victim. Finally, the gravedigger buries the corpse right there by the Biała River, near the bridge, in the very center of the village, a few dozen paces from the market square. As was usually the case in villages, the whole scene unfolded without any German involvement.

How is one supposed to understand this? Does it mean that in 1943, after a year of watching the Germans systematically murder the Jews, Jewish life ceased to have any meaning in the eyes of the residents of Ciężkowice? It is quite likely that, at least in the eyes of many Polish witnesses of the Holocaust, Jews became "the deceased

81 Assessment for release under amnesty, criminal proceedings in the case of Czesław Zander, ANKr, SAKr, 979/IV/230/49.

on leave," to once again borrow the expression used by Emanuel Ringelblum. In English-language Holocaust literature, historians often refer to the concept of bystanders, following in the footsteps of Raul Hilberg, the eminent Holocaust scholar. This term has a somewhat unfortunate Polish translation of *świadkowie*, which literally translates as "witnesses."[82] However, the word "bystanders" has a slightly different meaning. It implies a certain distance, a separation, an isolation, and a lack of impact on the observed events. None of the people crossing the bridge over the Biała River that day could be described as a bystander.[83] Each of them was a participating observer involved in the murder of an innocent man. Each of them in their own way had to relate to the events unfolding before their eyes and choose a response: to react, to look away, to walk away, or to stay. As far as Officer Zander is concerned, it could be said that in the fall of 1943, after a year of hunting Jews, murdering innocent people must have become an everyday occurrence for him, in some way coming naturally to him. The fact that it was possible for him to carry out a cruel execution in the center of town, in broad daylight, and in front of everyone is in itself proof that there had been a moral breakdown in society, the scale of which we cannot even begin to comprehend today.

Zander's act was not an isolated one. Many other police officers who have featured and will feature in this book behaved just like him. It is impossible to list them all here, but their actions replicate the same pattern in a painfully similar manner. The following incident took place in Zabierzów, near Kraków:

> Sometime in early October 1942, at noon, I was digging potatoes with the women. After a while...we suddenly heard shots from about a kilometer away. After a short while, we noticed a man running from the west to the east, along a

82 The French translation is equally unfortunate: *témoin*, which also means "witness."

83 A broader and more innovative discussion of this topic can be found in Elżbieta Janicka, "Obserwatorzy uczestniczący zamiast świadków i rama zamiast obrzeży: O nowe kategorie opisu polskiego kontekstu Zagłady," *Teksty Drugie*, 3 (2018), pp. 131–147.

> dirt path. When the man came closer, I recognized him as a Jew from Zabierzów named Szmul Metzendorf. The Jew was running at a distance of about fifty paces from us. As the Jew was approaching us, I noticed that a Blue policeman, Adolf Mierzwa from the Zabierzów post, was riding his bicycle on the same dirt path behind the fleeing man, with a rifle slung across his back. At one point, Officer Mierzwa jumped off his bicycle, threw it to the side, and began chasing the fleeing Jew on foot. After a few steps, the tired Jew stopped, and then Officer Mierzwa ran to him, grabbed him by the collar, kicked him in the back with his foot, and ordered him to run away. When the Jew Metzendorf started to run away, Officer Mierzwa fired three shots at him with his rifle, causing the instant death of Szmul Metzendorf, who fell to the ground.[84]

The described event is in many ways similar to the execution in Ciężkowice. The policeman carried out the murder in a public place, in daytime, in the presence of many people, and in front of villagers who not only observed the execution but were also able to identify the victim, unlike in Ciężkowice. One can assume that Officer Mierzwa could also have known Metzendorf as they hailed from the same village. However, the murder of an acquaintance or a neighbor—as long as the man was Jewish—was an act that was clearly just a part of everday life, perhaps even the norm, under occupation. Officers Ratajczak, Gaweł, and Kuczek, policemen from the station in Niepołomice near Kraków, acted no differently: After catching a local peasant who was hiding a Jew, they started to torture both victims, and whenever they lost consciousness, they were woken up with buckets of water. In the end, they shot both the Pole and the Jew. The purpose of the interrogation and torture was to extract information from the Jew about where he had hidden money.[85] A Polish witness

84 Files on the cases of Antoni Andrzejewski, Adolf Mierzwa, and Jan Ratajczak; and Edward Burkot testimony, March 16, 1946, AIPN, GK 164/6036, as quoted in Dagmara Swałtek-Niewińska, "Powiat bocheński," in *Dalej jest noc*, vol. 2, pp. 612–613.

85 *Z granatowego bagna*, November 30, 1943, AAN, AK, 203-VIII-2, p. 9.

claimed that Blue policemen near Proszowice murdered Jews in an equally public and open manner:

> The Blue policemen stopped several Jewish women, who were fleeing from the direction of Proszowice. As I heard from people whose names I don't recall, one of those Jewish women was covering her eyes with an apron when they were shooting her. The Jewish women were shot in the Bińczyckie fields near the river, next to Bronisława Kaczorowska's mill, and were buried there.[86]

The situation was somewhat different in the case of a murder committed against a native Pole, a fellow countryman "of flesh and blood." Here, the ties of social solidarity, however weakened, were still in force and dictated different rules of conduct. More importantly, the murder of a Pole could cost the Blue policeman dearly in the future. Only the most shortsighted officers or the most servile to the occupying authorities did not realize this. In the summer of 1943, a Blue policeman named Stanisław Kanciała from the Węgrów police station went to nearby Korytnica in order to arrest a wanted criminal. Setting out, the policeman mobilized a local peasant with a wagon to help. On his way back to the village of Liw, which is picturesquely situated on the Liwiec River, Kanciała saw a young man coming from the opposite direction on a bicycle. Shouting "Stop!" to the man, Kanciała reached for his rifle and, without waiting for the cyclist's reaction, fired in the direction of the rider. He then put the wounded man on the wagon and drove him to his parents' house, advising them to take the young man to the hospital. The gravely injured man, who turned out to be the innocent son of a local farmer, died of his wounds the next day.[87]

When trying to excuse himself, Kanciała told the distraught father that "he thought the man riding the bicycle was Jewish."[88] In this case, however, Officer Kanciała had made a mistake. The

86 Franciszek Czernek testimony, ANKr, SAKr, 1000/K39/50.

87 Investigation into the case of Stanisław Kanciała, AIPN, GK 318/568.

88 Ibid.

man riding the bicycle was a Pole, and the policeman had to face up to this error in court after the war. The killing of a member of one's own community was an act that could not be convincingly justified both during and after the war. From this point of view, a comparison of testimonies of Polish witnesses in trials involving the murder of Jews with that of testimonies regarding the murder of other Poles is tremendously informative.

A great deal of information about the participation of the Polish police in the hunt for Jews can be gleaned from the underground archive of Oneg Shabbat. Reports from the liquidated provincial ghettos had reached the still-existing ghetto in Warsaw and found their way into the hands of Ringelblum and his associates. Toward the end of 1942, news arrived in Warsaw from the Kraków district:

> In contrast to the "liberal" policy of the SS toward those criminals, it must be emphasized that in the countryside of the so-called Gen[eral] Gov[ernment] this practice [of murder] has taken truly tragic forms.
>
> This particularly concerns the Kraków district, where manhunts for "illegal" Jews take place in villages in the form of real hunts with dogs. The captured "game"—mostly women and children—are escorted to the nearest town, where they are publicly executed in the local Jewish cemetery. The following can serve as an example of this German practice: On December 5, this year, an execution took place at the cemetery in Wolbrom; a group of twenty-nine people surrounded by members of the Blue Police and a crowd of local onlookers were led out to the cemetery. Each of the condemned had to strip naked and lie down on the frozen ground covered with snow and ice. A shot to the head put an end to the suffering of the victims. The executioner was a German gendarme. Twenty-nine boys, girls, women, men, and children were killed that way. The pointless and tragic death of the victims was accompanied by laughter, derision, and words of abuse yelled by the local mob.[89]

89 "Wiadomości [Archiwum Ringelbluma]," no. 3, December 22, 1942, in Aleksandra Bańkowska and Tadeusz Epsztein, eds., *Archiwum Ringelbluma:*

The Hunt for Jews in the Countryside: The Battle of Racławice

Rabbi Józef Guzik was hiding near Dukla in the southeast of the Kraków district. He was aware of the threat that the Polish police posed to him and others in hiding. In his diary, he noted the following:

> Monday, 24 *Adar Aleph* 5703 [March 1, 1943]
>
> [As for] those who wished to flee and escape [from Dukla], there were scoundrels among the townspeople who tipped off the Germans or the Polish police. In particular, the little foxes [Song of Songs 2:15], the filthy vermin, their offspring, what madness gripped the vile and contemptible segment of the nation among which we dwelled that took part in these murders, and whenever they discovered some Jew's hideout, they swiftly betrayed [him].... Oh God, when will the day of these villains and their despicable accomplices come?[90]

A month later, an underground newspaper—judging by its tone, it was most likely the *Biuletyn Informacyjny*—found its way into the hands of Guzik and other Jews in hiding. It urged Poles to help those Jews escaping from ghettos and camps. Guzik wrote the following about this incident:

> It would be proper and worthwhile to give this newspaper to our Polish police. Then they could see what awaits them for their illusory heroism and actions toward the Jews. It would put some sense into them; they might realize that they shouldn't do such things in the future. Or perhaps they're just villains who will not repent even as they stand at the gates of hell.[91]

Konspiracyjne Archiwum Getta Warszawy, vol. 11, Ludzie i prace "Oneg Szabat" (Warsaw: Wydawnictwa Uniwersytetu Warszawskiego, 2013), pp. 267–286.

90 The diary of Rabbi Józef Guzik (original in Hebrew), YVA, O.33/1609, as quoted in Dreifuss, *Relations between Jews and Poles during the Holocaust*, p. 270.

91 Ibid., p. 271.

The "things" the Polish policemen did "toward the Jews," as Rabbi Guzik enigmatically phrased it, was an extension, a supplement, and often a refinement of the German extermination policy. To further explore what the officers in blue uniforms did, it is behooving to look at the post in Racławice in Miechów County, a village that in Polish history is mainly—if not exclusively—associated with the victorious battle against Russian forces fought by Tadeusz Kościuszko in April 1794. It is little known, however, that 150 years later, near the very same village, the Blue Police executed a number of hiding and defenseless Jews.

The Racławice post was not distinguished by any special features. It was simply a typical police station lost in the rural countryside of part of southern Poland known as Małopolska,[92] far away from larger towns and only rarely visited by gendarmes from Miechów. There was also one German serving locally—a man called Kupfer—but as officers' testimonies indicate, he never ventured outside Racławice. His Polish subordinates were entirely in charge of any activity in the field.[93] There were four Polish policemen serving in the area in question, including Stanisław Krawczyk, who acted as the officer in command. In 1943, Commander Krawczyk was forty-six years old. He was born in a town near Kraków and had started his police career in the early 1920s. His subordinate, Corporal Władysław Wesołowski, was born in 1889 and had commenced his police career in 1919. Wesołowski, a married man and father of three, hailed from the Wielkopolska region, and before the war, he served in several police stations in Konin county. He was first encountered in the introduction to this book, when in September 1939, he was complaining about the "disorganization" in the police force, and so he was retreating eastward "toward Warsaw."[94]

92 Małopolska ("Little Poland") is a geographic area in southern Poland. Kraków is its capital.

93 Officers' testimonies, the case of the officers of the Racławice police station (Józef Faryński, Władysław Wesołowski, and Piotr Jaworski), ANKr, SAKr, 1014/IVK/116/50.

94 Deposition of Władysław Wesołowski, April 6, 1949, ANKr, SAKr, 1014/IVK/116/50, p. 10.

After the Polish defeat in September 1939, Wesołowski returned to his hometown, but as he testified after the war, the Germans took him away in December 1939 and put him on police duty in the Generalgouvernement in Kraków, and from there to the Blue Police station in the municipality of Racławice.[95] Born in 1891, Józef Faryński was, like Wesołowski, a policeman with much prewar experience, and he also came from the Września area in Wielkopolska from where he was sent to work in the Generalgouvernement. Like Wesołowski, he was also a family man: He was married with three children. The fourth officer from Racławice, about whom we have some more detailed information, was Bolesław Kalinowski, born in 1896 and a prewar policeman from the area of Toruń.

The hamlet of Miroszów is situated less than 4 kilometers from Racławice. In early May 1943, four Jews from nearby Białoszyce came to the farmer Józef Bielawski's house in Miroszów. Bielawski knew three of them—a woman and two men named Spokojny. He did not know the fourth Jew personally. Over the following month, the Jews hid in the attic above Bielawski's barn. On June 11, 1943, a patrol of the Racławice Blue Police appeared in the village. It consisted of Commander Krawczyk and Officers Faryński and Wesołowski. The policemen had not come to catch Jews. Instead, it was one of the so-called quota patrols, collecting overdue deliveries of grains and meat from the peasants and to impose fines on the reluctant ones. "When we were in Miroszów," Wesołowski testified after the war, "we stopped at Piotr Jaworski's house, and he offered us half a liter of vodka."[96] During the conversation, Jaworski informed Commander Krawczyk that there were Jews hiding in his neighbor Bielawski's house a kilometer away. "After we got the order from Krawczyk, me and Faryński took the Jews to the so-called pits and shot them there."[97] It is worth adding that the policemen did not trouble themselves too much with looking for an isolated place: The "pits" were

95 Ibid.
96 Ibid.
97 Ibid.

only 150 meters from Bielawski's farm buildings. Wesołowski continues as follows:

> I myself, single-handedly, shot one Jewish man with my rifle, then I fired at the other Jewish man, whom Faryński finished off with a shot from his rifle on the ground, when that Jewish man fell over after my shot. Faryński, on the other hand, shot one Jewish man and one Jewish woman and shot the Jew I had wounded and did not kill on the spot. We carried out the shooting from a short distance—3 meters while marching, shooting in the back of the head from behind.[98]

Shooting people in the back of the head was German practice. German policemen were trained to murder civilian victims with a shot to the back of the head. The German language has a special word for such type of shooting: *Genickschuss*. It is difficult to say whether the Polish policemen were also specially trained for that purpose. They had probably become acquainted with the German *Genickschuss* technique during the liquidation of the ghettos in the summer and fall of 1942. After all, the Polish police participated in almost all the liquidation *Aktionen,* and as we have seen, the Blue policemen had no complaints about the lack of opportunities to closely observe German extermination practices. By June 1943, the Polish officers had undoubtedly mastered the various techniques of murdering Jews, using *Genickschuss* at least as skillfully as their erstwhile teachers.[99]

Faryński, who accompanied Wesołowski, remembered slightly more from that afternoon—or perhaps he was able to cite considerably more important details that are useful to a historian trying to make sense of the events in Miroszów. According to Faryński, after Krawczyk led the four Jews out of the barn, the commander allegedly said to Bielawski, "What should we do with them now?" After Bielawski replied that he did not know

98 Ibid.

99 Interrogation of Władysław Wesołowski, April 6, 1949, ANKr, SAKr, 1014/IVK/53/49, K10/50, pp. 57–59.

what to do, Krawczyk—after a moment's reflection—said, "There is nothing else to do but to shoot them, because when we take them to the station, the Germans will shoot them and others with whom they've been staying." Further on, Faryński's version of events corroborates Wesołowski's testimony: The two policemen, having received an order, took the Jews to the pits and killed them there. Finally, Faryński added, "Krawczyk ordered Bielawski to bury them, after that shooting we drank vodka and went to the village mayor, Jan Michta, and Krawczyk ordered him to see to the burying of the shot Jews."[100]

The murder of Jews by the Blue policemen in Miroszów in June 1943 was not an isolated incident. A year later, in June 1944, the German gendarme Kupfer ordered Wesołowski and Kalinowski to go to the village of Kościejów to investigate a report of a robbery. Kościejów was situated halfway between Racławice and Miroszów, where a year earlier, the farmer Bielawski had hidden four Jews. In the vicinity of Kościejów, Wesołowski "came across" some Jews. This time, it was two Jewish women with two children. We know neither the circumstances of the arrest nor who it was that pointed out the victims to the police, but the justification for the verdict reads that "the incident was witnessed by many local people."[101] During the interrogation that the police officers carried out in the village, "One of the Jewish women stated that she had previously been hiding at Bielawski's place and that she would indicate to the German gendarmes even more people who had been hiding them."[102] Although it is hard to believe, the Polish rescuer was supposedly the same Bielawski whose Jewish charges had been shot in the pits a year earlier.

It is unknown whether by quoting the words of one of the captured Jews, the testifying policemen were telling the truth or

100 Deposition of Faryński, the case of the officers of the Racławice police station, ANKr, SAKr, 1014/IVK/116/50. See also Interrogation of Faryński, February 8, 1949, ANKr, SAKr, IVK/53/49, pp. 99–101.

101 Verdict, the case of the officers of the Racławice police station, ANKr, SAKr, 1014/IVK/116/50.

102 Witness interrogation in the village, the case of the officers of the Racławice police station, ANKr, SAKr, 1014/IVK/116/50.

lying, trying to find both a rational explanation and a mitigating circumstance for the murder they then committed a moment later. Officer Kalinowski went to warn Bielawski that "the Jewess has betrayed," while Wesołowski loaded the two women with the children onto a cart and took them to Racławice. After some time, Kalinowski joined Wesołowski, but before they had a chance to leave Kościejów, they learned that a German patrol had arrived in the village. Facing the new threat of enemy retaliation against the villagers should the "betraying Jewess" fall into German hands, the Polish policemen went into action. The victims were rushed from the cart and shot on the roadside in a manner with which we are now familiar. We know nothing about the execution except that each of the policemen took care of two Jews, just as Wesołowski and Faryński had done the previous year.

One final incident about Racławice can also be mentioned at this point. A little earlier, in the winter of 1943, a Jewish woman was captured in the area and was brought to the police station. Kupfer, the now-familiar German gendarme, ordered a policeman named Krzywonos—we have no further details about him—to shoot the woman. Krzywonos refused to carry out the order, at which point Faryński volunteered, "demanding only a good gun, and then he took the gun from the desk."[103] Then, Faryński told the woman that he would take her back to Miechów and ordered her to walk ahead of him, along the roadside. According to one of the witnesses:

> In a moment he fired several shots at her, and when she fell into the ditch dead, he ordered Jarosz and Adamski [local people] to bury her corpse. When it was half covered with soil, Faryński ordered to dig her up and examine her for valuables, and when he found nothing, he ordered to bury her again.[104]

103 Witness testimony, the case of the officers of the Racławice police station, ANKr, SAKr, 1014/IVK/116/50.

104 Ibid.

The murder of Jews by Polish policemen from the Racławice post deserves some commentary and reflection. Not because their actions were in any way exceptional: On the contrary, what happened in Racławice may provide the key to understanding what happened at so many other rural police stations, some of which have already featured in this book. To begin with, the Polish policemen were very efficient. In the two cases already described, the officers acted on their own, without any German supervision or orders. The search for Jews was facilitated by their good knowledge of both the local area and the people, who—like the farmer in Miroszów—provided the Blue policemen with information about the whereabouts of the Jews. Furthermore, no evidence of resistance regarding the murder of Jewish men, women, and children can be found in the surviving documents. In addition, captured Jews were murdered in public places: in two cases right by the road, and in one case not far from the farm buildings. Also, the executions took place in front of witnesses each time. Apparently, the murder of innocent people—and to be more precise, the murder of innocent Jews—was not something shameful that should be hidden.

After the war, when the policemen stood trial, they rationalized their actions, explaining that the murders were meant to prevent any possible retaliation from the Germans. The court records for this trial read that a timely execution was a patriotic necessity, a form of struggle to preserve the national substance. It was argued that had it not been for the prompt action of the Polish policemen, the Jews would have fallen into the hands of the German police, and the Germans would have discovered which Poles were helping the Jews. That, in turn, would have paved the way for German retaliation against local villagers.[105] According to such logic, all murders of the Jews that were committed by the Blue policemen became a form of social self-defense and an act of higher necessity in the face of German terror. It can be added that this argument was accepted by both the Poles, who were in danger of being turned in during the occupation, and by postwar

105 Interrogation of Bolesław Kalinowski, March 7, 1949, ANKr, SAKr, IVK/53/49, pp. 37–39.

prosecutors and judges, who were ready to consider such an explanation as a mitigating circumstance.

The list of police officers who used these types of arguments both during and after the war is so long that it would fill an entire chapter. Therefore, here are two examples. A policeman from Kosów Lacki, a small village in the northern part of the Warsaw district and not far from Treblinka, justified his actions in almost exactly the same way as the policemen from Racławice. Józef Górski, the owner of the nearby Ceranów estate, described it in his very engaging memoir:

> From time immemorial there lived in Sterdyn a glazier named Całka. He took refuge in Ceranów and found hospitality with various farmers. Finally, he was discovered and a Blue policeman led him to the Gendarmerie station in Kosów. Then Całka threatened the village of Ceranów, waved his fists and shouted that he would give all those with whom he found shelter to the Germans. A policeman shot the Jew on the way, under the pretext that he was trying to escape. "Was I to allow them to burn down the entire village because of that one bastard?" he explained to me. In 1943, the Germans shot the foreman and several workers in the Paulinów farm, which belonged to the Sterdyn estate, for hiding Jews who had betrayed their benefactors.[106]

This kind of story—sometimes true, sometimes based on half-truths, and often entirely made up—effectively paralyzed people who were considering the rescue of Jews. Rumors about so-called Jewish betrayal were rife, and it was also discussed in the underground press, which had a demoralizing effect on the Poles who were rescuing Jews.

The commanding officer of the Garbów police station in the Lublin region acted in a manner very similar to the policeman from Kosów Lacki. This time it was the Morels, a Jewish family

106 Jan Grabowski, "Józef Górski, Na przełomie dziejów," *Zagłada Żydów, Studia i materiały*, 2 (2006), pp. 280–291.

of four. Józef Tkaczyk, a Pole who was later awarded the honor of Righteous Among the Nations, described their death as follows:

> The commander of the "Blue" police station probably knew where they [the Morels] were, because he had contact with them, but when someone went to the station and denounced them, he called the village elder, ordered him to gather the peasants to go and grab the Jews. The police didn't go. But the peasants went [and caught them], they brought them to the jail, and then the station commander ordered to shoot them, so that the Germans wouldn't get them. And so, they did. A "Blue" policeman lived in my house and he shot them. He led them out of the jail one by one and shot them. They were buried right there. After a few years or so, a communal cooperative was to be built in Garbów. A building. So, they dug up those bones. When they dug up those bones, someone let me know, and of course my wife, because my wife was a neighbor of the Morels. And I notified Salomon Morel, who was alive. And he came, and we took those bones, gathered them in a coffin, and buried them in the Garbów cemetery. And they are still lying there today. There were four people killed there. Both Morels, their son, and a sister-in-law. And two escaped, whom I later hid, of course.[107]

The key part of this account is the fact that the commander of the Garbów police station gave the order "to shoot them, so that the Germans wouldn't get them." Salomon Morel is a well-known figure in Poland: a Jew, a Communist, and a commander of the notorious postwar camp for "enemies of the people" in Świętochłowice. But hardly anyone knows the circumstances surrounding the death of his family members. Wikipedia, which unfortunately for many is still the first and only point of reference, simply says that the Morels organized a gang of robbers, which was later crushed by partisans from the People's Guard.[108]

107 Józefem Tkaczykie interview, VHA, 34989.

108 "Salomon Morel," Wikipedia entry, https://en.wikipedia.org/wiki/Salomon_

The time has come to revisit Racławice, because the patriotic narrative of the Polish officers to justify the murders committed against the Jews does not exhaust the list of intriguing topics. The discussion regarding the agency of the Polish officers in "Jewish affairs" could start with the aforementioned Constable Krzywonos, who simply ignored the order given to him by his German superior to kill the Jewish woman brought to the station. The problem of obedience during the Holocaust was discussed at length in the pioneering work by Christopher R. Browning.[109] The American historian described the behavior of German policemen who carried out mass executions of Jews in eastern Poland and concluded that participation in executions was, in principle, voluntary. German historians studying the actions of reserve battalions deployed in the Warsaw ghetto have come to very similar conclusions.[110] Policemen who refused to shoot Jews risked the disapproval of their superiors and the derision of their colleagues but not much more. The point is that there was never any trouble finding volunteers to fill the ranks of the firing squads. The situation seems to have been no different in Racławice, where Officer Faryński readily agreed to replace his colleague Krzywonos who refused to shoot the captured Jewish woman. The same happened in Warsaw, during the aforementioned execution in the Gęsia Street jail, when Constable Żelek from the XX precinct of the Warsaw Blue Police volunteered to shoot the Jews.[111]

Can any further conclusions be drawn from these examples? Were the Polish policemen who refused to kill Jews treated with the same leniency as German officers? The policeman Banaś, who previously described the liquidation of the Kraków ghetto and was awarded the title of Righteous Among the Nations, maintained that the policemen who refused to shoot were threatened with death by

Morel (accessed August 2019). The Blue policeman who murdered the Morel family is mentioned in Adam Dziurok, "23 lata, 6 miesięcy i 22 dni Salomona Morela," Biuletyn Instytutu Pamięci Narodowej, 6–7 (2004), pp. 42–45.

109 Browning, *Ordinary Men.*

110 See Stefan Klemp, *Vernichtung—Die deutsche Ordnungspolizei und der Judenmord im Warschauer Ghetto 1940–43* (Berlin: Prospero, 2013); and Curilla, *Der Judenmord in Polen.*

111 "Równia pochyła," *Biuletyn Informacyjny*, December 4, 1941.

the Germans, but that in Kraków, there were only three or four of them who took part in the shootings. Others, as we can infer, simply ignored German orders, and if Banaś is to be believed, they suffered no consequences for their disobedience. The problem warrants further research, because the subject of obedience, responsibility, and civilian courage concerns fundamental and universal issues. What is striking, however, is that we do not know of even a single case when a Polish policeman was punished for refusing to shoot the Jews. It was not uncommon for the occupation authorities to punish Blue policemen by death, but this usually concerned the loss of weapons, a serious breach of discipline, or contact with the armed underground. On the other hand, I have not come across any verdict of the VI SS and Police Court—to whose jurisdiction the Polish policemen were subject—that involved the crime of *Judenbegunstigung* (helping the Jews).

The Second Battle of Racławice: July 1943–January 1945

While the first battle of Racławice was over in less than a day, the second was more akin to positional war and lasted from July 1943 to January 17, 1945, with no ceasefire. Fighting on one side was the already familiar farmer Józef Bielawski along with his wife and children. On the other side of the fighting were the Bielawski's neighbors and the Blue policemen from the post in Racławice, who were supported by the Gendarmerie in Miechów. First, it is important to know some information about Bielawski from Miroszów.

All that is known about him is that he was born in 1897, he was married with seven children, and he owned 7 hectares of land. He served as an agronomist in the village, and one of his tasks was to collect the state-required quota of grains and meat from the farmers. On many occasions, the village agronomist resorted to threats and physical force, so it is not difficult to understand the long-standing enmity between Bielawski and many of the village residents, and why some were willing to give testimony against him after the war.[112] According to testimonies of his hostile neighbors, people knew that Bielawski was hiding Jews. They also suspected that he had denounced them to the police in an attempt to seek financial gain. As one resident testified in 1949:

> That he [Bielawski] hid those Jews in his house was known to me and to other residents of the hamlet. I myself saw them [the Jews] more than once when I was standing watch at night. I did not hear with my own ears that he betrayed them to the Germans, but he was there when the Germans shot them, and after the execution, they went to his house. It is clear that if they did him no harm, then he must have betrayed them himself. Apparently, those Jews had a lot of gold and money. Also, the aforementioned has [taken] twelve acres of land which belonged to the Jews, which he claims he supposedly bought from them.[113]

Several other neighbors gave similar testimonies, and as it turns out, each one of them felt wronged by Bielawski and each had long-standing disputes with him over undelivered quotas.

Indeed, it seems that Bielawski did not suffer any consequences for having harbored the Jews, and what is more, we know that on another occasion, a policeman warned him that "his" Jewish woman was ready to denounce him. This is all rather unusual, because in similar situations, the Blue Police usually imposed heavy fines on Polish rescuers and sometimes beat them. People in whose houses Jews were found remained on a list of suspects until the end of the war, and their neighbors, the police, and local bandits—not to mention the underground—paid close attention to them. The Ratyński family from Ziomaki near Grębków learned that the hard way.[114] Eight out of several dozen Jews hidden in the Ratyńskis' barn were betrayed and then killed by the Gendarmerie and the

112 Deposition of Franciszek Kulesa, January 20, 1949, ANKr, SAKr, 1014/IVK/53/49, pp. 8–8v.

113 Ibid.

114 This case is described in detail in Engelking and Grabowski, *Dalej jest noc*, vol. 1, pp. 492–499.

Blue Police. Several others were killed that same day by their Polish neighbors, who were members of the patriotic resistance. After those murders, the Ratyński family was targeted, and their house was repeatedly raided in search of "Jews and gold."

However, returning to Bielawski, as a result of incriminating testimonies from his neighbors, the village agronomist was interrogated by the police on suspicion of betraying the Jews in 1949. His wife Barbara was also brought in for questioning. Their statements are truly revealing. Bielawski explained himself as follows:

> I did not face any reprisals from the Germans for hiding Jews, because the "Blue" Police did not reveal that the Jews were with me. I gave them one and half of a quintal of wheat so they would keep to themselves that they found Jews at my place. There were three of them and I gave them 50 kilograms [of wheat] each. And that's why they didn't denounce me.[115]

Throughout this book, the question of the price of a human life is posed time and time again. Usually, such a price is impossible to estimate, but in the case of Jews, it often equaled zero. According to the above statement, the price of a Pole's life hiding Jews near Racławice in 1943 was valued at 150 kilograms of wheat, or about 1,500 zlotys at black-market prices. It is also now known why the agronomist Bielawski was not arrested by the police. Apart from the wheat, the Blue policemen took away from the Bielawskis all the belongings of the murdered Jews. According to Bielawski's wife: "The Jews who were shot didn't pay me anything for [keeping them] because they were from Działoszyce, and after they were shot, there was nothing left except for some linen and bedding, which the commander of the police station took."[116]

115 Józef Bielawski testimony, January 22, 1949, the case of the officers of the Racławice police station, ANKr, SAKr, 1014/IVK/53/49, pp. 8–9v. See also Barbara Bielawska testimony, the case of the officers of the Racławice police station, ANKr, SAKr, 1014/IVK/116/50, vol. 1, pp. 19–21.

116 Barbara Bielawska testimony, the case of the officers of the Racławice police station, ANKr, SAKr, 1014/IVK/116/50, vol. 1, pp. 19–21.

Although it is hard to believe, a month after the execution in the pits, Bielawski took in another group of Jews. As is well known, giving shelter to Jews was the riskiest form of underground activity. Giving shelter to Jews after such a massacre may be seen as a sign of recklessness, desperation, or murderous calculation. In the case of Józef Bielawski, however, it may have been a sign of determination, courage, and strong motivation. When interrogated after the war, the agronomist stated the following:

> Yes, I kept five more [Jews] for seventeen months, named [illegible] [?]rczyks, Szymon Czernacha, Wałek Lewkowicz, whom I kept in an empty room in the house behind a double wall until Poland was liberated. At first, I took money from them, about 7,000 złotys a month, and I took jewelry from them, which was about twenty gold rings and four pairs of [illegible] and 20 dollars in American coins. After liberation, I took them to Racławice and from Racławice I drove a car to Miechów.[117]

As it turned out, Bielawski was well acquainted with the Jews seeking rescue as their plot of land was in the nearby hamlet of Miroszów. This time, however, learning from his painful experience, Bielawski constructed a clever shelter inside his house, or rather an annex, where he hid five Jews behind a double wall. The agronomist's wife described hiding another group of Jews as follows: "One of them [was] Jarosz Stanisław, another Lewkowicz Wowek, and I don't know the rest of the names. There were five of them. My husband, Józef, made another wall in the house, and we hid them there until the liberation of Poland."[118]

As Bielawski himself admitted, those in hiding paid for the help they received. There is nothing strange about this: Keeping five people for a year and a half in conditions of extreme danger was neither easy nor cheap. Nevertheless, one is struck by the

117 Józef Bielawski testimony, the case of the officers of the Racławice police station, ANKr, SAKr, 1014/IVK/53/49, pp. 8–9.

118 Barbara Bielawska testimony, January 23, 1949, the case of the officers of the Racławice police station, ANKr, SAKr, 1014/IVK/53/49, pp. 22–23.

meticulousness with which Barbara Bielawska described the financial side of the rescue operation:

> They paid us in jewelry, which was gold, different rings [illegible], I don't know how much there was, because I wasn't interested in it. My husband was the only one who collected everything from them. And then when they ran out [of valuables], they left receipts, which meant that if they survived, they would pay accordingly. After Poland was liberated, my husband took them to Miechów, and then he bought a field from Lewkowicz Szmul, gave that jewelry back, and on the basis of an agreement in court, he bought that field. That field consisted of eight *morgs* [1 *morga* is equal to 0.5 hectares] with buildings.[119]

It is rare to find such a detailed calculation of the material benefits obtained by the rescuer. While not particularly important in itself, it nevertheless helps us to understand why the agronomist took the Jews to Miechów right after liberation. In almost all the cases known to this author, the rescuers hid their heroism from the world, and what is extremely symptomatic and important is that this conspiracy continued even after the liberation, often for decades. The reason was simple: By revealing themselves, the rescuers exposed themselves and their families to the hostility of their neighbors, for whom keeping Jews meant violating a taboo. It was commonly assumed that helping the Jews was the result of economic calculation, a desire to make a profit, to obtain the notorious "Jewish gold," which, instead of falling into the hands of the village collective, very unfairly ended up in the hands of a single farmer. When rescuers revealed themselves, they could encounter serious unpleasantness not only from their neighbors but also from ordinary bandits or the partisans, who were still very active after the war. This topic, however, while interesting and worthy of a separate discussion, is beyond the scope of this book. Under

119 Deposition of Barbara Bielawska, January 23, 1949, ANKr, SAKR 1014/IVK/53/49, p. 23.

such circumstances, Józef Bielawski, made a rational and balanced decision: If he wanted to acquire the rights to the coveted land, he had to accompany the rescued Jews to the notary in Miechów.

Finally, it is worth adding that Bielawski provided emergency aid to yet another group of Jews who fell into the hands of the Blue Police and the Gendarmerie in the summer of 1943. This time, it was a group of Jews—the testimonies are not specific—who were fugitives from Działoszyce and were also known to Bielawski by the following names: Lewkowicz, Kałurza, Kotan, and Majorek. These Jews were hiding in the woods between the villages of Kropidło and Miroszów with the help of Bielawski and two other farmers:

> Later, when the hunt for them was already in full swing and they were afraid to hide with any of the farmers, they hid in the field among the crops. This was until July 1943. While hiding, when they got cold and completely wet and had nothing to eat, they came to Marian Kolasa, who lived in Kropidło, and he told them to leave, which they did not do, because they wanted to stay with him for a while to dry off and rest a little.[120]

If Bielawski's testimony is to be believed, it was Kolasa who notified the Blue policemen from Racławice when the Jews refused to leave his house. The policemen arrived along with the gendarmes from Miechów: "[They] found Lewkowicz, Kotan and Lewkowicz (Majorek) in the attic, led them out, and beat them terribly and then shot them."[121]

In 1994, Józef Bielawski, his wife, and his eldest son were awarded the Yad Vashem honor of Righteous Among the Nations. Faryński and Wesołowski, the policemen from the Racławice station, were both sentenced to death in August 1950 by the Appelate Court in Kraków. The case reached the Supreme Court, which altered the sentence for both police officers from the death penalty to lengthy prison terms. Their sentences were further

120 Józef Bielawski testimony, the case of the officers of the Racławice police station, ANKr, SAKr, 1014/IVK/116/50, vol. 1.

121 Ibid.

reduced after the proclamation of the general amnesty of April 1956.

In order to learn more about the manhunts and the relentless hunt for the Jews conducted by the Polish police, it is worthwhile to revisit, however briefly, the village of Stanin, located just a few miles west of Łuków in the Lublin district, which was mentioned in the opening pages of this volume.

The commander of the local Blue Police detachment Sergeant Tomasz Klink kept a diary, which was essentially a record of his daily activities. It was a small notebook—a *notatnik służbowy* (work pocketbook), as he referred to it. Klink's diary, written in shorthand, barely legible and thus difficult to decipher, is a unique document, and the only such diary preserved in the archives.[122] The daily entries cover a period of nine months from mid-March to mid-December 1942, and they deal with thefts, assaults, banditry, grain and meat quotas that had not been met, and searches for people who had fled forced labor in the Reich. In mid-November 1942, the diary starts to bring news about the fate of the Jews, a theme that, until now, has been quasi-absent from the pages of the diary:

> *November 18 [19]42*: Special duty. 9 AM. On duty, in the bogs, we arrested three Jews, and in the Jeleniec Forest two Jewesses. Later—five [more] Jews, who have been delivered to the jail in Tuchowicz. Back at the station at 6 PM.
>
> *November 22 [19]42*: 6 PM. On patrol, in order to prevent crime…through Stanin and Tuchowicz, as required. Sgt. Klink and Constable Kozioł. While on duty, shots were heard from the direction of the village [of] Nowa Wróblina. Back at the [police] station at 2 AM.
>
> *November 24 [19]42*: 10 AM. Special duty. Together with the Gendarmerie to organize a manhunt in Stara Wróblina and to the woods. As required: Sgt. Klink; officers Miller,

122 I am grateful to Marta Pawlińska for her transcriptions of the sections of Klink's diary.

> Osenkowski, Kopeć, and Kozioł. During the manhunt, four Bolsheviks were killed; 4 rifles and 3 revolvers have been seized. During the manhunt in the forest, 23 Jews were killed. In Stanin, 4 Jews were killed, 5 civilians were killed in a grenade explosion. A cow was shot in Stara Wróblina. We returned [to the station] at 4 PM.
>
> *November 29, 1942*: 12 PM. On duty, in order to organize a manhunt for the Jews, taking a cart through Tuchowicz, Jeleniec, and Wesołówka; Sgt. Klink, [the] platoon leader Mazur, officers Kopeć Miller, Osenkowski, and Kozioł. During the manhunt, 4 Jews have been detained in Tuchowicz.
>
> *November 30, 1942*: 12 PM. On duty, in order to seize the Jews hiding in [the] Tuchowicz, Jeleniec, and Józefów [area]. As required: Sgt. Klink, plt. [platoon leader] Mazur, Osenkowski, Kopeć, Miller, and Kozioł. Four Jews have been shot in Tuchowicz, otherwise nothing important happened. Return [to police station] at 10 PM.
>
> *December 4, [19]42*: 9 AM. Special duty, in order to deliver the arrested Jews to Łuków and to surrender them to the Gendarmerie, on a cart. As required, Sgt. Klink and corporal Wierpachowski. The detained have been delivered to Łuków.[123]

From these few entries in Sergeant Klink's diary, over the course of twelve days in November and December 1942, the Polish policemen from the small Stanin detachment—acting either together with the Gendarmerie or on their own—intercepted thirty-nine Jews. Out of this number, twenty-seven were murdered on the spot, and the rest were arrested and taken to the local jail from where they were later transferred to Łuków for execution. Klink's notebook stops in mid-December 1942, barely a few days later. But from the report of platoon leader Mazur, who was Klink's deputy and whose report is quoted extensively in the introduction to this study, we can see that in early January 1943, the Polish policemen from Stanin

123 Sergeant Tomasz Klink diary, AP Lublin, Posterunek Policji Polskiej w Staninie, file 1035, dossier 15.

were holding another group of twenty-three Jews in custody. They executed eleven of them and failed to kill the rest because the Polish officers used duds, proving that the ammunition was of appallingly poor quality, as Mazur complained to his superiors.[124]

A Jew arrested by the Polish Blue policeman in the town of Goraj, c. 1943. Courtesy of Łukasz Biedka.

How can one explain these rather large numbers of Jewish victims present in the area? Some of them, no doubt, must have been fleeing the Łuków ghetto, which was the largest local ghetto and had been in the process of liquidation since October 1942. Understandably, some of the Jews who were fleeing the massacre and looking for shelter would have eventually reached the forests in the Stanin area. But the repeated manhunts and the steady stream of Jewish victims is, most likely, related to the two railway lines that passed through Łuków, one from Radom and the other one from Lublin in the direction of Siedlce and Małkinia. During the period of 1942–1943, both lines, which were located close to

124 Report of platoon leader Mazur, AP Lublin, Posterunek policji w Staninie, file 1035, dossier 13, pp. 1–3.

the Tuchowicz Commune, were used to carry the death transports on their way to Treblinka. The Jews who were intercepted and executed by the Polish Blue Police were, most likely, people who had managed to escape from the cattle cars, had survived the dangerous jump from the train cars, had dodged the shots fired by the soldiers guarding the trains, and had somehow reached the nearby woods only to be hunted down by the local peasants who were night guards or by the police. Sergeant Tomasz Klink's diary clearly describes this deadly efficiency of the hunting system deployed against the Jewish refugees in the Polish provinces.

The Toxic Proximity of the Camps

From time to time, Jewish testimonies from Collection 301 held in the archive of the Jewish Historical Institute in Warsaw are quoted in this study. Among Holocaust researchers, they are referred to simply as the 301s. There are over 6,000 such accounts, and they are all sources of exceptional historical value. The accounts were collected immediately after the war—some of them even during the war—by Jewish Historical Commissions operating in several parts of Poland with the aim of recording the "live" memories of Holocaust survivors. Unlike many other sources, the purpose of the 301s was solely to document the Jewish misfortune. It was not about compensation, medals, or anyone's raison d'être. The 301 accounts are usually brief and painfully concise: what the extermination of a given village looked like, who survived, where the extermination took place, who died, and under what circumstances. Some of them were written in Polish, some in Yiddish, some in Hebrew, and a few in German.

Report number 301/4660 is an exceptional document for many reasons. This account of an anonymous witness—or several witnesses—to the Holocaust, written in Yiddish, was erroneously attributed to Aleksander Lipiński in the ŻIH archives. However, Lipiński is simply the first name in a long list of names of Polish murderers of Jews who are referred to in the document. Although the author is unknown, there is not even the slightest doubt about their intentions. Their aim was to list and document in as much detail as possible the murders committed by Poles against Jews in hiding. Looking at the names of the towns, villages, and hamlets that are mentioned, we can guess the place where the author was hiding: the southern part of Sokołów Podlaski County, which was part of the amalgamated Sokołów-Wengrow County during the war. In addition to documenting what happened, the goal of the anonymous author must have been to bring those guilty to justice, hence the frantic listing of names of all the possible witnesses, which was, after all, difficult to find in the face of the complete annihilation of the Jewish population. Judging by the remarks scattered throughout the text, the account was written in mid-1945.

The quotations selected and presented below relate only to murders in which Blue policemen were involved. Readers who would like to get a more complete picture of Polish-Jewish relations in the southern part of the Sokołów district in 1942–1944 will find the entire record 301/4660 included in the Appendix:

> Stanisław Kurabiak was a policeman with the Germans. He murdered both Jews and Russians. He murdered the Jew Motl Feferkranc in Wólka Proszewska in Wiśniew Commune, and it was witnessed by Szalwar from Wólka Proszewska. The story goes like this: When Szalwar saw a policeman coming, he warned two Jews about it. One of them, Chaim Mordechaj Piaskowski, hid in Szalwar's shed, whereas the other, Motl Feferkranc, got nervous and ran out onto the road. As he ran away, Kurabiak shot him, pulled out his gold teeth, and removed the corpse's boots from his feet. Kurabiak and other policemen from Skupie went to the railroad tracks and murdered all the Jews who had saved themselves by jumping off the trains to Treblinka. In short, Kurabiak and his gang murdered almost 100 Jews. In a hiding place near the village of Zaliwie Szlacheckie, Niwiski Commune, there were seven [*sic*] Jewish women: Naska Góra, Naska Goldfarb, Szajndla Piaskowska with her 18-year-old daughter, Dwojra Feferkranc with her seven-year-old child, a girl. Together with Kurabiak Stanisław, the policemen Skanecki, Zimnacha, and Wichalak

came, rallied peasants with axes and pitchforks, surrounded the hiding place, took out the Jewish women and brought them to the jail in Mokobody. They stayed there all day. The next day the men took them, led them to the cemetery and shot them. Two women with children did not want to leave the jail, so they were killed on site. The bodies were taken outside the town on a wheelbarrow by Andrzej Gajowniczek from Mokobody and by Zwoliński Józef. They were buried there as well. The latter two could be witnesses in this case. In Osiny Górne, Skupie Commune, Stanisław Wojewódzki and the son of Jastrzębski from Osiny Górne caught Dawid Rużawa-Kwiata and his daughter, tied them up and took them to the police station in Mokobody, where the police shot them. Józef Zwoliński buried them. His payment was the clothes he could take off the dead. It was in March 1943....

Józef Babrik from the Smolaki colony, Skupie Commune. His father-in-law's name was Rybowski. Rywka Sadownik from Mokobody and the tailor Josl, her fiancé, and a six-year-old boy who had escaped from Treblinka and whose name was Abram Kasten [Kosten?], sold something to Józef Babrik. Babrik told them to come for the money in a few days. When the three of them came to collect the debt, the peasant, upon meeting them outside, told them not to enter because there were strangers there. He told them to go into the cellar next to his house.

Little Abramek did not enter the cellar, but hid in the bushes. From a distance he saw the peasant looking for him, and heard him say in Polish: "Where the hell did he go?" Abramek understood that it was not good, so he hid deeper in the bushes and from a distance he saw the peasant close the cellar where the Jews were and ride his bicycle to Bielany. He brought the Bielany police, who dragged the Jews out of the cellar and shot them in the forest on Babrik's land. The child saw how the peasant Babrik and his father-in-law stripped the Jews of their clothes and buried their bodies in the forest....

Janek Gąsiorek from Mokobody with his brother Franek took in a Jewish tailor and his fiancée, Sara Groszek. For two weeks the Jews sewed for them and then the Gąsiorek family called the policeman Michalak from Mokobody and he killed the Jews. This is how they were rewarded for their work.

Adaś Grzymowski, Heniek Ostaś and Heniek Lewicki from the Kapuściak family. Adaś on horseback, Lewicki and Tadek Gałecki with the whole gang were chasing three Jews, escapees from the Mokobody jail—Herszel Rużawa with his brother and another stranger from the forest, who had escaped from a train going to Treblinka. The gang caught the three Jews, beat them and handed them over to the Polish policemen, who shot them. They were killed in the field of Olek Talach, who buried them (he may be a witness). December 1942.

Zygmunt Fifa from Zaliwie Szlacheckie, Niwiski Commune, with a friend. February 20, 1943. Two boys from Kalisz [Kałuszyn?] aged 12 and 13 used to come to the barn to sleep in the hay. When the weather was bad, the boys did not leave the barn. Zygmunt Fifa and his friend went to the Mokobody police and reported that the two Jewish boys were hiding with a peasant named Jański Stanisław. The police arrived with a cartman, Bolek Król from Mokobody.

When the police arrived to take the boys away, Zygmunt Fifa came out of his smithy with an axe in hand and he and a friend surrounded the barn so that none of the children would sneak out. One managed to escape. They chased the boy for 3 kilometers, and when he got tired, policeman Wasikiewicz shot him....

Karabik Stach, Heniek Skanecki, and Maszukiewicz shot five Russians on a September morning in 1943. At the same time that those five Russians were being murdered, the peasants reported on a Jew who was just walking on this side of the Liwiec River, and the policemen shot him as well. His name was Szmulek Kiwedarbiuk. His mother, brother and sister are in America. Kiwedarbiuk was buried near the exit from the bridge, in the field of Giżański Heniek. Giżański, the peasant who buried Szmulek, is a decent man and never drives his plow near the grave of the shot Jew....

In the village of Kurabki [Korabie?], Kudelczyn Commune, Sokołów County, Czepelewicz from Sokołów and a girl were hiding at Janeczek's place. At first, they stayed for some time with Jan Dymowski in the [illegible fragment] commune near Sokołów. Jan Dymowski found them a hiding place with Janeczek from Kurabki, whom Czepelewicz had to pay 60,000 zlotys for three months. On Friday, June 16, 1943, at about 7 PM, Janeczek woke Czepelewicz and told him, "Get up and run away, because there is a gang here." Czepelewicz got up and left the room. As soon as he left, they shot at him. The bullet wounded him severely and he lay there next to the house for four days. He had to chase away barking dogs. He was hoping for help, but none of the residents helped him. And so he died. It turned out later that Janeczek sent for his brother from the village of Świniary, Skupie Commune.

Janeczek's brother shot Czepelewicz. The brothers deliberately spread a rumor that it was a gang that killed him. When Czepelewicz was shot, the girl from the printing house in Sokołów that was staying with him, ran away into the field of wheat and hid there. The following day she came to Janeczek's house and he told her to hide in the wheat because they were afraid. He promised her that they would bring food right away. Janeczek went to Bielany to get the police, and when one of the policemen came to Kurabki, Janeczek pointed out where the girl was hiding, and the policeman shot her.

On May 26, 1944, three Jews who had escaped from Treblinka [Treblinka I labor camp] appeared near the village of Paczuski—Sikory—Wiechetki, Sokołów county. The peasants, with the help of the Bielany police, surrounded the Jews and captured them. They first beat them until they bled, and then told them they could go. When the Jews started to run away, the policemen threw grenades at them, and all that was left of the Jews were shreds of flesh. After the bloody job was done, the policemen approached their victims and were very pleased. They buried them in the village of Wiechetki.[125]

125 Testimonies relating to the murders in which Blue policemen were involved, 1942–1944, ŻIH, 301/4660.

A horrible testimony, whose nightmarish tone is only further intensified by the diminutive names of the murderers—people apparently well known to the author of the account. The murderers were acquaintances, perhaps friends: Adaś, Heniek, Stachu, and Janek.

Some of the place names are difficult to decipher and identify, and sometimes the Yiddish transcription is not phonetically accurate or explicit. This tragic list of murders, victims, and perpetrators is not, however, an isolated document that may raise some doubts. Without much trouble and without further searching, one can find other testimonies that confirm the macabre enumerations included in the quoted 301. Romek Międzyrzecki came from Węgrów, from which he escaped with five other people on the day the local ghetto was liquidated, in September 1942. After some time, the group found shelter at the house of Antoni Bieliński, a good man and farmer living in Księżopol-Budki near Sokołów. In the following months, Międzyrzecki kept a diary in his hiding place. On Friday, December 18, 1942, he wrote as follows:

> In the morning Mr. Bieliński went to Węgrów.... Late in the evening he told us about the sad events that had taken place during the deportations in Sokołów. About how people were jumping off trains on the way to Treblinka. Masses of dead and wounded. There was also a woman lying there, she had been shot—as if that wasn't enough, Christian bullies had torn off her fingers and ears because she had gold rings and earrings. [He spoke] about many such incidents, and we were shaken to the core. I must add that everything he said is true, because thousands of such events took place in the forest, where Jews were robbed, left naked, barefoot and penniless. So we sat and listened to those stories, and then we went to sleep.[126]

The events described by Międzyrzecki took place somewhere between Sokołów and Treblinka, that is, in the immediate vicinity

126 Romek Międzyrzecki diary, YVA, O.33/4905.

of the place where the author of report 301/4660 was hiding. The vicinity described by the anonymous author was mainly the south and east of Sokołów County, an area not too distant from Treblinka II (the death camp) and Treblinka I (the labor camp). This is the area through which the now dismantled Lwów-Siedlce-Małkinia railroad line ran at the time. It was one of the two railroad lines used in 1942 and 1943 to transport the Jews to the death camp. The other ran from the west, from Warsaw through Łochów to Małkinia.[127] It seems that what happened along the Lwów-Siedlce-Malkinia railroad line did not differ in any way from what happened on the western line.

Here and there, the presence of Jews escaping from transports triggered the worst instincts in people. The news of Jews who were laden with gold and valuables circulated in the vicinity, and for people without mercy, conscience, or scruples, the hundreds of helpless Jews seeking rescue in the nearby villages constituted an irresistible temptation and a spoil not to be sneezed at. News about "Jewish gold" was also reproduced in underground reports and illegal newspapers, which further fueled the homicidal atmosphere. In the northern part of the Warsaw district—within the areas of interest of this study—there must have been fantastic rumors circulating about that, and echoes of these rumors can be found in intelligence reports sent from Sokołów to Warsaw. One such report from September 1943 reads as follows: "On September 5, 18 armed Ukrainians escaped from Treblinka to the surrounding forests, the following day another six escaped...; the latter took with them about 3,000,000 zloty in cash, gold and jewelry."[128] In another report, we read the following:

> The Jewish question in the area [the counties of Sokołów and Węgrów] is almost nonexistent. The wealthy Jews with money have long since "settled" and are waiting for the end of the

127 I have written extensively about this railway line in a recently published work devoted to the extermination of the Jews in the nearby Węgrów county. See Engelking and Grabowski, *Night Without End*.

128 Situation report, September 1943, AAN, Delegatura Rządu na Kraj, 202-II-23, pp. 19, 54.

> war together with the rest of the population. The Jews hiding in the woods are hated by the people. They are the cause of many troubles and misfortunes for the Polish population.[129]

The fact that "the Jewish question" was "almost nonexistent" was in large part due to the actions of the Blue Police, who had the necessary means, organization, and weapons to detect, detain, rob, and kill Jews. After all, incidents when victims were turned over to the Germans were not so frequent. As the account by the anonymous Jew indicates, Blue Police officers from the police stations in Bielany, Mokobody, and Skupie had become experts in committing murders without any German influence and often without the knowledge of the gendarmes, who would, after all, wish to receive their share in any loot or kill any Pole hiding Jews. On the one hand, Polish policemen committed murders independently, while on the other, they served the local peasants as useful executioners "by request," thus ultimately helping them solve their "Jewish problem."

Jagdkommandos: Nowak and Guzdek

From time to time, the police authorities organized so-called Rollkommandos, which are also sometimes referred to as Jagdkommandos (hunting units). These were mobile detachments composed of both German and Polish policemen, both Blue Police and Kripo officers. Such Rollkommandos were given special tasks, such as retaliatory operations, fighting partisans, collecting overdue quotas, catching people who refused to work for the Reich, and tracking down Jews in hiding. Rollkommandos of this type were established, among others, in the Lublin district. They usually consisted of a German gendarme, a German deputy, and between ten and fifteen Polish Blue Police officers, sometimes acting in tandem with Polish Kripo agents, and their task was to

129 BIP quarterly report for the period from July 15–October 15, 1943, AAN, AK, 203-X-68, p. 31.

liquidate "bandits and Jews," to borrow the language of the police documents.[130]

One of the best-known hunting units—80 percent of whom were Polish officers—operated in *Kreishauptmannschaft* Miechów. One of its commanders was Sergeant Major Kazimierz Nowak, a Poznań-born officer with many years of experience in the prewar police. We can reconstruct the activities of Nowak's Jagdkommando partly thanks to the surviving documents of AK intelligence and partly due to the extensive testimonies given after the war in the investigation by the aforementioned Piotr Sałabun.[131] Miechów's hunting unit was tasked with fighting common crime, such as smuggling or illegal slaughter of cattle or pigs. One of the most important tasks, however, was the search for and murder of hidden Jews. Dariusz Libionka writes about the activities of Nowak's Jagdkommando:

> In the testimony of a Jagdkommando member given before an AK investigator,[132] we find several descriptions of murders committed against Jews. On March 3, 1943, the unit arrived in Kozłów, where a policeman named Latacz reported that there were Jews hiding in nearby Klimontów. Together with Stanisław Brywczyński, they brought six Jews, whom they then shot. Several days later, in Pilica, an informer pointed out a house in Kąpiołki Małe, where Jews were supposed to be hiding. Having found no one, the officers beat the owner. In Wolbrom, after an anonymous letter, a Jew was found, and

130 Detailed Rollkommando reports from Krasnystaw and its surroundings have survived from the Lublin district. See commander of the Gendarmerie in Lublin, AIPN, GK 104/3 and 104/4. It is worth adding here that Rollkommandos became particularly useful in the period of increased activity of partisan units at the end of 1943 and the beginning of 1944. In the Lublin district alone, between February 14 and March 10, 1944, fifty-two gendarmes and policemen—including one major, four captains, and two lieutenants—were killed in battles against "Bolshevik bands." See Special order, March 19, 1944, AIPN, GK 104/24, p. 28.

131 Piotr Sałabun, *Kronika o Jagdkommando i jego dowódcy Nowaku Kazimierzu*, AIPN Ki, 128/210, p. 149.

132 Indictment (undated, mid-1944?), AAN, AK, 203-XI-21, pp. 1–3; Untitled report, undated, pp. 4–11, AAN, AK, 203-XI-21 (note in the original).

handed over to the Gestapo in Miechów. On April 20, the unit took part in a raid in the Sancygniów Forests. Another anonymous letter, sent to the police station in Kazimierza Wielka, helped to find three Jewish men and two Jewish women near Probołowice, who were executed on Beck's order. On June 4, during a manhunt near Dębiany, another Jew was killed.[133] It is unknown how complete this list is.[134]

A hunting unit made up of the Kripo and the Blue Police, Siedliszowice, 1943. AIPN Kr, 502/4069.

In addition to capturing and murdering Jews, Nowak's men were also active in operations against both the Polish underground and Polish civilians. The list of their victims includes several hundred names. Nowak was sentenced to death and died in an assassination attempt in July 1943. In Otfinów and Siedliszowice north of Tarnów, a similar mobile unit was formed in February–March 1943. Its leader was a gendarme called Engelbert Guzdek, who had several Polish policemen delegated from nearby stations

133 Untitled report, undated, AAN, AK, 203-XI-21, pp. 4–8 (note in the original).
134 Libionka, "Powiat miechowski," p. 147.

under his command. The tasks of the Otfinów Jagdkommando included guarding the supply of quotas, but by late fall, their primary concern was catching "bandits, Jews and other individuals," as summed up by one of Guzdek's Polish subordinates.[135] The Jagdkommando specialized in murdering Jews and Roma, and the murder of the entire Roma population of Szczurowa in early August 1943 went down in the history of terror. Soon afterward, Guzdek was killed in unexplained circumstances, and after his death, the Jagdkommando was disbanded.

Volunteer Fire Brigades

While the participation of the volunteer fire brigades (OSP) in liquidations was part of a plan developed by the occupying authorities, it was the firefighters' own initiative, methods of operation, and motivation that played the primary role in the later Jewhunts carried out until the end of the war. As is the case with all court documents, trial records, which today are among the primary sources of information for historians on the subject of hunting Jews, reflect only a small fraction of the scale of the phenomenon. As in the case of other crimes, most of these Jewhunts will never be fully explained and will forever remain shrouded in the darkness of oblivion. For this reason, it is worthwhile to quote extracts from the indictment drawn up after the war against the leader of a gang of firefighters from the Markowa area. The indictment is something of a blueprint of the crimes committed against the Jews:

> In the fall of 1942, together with other perpetrators, he captured two women unknown by name and Sara Hirszfeld, who were shot after being taken to the police.
> In the fall of 1942, together with other perpetrators, he captured Regina and Eliasz Brotspis and brought them to the German gendarmes, who shot them.
> In the fall of 1942, in Handzlówka, together with others, he

135 Interrogation of Stanisław Młynarczyk, APKr, SAKr, 1025/IVK/164/50, p. 12.

> took part in a manhunt and captured eight Jewish people, who were shot after being delivered to the gendarmes.
>
> In September 1942, going along with the authorities of the German state, he acted to the detriment of those persecuted by those authorities in the following way:
>
> - Together with other perpetrators, after capturing about forty people of Jewish nationality who were hiding, he took their money and valuable movables.
> - He extorted various benefits from Jakub Einhorn and, among other things, took away his household furnishings.
>
> In the fall of 1942, in Husów, he took part in a mass manhunt for Jews in the local forest, as a result of which several dozen people were captured.[136]

Over time, the firefighters became a constant point of reference and support for those catching Jews. If there was no police station in the area, it was the firefighters who were asked to help solve "the Jewish problem." Ber Ryczywół, who sought shelter near Łuków at the turn of 1942–1943, wrote the following in his memoir:

> I ended up in the village of Celiny [Włościańskie or Szlacheckie]. I thought of nothing else but a place to sleep, because it was very cold. I started talking, stammering, crossing myself, but the village elder didn't like my way of making the sign of a cross. I didn't know then how it was done, whether it ended on the left or on the right, and I ended on the left. He noticed this and said that I was a Jew. He told me to cross myself again. I answered him, "Lord Jesus does not want me to cross myself

136 In the 1953 trial in the Rzeszów Regional Court, the accused firefighter was acquitted, and during the trial, the witnesses—Polish neighbors—changed their earlier testimonies that had been given as part of the investigation. No one denied that the firefighters had murdered Jews—only the presumed innocence of the accused was defended. The whole process of changing testimonies and strengthening group solidarity in the face of external threat is described in Grabowski and Libionka, "Bezdroża polityki historycznej." The 1953 verdict was overturned by the Supreme Court and sent for retrial by the Provincial Court. In 1954, the Provincial Court in Rzeszów upheld the earlier ruling.

> twice." Without much thought, the village leader ordered to call the firemen to take me to the commune. The Jews were already gone, the firemen helped to look for them and catch them. The firemen wore two very wide belts on their jackets, that was their sign. The *sheygets*[137] had already run to fetch the firemen. There would have been no discussion with the Germans, they would have simply shot me.[138]

For Teofil Ryznar, a resident of the village of Sietesz near Łańcut, another search for escaped Jews began during the harvest time of 1943, when two policemen from the Markowa police station appeared, accompanied by a German policeman known as "Friszko." The officers immediately ordered the local firefighters to capture the Jews. The police were well informed about where the fugitives were hiding. Next, the entire group went to the head of the nearby Chodakówka hamlet and from there to the forest of the Sietesz hamlet. At the edge of the forest, Ryznar saw "about four Jewish men and women," who had been captured earlier by the firefighter, digging themselves a grave.[139] The same operation—as it is assumed—was described by Augustyn Wiglusz, head of the peasant night guard in Sietesz. He received an order from the police station in Markowa to carry out a "search for Jews" in the house of one of the villagers.[140] Since none of his own men were available, Wiglusz went to the guardhouse of the local fire brigade, where he enlisted the help of a few firefighters. The Jews were captured and first imprisoned in the guardhouse, which was turned into a makeshift jail, and then taken to Kańczuga and transferred into the hands of the German gendarmes.

Fire brigades operated in a very similar manner in the western part of the Kraków district and in the Kielce region. From one of the first works devoted to this issue, it is known that the heads of

137 The word "*sheygets*" is a slur, meaning a non-Jewish male.

138 Ber Ryczywół testimony, *Mayne iberlebungen*, ŻIH, 302/43.

139 Interrogation of Teofil Ryznar, June 18, 1949, AIPN Rz, 353/113, pp. 21–22.

140 Interrogation of the suspect Michał Boratyn, January 21, 1949, AIPN Rz, 353/113, p. 6; Interrogation of the suspect Augustyn Wiglusz, January 18, 1949, AIPN Rz, 353/113, p. 2.

the fire brigades were equally responsible for peace and security in the community as the village leaders, and they interpreted that duty in the same way. Alina Skibińska writes about Boronice in Pińczów County:

> Stanisław Noga, head of the fire brigade, was more involved in getting rid of the Jews. Judka Kluska with his wife and two small children were captured by members of the fire brigade in the attic of a barn on the estate. The signal to participate in the manhunt was the sound of a fire trumpet. The captured were taken to the police station in a fire engine. "The Jewish woman, crying, begged to be let go because she wanted to live."[141]
>
> In the confusion and under cover of darkness, her husband Judka escaped and hid in the village for another year. One night, Bolesław Biniek found Judka sleeping in the barn and immediately alerted Gołdyn, the village leader, and the head of the guards, Stanisław Noga, "to take him away, because if not, he would go to report him to the 'Blue Police.'" The court heard from village leader Gołdyn that he only came to the site and did not take any actions or decisions, as he did not have to. ("I did not give any orders, I only looked on.") Gołdyn sent Biniek to the fire brigade, "because they were in charge of all kinds of things." Gołdyn found several dozen people there, and Judka Kluska was tied up and held by Commander Noga. The three firefighters and their chief Noga drove Judka to the Proszowice police station. On the way Judka asked them to let him go. I replied that it was daytime and we could not. I added that I did it all out of fear that people in the village would report me to the Germans for not catching Jews.[142]

141 Feliks Bentkowski testimony, AIPN, GK 217/181–181a, p. 35 (in the original).

142 Alina Skibińska, "'Dostał 10 lat, ale za co?': Analiza motywacji sprawców zbrodni na Żydach na wsi kieleckiej w latach 1942–1944," in Barbara Engelking and Jan Grabowski, eds., *Zarys krajobrazu: Wieś polska wobec Zagłady Żydów 1942–1945* (Warsaw: Stowarzyszenie Centrum Badań nad Zagładą Żydów, 2011), pp. 362–363.

As previously indicated, the attitudes of Polish firefighters—members of voluntary brigades—toward the German policy of exterminating the Jews is a topic worthy of further research. Despite the availability of archival materials, they have yet to become a subject of thorough and systematic study. From the point of view of this study, two questions are crucial. The first one concerns the manner in which the OSP brigades took part in both the liquidations and the search for hidden Jews. Thanks to the source materials presented in this study, some preliminary answers to this question can be provided. Polish firefighters took an active part in the liquidations, sometimes on their own initiative and sometimes in response to the demands of the Germans. In the later period, the volunteer firefighters became some of the main participants in the pursuit of hidden Jews. As in the case of the Blue Police, the greater the distance from the center of German power, the greater the role of the firefighters. Thus, in rural areas where the German police presence was negligible, the role of the firefighters increased accordingly.

The second question concerns the motivation of those firefighters who were involved in the German extermination policy against the Jews. Can their actions really be explained by their fear of the Germans? Can voluntary participation in liquidations or the months- and years-long search for those in hiding be explained in the same way? And, in the case of such people whose profession and mission it is to save lives, perhaps the decision to take part in this mass murder sprang from much deeper and stronger motives than a simple fear of the occupying forces.

Chapter Six

Warsaw

My dear Sammern,
It seems to me that you are not up to the task and that you are not energetic enough.[1]

SS-Brigadeführer Jürgen Stroop to *SS-Oberführer* Ferdinand von Sammern-Frankenegg upon taking command during the Warsaw ghetto uprising in April 1943.

According to an order from the commander of Army Group "Warsaw" following the city's capitulation, the policemen were to remain in their positions in order to protect the city's population from the chaos and robberies that were due to follow in the wake of the collapse of state authority. German troops entered the conquered city of Warsaw on September 28, 1939. Within days, 120,000 German soldiers were deployed in the city and in the surrounding area.[2] By the end of September, German policemen and members of the Einsatzgruppen, whose task was to capture and arrest people considered by the occupying authorities to be particularly

1 Josef Wulf, *Das Dritte Reich und seine Vollstrecker—Die Liquidation von 500 000 Juden im Ghetto Warschau* (Berlin: Arani, 1961), p. 245.

2 Rudolf Meier, *Soldaten-führer durch Warschau* (Warsaw: Deutsche Buchh, 1941), p. 16.

dangerous, joined them in the conquered capital. In the first days of October, a ten-member team of the Berlin police vice squad—part of the Kripo—under the command of Commissioners Hennig and Bahr also arrived in Warsaw.[3] By the end of October, the process of taking over the Polish police was nearly complete. Since most of the Warsaw police had remained in the city, the transformation of the Polish State Police into the Blue Police followed relatively quickly, as evidenced by numerous investigation reports by Polish police officers dated from November and December 1939, which can be accessed in the Warsaw court records.

Given the exceptional importance and size of Warsaw, the actions of the Blue Police in the former capital of Poland must have differed considerably from those carried out by Polish police officers in other cities of the Generalgouvernement. The role of the Polish police in implementing the occupier's "Jewish policy" in this particular area therefore deserves a separate discussion. On December 14, 1943, Hans Frank declared:

> We have one point in this country from which all evil arises: It is Warsaw. If we did not have Warsaw in the Generalgouvernement, we would be spared 4/5 of the difficulties we have to fight. Warsaw is and will remain the focus of confusion, the point that spreads all the unrest in this country.[4]

There is no denying that in regard to this particular issue, the governor general was not wrong. Warsaw was not only the capital of the Polish Underground State where various currents of conspiratorial activity converged but also the location where the most serious economic crimes were being committed, often aimed directly against the occupying authorities or against the broader economy of the Reich. Until the summer of 1942, Warsaw had the largest concentration of Jews, and after the liquidation of the

3 The same happened in Kraków, where as early as September 13, 1939, the German authorities demanded that the city magistrate open brothels for the army. See Kubalski, *Niemcy w Krakowie*, pp. 29, 80.

4 Piotrowski, *Dziennik Hansa Franka*, p. 139.

ghetto, it was the city with the largest number of Jews in hiding. For all these reasons, increased police control over Warsaw was a priority for the German authorities. On April 1, 1941, 4,662 officers of the Blue Police were serving in the Warsaw district, which stretched from Łowicz in the west to Siedlce in the east.[5] Of that number, 3,273 were stationed in Warsaw itself, and another 456 were deployed in the suburban areas (*Kreiskommando Warschau*).[6] Thus, it is evident how important the Germans considered the role of the police in the largest city in the Generalgouvernement. As the years passed and despite the worsening public safety situation, the strength of the Warsaw Blue Police remained more or less the same, with the exception of some officers who were transferred to suburban police stations in the Warschau-Land district. The strengthening of the Polish Criminal Police in Warsaw will be discussed later in this volume.[7]

With few exceptions, the police stations in occupied Warsaw retained their prewar locations and numbering.[8] All in all, there were twenty-seven regular police stations in Warsaw, two railroad police stations—one near the main railway station and the other one in Praga, near the railway station in Wschodnia—and a river police station located on the shore of the Vistula.

5 See the following documents in AMSW, Starostwo Powiatowe Warszawskie, 1140: Personnel numbers of the Polish and Ukrainian police in the Warsaw district, April 1, 1941, p. 38; Summary of the personnel of the Polish police in the Warsaw district, October 1, 1943, p. 72; and List of Polish police forces from 1944, p. 80.

6 German officials are, however, also likely to have included officers of the Polish Kripo in this number.

7 For more information about the involvement of the Polish Criminal Police in the murder of Polish Jews, see chapter 7.

8 The list and locations of police stations can be found in Office of the Governor of the Warsaw District, The SS and Police Leader for the Warsaw District, 1939–1944, AMSW, file. 156, pp. 15–23; Marek Getter, "Policja granatowa w Warszawie 1939–1944," in Krzysztof Dunin-Wąsowicz et al., *Warszawa lat wojny i okupacji, 1939–1944*, vol. 2 (Warsaw: Państwowe Wydawn. Naukowe, 1972), p. 214.

The Number of Police Officers in Warsaw and the Warsaw District as of January 15, 1943[9]

Formation	Germans	Poles
CITY OF WARSAW		
KdS, Department V (Kripo)	31	400
KdS, Department IV (Gestapo)	160	–
KdS, Department III (intelligence)	20	–
Protective Police (Schupo)	180	–
Polnische Polizei im Generalgouvernement (Blue Police)	–	2,700
Railroad Security Police (Bahnschutzpolizei)	170	100
Forest Guard (Forstschutzkommando)	8	?
Field Gendarmerie (Feldgendarmerie)	100 (1 company)	–
WARSAW DISTRICT (Outside the city of Warsaw)		
Kripo	12	119
Gestapo	40	–
Intelligence	5	–
Gendarmerie	451	–
Blue Police	–	1,250
Railroad Security Police	200	100

The first commander of the Warsaw police was Lieutenant Colonel Marian Kozielewski—the brother of well-known underground courier Jan Karski—who was sent to Auschwitz shortly after his arrest by the Germans in May 1940. Along with Kozielewski, a large group of Warsaw police officers was arrested. Little material has survived about Kozielewski's role in

9 Comments to the Special Investigation Plan of the Security Police for the Warsaw district, March 7, 1943 (as of January 15, 1943), AIPN, GK 714/19, pp. 20–21.

implementing the occupation's first regulations. It is known that he was closely acquainted with Captain Józef Szeryński who later became the commander of the Jewish police in the ghetto, something which may or may not have impacted his future choice of head of the Jewish police.[10] At this point, it is worth referring to a brief characterization of the first commander of the Blue Police, written by AK underground intelligence agents:

> Not very intelligent and a stickler for regulations. As soon as the Germans entered Warsaw, he declared to his staff officers from the city headquarters that "for him the Polish-German war is already over" and tried to establish as good a rapport as possible with Colonel Brenner of the German police.[11] When, after his imprisonment, he learned that the Germans had dismissed him from office, he fell into a temporary depression and then needlessly manifested his hostile attitude toward the occupier at every turn. This was the main reason why, while the others were released after a month, Mr. Kozielewski was sent to Auschwitz, where he spent several months. After his release from Auschwitz, he was employed in the printing plant of the Warsaw Municipal Board. He was basically a righteous man, but pretentious beyond measure, characterized by an unbridled desire for career advancement, which, along with a lack of understanding for his subordinates, created an unpleasant atmosphere around him...among the police noncommissioned officers, he was simply hated.[12]

After his release from the camp, Kozielewski joined the resistance and became head of the State Security Corps, an underground organization subordinate to the Government Delegation for

10 Katarzyna Person, *Policjanci: Wizerunek Żydowskiej Służby Porządkowej w getcie warszawskim* (Warsaw: Żydowski Instytut Historyczny im. Emanuela Ringelbluma, 2018), p. 25.

11 Karl-Heinrich Brenner, the first Orpo commander in the Warsaw district.

12 Note about Lieutenant Colonel Marian Kozielewski, undated, AAN, AK, 203-III-124, p. 113.

Poland that was designed to be the nucleus of the future police force in the reborn Poland.

Aleksander Reszczyński, at the time the chief of police in Kraków, in conversation with Kazimierz Dobija, the director of the press conglomerate IKC, in 1934. NAC, 1-B-31-2.

Kozielewski was succeeded by Lieutenant Colonel Aleksander Reszczyński, who was killed in March 1943 by an execution squad of the People's Guard. The last commander of the Blue Police in Warsaw was Major Franciszek Przymusiński, who held that position until the outbreak of the Warsaw Uprising in August 1944. We know quite a lot about both Commanders Reszczyński and Przymusiński, and their role in enforcing the German *Judenpolitik* will be discussed in the coming pages.

The Role of the Warsaw Police in the Fight against the Jews

The activities of the Warsaw Blue Police and the first tasks related to the implementation of anti-Jewish German regulations in the initial period of the occupation have been discussed previously.

Of particular significance were, undoubtedly, the enforcement of the armband regulation as well as the arrest and resettlement in the ghetto of those Jews who had remained on the Aryan side after the ghetto was sealed in November 1940. From that point on, the arrests of Jews sneaking out of the ghetto—usually in search of food—became an integral part of the work of the Polish policemen. For example, on December 22, 1940, on Graniczna Street, the Blue Police stopped a twenty-year-old Jewish woman called Sura Honiksman who was trying to cross to the Aryan side. The young woman began to struggle with the policeman Roman Brzozowski of the XII precinct who stopped her. She shouted: "You son of a bitch, you German stooge, you won't let people live! One day we're going to pay you back and you'll be hanging from lampposts!"[13] Brzozowski was assisted by another policeman on duty nearby, and they both led the struggling woman to the nearest police station. Contrary to Sura Honiksman's wishes, the Blue policemen were not hanged from lampposts, but the Jewish girl was sentenced to eight months' imprisonment by the *Sondergericht* for her insolence. Given the rulings of the Warsaw Special Court at the time, the punishment imposed on Sura Honiksman was relatively mild: German judges often handed down much harsher sentences in similar cases. As we know, at the end of October 1941 after the Third Regulation Concerning the Limitations of the Right of Residence in the Generalgouvernement came into force, death sentences became the general rule.

The arrest of Sura Honiksman is just an illustration of the way in which the Warsaw police treated Jews who tried to leave the ghetto or were caught outside it on the Aryan side. The actions of the Polish police officers not only sealed the fate of thousands of Warsaw Jews arrested in the city but also helped tighten the death ring around the ghetto by effectively deterring many others from the risky expedition. Preserved in Ringelblum's underground Oneg Shabbat Archive are reports about the effectiveness of the

13 Files of the criminal case against Sura Honiksman, a Jewish woman accused of not wearing a Jewish armband, insulting a policeman, and resisting the police. See Report of policeman Roman Brzozowski for the head of XII Commissariat, October 22, 1940, AMSW, Sondergericht Warschau, 414, p. 3.

Polish police in sealing the ghetto's borders. One of them reads as follows:

> Thus, in May 1941, Polish police brought 823 Jews, detained on the Aryan side, into the Jewish District, and in the following months the number steadily increased. The report mentions that the Gen[eral] Governor's decree of October 15, 1941, on the death penalty for leaving the Jewish District had only an inhibiting effect in this respect.[14]

Polish and Jewish policemen check passes upon entry into the ghetto, Warsaw. Photo Collection, YVA, 1605/455.

According to a report drawn up in the spring of 1942, the number of people caught either on the Aryan side or trying to cross the wall rose steadily. This trend stopped in the fall of 1941 when the Germans introduced the death penalty for leaving the ghetto. It was in August 1941, during this period of rising arrests, that Emanuel Ringelblum noted in his diary: "The Polish police have no mercy, neither for women nor children [begging on the

14 Author unknown, "One Year under the Rule of the Commissioner for the Jewish District in Warsaw" (after May 1942), in Janczewska, *Archiwum Ringelbluma: Konspiracyjne Archiwum Getta Warszawy, vol. 12*, p. 96.

Aryan side]. The Polish police in general wrote a sad page in the history [of the occupation]."[15] While Ringelblum was writing about the indubitable "efficiency" of the Polish policemen in sealing the ghetto borders, 4,000–5,000 people a month were dying of starvation inside the Jewish ghetto. Although it is difficult to estimate the extent of the Polish policemen's complicity in this phenomenon, it certainly cannot be said that they bore no responsibility for this tragic situation.

Apart from tracking down Jews around the ghetto and on the Aryan side of the city, another task of the Polish police in the capital included the enforcement of the occupation's regulations prohibiting Jews from moving around Warsaw without the proper passes. On the one hand, the German regulations were meant to cut off the ghettos from illegal food supplies, whereas on the other hand, they had a symbolic meaning: to stigmatize Jews in the eyes of the general population. However, as discussed, the identification of Jews who ventured outside the ghetto without armbands was a great challenge for the Germans. For the German authorities, the experience of the Blue policemen, who prided themselves on being able to "distinguish Jews from people," as we can read in reports from that period, was particularly valuable. An example of such police physiognomy in action can be found in a Jewish account about an incident in 1940:

> There were sixteen more Christians from Sochaczew on the wagon, the owner of the wagon was a good friend of my neighbor, whom he promised to watch out for me all the way. I said goodbye to my neighbor and we hit the road. We drove eighteen kilometers like that, and suddenly we were stopped by German gendarmes and two Polish policemen. One Polish policeman got on the wagon and asked with malice, "How many Jews are there among you?" I then looked right at him, without turning my face the other way, so as not to draw attention to myself. One Christian woman spoke up, "Take a good look, you might find one." The policeman replied that he could recognize Jews by their eyes, and then his gaze fell

15 Ringelblum, *Kronika getta warszawskiego*, p. 300.

on a young Christian woman who had dyed her hair: it was neither light nor brown, and he told her to show him her papers. Everything was in the best order, for he came across a Christian woman; her brother-in-law was our driver, and he made fun of the policeman for being sure that he had caught himself a pike, but he was mistaken.[16]

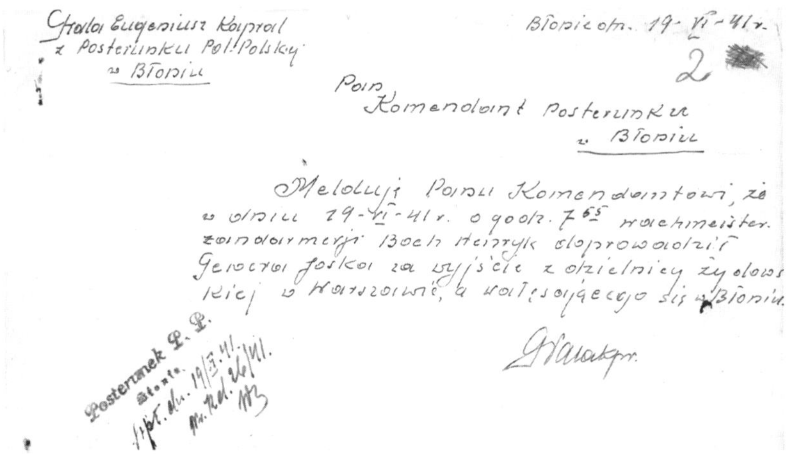
Gała Eugeniusz Kapral
z Posterunku Pol. Polskiej
w Błoniu

Błonie dn. 19-VI-41 r.

2

Pan
Komendant Posterunku
w Błoniu

Melduję Panu Komendantowi, że w dniu 19-VI-41 r. o godz. 7^{65} wachmeister żandarmerji Boch Henryk doprowadził Gerszę Joska za wyjście z dzielnicy żydowskiej w Warszawie, a wałęsającego się w Błoniu.

Gała kpr.

Report of a Jew arrested in Błonie (close to Warsaw) by the Blue Police for "roaming outside the ghetto," 1941. AMSW, Sondergericht Warschau, 385.

One of the more visible forms of Blue Police activity inside the ghetto was the so-called sanitary control operations that had been ordered by the German Health Department. In theory, the aim of such operations was to combat the typhus epidemic. That is why there was a quarantine order for houses where outbreaks of the disease were reported, after which the inhabitants were forced to take baths and to disinfect the houses, bedding, and clothes. In principle, these were sham operations with low effectiveness, whose main advantage—from the point of view of the Polish policemen in charge of such operations—was an opportunity to extort

16 Rela [Renia] Sapot, *Strona aryjska*, ŻIH, 302/150.

considerable amounts of money from desperate tenants.[17] A typical sanitary operation, which involved the officers of the Blue Police, members of sanitary columns, and sometimes representatives of the German authorities, could last anywhere from several hours to more than twelve hours and was carried out with great brutality. People were driven outdoors and brought to a bathhouse—regardless of the weather—and their clothes and bedding were usually destroyed during the disinfection. Peretz Opoczyński provided a haunting description of such an event in the Warsaw ghetto. It is worth noting the role of the Blue policemen who oversaw the operation and on whose whim the fate of the tenants depended:

> The women return to their apartments and try to do what Perele did—take whatever they can to their neighbors and relatives. They are running around, bustling about, because they don't know when the torturers will come—maybe in a moment, or maybe tomorrow. Before they know it, however, in the yard you can already hear the angry, sinister shouts of the Polish policemen herding them to the bathhouse. Oh, it's not good. People run to the windows and look out on the yard—the gate is already closed, there is no place to run, no place to hide, they have them in their grip. Suddenly, shouts are heard in the courtyard, policemen hitting people with their rubber truncheons. They surrounded all the staircases, no one can leave except to join the queue of people marching to the bathhouse. Some of the policemen are standing at the entrances, others are running around the apartments and chasing tenants out. Wailing and shouting are coming from everywhere. The wife of a trader in the hall, who is about to give birth, tries to explain to a policeman that she cannot go to the bathhouse in such a state, but he bludgeons her over the head and the woman's painful scream echoes up the stairs. Police cruelty is an effective measure! There is a butcher, who

17 Descriptions of such "sanitary operations" can be found in *Dwie relacje na temat: "Akcja sanitarna na ulicy Krochmalnej" [we wrześniu 1941] z 27.03 i 29.03.1942* (unknown author), ŻIH, Ring I/93 and I/291.

> calls a couple of cops and locks the door behind them from the inside, takes a bottle of vodka out of the cupboard, puts a plate full of sliced sausage on the table and…opens his wallet. Then the policemen walk out with red faces, quietly, hush hush. The butcher stands by the window, unperturbed, and watches the crowd rushing into the bathhouse.[18]

In the third year of the occupation, the Blue policemen did not need German regulations to extort money from the Jews. With every month, the power of the police over the Jews grew, and the victims could hardly go and complain to the authorities. Rabbi Szymon Huberband, one of Ringelblum's associates, gave an example of the Blue Police officers' ingenuity in his diary. On Sunday, May 17, 1942, Blue policemen were stopping Jews at the corner of Zamenhofa and Gęsia Streets. Each person, one by one. They threatened to take them to the Pawiak Prison for investigation. "They didn't charge much," Huberband added. "You could buy yourself out for as little as 25 zlotys."[19] Over time, robberies by Polish policemen in broad daylight became an everyday occurrence. As Daniel Fligelman noted in his diary in an entry dated May 28, 1942, "There was a line of Jews standing in front of the court building in Leszno, intending to pay some due taxes. Suddenly, the group was surrounded by Polish policemen, who took away all the money, and told them to pay the tax the next day."[20] A week earlier, a similar incident occurred at the market on Ciepła and Nowolipki Streets, where policemen surrounded a crowd of shoppers, dragged out the better-dressed ones, and robbed them.

This does not mean, however, that the Blue policemen were not punished for misconduct, bribery, and other arbitrary actions. On the contrary, albeit not as a result of the victims' complaints but based on the decision of the Germans themselves, who punished

18 Perec Opoczyński, "Dom numer 21," in Polit, *Reportaże z warszawskiego getta*, p. 51.

19 Anna Ciałowicz, ed., *Archiwum Ringelbluma: Konspiracyjne Archiwum Getta Warszawy, vol. 32, Pisma Rabina Szymona Huberbanda* (Warsaw: Żydowski Instytut Historyczny im. Emanuela Ringelbluma, 2017), p. 60.

20 Daniel Fligelman diary, in Person, *Archiwum Ringelbluma: Konspiracyjne Archiwum Getta Warszawy, vol. 5*, p. 78.

Polish policemen caught violating the regulations of their service. German court records as well as Jewish and Polish testimonies provide numerous descriptions of such situations. A noteworthy, unpublished diary from the wartime period provides a description of a rather unusual case when the Polish prosecutor's office opened an investigation into a Blue policeman accused of beating Jews in the ghetto. According to the well-informed chronicler, who was a prewar lawyer and judge, "Judge Rybczyński of the District Court sentenced him (having summoned Jewish witnesses) to a prison term."[21] If true, this would be a precedent-setting case. The records of these proceedings, however, have not been preserved in the archives, which is not surprising since very few dossiers of the Warsaw District Court survived the war.

Supervision of the Jewish Police in the Warsaw Ghetto

As briefly discussed with the example of Opoczno, the Blue Police controlled the Jewish police and were their superiors. At the highest levels, however, such supervision was carried out with a certain professional etiquette, courtesy, and police *savoir vivre*. This etiquette was violated by the head of one of the Blue Police commissariats, who in January 1942, sent a written order to the commander of the Jewish police, the aforementioned Lieutenant Colonel Józef Szeryński, to isolate designated Jewish houses in the ghetto. At this point, Blue Police Commander Aleksander Reszczyński reminded his subordinate that only he was authorized to give orders to Szeryński, and that the heads of the individual police precincts could only give orders to the heads of the Jewish Order Service areas.[22]

21 Karol Pędowski, *Pamiętnik: Powrót do mojego miasta* (handwritten manuscript), Biblioteka Narodowa (BN), Magazyn Rękopisów, ref. 12254 (mf 104106), p. 6.

22 Briefing with the Blue Police commander of the city of Warsaw, January 27, 1942, AAN, AK, 203-III-123, p. 4. The ghetto was divided into several *rejony* (regions), which were the equivalent of the patrolling areas of the Polish police precincts.

In terms of organization and management, there were three Blue Police precincts in the Warsaw ghetto (VI, VII, and VIII), and in the winter of 1942, an additional special detachment was created whose main task was to supervise the sealing of the ghetto borders. Polish officers served at the ghetto gates side by side with both Jewish and German policemen. In addition to guarding duties, the Blue Police carried out both investigative and intelligence activities within the Jewish district. The Jewish police tried as much as possible to solve minor cases on their own, but regarding more serious investigations, the cases were automatically handed over to the Blue Police.

The tangled web of connections and mutual dependencies between the Jewish police, the Blue Police, and the German police in the Jewish quarter is best illustrated by the case of Szlama Klajnberg.[23] Klajnberg, a Jew and a career thief from Warsaw with eight prewar convictions, was the leader of a gang operating in the ghetto, which also included two other experienced thieves: Icek Hoppenblum and Majer Margulies. The gang preyed on the most vulnerable inhabitants of the Warsaw ghetto: the displaced persons. From time to time, groups of Jews expelled from towns in the Warsaw district were "resettled" in the ghetto. With no support in Warsaw and unaware of big-city customs, they were particularly easy prey for criminals of various kinds. On March 7, 1941, Klajnberg robbed three displaced persons living "at the point"—referring to houses for the refugees and the poor—at 100 Pawia Street. His loot was 670 zlotys, but several hours later, the victims caught the perpetrator in the street and handed him over to the Jewish police. Normally in such a situation, the Blue Police would then enter the scene and hand over the results of their investigation to the Polish prosecutor, who would file an indictment with either the Warsaw District Court or the Municipal Court, depending on the seriousness of the crime. As a matter of fact, the Germans did not care about Jewish petty crime, and they left both the investigation and further legal proceedings in the hands of the Polish police and Polish courts. The German public

23 The proceedings and testimonies of the criminal case of Szlama Klajnberg and others, AMSW, SSW, 1636.

prosecutor's office only intervened if a German citizen was involved in the crime or if there was a violation of "the vital interests of the German people," as the official legal formula claimed.

In Klajnberg's case, however, things turned out differently. On the very first day of the investigation, the commanding officer of the II Region of the Jewish Police decided that the case went beyond his jurisdiction and sent a letter requesting help to the chief of the VIII Commissariat of the Polish police. According to preliminary inquiries, Klajnberg's gang operated with the help of a Polish policeman, whose presence guaranteed the compliance of the victims. When the case of a simple theft in the ghetto turned into an investigation of corruption within the ranks of the Polish police, the Germans took an interest in the case. The first sign that the Blue Police had lost control of the investigation was a letter dated March 10, 1941, sent by Captain Leon Dymiński, head of the VIII Commissariat to the Criminal Police (Kripo) authorities. In the letter, Captain Dymiński wrote, "I am sending the investigation file together with the detained Szmuel [Szlama] Klajnberg, for your consideration because one of the suspects is allegedly a Polish policeman, who was said to have acted with a weapon in his hand."[24] As a result of the German intervention, the Jews who had been robbed were asked to identify the culprit among the entire personnel of the VIII Commissariat. However, none of the Jews recognized the wanted officer among the Blue policemen. After the unsuccessful confrontation, the Germans lost interest in the case, and the story of the corrupt Blue Police officer was dropped when the investigating Kripo officer concluded that the identity of the wanted man could not be established. In a lengthy note, the Polish Kripo officer wrote, "Since this policeman has been seen entering the premises of the VIII Commissariat, therefore all the policemen of that commissariat were shown to the victims, but the victims did not recognize any of them."[25]

24 Letter sent by Captain Leon Dymiński, head of the VIII Commissariat to the Criminal Police (Kripo) authorities, March 10, 1941, the case of Szlama Klajnberg and others, AMSW, SSW, 1636.

25 Note from Polish Kripo officer, the case of Szlama Klajnberg and others, AMSW, SSW, 1636.

Since German interests were not violated in that case, Klajnberg, Hoppenblum, and Margulies were detained by the Directorate of Criminal Police and sent to be tried by the Polish District Court in Warsaw at 53 Leszno Street. Finally, Lieutenant Colonel Stanisław Wasilewski, the liaison officer of the Polish Criminal Police in Warsaw, sent an indictment to the District Court. As far as the management of the Jewish police was concerned—as evidenced by the example of the Klajnberg case—the power of the Blue policemen ended whenever the Germans entered the scene. This was true not only for the investigations but also for any other activities of the Blue Police in and around the ghetto.

The Guard-Convoy Unit

Captain Karol Stanisław Moniak was a Blue Police officer deeply involved in black-market scandals, who had also been designated as a person without honor by the underground resistance.[26] Moniak was head of the XV Commissariat (Praga) whose officers were often deployed in and around the ghetto. In October 1941, during a briefing, Captain Moniak declared to his subordinates, "The protection of the borders of the Jewish district is the sole responsibility of the Polish police and in matters of combating illegal border crossing, as well as the transfer or transportation of goods, the police should show initiative and utmost severity."[27] Captain Moniak was mistaken, because "the protection of" the borders of the ghetto was also the duty of both the German and Jewish Police, but these strong words delivered by the head of the commissariat were a nod to his German superiors. Captain Moniak was undoubtedly aware of the pressure from Lieutenant Colonel Alfred Jarke of the Schupo, who in the summer of 1941 had threatened Polish policemen with severe punishments for

26 Hempel, *Pogrobowcy klęski*, pp. 152–153.

27 *Informacja Bieżąca*, October 20, 1941, as seen in Note of Arnold Gubiński, chief of the 3rd Department of the Ministry of Justice to the prosecutor attached to the Warsaw District Court in Warsaw, January 5, 1949, AIPN, GK 453/1291, p. 1.

insubordination. Serious consequences were to be meted out, for example, to those policemen who refused to use their weapons against Jews illegally crossing the ghetto border.[28]

The harsher tone of the German superiors and the increasing terror against the Jews were in direct connection with the oft-cited Third Regulation, which introduced the death penalty for leaving the ghetto. It was in connection with this ordinance that the Germans decided to intensify their supervision over the Blue Police in the Jewish district. Lack of discipline, corruption, and outright criminal activity in the ranks of the Blue Police resulted in a firm response from the Germans from the beginning of 1942. In a letter to Commander Reszczyński of the Blue Police, Jarke threatened Polish police officers caught helping Jews "to leave the Jewish district" with severe punishments, including the death penalty, and the letter, translated into Polish, was sent to all high-ranking policemen of the Warsaw commissariats with an instruction to spread the word to the other police officers.[29]

A German gendarme cuts off the beard of a Jewish pedestrian with the assistance of two Polish officers. Courtesy of Łukasz Biedka.

28 Information, Protective Police Command in Warsaw, August 25, 1941, AAN, AK, 203-III-110, p. 12.
29 Letter of Colonel Jarke to Reszczyński, the commander of the Blue Police,

Polish and German police officers inspect the papers of a Jewish pedestrian, Warsaw 1941. Photo Collection, YVA, 3307/22.

In December 1941, Lieutenant Józef Skrzypiński, deputy head of the Kripo Commissariat V, was dismissed from service for "machinations" related to the illegal trade in furs confiscated from the Jews. As mentioned earlier, the scandals surrounding the furs requisitioned by the police in the ghettos were the cause of many arrests among Polish officers.[30] Rumors about German reprisals against the Blue Police spread around Warsaw. The Warsaw chronicler Franciszek Wyszyński noted the following in an entry dated December 31, 1941:

> As everyone here knows, smuggling and terrible bribery and corruption flourished at the entrances to the ghetto; with the money that the German guards and Polish policemen shared, everything could be carried into the ghetto and taken out of there. The same was now happening with furs, which supposedly could be bought very cheaply in the Jewish district. Well, now this boil is said to have burst: supposedly today at

January 8, 1942 and translation and commentary by Lieutenant Colonel Reszczyński, January 12, 1942, AAN, AK, 203-III-124, p. 25.

30 Warsaw police matters, undated, AAN, AK, 203-III-124, p. 114.

> 6 AM, eleven Polish policemen from the VII Commissariat were shot, and 46 are under arrest.[31]

In fact, it was Commissariat VI rather than Commissariat VII, no one was shot, and only two policemen were arrested. However, there is no doubt that the German authorities were concerned not only about the theft of Jewish furs but also about the general breakdown of discipline among the Polish policemen. On January 8, 1942, Lieutenant Colonel Jarke cautioned Polish officers against "bribery, careless approach to duty"[32] and stressed the increasing number of incidents of the Jews being led out of the ghetto in exchange for payment. "In cases of aiding and abetting clandestine trade, assisting and helping Jews to leave the Jewish district, etc., a death sentence may follow," he concluded emphatically.[33] Four days later Lieutenant Colonel Reszczyński sent out a Polish translation of the warning to all Blue Police officers serving in Warsaw.

Jarke's complaints, however, were not entirely justified. Regardless of the Germans' criticism, the Polish police was the most effective tool in the fight to seal the ghetto's borders. As the underground press reported:

> It was found that nearly 80 percent of the Jews caught on that [Aryan] side were handed over to the German authorities by the Polish police. Premeditatedly, deliberately, with a smile of duty well done, aware of the fact when passed into the hands of German tormentors, those people are crossing the border of life and death, "Polish policemen" pursue their victims.... Even German gendarmes are sometimes more understanding and less diligent on duty.[34]

31 Wyszyński, *Dzienniki z lat 1941–1944*, pp. 42–43.

32 Letters on bribery and careless approach to duty in the Polish police, January 8 and 12, 1942, AAN, AK, 203-III-124, p. 25.

33 Ibid.

34 "Za Naszą i Waszą Wolność," *Nasza Policja*, January–February 1942, no. 1 (10), ARG I 1340 (I/700), as quoted in Person, *Policjanci*, p. 141. For more information on the subject see the investigation of Officer S. Krzemiński accused in December 1941 of taking bribes from the Jews who were caught on the Aryan side, AMSW, Komenda Policji Polskiej Miasta Warszawy, fol. 17, investigation files VII.S.108/41.

Despite Jarke's complaints, the Polish officers seem to have been very vigilant, as long as the bribes did not diminish their devotion to duty. These bribes as opposed to their regular salaries constituted the essential part of the Polish policemen's budget. Eventually, the efficiency with which the Blue policemen hunted their victims around the ghetto began to worry the command of the Warsaw Blue Police. It was not the Jews, as they found out, but innocent Poles who fell prey to the overzealous policemen. On January 20, 1942, Lieutenant Colonel Reszczyński admonished his subordinates that "they too often detain Poles wrongly suspected by the police of hiding their Jewish ancestry. Many wrongly detained people were put in prison," the Blue Police commander added, "even though it could have been immediately established that the suspicion of Jewishness was unfounded."[35]

In early 1942, most likely in response to increasing German pressure and a breakdown in discipline, the leaders of the Warsaw Blue Police came up with a plan to create a special unit to intervene in and around the ghetto. The Guard-Convoy Unit (Oddział Wartowniczo-Konwojowy in Polish, OWK), also known as the Temporary Guard Unit, was established by order of Lieutenant Colonel Reszczyński in mid-February 1942. This unit took over the court-convoy platoon, the raiding platoon, the guard platoon in the Jewish district, and all police guards posted near the prisoners. As one of the underground reports reads: "The largest and tasked with particularly arduous and unpleasant duties is the so-called Guard Unit (ghetto duty). Its former commander, Second Lieutenant Michalski, was dismissed and replaced by the notorious fool and liar, Second Lieutenant Franciszek Kaczmarek."[36]

From the very beginning, service in this new unit, which was deployed around the ghetto and composed of policemen delegated from various stations, aroused much controversy. In theory, the members of the unit were supposed to work in rotation, but in practice—as the chief of the Blue Police pointed

35 Meeting with Lieutenant Colonel Reszczyński, January 20, 1942, AAN, AK, 203-III-123, p. 3.

36 Warsaw police matters, undated, AAN, AK, 203-III-124, p. 114.

out—it was always the same officers serving, and to make matters worse, they were always delegated by the same police stations. This, according to Lieutenant Colonel Reszczyński, encouraged corruption and demoralization.[37] The establishment of the OWK, intended as a countermeasure against bribery, turned out to be a complete mistake. Some commissariats resentfully defended their "monopoly" on access to the ghetto. Various arguments were put forward, including the question of vaccinations against typhus. In the summer of 1941, one of the Blue Police commissariats in the ghetto was quarantined after several of its officers became ill with typhus.[38] As a result, in the winter of 1941, all police officers on duty in the ghetto were vaccinated against louse-borne typhus. Consequently, efforts were made to limit the rotation of officers from other police stations where vaccinations had not been given.[39]

The first weeks of service of the newly formed OWK provided further evidence that the demoralization of the Polish police was progressing, regardless of the type of formation supervising the Jewish district.[40] The results were not long in coming. In April 1942, the new commander of the Orpo in Warsaw, Lieutenant Colonel Joachim Petsch, summoned Lieutenant Colonel Reszczyński to his office to warn him that should the situation fail to improve radically, he would not hesitate to arrest all the higher officers of the Warsaw Blue Police. Such a threat had to be treated seriously. After all, two years earlier in May 1940, the Germans had done exactly that to several dozen high-ranking officers from the Warsaw Blue Police headquarters, including the then-commanding officer of the Blue Police, Lieutenant Colonel Marian Kozielewski, who—as previously mentioned—was later sent to Auschwitz. Reszczyński acknowledged the validity of the Orpo commander's remarks, even adding that "policemen in the Guard-Convoy Unit do not collect their bread rations, not caring that they turn moldy, and a

37 Report, AAN, Delegatura Rządu na Kraj, 202-II-11, p. 6a.

38 Ibid.

39 Meeting with Lieutenant Colonel Reszczyński, January 20, 1942, AAN, AK, 203-III-123, p. 3.

40 Protocol no. 5 from the briefing with the police commander of the city of Warsaw, January 20, 1942, AAN, AK, 203-III-123, pp. 3–4.

policeman who was drunk and stopped at the ghetto border had 900 zloty in cash on him—one can come to the conclusion that Polish policemen are not always so poorly off."[41] At the same time, and approaching the matter from a slightly different angle, Petsch threatened to arrest the heads of any police stations whose walls "are covered with various inscriptions,"[42] which was most likely a reference to the anti-German slogans painted in public spaces by the illegal scout teams of Polish youths.

During the winter and spring of 1942, the issue of an effective blockade of the ghetto became one of the most serious challenges faced by Commander Reszczyński. The chief of the Polish police was particularly concerned with Jewish children, who were getting out of the ghetto by some unknown means. The commander's order no. 3617 of March 10, 1942, reads as follows: "It is ordered to combat more thoroughly the presence of Jewish minors in the Aryan district. Detained Jews are to be sent directly to the Jewish stage point in 5/7 Stawki Street."[43] The "Jewish stage point" mentioned in the order was a section of railroad tracks inside the ghetto, which would soon go down in history as the *Umschlagplatz*. Until July 1942, before the liquidation of the ghetto, this so-called stage point served as a concentration point for Jews sent to labor camps, primarily to the dreaded Treblinka I labor camp.

It seems that order no. 3617 did not bring about the desired results, as one month later, on April 16, 1942, Commander Reszczyński called a meeting of the heads of the Blue Police commissariats, during which the necessity of increased control over the Jews outside the ghetto was raised once again. The commander was concerned with recurring reports of Jewish children begging in the area of Marszałkowska and Świętokrzyska Streets, in Krakowskie Przedmieście, and Nowy Świat—the very core of downtown Warsaw and the most prestigious parts of the

41 Briefing with the commander of the Polish police, April 18, 1942, AAN, AK, 203-III-123, p. 6.

42 Ibid.

43 Minutes of the meeting of the police stations' chiefs, March 10, 1942, AMSW, II Komisariat PP, file 11, p. 52. An SS unit who served around the *Umschlagplatz* was stationed in this building.

city. The heads of the commissariats were ordered to spare no effort in the capture and arrest of Jewish children found outside the ghetto. There is no doubt that Commander Reszczyński's concern was directly related to a series of conferences during which the Germans demanded that the Blue Police strengthen their control over the ghetto. In the eyes of the German authorities, the question of Jewish children was important insofar as, with regard to people under fourteen years of age, the German prosecutors could not request the death penalty in the *Sondergericht*, so they did not know what to do with them. Ghetto commissioner Heinz Auerswald assured the German justice officials that underage Jews captured by the Polish police would be deported to the East. Incomplete documentation from the German courts shows that between April and July 1942, several hundred juvenile ghetto escapees were sent to their deaths, in accordance with the new policy.

Adam Chętnik, the previously mentioned ethnographer and social activist who was living in Warsaw during the war, mentioned Jewish children roaming the streets of Warsaw in his diary. "At the end of 1941, there were more and more shabby Jewish children walking around the city, begging for bread. This year (1942) you hardly meet them. The Germans caught them and shot many of them."[44] Lieutenant Colonel Reszczyński's problem with Jewish children illegally crossing to the Aryan side of Warsaw would, however, soon be truly over. On July 22, 1942, the Germans began liquidating the ghetto, which resolved the issue once and for all.

From the *Grossaktion* to the Ghetto Uprising

July 22, 1942, marks the beginning of the liquidation of the Warsaw ghetto or, as the Germans called it, *Grossaktion Warschau*.[45] The operation lasted until September 21, 1942, and resulted in the

44 Chętnik, *Wspomnienia z lat okupacji*, p. 96.
45 In Polish nomenclature, the term "*Wielka Akcja*" (Great Action) was adopted.

deportation of more than 300,000 Warsaw Jews to the gas chambers of Treblinka. Many accounts of the liquidation of the Warsaw ghetto have survived in Holocaust literature, including one of the most haunting: Abraham Lewin's *Dziennik wielkiej deportacji* (Diary of the Great Deportation).[46] However, the aim of this study is not to discuss the course of the operation itself—this has been described many times by survivors, non-survivors, and Holocaust scholars—but to try to understand the actions of the Polish police during that time.

On July 18, 1942, a special liquidation squad (Liquidierungskommando) consisting of more than 800 men arrived in Warsaw from Lublin. The headquarters and most of the Liquidierungskommando operating in the ghettos of the Warsaw district were located in Lublin from where they were "delegated" to carry out the deportation operations in both the Lublin and Warsaw districts. The concentration of both police and SS forces in Lublin was related to the leadership ambitions of Odilo Globocnik, who was charged with implementing Operation Reinhard. The "death commando" was led directly by *SS-Sturmbannführer* Hermann Höfle, the staff commander of Operation Reinhard and one of Globocnik's deputies and trusted men. For this reason, the unit sent to Warsaw was referred to as Kommando Höfle.[47] The commando consisted of SS and SD officers along with Ukrainian and Latvian auxiliary formations, joined on site by the Polish police, the Kripo, and the Jewish Order Service.

With the arrival of the liquidation commando in Warsaw, the Blue Police were put on alert. At the time when Höfle's men entered the ghetto, the Polish police officers were on so-called protective duty outside the walls. The job of the Blue Police was to cut off any escape routes from the liquidated ghetto, a particularly important role because in the face of death, thousands of Jews panicked and

46 The English publication of Abraham Lewin's *Dziennik wielkiej deportacji* is *A Cup of Tears: A Diary of the Warsaw Ghetto*, ed. by Antony Polonsky (Oxford: Basil Blackwell and the Institute of Polish-Jewish Studies, 1988).

47 Transcript of the interrogation of Hermann Höfle, October 20, 1961, in Charles Ajenstat et al., *Hermann Höfle: L'Autrichien artisan de la Shoah en Pologne* (Paris: Berg, 2007), pp. 140–141.

looked for ways to reach the Aryan side. As one survivor noted, "Blackmailers and paid agents were rampant. On average 30–40 Jews were captured every day in the city."[48] The activities of the *szmalcowniks* (blackmailers) went hand in hand with intensified police action. Reinforced patrols of both the German Gendarmerie and the Blue police appeared in the city, and their main job was to catch Jews. The desperation of those escaping the ghetto provided the Polish police officers with an opportunity to make additional profit. In a few known cases, police officers helped selflessly, but most often they were paid dearly for turning a blind eye.[49] There is no question that turning a blind eye during the *Grossaktion* became a rather risky business. Blue Police patrols were reinforced by a strong contingent of German police, and it became increasingly commonplace to see Ukrainian and Latvian auxiliary formations along the ghetto walls.

Guard duty around the liquidated ghetto must have been draining, since on July 25—the fourth day of the *Grossaktion*—policemen from the company whose job it was to "protect the Jewish district" had their service reduced to six hours because of the "hard work" it involved.[50] This type of service was indeed hard, as evidenced by an underground report that reads: "At 2:50 PM, policemen Mioduszewski Franciszek and Lewandowski Roman shot the Jew Chaim Kon, for escaping from a transport taken to Stawki Street."[51] The policemen Lewandowski and Mioduszewski had shot at one of the thousands of Jews who were being herded to the *Umschlagplatz*—and then to Treblinka—day after day. It is difficult to deduce from the laconic report whether the Polish policemen were inside the ghetto at the moment they opened fire or if they were securing the liquidation operation from the outside. However, there is no doubt that some were on duty at the loading ramp in the ninth circle of hell—the *Umschlagplatz* itself.[52] It was there that the tailor Błędowski ended up along

48 Recollections of Bronka Kalibanski, YVA, O.33/684.

49 For more on this subject, see chapter 8 of this volume.

50 Note "P.17", July 25, 1942, AAN, AK, 203-III-119, p. 13.

51 Report, September 8, 1942, AAN, Delegatura Rządu na Kraj, 202-II-44, p. 19.

52 It should be noted here, however, that at the same time, one of the Blue

with his wife and three daughters. Having waited in hiding until the death transport departure, Błędowski had emerged from his hiding place and encountered three Blue policemen sitting on a bench in front of the building:

> He asked them to help him escape, said that he was a Polish citizen who had been wounded in the war in 1920, that Poland would soon be resurrected, and he would like to live to see that, that they, Polish police, as Poles would best understand his plight and help him. But the "Polish police" were not convinced by his pleas. One of them even said: "Poland is far away, it may come to pass or it may not, it remains to be seen, but in the meantime, I have to live."[53]

This appeal to the civic community turned out to be completely misguided. For the majority of Poles in the third year of the war, civic community—already a very weak concept in prewar Poland—had been replaced by a narrowly defined national community. It is worth noting at this point that as the occupation continued, even this narrow notion of belonging based on ethnicity had eroded. A Jew hiding in the Bielany district during the Warsaw Uprising in August 1944 noted in his diary:

> All the local Poles buy from the [German] soldiers the loot brought from the city, because these soldiers go in their tanks to fight the insurgents in the city. They bring food, sugar, etc., as well as rags, and the brothers of the insurgents, Poles, eagerly buy the loot taken from their brethren who are fighting and dying in the burning Warsaw, oh, the irony of fate.[54]

policemen informed the underground authorities. "Polish policemen have nothing to do with the ghetto liquidation. The fact that the occupier did not use the Polish police for this purpose is certainly proof of a lack of trust in the Polish police, resulting from the attitude of the entire Polish society." August 11, 1942, AAN, Delegatura Rządu na Kraj, 202-II-28, pp. 58–59. I am grateful to Dariusz Libionka, who pointed out this quotation.

53 Obremski, *Wśród zatrutych*, p. 163. The described scene at the *Umschlagplatz* took place in January 1943 during the second deportation from the Warsaw ghetto.

54 Mordka Purman testimony, YVA, O.3/260.

Toward the end of the *Grossaktion*, one of the leaders of the underground police infrastructure (State Security Corps, Państwowy Korpus Bezpieczeństwa)—most likely Lieutenant Colonel Stanisław Wasilewski, who had been in hiding since the spring of 1942—had a long conversation with Commander Aleksander Reszczyński of the Blue Police. Reszczyński did not hide his bitterness about cooperation with the underground and complained about unfavorable opinions spread about him by the underground press. As far as general matters were concerned, the police chief expressed his disapproval of increasingly frequent attempts to involve his men in the underground resistance. According to Reszczyński, such actions were pointless, as they only led to great losses in the police ranks. In his opinion, about half of the Blue policemen were involved in the resistance in one way or another, and their further recruitment would cause "a culling of the valuable element," as a result of which Commander Reszczyński would be "left with dredges" when the hour of trial came.[55] It is worth noting the commanding officer's estimates regarding the scale of the Blue policemen's involvement in the activities of the Polish underground.

In the aftermath of the *Grossaktion,* about 50,000 Jews remained in the Warsaw ghetto, 30,000 of whom were there legally, working in the so-called *szopy* (German-owned workshops in the ghetto), while the rest were "illegals," people hiding in bunkers and other hideouts within the significantly reduced Jewish district. Franciszek Wyszyński recorded the following in his diary: "October 5, [1942]. Jewish front. It is no longer the Latvians that guard the ghetto walls, but our 'Blue' Police. The remaining 30,000–33,000 Jews are housed in the ghetto."[56] However, the Blue Police had reclaimed control of the ghetto walls under dramatically different circumstances. The underground *Kronika wydarzeń na terenie m.st. Warszawy od 1 sierpnia 1942 do 30 kwietnia 1944* (Chronicle of Events in the

55 Conversations held with Aleksander Reszczyński, September 19–20, 1942, AAN, AK, 203-III-115, pp. 10–10a.

56 Wyszyński, *Dzienniki z lat 1941–1944*, p. 224.

City of Warsaw from August 1, 1942–April 30, 1944) records a number of incidents when Polish policemen were forced to open fire.[57] They usually shot at people trying to rob abandoned houses. Previous ordinances and legal arrangements ceased to have any meaning. As soon as the implementation of the "Final Solution to the Jewish Question" began, the Jews lost their right to live, except those few who were working for the Germans in secondary ghettos and whose death sentence was therefore deferred for several months. The new policy of the authorities was expressed in an order from the chief of the SS and police for the Warsaw district, which as of December 10, 1942, applied to both German and Polish officers: "Jews encountered outside the perimeter of the residential Jewish district, without having permission to do so, are to be shot immediately without opening any investigation."[58]

In early January 1943, Heinrich Himmler visited Warsaw on his way back from an inspection of the Eastern Front. During his short visit, the chief of the SS and police ordered the liquidation of the remaining ghetto. According to the plan, the Germans first wanted to transport about 8,000 "illegal" ghetto inhabitants to their deaths. The *Aktion* began on January 18, 1943. This time, however, the unsuspecting Germans encountered armed Jewish resistance. As the *Kronika wydarzeń* reports:

> The liquidation was carried out by a team consisting of 40 G[estap]o officers and 500 gendarmes. During the operation, there were a few acts of defense, Jews shot at the gendarmes with revolvers and threw grenades. Three gendarmes were killed and several wounded. These manifestations were sporadic, there was no large-scale activity. Mostly people who were not employed or who worked in *szopy* of lesser importance for the army, were to be deported. This *Aktion*

57 *Kronika wydarzeń na terenie m.st. Warszawy od 1 sierpnia 1942 do 30 kwietnia 1944*, AAN, Delegatura Rządu na Kraj, 202-II-44.

58 Order of the SS and police commander to the commanders of the Order Police in Warsaw, December 10, 1942, AMSW, Komenda Policji Polskiej "Obwód Praga" 1939–1944, 1710, file 10, p. 1.

> finished today. Jews were transported to Treblinka. The wagons were disinfected in Warsaw, and these trains had priority over military trains.[59]

Among those transported to their deaths that day was Abraham Lewin—the ghetto chronicler, Ringelblum's associate, and a member of the Oneg Shabbat group—and his daughter Yehudit.

Following the January *Aktion*, preparations for the Warsaw Ghetto Uprising intensified. Jewish fighters began to rearm on the Aryan side of the city by either buying weapons on the black market or disarming Germans.[60] For the Polish police, this meant risky interventions and sometimes an exchange of fire. The Jews, who were thus far considered as easy prey, began to put up armed resistance. As the underground *Kronika wydarzeń* reports:

> 13 [March 1943]. In the morning, a Blue Police investigator stopped two Jews on Leszno Street, because they seemed suspicious to him. The Jews started to run away, and during their escape they used weapons and killed a German guard who wanted to stop them. The guard also used a gun, wounding one of the Jews. A pistol and ammunition were found with the wounded man. At the sound of gunfire, another German sentry came running and stopped the other fleeing man. When the detainee was being escorted, a group of Jews attacked the convoy in an attempt to free him. A shootout ensued, resulting in the wounding of two Germans and Detective Wasilewski. The escorted Jew was killed. In the evening of that day, the Germans killed about 300 Jews in retaliation.[61]

59 *Kronika wydarzeń*, AAN, Delegatura Rządu na Kraj, 202-II-44, as quoted in Dariusz Libionka, "Zapisy dotyczące Żydów w warszawskich kronikach policyjnych z lat 1942–1944," *Zagłada Żydów, Studia i materiały*, 10 (2014), pp. 592–621.

60 Icchak Cukierman ("Antek"), *Nadmiar pamięci (Siedem owych lat): Wspomnienia 1939–1946* (Warsaw: PWN, 2000), pp. 183–185; Simcha Rotem ("Kazik"), *Wspomnienia bojowca ŻOB*, ed. by Iwona Śledzińska-Katarasińska (Warsaw: PWN, 1993), pp. 36–39.

61 As quoted in Libionka, "Zapisy dotyczące Żydów."

Perhaps this killed man was a member of the Jewish Military Union (Żydowski Związek Wojskowy, ŻZW), as suggested by Dariusz Libionka and Laurence Weinbaum.[62]

On March 23, 1943, the Schupo command sent a circular to the chief of the Polish police, requesting the distribution of the circular to all Polish policemen. The circular stated that many Jews were hiding outside the ghetto, using Polish documents and Aryan papers. Police officers were ordered to intensify the search for all those Jews and to coordinate their activities with Kripo agents. The order from the Schupo commander reads: "Detected Jews are to be arrested immediately, their apartments secured and sealed, and *Untersturmführer* Brandt is to be notified of the fact."[63] As a reward for discovering a Jew, policemen were promised a bonus: one-third of the secured Jewish property. This Schupo command contradicted von Sammern-Frankenegg's December directive to shoot immediately, but from the point of view of the captured Jews, the difference was not at all significant: In both cases, the victims were ultimately going to die.

The March order, however, introduced a certain modification to police practice, namely the incentive bonus paid out in the form of a percentage of the property found on the captured Jews. The idea was certainly the result of a meeting of the chiefs of the civil local German administration (*Kreishauptmänner*) of the Warsaw district, which took place in Łowicz on March 11, 1943. During the meeting, material incentives were promised to policemen and informers, and a uniform and consistent system of searching for fugitive Jews was put into effect. The German administrators placed special emphasis on the participation of "the Sonderdienst, Polish police and informers [*V-Männer*]. The broadest possible masses of Polish society should also be involved in this action [the search for Jews]," the German officials urged.[64]

62 Dariusz Libionka and Laurence Weinbaum, *Bohaterowie, hochsztaplerzy, opisywacze: Wokół Żydowskiego Związku Wojskowego* (Warsaw: Stowarzyszenie Centrum Badań nad Zagładą Żydow, 2011), pp. 339–340.

63 Report no. 11, April 7, 1943, AAN, Delegatura Rządu na Kraj, 202-II-37, pp. 42–43.

64 Ferdinand von Sammern-Frankenegg's notes, March 13, 1943, BAL, B162/2158, p. 2549.

In the concluding sentence of the March order, the Schupo instructed Polish policemen to notify *SS-Untersturmführer* Brandt of any discovered victims. Karl Brandt was one of the heads of the Jewish Section (Judenreferat) in the Warsaw Gestapo, and his headquarters were on Żelazna Street. It was to there that in April 1943, in accordance with the Schupo order, Polish policemen brought Stanisław Holckener, who had escaped to the Aryan side two months earlier. At the beginning of April, Holckener visited his prewar employee Stanisław Kamiński, who he had entrusted with his belongings for safekeeping. This was the remainder of his property, the recovery of which was a matter of life and death for the owner. Instead of Kamiński, however, two Blue policemen were waiting for the terrified Jew at the gate of the house. In his testimony, Holckener even noted the service numbers of the two officers—badges 1787 and 2688:

> The house at 33 Freta Street, where Kamiński lives, belongs to the II precinct, and those policemen were from the I precinct and had no right to arrest anyone in the area of another commissariat. At the gate, they jumped at me, revolvers in hand, shouting "Hands up!" They knew my name and prewar profession, apparently Kamiński had informed them about everything, I tried to reason with them, saying that I was also a Pole and that I had served as a volunteer in the Polish army in 1918, 1919, and 1920, and that I was a Knight of the Cross of Valor and two Crosses of Merit, but they would not hear any of that, they only called me a Jew and a Bolshevik and hit me several times with their revolver butts so that I had a hollow in my skull the size of an egg. I had a "Tissot" watch worth 2,500 zlotys on my wrist, 350 zlotys in cash, and I was wearing an overcoat. I wanted to give it all to them. They refused and took me to the I Commissariat instead. The next day, that is April 14, 1943, the same two policemen came to the apartment on Ciepła Street, looking for my wife, who was hidden in a shelter with 13 people. They let her go for a larger ransom because she had Aryan documents. The search and the visit of these policemen cost the lives of four people who

became so frightened that they returned to the ghetto. Most likely the Kamińskis had planned that crime, followed me, and tracked down this address. At the I Commissariat, where I was brought on April 13, 1943, at 8:00 AM, the deputy chief of the station was Sergeant Stodulski, my acquaintance, who told me that there was nothing he could do for me because he was afraid of those policemen who had arrested me, as they were outcasts, specializing in catching Jews. The only thing he could do for me was to send me to the Befehlstelle at 101 Żelazna Street, instead of the Gestapo on Szucha Avenue. And, so he did.[65]

On April 15, 1943, two days after Holckener's arrest and his transfer to *SS-Untersturmführer* Brandt's office on Żelazna Street, Major Przymusiński, the new commander of the Warsaw Blue Police, issued the following message lamenting the declining morale of the officers:

> After all, it is experience that should teach every policeman that criminals are recruited from among the uncultured, uneducated spheres and from among dark and lazy individuals, meaning that work and knowledge usually protect one from falling into the abyss of crime. Unfortunately, numerous cases of illegal trafficking, bribery, and extortion among police officers prove that lack of work and unwillingness to expand one's knowledge and education go hand in hand. Such a policeman, who does not care about his intellectual and moral standards, is lost for his profession, his family, and for the society.[66]

To be clear, Major Przymusiński was not concerned about the capture and handover of Jews to the Gestapo. What worried the chief of the Polish police was the apparent lack of enthusiasm for

65 Stanisław Holckener, *Zapiski z getta warszawskiego, styczeń–maj 1943*, GFH, Adolf Berman Collection, 6086, pp. 7–9.

66 Order No. 81 of the Blue Police Commander in Warsaw, April 15, 1943, AMSW, Komenda Policji Polskiej "Obwód Praga" 1939–1944, 1710, file 5, pp. 3–3a.

learning German among Polish policemen. Four days later, the uprising broke out in the Warsaw ghetto.

"'Brave' Associates in Murder": The Blue Police during the Ghetto Uprising

On April 19, 1943, upon hearing the news that German liquidation units were entering the district, an uprising broke out in the Warsaw ghetto. The Germans deployed considerable forces to suppress it: 440 SS Panzergrenadiers, 380 SS cavalry soldiers, 220 Orpo officers, 340 Ukrainians from the Trawniki training camp (the so-called Trawniki men who also served in the extermination camps), artillerymen, and armored forces. On the Polish side, about 360 policemen from various commissariats took part in the fight against the Warsaw Jews on a daily basis, and 166 Warsaw firefighters were assigned to extinguish the fires. Eighty-five soldiers and policemen were killed or wounded in the fight against the insurgents in the ghetto. In the conclusion of his report "The Jewish Residential District in Warsaw Is No More!", the commander of the whole operation, *SS-Gruppenführer* Jürgen Stroop, preceded the list of dead and wounded with a brief comment: "They put on the line what they had most precious: their own lives. We will never forget them!"[67]

The last name on the list of causalities belonged to Julian Zieliński, a Blue policeman from the XIV Commissariat killed "in the performance of his duties" on the first day of the uprising.[68] It is worth mentioning that among those wounded in the fight against the Jewish insurgents were Polish policemen from the I, VII, and VIII Commissariats as well as officers from the regular stations located around the ghetto.[69] In his report, Stroop devoted

67 Jürgen Stroop, *Żydowska dzielnica mieszkaniowa w Warszawie już nie istnieje!*, ed. by Andrzej Żbikowski (Warsaw: Instytut Pamięci Narodowej and Żydowski Instytut Historyczny, 2009), p. 24.

68 In fact, Zieliński was killed on April 19 during an exchange of fire with a Kedyw sabotage unit.

69 Stroop, *Żydowska dzielnica mieszkaniowa w Warszawie*, pp. 24–29.

one more sentence to the Polish police. Under the entry dated May 6, 1943, when organized resistance in the ghetto had practically ceased, the following is written: "The Polish police, encouraged by the monetary rewards paid out, are trying to bring every Jew that shows his face in the city to the authorities."[70]

The short, dry phrases of Stroop's report, however, do not fully present the contribution of the Polish police to the suppression of the uprising. A good starting point is the *Kronika wydarzeń* and the *Kronika policyjna* (The Police Chronicle), two—sometimes overlapping—records of events on the front lines of the fight against crime in occupied Warsaw.[71] Both sources were compiled for the purposes of the underground, which scrutinized the activities of the Orpo, Kripo, and the Blue Police. There is no doubt that the information on which the entries in the *Kronika wydarzeń* and the *Kronika policyjna* were based was taken—at least in part—from reports filed by Blue policemen involved in underground work. Dariusz Libionka writes more extensively on this subject in the introduction to the first printed edition of excerpts from both chronicles.[72]

The first indication of the impending liquidation of the ghetto came from the Polish police commander Major Franciszek Przymusiński, who was summoned to a meeting with von Sammern-Frankenegg, the SS and police commander in the Warsaw district. The invitation was issued by von Sammern-Frankenegg, but it was Jürgen Stroop who presided over the meeting, having arrived in Warsaw that day—on Himmler's orders—to take charge of the liquidation of the ghetto. Von Sammern, who Stroop publicly declared "was not up to the task and did not show enough energy,"[73] was removed from command. Born in Pomerania in the Prussian partition, Przymusiński enjoyed a certain amount of respect from the Germans. He was one of the few Polish

70 Ibid., p. 84.

71 The previously mentioned *Kronika wydarzeń na terenie m.st. Warszawy od 1 sierpnia 1942 do 30 kwietnia 1944*, AAN, Delegatura Rządu na Kraj, 202-II-44; and the *Kronika policyjna*, AAN, Delegatura Rządu na Kraj, 203-III-122.

72 Libionka, "Zapisy dotyczące Żydów."

73 As quoted in Wulf, *Das Dritte Reich*, p. 245.

policemen who spoke fluent German, graduated from a German police school before World War I, and was later distinguished in service of the German army for which he was awarded the Iron Cross in 1917. In the Second Polish Republic, Przymusiński served in the police force in Bydgoszcz, Środa Wielkopolska, and Rypin respectively. In 1934, he was promoted to the rank of captain. After the September defeat, he came to the capital and, for a time, served as commanding officer of the Warsaw Blue Police, later becoming Lieutenant Colonel Reszczyński's deputy.

When he received the invitation to the meeting with von Sammern-Frankenegg, Przymusiński had only been the Blue Police commander for three weeks, having succeeded Lieutenant Colonel Reszczyński following his assassination on March 4, 1943.[74] The underground informants monitoring the Blue Police did not have a good opinion of the new commander. As counterintelligence reports from the fall of 1943 read:

> Blue Police Commander, residing at 23 Miodowa St., apartment 48, speaks better German than Polish. He tried to register as an ethnic German (*Volksdeutsch*). In his office at the headquarters he put up Hitler's portrait that he took down when he heard that his request to change the citizenship had been turned down. He bowed humbly to every German. He instructed that in case of a German visit, Poles should report in their offices in German.[75]

Under the report dated November 2, 1943, there is a note that reads: "According to 'Balcer' Przymusiński did not apply to be

74 Quite a bit has been written about the assassination of Colonel Reszczyński (the discussion of which is beyond the scope of this volume). See, for example, among others: Maciej Bernatt-Reszczyński, *Niewygodny Polak* (Poznań: Wydawnictwo Poznańskie, 2017). According to police intelligence, shortly after Reszczyński's assassination, Commissioner Kierski of the Blue Police headquarters was killed by bullets from the same assassins—"one of the assassins with an eminently Semitic appearance." See Report no 12, April 12, 1943, AAN, Delegatura Rządu na Kraj, 202-II-37, pp. 47–48.

75 Report, Home Army intelligence and counterintelligence documents from the Warsaw area, November 2, 1943, AIPN, BU 380/30, vol. 3, p. 204.

counted among the *Volksdeustche*. He confirms, however, that for a short time a portrait of Hitler was hanging in his office."[76]

The meeting with the commander of the SS and the police began on April 18, 1943, at 2:30 PM. Aside from Major Przymusiński, also invited were: Alfred Jarke, the previously mentioned commander of the Schupo in Warsaw; his deputy, Captain Veesinger; and Lieutenant Colonel von Zammore, Gendarmerie commander in the district. During the briefing, Major Przymusiński was ordered to summon a special detachment of five higher-ranking officers and 215 policemen at 1:00 AM. "The task of the Polish police," reads the underground *Kronika wydarzeń*, "was to guard the outer walls of the ghetto and prevent Jews from escaping beyond those walls."[77] In the following days of fighting, the amount of Polish police forces deployed around the ghetto would increase. The scope of their duties would also change.

Considering the number of officers involved in suppressing the ghetto uprising, it is safe to assume that all of Warsaw's police commissariats participated in the *Aktion*. Mietek Pachter, a Jewish insurgent brought to the *Umschlagplatz*, noted the following scene:

> My thoughts are interrupted, here we are passing a *wacha* [sentry unit] on Dzika Street. There are Polish Blue policemen. They were standing there, watching the death march. A few of them, standing a little further from the Germans, are saying quietly: "Come on, throw your money and diamonds, you won't need them anyway..." Who could be more awful than these greedy leeches. I would throw something at them, all right, but a grenade, for those words, but one must remain silent. However, a scream full of hatred bursts out of my chest involuntarily, "And you are not safe, the same thing will happen to you too, I can only throw a curse at you...!" I would be cursing them now with all my soul. A fire simply burned in my heart. All I heard in my ears was: "You won't need them anyway…" A few people responded to their words

76 Ibid.

77 *Kronika wydarzeń*, April 18, 1943, AAN, Delegatura Rządu na Kraj, 202-II-44.

> with a series of curses. The crowd went wild because of that, their insolence had reached its peak. But what can you expect of them, why would they be better than their employers? They form a well-knit set. Someone even spat in the Blue policeman's face when he said that again. How much sadism and hatred there was in those few words!!![78]

Other Blue policemen were waiting for the insurgents who were trying to escape from the encirclement. Standing on Świętojerska Street—more or less in the area of today's Chinese embassy—Alina Margolis saw a hole in the wall:

> Through this hole a girl was crawling toward us with snakelike movements. Now everyone was staring at her. She got out. She was all black and smeared with soot. She screamed so loud that I heard her. "I JUMPED OFF FROM THE FLOOR!!! EVERYONE WAS BURNED!!!" It seemed to me that a firefighter [a Polish fire brigade was deployed by the wall] shouted back, "GOOD LUCK, MISS!!!" A moment later, a "Blue" policeman broke through the crowd, grabbed her by the shoulder and dragged her away.[79]

Hela Rufeisen Schüpper and a group of her comrades from the Jewish Fighting Organization (Żydowska Organizacja Bojowa, ŻOB) got to the other side of the wall through the sewer. Instead of taking them to the manhole on Bielańska Street, the guide left them on Długa Street. That was where they came face-to-face with Polish Blue policemen. "As soon as I got out of the sewer, I heard, 'Go into the entrance of that house and we'll sort everything out.' 'We're not going to any entrance,' I said. 'I handle all the money matters, if that's what you mean.'"[80] This went on long enough for the Germans to take notice of the group of ŻOB members. They began to shoot. The group dispersed. The policemen did not stop them.

78 Pachter, *Umierać też trzeba umieć*, pp. 413–414.

79 Alina Margolis-Edelman, *Tego, co mówili, nie powtórzę…* (Wrocław: Siedmioróg, 1999), p. 93.

80 Rufeisen-Schüpper, *Pożegnanie Miłej 18*, p. 114.

As mentioned previously, the *Kronika policyjna* and the *Kronika wydarzeń*—day by day and sparing little detail—reported the activities of the Blue Police, its casualties, and the situation in the city in connection with the uprising. On the very first day of the uprising, Corporal Julian Zieliński of the XIV Commissariat, who was mentioned in Stroop's report, was killed, Corporal Franciszek Kluziński of the VII Commissariat was shot in the hand on Bonifraterska Street, and Sergeant Frydrykiewicz of the I Commissariat was shot in the stomach.[81] All three took part in a clash with a unit of the Home Army. A day later, Corporal Stanisław Gruszecki received bullet wounds to his legs, and in the Mokotów district, "a policeman named Rozpędowski Marian from the XVI Commissariat was shot dead. The perpetrators were two Jewish men and one Jewish girl who escaped. A SS unit was training in the area, but they did not take part in the chase because of the lack of ammunition."[82] On May 10, 1943, at 2:30 PM, the *Kronika policyjna* reports:

> Two Jews riding in a cab on Żabia Street, upon seeing a policeman, Corporal Wacław Zasada, fled in haste, shooting at him with pistols and throwing grenades behind them, the shrapnel of which wounded the corporal. Despite the wound, he did not stop his pursuit and continued it with the help of Corporal Głownia. One of the Jews was killed, the other was shot by an SS officer after the capture.[83]

As a result of the swift action of Corporals Zasada and Głownia together with an unknown SS officer, the Jews on the Aryan side of Warsaw were killed. Nevertheless, the murder of Platoon Sergeant Rozpędowski and the wounds of Corporal Zasada provided tangible proof that the insurgents escaping from the ghetto moved the fight against the enemy to the Aryan side of the city, something that disturbed not only the Germans but also the Home Army

81 *Kronika policyjna*, entry dated April 19, 1943, AAN, Delegatura Rządu na Kraj, 203-III-122.

82 Libionka, "Zapisy dotyczące Żydów," p. 589.

83 Police reports, *Kronika policyjna*, AAN, Delegatura Rządu na Kraj, 203-III-122.

command, who feared German reprisals in case of uncoordinated acts of resistance in the city.

The ghetto uprising caused a veritable "blackmail fever" on the Aryan side. As the *Kronika policyjna* noted: "The number of robberies in this reporting week has not decreased. The attackers pose as men searching for Jews, checking meters, and most often try to pass off as G[esta]po or Kripo."[84] The Delegatura records include a report sent by a Jewish witness. He described the sudden upsurge of blackmail during the liquidation of the ghetto as a "mania":

> The Aryan side—tragic news was coming from there. Even the first steps [on the Aryan side] were often nightmarish. *Szmalcowniks* would greet newcomers by robbing them completely, often even taking their clothes. Blackmail was practiced by landlords, street urchins, policemen and agents, and was so common that it verged on a mania.[85]

As the secret informer wrote:

> They saw a Jew in everyone. Policemen would stop people in cabs and in the street if they thought someone looked Jewish. On May 6, at Bankowy Square two policemen stopped a cab—the passengers did not even look like Jews—one of them threw a grenade at the policemen, a shoot-out ensued, and the policemen killed both Jews.[86]

Reinforced German patrols circled the liquidated ghetto. Their presence exposed some Polish policemen to unforeseen and unwelcome challenges that they unexpectedly had to face. Sergeant Edward Dębek learned about this when he was captured by agents

84 *Kronika policyjna*, April 1943, AAN, Delegatura Rządu na Kraj, 203-III-122.

85 Report by a Jewish witness in the Warsaw ghetto, April 1943, AAN, Delegatura Rządu na Kraj, 202-II-28, p. 92.

86 *Kronika policyjna*, entry dated May 6, 1943, AAN, Delegatura Rządu na Kraj, 203-III-122.

of the German Security Police "while plundering the Jewish district," and he was later taken to the Żelazna Street guardhouse, where he was left in the care of *SS-Untersturmführer* Brandt from the Warsaw Gestapo.[87]

Returning to the liquidated ghetto for a moment, while the quoted accounts and documents place the Polish policemen mostly at the ghetto gates or outside the ghetto walls, Leon Najberg's diary leaves no doubt that the Blue officers were also directly involved—together with the Germans—in the murders of defenseless civilians inside the ghetto:

> On Wednesday, 26 May [1943], all day long it was uneasy in our area, machine guns were barking, LMGs were howling, and bandits were running like mad through the yard; at 7 PM, we could hear the screams of Jews. A gang of German bandits with bloodthirsty sellouts from the "Blue" Police entered the courtyard of the house at 4 Wałowa Street, dragging new Jewish victims. The "Blue" policemen rushed to the disoriented and terrorized people and shot them. Then the bandits drove away the last three victims. I recognized them as Ajzenberg, Weinberg, and Fugman. They walked calmly, composed and resigned. When Fugman noticed Browning pistols aimed at them by the "Blue" policemen, he said his final words to them: "German lackeys, I will be avenged!" The steel barrels in the hands of the policemen fired their last rounds into the living.[88]

It did not stop there. In addition to committing murder, the Blue Police also participated in looting, as Najberg writes:

> *Thursday, 27 May*: All that was not enough for our fellow citizens, our "brave" associates in murder—the "Blue"

87 *Kronika policyjna*, entry dated May 4, 1943, AAN, Delegatura Rządu na Kraj, 203-III-122.

88 Leon Najberg, *Ostatni powstańcy getta* (Warsaw: Żydowski Instytut Historyczny w Polsce, 1993), pp. 89–90. See also the original manuscript: Leon Najberg, *Ostatni walczący w getcie warszawskim*, ŻIH, 302/113.

> Police: after yesterday's killings, today they came to loot. Policemen from the XVI and XVII Commissariats in Warsaw[89] came today at 4:00 AM to the courtyard of the house at 4 Wałowa Street and pulled off clothes, underwear, and shoes from the still warm Jewish bodies from the Drykiers' bunker, leaving the "carcasses" naked. They did the same with the corpses of women from 2 Wałowa Street. The robbers packed the clothes into bags and at 5:00 AM, they took them to the Polish district. When stripped, the corpses were tossed around like animal carcasses. Twenty-five hyenas, armed to the teeth with a variety of automatic weapons and grenades, took part in the sacrilege.[90]

The Blue policemen from the XVI Commissariat located at 172 Grochowska Street—included in the operational area of Praga—had already gained a notorious reputation for fighting the Jews of Warsaw. In February 1943, two of its officers Antoni Kołomoński and Andrzej Szlęzak were sentenced by a German court to nine months' imprisonment for extorting Jews.[91] They were joined by a certain Michał Wojciechowski, who according to the AK police department, "was known in the area of the XVII Commissariat as a Jew-killer."[92]

89 XVII and XVIII Commissariats were part of the "Praga" circuit. In 1943, the head of the XVII Commissariat was Captain Piotr Kruk. For more on him, see chapter 8. The head of the XVIII Commissariat was Lieutenant Marian Obrembski, who was described in the underground report as a paid guardian of dangerous bandits prowling around Warsaw. See Special report no 25, December 21, 1943, AAN, Delegatura Rządu na Kraj, 202-II-36, p. 33.

90 Najberg, *Ostatni powstańcy getta*, p. 92.

91 Blue Police, AMSW, Komenda Policji Polskiej "Obwód Praga" 1939–1944, 1710, file 5, p. 11. Henryk Kluska of the River Commissariat was also suspected of extorting Jews, and Stanisław Łuczyński was arrested for the same offense in February 1943 and incarcerated in the Pawiak Prison. He was reinstated in April 1944.

92 Report, May 22, 1944, AAN, AK, 203-III-112, p. 43.

Activities of the Blue Police after the Ghetto Uprising

By the first days of May, the resistance of the Jewish fighters had virtually ceased. Groups of insurgents and civilians still remained in bunkers, and Stroop's men burned the tenements over their heads, block after block. In late April and early May 1943, facing imminent death, thousands of Jews made their way through the sewers to the Aryan side of Warsaw. A shocking account from Simcha Rotem ("Kazik") on his escape from the burning ghetto through the sewers was included in Claude Lanzmann's documentary film *Shoah*. Some insurgents fell immediately into the hands of the Germans or their Polish helpers, but many managed to escape the hunters and find temporary shelter on the Aryan side of the city—temporary because in the face of the ongoing hunt, Jews often had to flee from one burned hideout to another. As in the previous period, the Blue policemen played a significant role in the hunt for the hiding insurgents.

In the work of a Holocaust historian, official documents of the German authorities are of particular importance, first and foremost because the Germans did not want to boast about the "Final Solution to the Jewish Question." On the contrary, German soldiers and policemen were threatened with prison sentences for spreading information about the crimes committed against the Jews. Of course, the issue did not concern the actual crimes themselves—the murders of Jews—but rather the betrayal of state secrets, as in the case of Max Täubner, the SS officer who decided that it would be a good idea to share photographs with his family of various executions carried out "in the East."[93] Täubner was an ardent Nazi who was sentenced by an SS court to several years in prison for his lack of discretion. For this reason, correspondence concerning the murder of European Jews was kept to a minimum.

Documents directly related to the planned and ongoing genocide were kept secret and destroyed. Reports by Stroop (Warsaw), Katzmann (Galicia), or Jäger (Lithuania), in which

93 Bühler, "Unworthy Behavior."

the technique of mass murder was directly presented in vivid detail, were indeed exceptions. Nevertheless, it is impossible to exterminate millions of people and leave no written trace. In this volume, one can see several types of official documents that give us an insight into the policy of genocide formulated by the occupying forces and developed with the help of the Blue Police. These include police reports on the detection of a crime—the aforementioned *Strafanzeigen*—which also includes lists of the number of bullets fired by Polish policemen or accounts of the travel costs to liquidation operations. After the Warsaw Ghetto Uprising, these reports were supplemented by additional reports submitted to the Blue Police commander by individual commissariats. In accordance with an earlier order of the German authorities, those reports included data concerning Jews captured by the Blue Police officers on the Aryan side.[94]

As mentioned earlier, an order was given on December 10, 1942, about which von Sammern-Frankenegg demanded that "by the 30th of each month...a report be submitted [to him] on how many Jews were shot based on this order."[95] It could have been that for almost half a year prior to this, the Warsaw commissariat had not submitted any such report. It is much more likely, however, that the documentation was lost or destroyed. It is also possible that until the end of the ghetto uprising, the Germans were quite lenient in regard to the submission of reports or lack thereof. After the ghetto uprising, however, Jewish affairs again became the focus of the German police in Warsaw. The hundreds, if not thousands, of Jews that had managed to reach the Aryan side of the city before, during, and after the uprising must have been a challenge for the occupation authorities, and as a result of which, the role of the Polish police had to be intensified.

94 Reports, AMSW, II Komisariat PP, file 16. A selection of these documents has appeared in print. See Grabowski and Libionka, "Meldunki Obwodu 'Praga.'"

95 Order of the SS and police commander to the commanders of the Order Police in Warsaw, December 10, 1942, AMSW, Komenda Policji Polskiej "Obwód Praga" 1939–1944, 1710, file 10, p. 1.

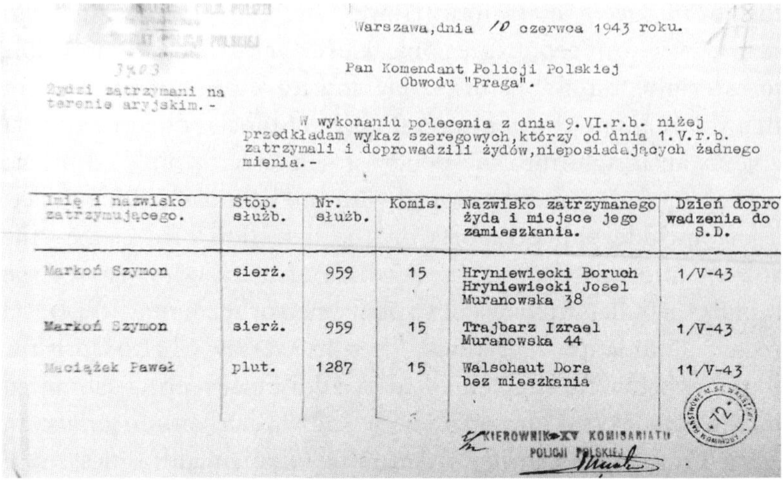

Warszawa, dnia 10 czerwca 1943 roku.

3903

Żydzi zatrzymani na terenie aryjskim. -

Pan Komendant Policji Polskiej Obwodu "Praga".

W wykonaniu polecenia z dnia 9.VI.r.b. niżej przedkładam wykaz szeregowych, którzy od dnia 1.V.r.b. zatrzymali i doprowadzili żydów, nieposiadających żadnego mienia. -

Imię i nazwisko zatrzymującego.	Stop. służb.	Nr. służb.	Komis.	Nazwisko zatrzymanego żyda i miejsce jego zamieszkania.	Dzień doprowadzenia do S.D.
Markoń Szymon	sierż.	959	15	Hryniewiecki Boruch Hryniewiecki Josel Muranowska 38	1/V-43
Markoń Szymon	sierż.	959	15	Trajbarz Izrael Muranowska 44	1/V-43
Maciążek Paweł	plut.	1287	15	Walschaut Dora bez mieszkania	11/V-43

KIEROWNIK XV KOMISARIATU POLICJI POLSKIEJ

Report of the chief of XV precinct of the Blue Police in Warsaw about the capture of Jews, June 10, 1943. AMSW, II Komisariat PP, file 11.

Surviving reports preserved in the Warsaw City Archives were produced in the commissariats of the Warsaw-Praga[96] police area in the spring and summer of 1943. The following commissariats belonged to the Praga area: XIV (11 Wileńska Street); XV (9 Jagiellońska Street); XVII (172 Grochowska Street); XVIII (1 Kartuska Street); XXIV (16 Tykocińska Street); XXV (no information about the address); the II Railway Commissariat (at the Warsaw-East Railway Station); and the River Commissariat (Helski embankment). It can be assumed that the same reports were also sent to the main headquarters of the Polish Home Army by the commissariats located in other parts of Warsaw. Unfortunately, only the reports from the commissariats in Praga survived, and even those are poorly preserved and incomplete. Nevertheless, reading them is extremely informative, and the documents are so important that it is worth devoting more space to them.

On June 23, 1943, the commander of the Praga area "*Magister* Wnękiewicz, Major of Police"—evidently it was a time when the title of *magister* (the equivalent of a graduate degree) carried more weight

96 Praga is a part of Warsaw located east of the Vistula River, which cuts through the city.

in the police than the rank of a major—wrote the following to Major Przymusiński: "I report that from 23 May to 23 June 1943, on the territory of the units of the 'Praga' area, 20 Jews were arrested and handed over to the SD [Gestapo], at 25 Szucha Av[enue]. There were no cases of shooting of Jews trying to escape."[97] On July 22, 1943, the previously discussed head of the XV Commissariat Captain Moniak reported that three Jews had been arrested and handed over to the Gestapo, while Captain Piotr Kruk of the XVII Commissariat reported the arrest of four "persons of Jewish origin, three of whom were sent to the German Police Headquarters, 23 Szucha Avenue and one to the German Police Post, 74 Targowa Street."[98] Some reports are more detailed. On July 21, 1943, Second Lieutenant Banach, head of the XVIII Commissariat, informed Commandant Przymusiński "that the following Jews were detained in the area of this Commissariat: Frydman Abram, Frydman Regina, Frydman Szymon, and Frydman Icek. The abovementioned were sent to the SD on July 3, 1943, as well as Rozenberg Sura vel Lewandowska Teresa, sent to the SD on 17 July 1943."[99]

Police reports fail to convey the horror of the described events. In order to do so, one must turn to the accounts of the Jewish survivors. The aforementioned Leon Najberg, one of the last Jewish insurgents still armed and hiding in the ghetto ruins, was preparing to cross over to the Aryan side on September 26:

> I climbed the ladder. As soon as I peeked out, my gaze fell on a gendarme, assisted by a "Blue" policeman, on patrol at the corner of Świętojerska and Bonifraterska Streets. We managed to escape, but a moment later we were surprised by another Polish policeman. He spoke to us very politely, "Boys, give me your money and go with God." There was no time for reply. We gave him the 1,000 zloty, stressing that if he was going to blackmail us further, then we would pay him...with a bullet.[100]

97 Letter from *Magister* Wnękiewicz to Major to Przymusiński, AMSW, II Komisariat PP, file 16.

98 Ibid.

99 Report, July 21, 1943, AMSW, II Komisariat PP, file 16.

100 Najberg, *Ostatni powstańcy getta*, p. 161.

Najberg and his comrades had guns. Almost none of the other Jews escaping from the ghetto had any weapons, and the only thing they could offer the officers was money. When there was not enough money, the names of the captured Jews were included in the reports that were then sent to the headquarters by the commissariats, and the Jews themselves—accompanied by the Blue policemen—were sent to the Gestapo on Szucha Avenue. However, even weapons did not guarantee their safety. In May 1943, a group of over forty fighters from the Jewish Military Union (ŻZW) made their way to Michalin near Warsaw, where they were hiding. There, they were discovered by the Blue Police, who opened fire on the Jews, wounding the sentry guarding the house. As a result, the ŻZW unit was forced to move back behind the Świder River, in the direction of the nearby forest. There, however, the fighters were fired upon from German gendarmes, and twelve people were killed.[101]

In some reports, the heads of the commissariats included the names of officers who had made the arrests as well as the names of the captured Jews. Thus, we learn that Platoon Sergeant Jan Czuboni (service number 1773) from the XIV Commissariat captured Jew Bronisław Horodyński; Sergeant Józef Jagodziński (service number 669) from the same commissariat captured Helena Gisa on the Aryan side; Corporal Władysław Borzęcki (service number 1284) from the XIV Commissariat delivered Róża Pesa into the hands of the Germans; and Platoon Sergeant Mieczysław Nowak (service number 2085) from the XVII Commissariat—the same one whose officers had murdered Jews in the bunker at 4 Wałowa Street—captured Chaim Rosenberg. In all these cases, next to the names of the captured Jews in the column "Payment awarded," we see the annotation "None."[102] Once again, looking at the orders of the German district governors from March 1943, a policemen could count on one-third of the property found on the arrested Jews under those decrees. If these reports are to be believed, all of the victims who fell into the trap of the Warsaw policemen were

101 Revisionist account, GFH, 5970, as quoted in Libionka, "Polska konspiracja wobec eksterminacji Żdó w dystrykcie warszawskim," p. 473.

102 For example, see Jews detained in Aryan territory, June 15, 1943, AMSW, II Komisariat PP, file 16, p. 32.

penniless. This may well have been true but seems rather unlikely. What is more likely is that the Jews were robbed completely by the policemen at the moment of arrest—why give two-thirds of the loot to the Germans if you can steal everything? Alternatively, only those specific Jews who had no money left whatsoever were arrested as they had no means to buy themselves out. Both of these hypotheses are defendable, although neither will ever be verified. Finally, it's important to add that the Polish policemen knew how to exact tribute of a physical nature from women. And sometimes, these victims of rape were later delivered to the Germans for execution.

Between May 1 and June 28, 1943, a total of forty-three Jews were arrested in the Praga precincts, of whom twenty-two victims were recorded under their last names. The arrests were made by twenty-one officers from seven commissariats. Only the XXIV Commissariat did not report any arrests of the Jews. The data in these reports of the Praga commissariats are fragmentary and underestimated, since they concern only those Jews who were officially handed over to the Gestapo by the Blue Police. It is difficult to say how many of them the policemen released after blackmailing them and extorting them for ransom. It is also unknown how many people the officers handed over to the Germans without notifying their superiors. There is no doubt that preying on Jews was one of the most important sources of income for the Warsaw policemen from the beginning of the occupation. Hunting down those in hiding became even more important after the final liquidation of the ghetto, when the police officers could no longer count on the income from bribes and extortion collected at the gates of the Jewish district. Emanuel Ringelblum summed it up as follows:

> The Polish agents of the criminal police, Gestapo agents and Polish Police are all under orders from the German authorities to pursue Jews. When the police—both agents and uniformed policemen—were deprived of their ample takings in the Jewish district, where the scope for their activity was constantly dwindling, they passed over to

> the "Jewish region" on the Aryan side. It was not so much a matter of giving the Jews away to the Germans as of making profits, and ample ones at that, for themselves. Jews of limited means who were not able to buy themselves out of the hands of their tormentors, were given away to the Gestapo.[103]

The Home Army intelligence reports issued in the fall of 1943 confirm Ringelblum's bitter remarks. These lists of policemen who were involved are fragmentary and patchy, and those police officers who dealt exclusively with blackmailing Jews, without attempting to fight the underground, were essentially outside the scope of AK intelligence interest. Nevertheless, in the Home Army intelligence reports, we find a small amount of information on the subject in question:

> From the VII Commissariat:
>
> Platoon Sgt. Sylwestrzak Ignacy, 34/57 Młynarska St., known extortionist, unethical, constantly preyed on Jews in the Aryan district. An individual of little value.[104]
>
> Cpl. Affelt Roman, 56/30 Krochmalna St., known extortionist, preyed on Jews.
>
> Cpl. Rupiński Józef, 48 Karolkowa St., of little moral value, shady individual, preyed on Jews.
>
> Cpl. Prokop Józef, 4/15 Opolski Square, known as a crook, an extortionist, unethical, constantly preyed on Jews. He was of little moral value.
>
> Cpl. Rogoziński Władysław, 5/22 Marynarska St., an extortionist, constantly preyed on Jews.
>
> Cpl. Sawicki Stanisław, 89/9 Wolska St., constantly preyed on Jews.

103 Ringelblum, *Polish-Jewish Relations*, p. 120.

104 Officer profiles, 1943 (?), AAN, AK, 203-III-124, p. 38.

> Cpl. Szulc Jan, 55/23 Ogrodowa St., known as a strangler, constantly preyed on Jews.
>
> Platoon Sgt. Boniecki Roman and Cpl. Durant, together with civilian Józef Zalewski extort money from hiding officers and Jews.[105]
>
> Policemen Władysław Skrzypek, Władysław Górczewski and Antoni Kalinowski—looking for Jews, blackmailing their victims.[106]
>
> Stefan Jaźwiec, corporal of the XVI Commissariat (police ID number 2632), 49 Puławska Str., corner of Dworkowa Str. He is a complete scoundrel. He will do anything for money. He is friends with local scum and so on. Usually, they search for Jews together. J. is a drunkard.[107]

The intelligence and counterintelligence reports of the Home Army include many lists of people identified by the underground as working for the enemy. Among them, a prominent place is occupied by Polish policemen, for whom "Jewish business"—blackmail, extortion, and murder—after the liquidation of the ghetto became the only profitable occupation they really knew how to do.

105 The order to conduct an investigation, September 13, 1943, AAN, AK, 203-III-118, p. 79.

106 Home Army intelligence and counterintelligence documents from Warsaw (duplicates), AIPN, BU 380/30, vol. 3, p. 190. This volume contains duplicates of documents from various AK intelligence and counterintelligence units from the Warsaw area. Most of the documents are lists of people suspected of collaboration with the Germans, officers of German police and of the Blue Police. Many documents contain the characteristics of those officers. The selection contains mostly reports and denunciations from the area of operations of the Blue Police.

107 See the following reports in AAN, AK, 203-III-111: Report 993, April 3, 1944, p. 8; Report 993, April 22, 1944, p. 58.

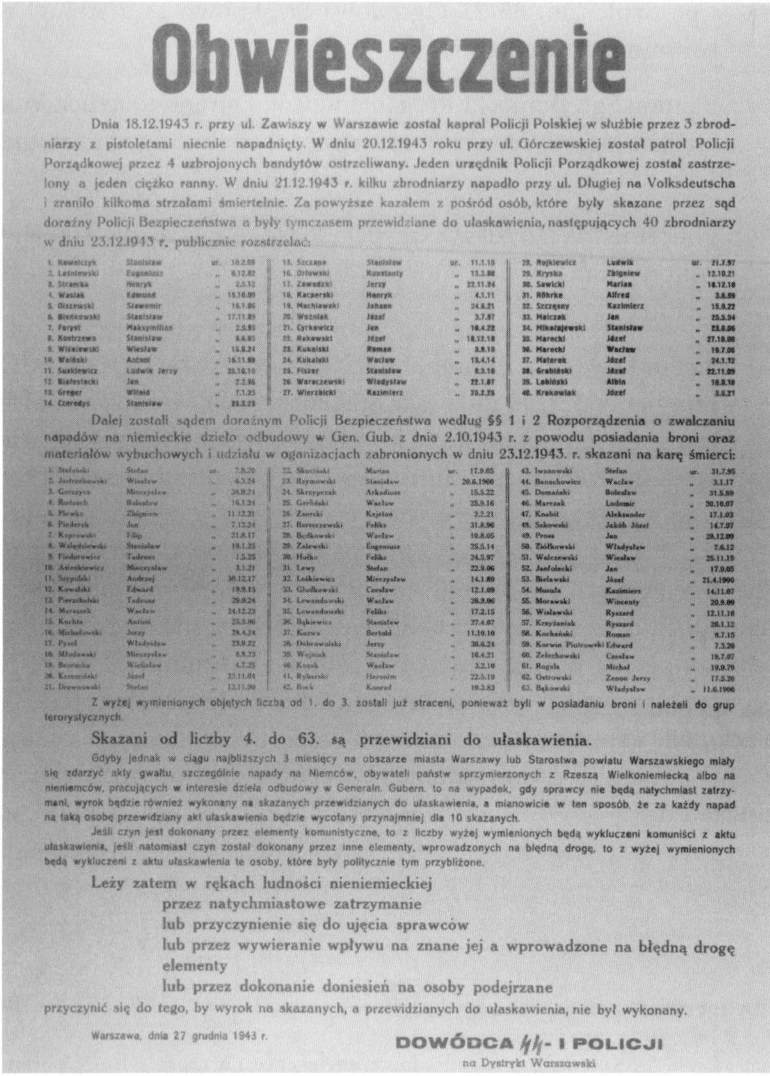

Obwieszczenie

Dnia 18.12.1943 r. przy ul. Zawiszy w Warszawie został kapral Policji Polskiej w służbie przez 3 zbrodniarzy z pistoletami niecnie napadnięty. W dniu 20.12.1943 roku przy ul. Górczewskiej został patrol Policji Porządkowej przez 4 uzbrojonych bandytów ostrzeliwany. Jeden urzędnik Policji Porządkowej został zastrzelony a jeden ciężko ranny. W dniu 21.12.1943 r. kilku zbrodniarzy napadło przy ul. Długiej na Volksdeutscha i zraniło kilkoma strzałami śmiertelnie. Za powyższe kazałem z pośród osób, które były skazane przez sąd doraźny Policji Bezpieczeństwa a były tymczasem przewidziane do ułaskawienia, następujących 40 zbrodniarzy w dniu 23.12.1943 r. publicznie rozstrzelać:

1.	Kowalczyk	Stanisław	ur. 10.2.09
2.	Leśniewski	Eugeniusz	„ 8.12.02
3.	Stramka	Henryk	„ 2.5.12
4.	Wasiak	Edmund	„ 15.10.09
5.	Olszewski	Sławomir	„ 16.1.06
6.	Bieńkowski	Stanisław	„ 17.11.89
7.	Foryst	Maksymilian	„ 2.9.95
8.	Kostrzewa	Stanisław	„ 8.6.05
9.	Wiśniewski	Wiesław	„ 15.8.24
10.	Walński	Antoni	„ 16.11.89
11.	Suskiewicz	Ludwik Jerzy	„ 25.10.10
12.	Białostocki	Jan	„ 2.2.96
13.	Greger	Witold	„ 7.1.25
14.	Czeredys	Stanisław	„ 23.2.23
15.	Szczapa	Stanisław	ur. 11.1.15
16.	Orłowski	Konstanty	„ 13.3.08
17.	Zawadzki	Jerzy	„ 22.11.24
18.	Kacperski	Henryk	„ 4.1.11
19.	Machlawski	Johann	„ 24.6.21
20.	Woźniak	Józef	„ 3.7.97
21.	Cyrkewicz	Jan	„ 18.4.22
22.	Rakowski	Józef	„ 18.12.18
23.	Kukalski	Roman	„ 3.8.10
24.	Kukalski	Wacław	„ 13.4.14
25.	Fiszer	Stanisław	„ 8.5.10
26.	Wareczewski	Władysław	„ 22.1.07
27.	Wierzbicki	Kazimierz	„ 25.2.25
28.	Rojkiewicz	Ludwik	ur. 21.7.97
29.	Kryska	Zbigniew	„ 12.10.21
30.	Sawicki	Marian	„ 18.12.18
31.	Röhrke	Alfred	„ 3.6.09
32.	Szczęsny	Kazimierz	„ 15.9.22
33.	Malczak	Jan	„ 25.5.94
34.	Mikołajewski	Stanisław	„ 23.8.06
35.	Marecki	Józef	„ 27.10.08
36.	Marecki	Wacław	„ 19.7.06
37.	Materek	Józef	„ 24.1.12
38.	Grabiński	Józef	„ 22.11.09
39.	Lebiński	Albin	„ 18.8.18
40.	Krakowiak	Józef	„ 3.6.21

Dalej zostali sądem doraźnym Policji Bezpieczeństwa według §§ 1 i 2 Rozporządzenia o zwalczaniu napadów na niemieckie dzieło odbudowy w Gen. Gub. z dnia 2.10.1943 r. z powodu posiadania broni oraz materiałów wybuchowych i udziału w oganizacjach zabronionych w dniu 23.12.1943. r. skazani na karę śmierci:

1.	Stefański	Stefan	ur. 7.8.20
2.	Jastrzębowski	Wiesław	„ 6.3.24
3.	Gorczyca	Mieczysław	„ 30.9.21
4.	Rodzoch	Bolesław	„ 16.1.24
5.	Plewko	Zbigniew	„ 11.12.21
6.	Pinderak	Jan	„ 7.12.24
7.	Kaprowski	Filip	„ 21.8.17
8.	Walędziewski	Stanisław	„ 19.1.25
9.	Fiedorowicz	Tadeusz	„ 1.5.25
10.	Asienkiewicz	Mieczysław	„ 3.1.21
11.	Szypulski	Andrzej	„ 30.12.17
12.	Kowalski	Edward	„ 19.9.15
13.	Pierzchalski	Tadeusz	„ 29.9.24
14.	Maraszek	Wacław	„ 24.12.23
15.	Kuchta	Antoni	„ 25.5.86
16.	Michałowski	Jerzy	„ 28.4.24
17.	Pyzel	Władysław	„ 23.9.22
18.	Młodawski	Mieczysław	„ 8.8.23
19.	Bezrucka	Wiesław	„ 4.7.25
20.	Krzemiński	Józef	„ 23.11.04
21.	Drewnowski	Stefan	„ 12.11.90
22.	Skuciński	Marian	ur. 17.9.05
23.	Rzymowski	Stanisław	„ 20.6.1900
24.	Skrzypczak	Arkadiusz	„ 15.5.22
25.	Gerliński	Wacław	„ 25.9.16
26.	Zaorski	Kajetan	„ 2.2.21
27.	Barszczewski	Feliks	„ 31.8.96
28.	Będkowski	Wacław	„ 10.8.05
29.	Zalewski	Eugeniusz	„ 25.5.14
30.	Holke	Feliks	„ 24.5.97
31.	Lewy	Stefan	„ 22.9.06
32.	Leśkiewicz	Mieczysław	„ 14.1.89
33.	Gludkowski	Czesław	„ 12.1.09
34.	Lewandowski	Wacław	„ 28.9.06
35.	Lewandowski	Feliks	„ 17.2.15
36.	Bąkiewicz	Stanisław	„ 27.4.07
37.	Kuzwa	Bertold	„ 11.10.10
38.	Dobrowolski	Jerzy	„ 30.6.24
39.	Wojniak	Stanisław	„ 16.4.21
40.	Kozak	Wacław	„ 3.2.10
41.	Rybarski	Heronim	„ 22.5.19
42.	Bock	Konrad	„ 10.3.83
43.	Iwanowski	Stefan	ur. 31.7.95
44.	Banachowicz	Wacław	„ 3.1.17
45.	Domański	Bolesław	„ 31.5.89
46.	Marczak	Ludomir	„ 30.10.07
47.	Knabit	Aleksander	„ 17.1.03
48.	Sakowski	Jakób Józef	„ 14.7.97
49.	Pross	Jan	„ 28.12.09
50.	Ziółkowski	Władysław	„ 7.6.12
51.	Walczewski	Wiesław	„ 25.11.19
52.	Janfolecki	Jan	„ 17.9.05
53.	Bielawski	Józef	„ 21.4.1900
54.	Musuła	Kazimierz	„ 14.11.07
55.	Morawski	Wincenty	„ 20.9.09
56.	Wisławski	Ryszard	„ 12.11.10
57.	Krzyżaniak	Ryszard	„ 26.1.12
58.	Kochański	Roman	„ 8.7.15
59.	Korwin Piotrowski	Edward	„ 7.3.20
60.	Zelechowski	Czesław	„ 18.7.07
61.	Rogala	Michał	„ 19.9.79
62.	Ostrowski	Zenon Jerzy	„ 17.5.20
63.	Bąkowski	Władysław	„ 11.6.1900

Z wyżej wymienionych objętych liczbą od 1. do 3. zostali już straceni, ponieważ byli w posiadaniu broni i należeli do grup terorystycznych.

Skazani od liczby 4. do 63. są przewidziani do ułaskawienia.

Gdyby jednak w ciągu najbliższych 3 miesięcy na obszarze miasta Warszawy lub Starostwa powiatu Warszawskiego miały się zdarzyć akty gwałtu, szczególnie napady na Niemców, obywateli państw sprzymierzonych z Rzeszą Wielkoniemiecką albo na nieniemców, pracujących w interesie dzieła odbudowy w Generaln. Gubern. to na wypadek, gdy sprawcy nie będą natychmiast zatrzymani, wyrok będzie również wykonany na skazanych przewidzianych do ułaskawienia, a mianowicie w ten sposób, że za każdy napad na taką osobę przewidziany akt ułaskawienia będzie wycofany przynajmniej dla 10 skazanych.

Jeśli czyn jest dokonany przez elementy komunistyczne, to z liczby wyżej wymienionych będą wykluczeni komuniści z aktu ułaskawienia, jeśli natomiast czyn został dokonany przez inne elementy, wprowadzonych na błędną drogę, to z wyżej wymienionych będą wykluczeni z aktu ułaskawienia te osoby, które były politycznie tym przybliżone.

Leży zatem w rękach ludności nieniemieckiej
przez natychmiastowe zatrzymanie
lub przyczynienie się do ujęcia sprawców
lub przez wywieranie wpływu na znane jej a wprowadzone na błędną drogę elementy
lub przez dokonanie doniesień na osoby podejrzane
przyczynić się do tego, by wyrok na skazanych, a przewidzianych do ułaskawienia, nie był wykonany.

Warszawa, dnia 27 grudnia 1943 r.

DOWÓDCA SS- I POLICJI
na Dystrykt Warszawski

A poster announcing the mass execution in retaliation for the murder of a Blue Police officer. On December 23, 1943, the *Kronika policyjna* reported the attack mentioned on the poster, which occurred on December 18, 1943: "At 9:30, close to Zawisza Square, three armed men attacked and killed Officer Wojciech Szczudło of XXII precinct and took away his service revolver and fourteen bullets." Courtesy of the personal archive of Jan Grabowski.

The end of the Blue Police activity in the capital city coincided with the outbreak of the Warsaw Uprising. On August 1, 1944, the Germans executed police officers from the XXII Commissariat in Wola, and officers from the headquarters were disarmed and imprisoned.[108] Some policemen—several hundred members of the underground State Security Corps—joined the insurgents, while others withdrew with the Germans westward, where they reinforced the police stations in Łowicz, Sochaczew, and other towns in the Warsaw district that were still under German control.

108 See Getter, "Policja polska w Generalnym Gubernatorstwie 1939–1945."

CHAPTER SEVEN

The Role of the Polish Criminal Police in the Murder of Polish Jews

For information and intelligence purposes, detectives must speak local and foreign languages, as well as the Jewish jargon.[1]

Instruction on surveillance from the Regulation of the Minister of Internal Affairs, January 4, 1924.

In the spring or early summer of 1941, the staff of the Polish Criminal Police Commissariat I—the so-called banditry division—of the Polish Criminal Police in Warsaw took a photo together (the photo appears on the next page). It is worth taking a closer look at those men, as some of them played a significant role in the events described below.[2] In the foreground, in the center, there are four uniformed Germans. First from the left, Gestapo officer *SS-Hauptscharführer* Kaiser is looking grimly into the camera. Next to him. wearing an ankle-length leather coat, is Andreas von Amburger, head of Commissariat I who in late July 1941 was transferred from Warsaw

1 Andrzej Misiuk and Andrzej Pepłoński, eds., *Organizacja instytucji policyjnych w II Rzeczpospolitej 1918–1926: Wybór źródeł i dokumentów* (Szczytno: Wyższej Szkoły Policji, 1992), p. 189. In this chapter, I have used fragments from my article: Jan Grabowski, "Tropiąc Emanuela Ringelbluma: Udział polskiej Kriminalpolizei w 'ostatecznym rozwiązaniu kwestii żydowskiej,'" *Zagłada Żydów, Studia i materiały*, 10 (2014), pp. 27–56.

2 Lists of Warsaw Kripo employees, AMSW, II Komisariat PP, file 5.

to the Eastern Front, where he joined Einsatzkommando 8, part of Einzatzgruppe B, commanded by Arthur Nebe. It is his presence in the picture that helps us determine the cut-off date of the group photograph with relative accuracy. Seated next to von Amburger, smiling lightly, is *SS-Hauptscharführer* Bard. The last of the uniformed Germans is Rudolf Kosmala, who suffered wounds fighting Jews on April 19, 1943, the first day of the Warsaw Ghetto Uprising. The four Germans in the middle of the picture are those who supervised the work of the Polish detectives who formed the core staff of the so-called banditry division. Also worth mentioning are the names of several Polish detectives (*Kriminalbeamten*). In the first row, second from the left, is Karol Bartl, a detective in the prewar Investigative Service, who discovered his German roots after the German invasion, signed the *Volksliste*, and was soon promoted to the rank of sergeant. Bartl would later be executed by a Directorate of Sabotage (Kedyw) unit in December 1943.[3]

Officers and employees of the I Criminal Commissariat, Warsaw, spring/summer 1941. AMSW, II Komisariat PP, file 5.

3 Kedyw (Directorate of Sabotage of the Home Army) was founded in early 1943. This specialized branch of the underground was responsible for armed reprisals against the occupant—for the assassination of the German officials, spies, and other agents.

Third from the right sits a thin man with a pained expression on his face, uncomfortably squeezed between Rudolf Kosmala and another detective. This is Wacław Lange, described by an underground informant as follows: "Pole, former head of the Banditry Com[missariat], now its deputy. Bribe-taker, man capable of any cruelty if there is enough money in it for him. Dangerous in every way."[4] To the right of Lange, seated comfortably, is Feliks Rydlewicz, described as "master corporal, probably a VD [*Volksdeutsch*], corrupt, dangerous in every way."[5] According to the intelligence service, Rydlewicz "sucked up to" the Germans.[6] On March 11, 1944, he was shot and wounded in a Warsaw street, possibly as a result of an underground court sentence. He survived the war.[7]

Sergeant Major (*Stabsfeldwebel*) Karol Bartl, Warsaw, 1941. AMSW, II Komisariat PP, file 5.

Wacław Lange, deputy chief of the banditry commissariat of the Polish Criminal Police in Warsaw, 1941. AMSW, II Komisariat PP, file 5.

4 Lists of Warsaw Kripo employees, AMSW, II Komisariat PP, file 5.

5 Ibid.

6 Ibid.

7 Maria Dzięgielewska hearing testimony, January 3, 1950, AIPN, BU 0423/3402, p. 246. Information about the assassination attempt on Rydlewicz was reported in the *Kronika policyjna*, AAN, Delegatura Rządu na Kraj, 203/III-122. An extensive AK intelligence report on Rydlewicz can be found in AIPN, BU 380/30, vol. 1, p. 140.

In the last row, sixth from the right, against the white door, stands Józef Osipiak. In 1941, an underground report described him as "corrupt but harmless."[8] Over time, this classification would change, and the "harmless" bribe-taker became one of the most dangerous hunters of Jews. At the same time, much to his own chagrin, he was an undercover agent helping the Germans to track down members of the underground. For collaborating with the Gestapo, Osipiak was sentenced to death by the underground court, and he was executed on January 5, 1944, on Płocka Street in Warsaw.

In the second row, third from the right, stands Stefan Chamski, "bribe-taker, acting as some kind of dignitary, and snooping around to make money," to quote an underground informant's assessment.[9] With time, Chamski became more involved in the search for and blackmail of Jews, and as we know, since the *Grossaktion*, this was one of the most profitable trades in the capital and a field in which the detectives of the banditry division were particularly successful. On January 4, 1943, Chamski was wounded in an attack on Zamkowy Square. As we learn from the oft-quoted *Kronika policyjna*, the officer "was seriously wounded and taken to hospital. He refused to testify, only asking that a police guard be set up near him because he feared another assassination attempt."[10] Chamski died several months later from his wounds. Working at the intersection of the German authorities and the Polish underground was particularly dangerous, as one of the three women in the photograph found out. On August 18, 1943, under the sentence of the Special Civil Court in Warsaw, Maria Giedroyć-Mordasiewicz—first on the right in the group of women, standing directly above Gestapo officer Bard—who worked as a translator and a clerk in the Directorate of Criminal Police in Warsaw, was executed for collaboration with the Gestapo.[11]

8 *Kronika wydarzeń*, entry dated January 4 1943, AAN, Delegatura Rządu na Kraj, 202-II-44.

9 List compiled by "M", March 1942, AMSW, II Komisariat PP, file 5, unpaginated.

10 The underground report reads: "Police agent Chamski, on whom an assassination attempt was made in early January, died on March 8 from wounds received. It is customary among police employees to lay a wreath for their deceased colleagues, but it is notable that no one gave a penny for Chamski's wreath." See Report no. 10, March 31, 1943, AAN, Delegatura Rządu na Kraj, 202-II-37, p. 37.

11 Report "P.17", August 20, 1943, AAN, AK, 203-III-118, p. 67.

A report by the AK intelligence service—two pages long, poorly preserved, and at times illegible—which describes other detectives serving in the Directorate of Criminal Police in Warsaw in February 1942, adds more information about the characteristics of the Polish Kripo officers. The few legible excerpts give some idea of the type of officers who were making a career in the Polish Kripo at the time:

> Head of Commissariat I: Klimowicz Czesław. He has a reputation as a "bribe-taker" and a man of poor morals. Allegedly married to a German woman. He keeps in touch with Lieutenant Grabowska Karolina (from the vice squad com[missariat]), who is a deeply negative individual.... Mańkowski Jan—sucks up to the Germans, known for torturing the arrested during the [illegible], bribe-taker, drunkard, professional informer; ...provocateur, Pole-hater.... Commissariat I had 47 functionaries in total, including 2 commissioned officers, 2 female clerks, 3 senior sergeants, 23 master corporals, 11 corporals, and 2 janitors. Commissariat II—Chief: Lieutenant Plucinski, Waclaw, no national awareness, great coward, worthless for the Cause.[12]

Although considered "worthless for the Cause," who were these people that played a significant role in tightening the noose around the throats of those Jews seeking help?

The Warsaw Directorate of Criminal Police

Even before the end of 1939, the Warsaw Investigative Service was divided into seven commissariats, as mentioned above. These should not be confused with the Warsaw Blue Police commissariats. Among them, the most important were: Commissariat I—the so-

12 Report, Directorate of the Polish Criminal Police by police stations, February 16, 1942, AAN, AK, 203-III-124, p. 118–199. The characteristics includes lists of officers deemed trustworthy. See also List of employees of the Directorate of Criminal Police in Warsaw, June 25, 1941, AAN, AK, 203-III-110, p. 6.

called banditry division; Commissariats II and III—theft divisions; Commissariat IV—forgery division; and Commissariat V—vice squad.[13] The first head of the Directorate of Criminal Police in Warsaw, with the official title of liaison officer, was Lieutenant Colonel Stanisław Wasilewski, who held that position until June 11, 1942, when he left the service and went into hiding from the Germans. From 1943, Wasilewski—codename "Rogala"—was among the leaders of the Security Department of the Warsaw branch of the Government Delegation for Poland.[14] Wasilewski was also one of the founders of the previously mentioned State Security Corps, the underground police apparatus that became part of the structure of the Government Delegation for Poland.[15] Following Wasilewski's departure, Lieutenant Colonel Chmaj took over as head of the Directorate of Criminal Police. After Chmaj's death—he died of a heart attack in April 1943—Captain Seweryn Rosiński became head of the Polish Kripo. Rosiński was also head of Commissariat I.[16]

Little is known about the personnel transfers within the Polish Kripo in the first months of the occupation. In Warsaw where, relatively speaking, much source material has survived, most of the police officers continued in their previous roles following a hasty background check. For obvious reasons, the exception was the Intelligence and Counterintelligence division—the I–IV brigades of the prewar Investigative Service. These divisions were disbanded by the Germans. Some of the detectives were arrested, whereas some were transferred to newly created criminal commissariats. For example, Antoni Haar and Wincenty Wilczyński, who had fought against the Communists before the war, were placed in Commissariat I.

13 Maria Dzięgielewska testimony, AIPN, BU 0423/3402, pp. 35–44, 227–229, 251–257. The structure of the Investigative Service has been reconstructed in part from the testimony of this longtime secretary of the Investigative Service of the Directorate of Criminal Police during the war. Commissariats VI and VII did not have any specific names.

14 Waldemar Grabowski, *Polska tajna administracja cywilna 1940–1945* (Warsaw: Instytut Pamięci Narodowej, 2003), p. 202.

15 Hempel, *Pogrobowcy klęski*, pp. 220–221. For more on the organization and structures of the State Security Corps, see ibid., pp. 343–345.

16 Interrogation of Maria Dzięgielewska, December 30, 1949, AIPN, BU 0423/3402, pp. 226–227.

The same happened to detectives Kazimierz Duchiński and Bronisław Chudzikowski, who were transferred from Intelligence to Commissariat II, while Józef Skrzypiński, who had been the head of the II Brigade before the war, was transferred to the vice squad.

Organization Chart of the Directorate of Criminal Police in Warsaw[17]

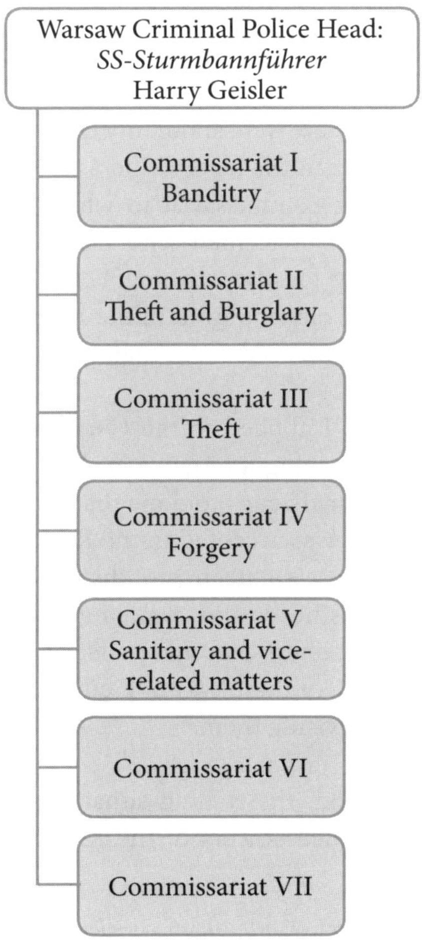

17 Organization chart of the Directorate of Criminal Police in Warsaw according to the testimony of Gestapo officer Fritz Nowack, June 26, 1948, AIPN, GK 714/17, p. 6/1.

This organizational transformation was followed by significant personnel changes, when officers delegated to "work in the East"—*Osteinsatz* was the specific German term for this type of deployment—arrived in Warsaw from the Reich. At the end of 1939 and the beginning of 1940, a number of Germans joined Commissariat I to supervise Polish officers. Some of them have already been identified in the photo of the banditry division from the spring or summer of 1941. Another German employee of the Polish Kripo was criminal commissioner *SS-Hauptsturmführer* Wilhelm Tewes, who had been sent to Warsaw in early 1940.[18] According to Tewes, there were about fifty German officers and 700 Polish officers serving in the local Kripo as well as four Germans and fifty Poles in the commissariat to which he was attached.[19] In time, the German policemen who had been sent from the Reich were joined by locally recruited *Volksdeutsche*. Kazimierz Garbowski, a young Pole employed in the Polish Kripo at the end of the occupation, reminisced about them as follows:

> In March 1944, I applied to the German "Kriminalpolizei" because I was earning a pittance at the railway, not enough to live on, and my friends told me that the Kripo paid better. In mid-March I was accepted to the Kripo for a trial period, which was to last eighteen months. There were Germans working there as heads and commanders, and the rest were Poles from the prewar criminal police and *Volksdeutsche*, so that proportionally there was one ethnic German for every four Poles supervising them.[20]

By way of comparison, the staffing situation was also relatively stable among the police officers of the Kraków criminal police.

18 Interrogation protocol of Wilhelm Tewes, questioned by the British occupation authorities in Germany, August 23, 1946, AIPN, GK 164/3754, pp. 1–2. At first, Tewes worked at the commissariat at Teatralny Square, but later, in 1943, he was transferred to Ujazdowskie Avenue.

19 Ibid., p. 3.

20 Interrogation of Kazimierz Garbowski, January 26, 1950, AIPN, BU 0423/4447, pp. 14–15.

Before the war, there were 120 detectives in the Investigative Service in Kraków, including nine commissioned officers under the command of Lieutenant Colonel Wojciech Stano. The staff size did change somewhat during the occupation, albeit not drastically. In 1943, there were still slightly more than 100 officers working for the Kripo in Kraków, but their number included only ten German policemen. The rest were Poles who were prewar policemen from the local Investigative Service.[21] In spite of the personnel changes and a radically different form of operations, the Polish Criminal Police had already resumed its statutory tasks by the end of 1939. Theoretically, according to the internal regulations of the Sipo, the Polish Kripo was tasked with combating common crime. In reality, however, it became one of the key links in the Nazi terror apparatus, and in the following years of the occupation, an important area of its activity was the fight against Jews who had managed to avoid transportation to the extermination camps and who were trying to survive on the Aryan side.

The Polish Kripo was organizationally separate from the Blue Police, but in practice, uniformed officers and undercover agents worked side by side, and as mentioned earlier, Kripo commissariats were often housed within the Polish police stations. In smaller towns, Kripo officers not only shared space with the Blue Police but also acted virtually without any direct German supervision, like their uniformed counterparts.

The Stifling Year of 1944: Special Units of the Polish Kripo

In the history of the German occupation, several periods can be distinguished. Historians differentiate the following periods: early occupation; the consolidation of the Polish resistance movement or the solidifying of the Polish Underground State; and the period of increased terror of the occupation forces from mid-1943 onward. A specific turning point in such a classification of these periods is

21 See BAL, B162/2149, p. 363.

the concept of "the stifling year of 1944."[22] It was stifling for many reasons but mainly because, with the end of the war approaching, the divisions within the underground became more prominent, and the increasing number of acts of fratricidal violence turned into waves of politically motivated murders, such as the murders of Ludwik Widerszal and Jerzy Makowiecki, members of the main headquarters of the Bureau of Information and Propaganda of the ZWZ-AK, by Polish right-wing nationalists on June 13, 1944.[23]

If 1944 was a particularly difficult year for Poles, then for the remaining Jews who were fighting for survival, each consecutive month brought an increased and often impossible burden to bear. The Jews in hiding were running out of money—in the case of those few who could count on Żegota's support, the aid covered only a small part of the costs of shelter—and their Polish hosts often did not have enough courage or patience for further sacrifices, all the more so because the hunt for Jews did not slow down. The *Judenjagd* continued until the very end of the occupation. One could even say that with the approaching front it grew stronger, and this phenomenon was observed not only in Poland but also in other countries in occupied Europe.

On January 4, 1944, Adolf Berman (alias Adam Borowski), who before the war was a politician in the Poale Zion Left party and during the occupation was one of the most important members of Żegota and the head of the Jewish National Committee, fell into the hands of a gang of *szmalcowniks*. The blackmailers were well aware of who they had captured and how much they could demand for his release. The sums they named were indeed exorbitant. At first, they demanded half a million zlotys, a staggering sum at the time. After the ransom was paid—200,000 zlotys—the blackmailers released Berman, who soon produced a detailed report on the

22 This expression was originally used in this context by Colonel Jan Rzepecki, the chief of the underground Bureau of Information and Propaganda of the Home Army. See Janusz Marszalec, "Morderstwo na Makowieckich i Widerszalu: Stara sprawa, nowe pytania, nowe wątpliwości," *Zagłada Żydów, Studia i materiały*, 2 (2006), p. 25.

23 Note 993/W, July 10, 1944, AAN, AK, 203-III-105, p. 113. See also Marszalec, "Morderstwo na Makowieckich i Widerszalu."

attack.[24] According to the report, three agents were involved in Berman's arrest. One, short and black-haired, a "typical flatfoot," as Berman described him, "kept waving a revolver in front of my eyes, kept threatening and yelling that he would 'finish me off', that we were 'going to the Directorate.'"[25] By this, the blackmailer was undoubtedly referring to the Directorate of Criminal Police, located on Ujazdowskie Avenue. The second undercover agent, "a rather handsome dark-haired man of medium height," seemed to be "a professional, well-qualified detective."[26]

After collecting the ransom, the "well-qualified" policeman became "downright gallant" and confessed to Berman that he had long had dealings with Jews because he had worked for some time as a detective in the ghetto. Berman believed that the blackmailer might have previously served in the intelligence unit of the Blue Police in the ghetto. The third undercover agent was a man "of the most vulgar appearance, medium height, fat, stocky, a typical primitive cop, had a bloated and hostile face."[27] The fact that these were not ordinary, amateur *szmalcowniks*, hundreds of whom were operating in Warsaw at that time, became clear the moment the three agents brought Berman to the Blue Police railway commissariat on Jerozolimskie Avenue. The blackmailers felt visibly at home there, as Berman noted. Everything seemed to be running smoothly: The undercover agents delivered the victims to the station, while their uniformed colleagues carried out further "processing" of the captured Jews. All three detectives were visibly nervous, because they were very much aware of their victim's connections with the underground. While Jews could be blackmailed and murdered with relative impunity and without much fear of reprisals from the underground, raising a hand against a member of the resistance

24 Adolf Berman, additional information, short description of the participants in the attack of January 4, 1944, GFH, Adolf Berman Collection, 6049. See also Dariusz Libionka, "Polska Podziemna wobec szantażystów i szmalcowników w Warszawie: Korekta obrazu," *Zagłada Żydów, Studia i materiały*, 14 (2018), pp. 115–164.

25 Adolf Berman, additional information, short description of the participants in the attack of January 4, 1944, GFH, Adolf Berman Collection, 6049.

26 Ibid.

27 Ibid.

movement—even a Jew—could result in serious unpleasantness. In fact, one of the undercover agents told Berman that he had already been wounded once "on the job," and he feared that armed conspirators would attempt to liberate the Żegota activist by force.[28]

Adolf Berman giving a speech during the commemoration of the victims and heroes of the Warsaw Ghetto Uprising, April 19, 1946. Ghetto Fighters' House Museum, Israel, Photo Archive, 31091.

Tadeusz Obremski, who was hiding in Warsaw, noted the following several months after Berman's capture:

> Yesterday there was a shooting on Mariańska Street. The agents of the Secret Police (Poles) and the Polish police were chasing a young Jew, who was recognized by the agents. The Jew was running away. The agents, afraid to let the "game" slip

28 Ibid.

> out of their hands, fired shots after him. By mistake, they hit and killed a woman passing by. The Jew, seeing that he would not be able to escape pursuit, ran into a large house where he apparently intended to take refuge. Agents and police rushed in after him. The gate was locked and the entire building was cordoned off. The police and agents arrived. The hunt for the poor Jew began, with revolvers and handguns. The Poles, "heroes" of the security service, searched for the "criminal" in all corners of the house. Of course, he was found, handcuffed and brought out [to the street]. There was already a German car with a dozen or so gendarmes in it. They put the handcuffed Jew into the car and, assisted by about twenty-five gendarmes, agents and Polish [u]niformed policemen, that is, assisted by about twenty-five people, defenders of "racial purity," took him to the Pawiak Prison.... Had it not been for the Polish agents and the Polish police, would this unfortunate young Jew have been apprehended? If there had been a bit of good will and love of humanity on the part of the Polish "guardians of peace," would this tragedy have happened? Now, when it seems that the time of such terrible, nightmarish murder of people is coming to an end, this unfortunate Jew died at the hands and through the fault of the Polish security organs.[29]

Both in the case of Berman's arrest and in the incident described by the hidden Obremski, the Polish detectives played a crucial role in the capture of the Jews. It is worth noting Obremski's words emphasizing the efficiency of the Polish officers, who could have been less zealous in the hunt, were not supervised, and could have turned a blind eye to the last Jews in hiding, especially since the end of the war was so near. In both cases, the detection and the arrest were the result of the work of Polish secret agents from beginning to end. The Germans appeared somewhere on the periphery of these events. Berman secured his release, having paid an enormous ransom. The name of the Jewish woman from Mariańska Street

29 See the entry dated the end of April 1944 in Obremski, *Wśród zatrutych noży*, pp. 245–246.

who paid for the zeal of the Polish detectives with her life remains unknown. While the undercover agents who Obremski described remain anonymous, we know the names of two of the three detectives who arrested Berman. They were Corporal Marian Szwed and Corporal Kazimierz Lubarski, both members of the so-called banditry division of the Warsaw Polish Kripo.[30]

The Sonderstreife of *SS-Hauptsturmführer* Richter

In the fall of 1943, the Warsaw Office of the Chief of Security Service (KdS) created a special unit tasked with "liquidating gangs and persons suspected of possessing weapons": in other words, combatting the underground.[31] An additional duty for the members of this unit was to solve broadly defined "Jewish matters." Officially, the new commando was called Section A. Unofficially, among Polish detectives, it was referred to as Richter's Sonderstreife (special commando), after its commander *SS-Hauptsturmführer* Georg Richter who was brought over from Berlin specifically for this purpose. The special commando consisted of a dozen or so Polish Kripo detectives, but the largest number of officers came from Commissariat I banditry division.[32] Richter's right-hand man was the aforementioned Senior Sergeant Karol Bartl, and one of his pupils was Detective Piotr Pupysz, who was born in 1908 in Vilna (Vilnius) and was a plainclothes officer with much prewar experience who joined the Investigative Service in 1933. As reported by an underground informant, Pupysz together with Wilhelm (Przemysław) Leitgeber took part in nighttime executions of the members of the Polish patriotic resistance.[33] One of the many reports on the underground's investigation of the commando members reads as follows:

30 Libionka, "Polska Podziemna wobec szantażystów i szmalcowników w Warszawie," p. 155.

31 Hempel, *Pogrobowcy klęski*, pp. 204–205.

32 Report 993, investigation of Piotr Pupysz, AIPN, BU 0423/4999, p. 3.

33 Service history of Piotr Pupysz, AIPN, GK 714/20, pp. 191–194. For more on Leitgeber, see Wojciech Königsberg, *AK 75: Brawurowe Akcje Armii Krajowej* (Kraków: Znak Horyzont, 2017), pp. 198–202. Leitgeber served time for murder before the war.

> It has been established that he [Pupysz] has been losing large stakes at the casino. The G[estap]o took an interest in this. In the evening, *Hauptmann* Richter entered the casino at the very moment when Pupysz had 100,000 zlotys on the table. When the Pol[ish] Pol[ice] offered to carry out a disciplinary inquiry, Richter refused, saying that he would deal with Pupysz himself. That was the end of the whole incident.[34]

According to AK intelligence, Pupysz behaved in the following way during interrogation and examination:

> [He] sadistically mistreats the detainees, beating them on the face and knocking their teeth out. Recently, one of the Polish officers, upon entering the room where Pupysz was interrogating an individual suspected of sabotage on the railway and alleged murders of detectives, P[upysz] tried to beat a confession out of him and make him inform on his colleagues. When told that he should not mistreat a fellow Pole in such a way, Pupysz shouted, "he was killing our detectives."[35]

The quoted report from September 1943 concluded that Pupysz had most likely been sentenced to death. As "Hanna" who was in charge of gathering intelligence reported, from as early as October, Pupysz left his house "in fear of our company."[36] The impunity of the Sonderstreife officers is well illustrated by the behavior of Kazimierz Lubarski, another member of Richter's commando who was investigated by the underground. On Saturday, October 30, 1943, Lubarski "shot a boy in the street, putting five bullets into him, and wounded another."[37]

While on duty, Pupysz was usually accompanied by Władysław Więckowski and Marian Szwed—the same person who captured and blackmailed Adolf Berman in January 1944—

34 Investigative report by "Hanna," October 23, 1943, AIPN, BU 0423/4999, p. 15/6.

35 Ibid.

36 Ibid., p. 15/1.

37 The report by "Paweł," November 4, 1943, AIPN, BU 0423/4999, p. 16.

and other Polish detectives active in Richter's Sonderstreife. As we learn from underground reports, on the one hand, the agents "were involved in capturing Jews and Poles harboring Jews," whereas on the other hand, "it has been established beyond doubt that they liquidated a whole number of Poles, completely innocent people, solely for their own material benefit and for the plunder of valuables."[38] If one of the AK reports written in the late fall of 1943 is to be believed, Pupysz apparently contributed to "the liquidation of the main Jewish Fighting Organization (ŻOB) unit, 70 people in all."[39] It is difficult to verify that information today because it is unclear to what timeframe this is referring. Are we talking about the detective's activity in the ghetto during the uprising? Rather doubtful. Does it concern escapees from the ghetto at the end of the uprising? Perhaps, although the largest groups of ŻOB fighters who managed to reach the Aryan side were smaller and numbered a dozen or so people.[40]

Piotr Pupysz, Polish Kripo agent and member of Richter's Sonderstreife. AIPN, GK 714/20.

It can be assumed that the Jews were blackmailed on the side, with neither the authorization nor knowledge of the German superiors. After all, it is unlikely that Lubarski and Szwed would

38 Ibid.

39 The investigation of Pupysz, undated, AIPN, BU 0423/4999, p. 5.

40 Grabowski and Libionka, "Meldunki Obwodu 'Praga' Policji Polskiej."

inform Richter about both the capture of Adolf Berman or about the ransom collection and subsequent release of the Jewish leader of Żegota. Archived AK intelligence reports clearly indicate that Richter's men were primarily interested in Polish underground organizations.[41] What concerned the Polish resistance the most were not so much the activities on the so-called Jewish front as attempts to infiltrate the underground made by members of the new commando. The investigation of the Sonderstreife continued throughout the autumn. On November 4, 1943, "Pawel", who was in charge of the AK investigation, wrote about Polish detectives who were part of the group:

> All the above mentioned constitute a special raiding party in the Kripo for the handling of "wet" jobs [murders] assigned to them by the German authorities. They execute all sentences on Poles and carry out official robberies on specific persons. They have their own separate intelligence network. They carry out their tasks by hook or by crook and their power is unlimited. They handle all matters and orders at night. They have a car with a permanent available staff at their disposal.[42]

From the underground's point of view, attempts at reconnaissance and attacks on underground structures were undoubtedly the most dangerous pursuits of the unit. This was the reason behind the alarm regarding the contact between Polish Kripo agents and a certain Willy Hildebrand, agent of the Gestapo and German intelligence.[43]

Upon their return from their nighttime liquidation expeditions, Sonderstreife members would bring the loot to the

41 For obvious reasons, the AK intelligence and counterintelligence paid much more attention to the so-called WBB operations (*Wiederstandbewegung Bekämpfung*) combatting the underground than to any actions aimed at tracking down Jews.

42 Investigation of Pupysz, undated (presumably February 1944), AIPN, BU 0423/4999, p. 16.

43 Investigation of Pupysz, November 18, 1943, AIPN, BU 0423/4999, p. 15/3.

Directorate of Criminal Police, which would then be deposited in the office of Kripo officer Kaiser, who appeared in the 1941 photo sitting next to von Amburger, looking grimly into the camera. Then Kaiser, "upon arriving at the office, selects the best things and tosses the rest to his obedient subjects," according to another reconnaissance report.[44] While Kaiser shared in the profits of the thefts, extortions, and seizures, Richter was in control of the city's operations. The AK reported that Polish officers, "do their work willingly, with dedication and enthusiasm. They are all young and keen."[45]

In theory, according to the Kripo organization chart, Polish detectives reported to Senior Sergeant Sylwester Rusiniak,[46] but in practice, Pupysz and others bypassed their Polish superior and communicated directly with the Germans. Rusiniak was described by AK intelligence as follows: "He extorts bribes together with his boss. A drunkard and a troublemaker. During searches in hotels he sometimes beat the searched persons without any reason. He will do anything for money, but does not interfere with political matters."[47] As for hunting Jews, Sergeant Rusiniak did not lag behind his subordinates and also worked on his own. On February 11, 1943, the AK intelligence service reported that Rusiniak "in partnership with [the] G[estap]o, seized a box of gold from Jews hiding from [the] G[estap]o."[48] In any case, as long as a Polish policeman did not interfere with political matters—and such matters did not include catching Jews—retaliation by the underground was unlikely. In January 1944, after a series of arrests, the AK counterintelligence report reassuringly stated that "'Biały' informs that what 'Miś' is saying is 'baloney,' because political matters are settled in the

44 Ibid.

45 Ibid.

46 Investigation of Sylwester Rusiniak, October 30, 1943, AIPN, BU 0423/5006, p. 6. The note about him reads as follows: "(3 Ciepła apartment 29), a sergeant of the crim[inal] pol[ice]...born in 1910. For the summer he moved to Nowy Międzyszyn near Falenica, 3 Zawiszy Street apartment 8. During the war he was advanced through the ranks. He works in the [Commissariat] IV of the Criminal Police under *Hauptscharführer* Ogórek."

47 Ibid.

48 Investigation of Sylwester Rusiniak, October 30, 1943, AIPN, BU 0423/5006.

political branch, not in the Jewish branch, and 'Miś' was being held in the Jewish branch."[49] In late 1943 and early 1944, Ringelblum commented bitterly:

> Blackmailers, *szmalzowniks*, agents, uniformed police and all sorts of other scoundrels held and still hold their revels with impunity in the streets of the capital. The murder of thousands of Jews, sentenced to death by the Gestapo after being caught, is their handwork. Yet no harm befalls them. They know that where Jews are concerned, there is no law and no punishment, nobody will stand up for them. Jewish political and social organizations constantly demand that extortion and blackmail be fought. The Polish Underground, however, has as yet done nothing to save the handful of Polish Jews on the Aryan side. The Home Plenipotentiary of the Polish Government [in Exile] has indeed issued a very belated warning that blackmailing Jews is a crime, which the Government will punish now and after the war. Words have not been followed by deeds. Though energetic action was taken to liquidate denunciators and informers, very little has been done in the sphere of fighting blackmailing of Jews. This complete impunity for the blackmailers and *szmalcowniks* has wounded and still wounds the handful of Jews, who see in this a clear sign that nobody is anxious to save Polish Jews.[50]

In the winter of 1943–1944, Jan Putrycz, a detective from Sokołów Podlaski, joined Richter's commando, after his cover had been blown in the previous area of activity. Putrycz—"about 45 years old, height: above average, corpulent, full face, wears a small moustache and a beard in the English style, dressed smartly (in knickerbockers), in a green hat"—became an obedient executor of the orders of his German superiors and, as the informants of the underground reported, he "dealt mainly with Jews" but was also

49 Report, WK-10, January 20, 1944, AIPN, BU 380/30, vol. 3, p. 274.
50 Ringelblum, *Polish-Jewish Relations*, p. 128.

"the soul of all actions."[51] Putrycz is worth remembering because he was one of the few Richter agents who would soon go on to become part of a more specialized commando aimed exclusively at fighting Jews.

Richter's Sonderstreife was recognized by the AK as a serious threat to their underground work. It did not take long for the effects of that conclusion to be seen, and in November and December 1943, the underground courts handed down numerous death sentences against Kripo agents. These sentences were followed by executions of the condemned policemen. Ludwik Landau—an economist, statistician, and employee of the Bureau of Information and Propaganda of the ZWZ-AK headquarters—noted the following in his diary in an entry dated December 21, 1943:

> Again, today there was an incident that could serve as a pretext for an official murder—the killing of some German in Długa Street. He was in civilian clothes, nevertheless, rumor has it that it was a man from the police, the "chief of police" at that, which sure is patently untrue. It is not known whether it was in connection with this that today there were tanks in the streets and numerous patrols, as usual, stopping, checking IDs and inspecting passers-by.[52]

This time, however, the rumor was not unfounded: The person killed on Długa Street turned out to be Senior Sergeant Karol Bartl—Richter's right-hand man, who appears in the 1941 photo seen earlier.[53] The execution on Długa Street was directly linked to the activities of Section A, and Bartl's death was a clear sign that the underground considered the specialized Kripo unit a serious threat to its activities. On January 5, 1944, another detective from the commemorative photo, Józef Osipiak, was killed by a combat

51 War report 2664, undated, AAN, AK, 203-III-109, p. 31. "Infor[mer] Łukasz reports that a Belarusian man, PUTRYCZ Jan, has been assigned to Kripo to serve in the Sonderstreife, Sergeant P. is the successor to the ideas of W. Leitgeber, Szwed, Więckowski, Pupysz and others."

52 Landau, *Kronika lat wojny i okupacji, vol. 3, Lipiec 1943 – luty 1944*, p. 494.

53 Władysław Bartoszewski, *1859 dni Warszawy* (Kraków: Znak, 1974), p. 489.

unit of the resistance. On January 13, 1944, another detective, Władysław Więckowski, was shot and wounded.[54] The shooters were members of the Warsaw Kedyw (sabotage unit), and the wounded agent was taken to the Sisters' of Saint Elizabeth Hospital with an injured leg. During this exchange of fire, Więckowski shot one of the fighters, and he ended up in the same hospital, although under an assumed name.

Panicked, Polish members of the Sonderstreife began to look around for better hiding places in Warsaw: "Pupysz is holed up with Tadeusz Burcher somewhere in the vicinity of Wolska Street," an AK report reads.[55] Another detective, Wiktor Neuman, also disappeared from his place of residence, and Szwed—who had been living at 16 Solna Street—asked the Germans to give him another place to live, somewhere closer to where he worked, "because he is afraid for his life."[56] Richter and his men could not leave these attacks on their subordinates unanswered. On the night of January 26, 1944, the Sonderstreife launched a counterattack. Although the AK intelligence did not have detailed information about the scope of this action, it was known that Richter's commando struck several places in Warsaw and arrested many people. One of those arrested was Bolesław Żukowski. He was taken by detectives to the Kripo jail—probably to the Directorate of Criminal Police on Ujazdowskie Avenue—where he was beaten to death during interrogation. The Kripo officers showed up in the hospital where the member of the liquidation group who had been shot by Więckowski was taken. Doctors who had operated on the wounded man were interrogated: It turned out that the name Kowalski that he had given was false. Polish Blue Police officers were also interrogated on suspicion of informing the underground about the identity and activities of Kripo agents—a suspicion not without foundation. It was due to those suspicions that Richter arrested and brutally interrogated the

54 Hanna Rybicka, ed., *Obwodowe oddziały dywersji bojowej Okręgu AK Warszawa: Dokumenty warszawskiego Kedywu z lat 1943–1945* (Warsaw: Wydawnictwa Uniwersytetu Warszawskiego, 2010), p. 165.

55 The investigation of Pupysz, undated, AIPN, BU 0423/4999, pp. 16–17.

56 Ibid.

head of the XIV Commissariat (Warsaw-Praga). Such leaks from the Blue Police were a common occurrence.

What Richter did not know was that the man who was collaborating with the underground State Security Corps—with Lieutenant Colonel Stanisław Wasilewski—was one of the chiefs of the theft commissariat Lieutenant Pluciński, who in 1942 was described by the resistance movement as "a great coward" and a man "worthless for the Cause."[57] Wasilewski and Pluciński took a list of 600–700 Kripo men from the Polish Kripo secretary's office, which they divided into three groups: those who retained "a healthy political and moral backbone"; those who retained only a healthy political backbone, but "faltered morally"; and those who collaborated closely with the Germans and abused their positions to enrich themselves.[58] The lists of Polish Kripo employees also contained the private addresses of detectives. Under such circumstances, it is hardly surprising that the liquidation of the policemen convicted by the underground courts was greatly facilitated.

The End of the Richter Commando

As a result of the January liquidations and well-aimed strikes by the underground, Richter's Sonderstreife was largely paralyzed. This does not mean that the commando suspended its activities altogether, but there is no doubt that from that moment on, Polish detectives—even those most devoted to the Germans—understood that acting openly against the underground Polish state could be lethal. A brief review of the fate of the Sonderstreife members leaves no doubt that Richter's men were, indeed, engaged in a very dangerous line of work. Józef Osipiak, as mentioned previously, was sentenced to death by an underground court and executed in January 1944. Another member of the commando,

57 Report, Directorate of the Polish Criminal Police by police stations, February 16, 1942, AAN, AK, 203-III-124, pp. 118–199.

58 Interrogation report of Stanisław Wasilewski, December 29, 1949, AIPN, BU 0423/3402, p. 85

Władysław Urbański, having received a death sentence, had to go into hiding. In June 1944, he was wounded during an assassination attempt on another agent, Wilhelm Leitgeber. The underground fighters who carried out this assassination attempt on the German were unaware that they should have also killed Urbański. While ultimately the underground failed to execute him, Urbański was tried after the war and sent to prison for several years. Detective Władysław Więckowski was seriously wounded in an assassination attempt in December 1943. Karol Bartl was killed on December 21, 1943, by members of an underground liquidation cell. Kazimierz Lubarski was executed on February 16, 1944, in his apartment on Pańska Street, following a death sentence passed in November 1943. Lubarski had been under investigation for a long time since he was on the list of Gestapo informers that had been prepared by AK counterintelligence on May 21, 1943.[59] Marian Szwed was killed on April 15, 1944, by an AK liquidation cell. As Stanisław Likiernik, a participant in the operation, recalls:

> There were four of them in all. It was Marian Szwed that looked the most dangerous. Master corporal of the criminal police, and a Gestapo agent. A towering man, about two meters tall, a powerful figure, athletic, a real gunfighter. He could hit the very center of a playing card from a great distance. I know it from Rybicki's report.... Szwed, running, was shooting at us and one of us got hit right in the middle of his hat, the bullet went right over his head, burnt his hair but didn't hurt him. Shooting on the run like that? That takes skill. And he did have it, because he fired six bullets from each revolver.... When Szwed reached the window of the house, someone fired. Szwed had already been wounded and was dripping blood as he ran. After this shot, he fell down on the street. He was finished off a moment later. As soon as the truck pulled up, I was tossing the bodies onto the back.[60]

59 "Naczelna Komenda Narodowego Wyzwolenia," *Biuletyn Informacyjny*, May 21, 1943, AIPN, BU 380/30, vol. 3, p. 149.

60 Emil Marat and Michał Wójcik, *Made in Poland: Opowiada jeden z ostatnich*

Despite being sentenced to death, Detective Piotr Pupysz avoided the punishing hand of the underground, and after the August 1944 uprising, he disappeared without a trace. After the war, the authorities sent out an arrest warrant for him but to no avail. The search for Pupysz lasted until 1972. No further information about Corporal Tadeusz Burcher (aka Burchard) and Sergeant Wiktor Neuman from Commissariat I has been found. Both disappeared after the war without a trace, which was not so difficult for men who had easy access to false documents until the end of the occupation.

German members of the Sonderstreife fared little better. Fighting the underground was a very risky business, especially after the AK command launched Operation Little Heads, the liquidation of the most troublesome members of the occupation regime. Wilhelm Leitgeber, who in October 1943 was sentenced to death by the Civilian Special Court of the Warsaw District, survived the first assassination attempt on February 21, 1944, but died during the second attempt on June 13, 1944. All that is known about Richter himself is that he died before the end of the war, presumably in 1944.[61]

Polish Criminal Police on the Trail of Emanuel Ringelblum

As we know, one of the Jews hiding on the Aryan side was Emanuel Ringelblum, founder of the underground Oneg Shabbat Archive and chronicler of the Warsaw ghetto who spent the last months of his life in the Krysia bunker at 81 Grójecka Street. The bunker was dug under a hothouse owned by gardener Mieczysław Wolski, and it was located on the outskirts of the city where the southern

żołnierzy Kedywu Stanisław Likierni (Warsaw: Wielka Litera, 2014), pp. 84–87. Szwed was liquidated during an operation against Lieutenant Jerzy Tabecki, codename "Lasso." Another dramatic description of Szwed's liquidation can be found in Rybicka, *Obwodowe oddziały dywersji bojowej Okręgu AK Warszawa*, pp. 88–90.

61 Handwritten note on the last page of a long dossier containing organizational charts of KdS Warschau, AIPN, GK 714/17, p. 8/2.

fringes of the Ochota district gradually became more rural. The hiding place was unusual in that more than thirty people hid there during this time, including Ringelblum and his wife Judyta and their fifteen-year-old son Uri. In 1944, a bunker of this kind was a complete rarity in Warsaw. Literature on the subject of hiding does not mention any other equally impressive hideout where its inhabitants managed to survive for so long. Of course, chroniclers of the ghetto uprising noted the existence of large shelters, sometimes accommodating several hundred residents, but all of those hiding places were discovered and destroyed by the Germans by the end of May 1943. And, of course, those bunkers were located within the ghetto. On the Aryan side, Jews hid in small groups, sometimes with families and sometimes individually.

Inspecting the area where the Krysia bunker once stood, Warsaw, 1945. Adolf Berman stands in the lower row, second on the right. From the collection of the POLIN Museum of the History of Polish Jews, Warsaw, MHŻP-B291.

The historian and Ringelblum's biographer Samuel D. Kassow writes the following about the discovery of the Krysia bunker:

> In early March 1944 the Krysia's luck ran out. According to three different sources, Wolski was betrayed by his girlfriend after a falling out. The Jagurs[62] stated that the Krysia was betrayed by an eighteen-year-old named Jan Łakiński, who was subsequently executed by the Polish underground. On March 7 Germans and Polish police appeared at the Wolski house. They knew exactly where to look. While one group burst into the house, another ran toward the garden and into the hothouse. Some of the Germans threw themselves on Mieczysław [Wolski] and yelled, "You damned Jewish lackey, you wanted to hide Jews, you will pay for it, fool!"[63]

The Germans then circled the bunker's exit and, shooting into the air, threatened to "kill all the Jews like rats" if they did not come up on their own.[64] After the Jews finally left the bunker, they were taken to Pawiak Prison. Several days later they were all shot in the ruins of the ghetto. Gardener Mieczysław Wolski and his fifteen-year-old nephew, Janusz Wysocki, shared their fate.

The discovery of the bunker was described in a similar way by a Blue policeman who was loyal to the patriotic underground. In the *Kronika* of March 7, we read the following:

> At 81 Grójecka Street, in the buildings of Wolski, a gardener, 38 Jews hiding there were arrested. There was a

62 This is referring to Orna and Józef Jagur, who moved out of the bunker shortly before it was denounced.

63 Samuel D. Kassow, *Who Will Write Our History? Emanuel Ringelblum, the Warsaw Ghetto, and the Oyneg Shabes Archive* (Bloomington: Indiana University Press, 2007), pp. 383–384.

64 It is difficult to say to what extent the description of the police raid on the Wolski's buildings reflects the actual events. The information in Kassow's book comes from the accounts of Wanda Szadurska and Halina Michałecka, sisters of the murdered gardener, submitted to Yad Vashem in July 1988. See Wanda Szadurska's file and Halina Michałecka's file, YVA, M.31.2/4252. However, according to the report discussed later, both women were away from home at the time of the raid.

> few-days-old baby among them. Those Jews were hiding in a well-appointed hothouse. They had water, bathroom, and electricity, and gardener Wolski provided food. The Jews had been hiding there since March 5, 1943. They were rich and well-known people in the area of the XXIII commissariat ([the] baker Gitter, [the] restaurateur Rawicz, [the] doctor Cendrowicz, and others). German gendarmes spotted them following an informer's report. Also present during the liquidation of the shelter was the police from the XXIII Commissariat. The Jews were taken away along with their property (furs, jewelry, 4 kilograms of gold, etc.). The hothouse and all its equipment was destroyed with grenades and burned. Wolski was arrested together with his sister and nephew, and his private apartment was sealed.[65]

This description is supplemented by materials from an investigation of an entirely different case carried out by the security authorities less than six years after the discovery of the bunker and Ringelblum's subsequent death. As part of an investigation that focused on the activities of the prewar Political Police, it was revealed that the hideout had caught the attention of the Citizens' Militia by chance. The murder of Jews during the war was one of the secondary lines of inquiry in this investigation, thus making the findings all the more credible. On January 26, 1950, an anonymous Citizens' Militia officer from the Warsaw-Ochota station wrote a preliminary report,[66] which while not free from numerous errors mainly concerning chronology, provides a lot of information previously unknown to historians. The findings concerning the liquidation of the bunker are particularly interesting, and as the information comes from a period not too distant from the described events, it is particularly valuable. In view of this, it is worth quoting extensive passages of this report:

> Today I have conducted interviews to determine the shelter in Ochota and the witnesses and have established that:

65 *Kronika wydarzeń*, entry dated March 7, 1944, AAN, Delegatura Rządu na Kraj, 202-II-44.

66 Report, January 26, 1950, AIPN, GK 317/248, pp. 67–67v.

> Mieczysław Wolski, a Warsaw-based gardener, who owned the house and the large lot at No. 81 Grójecka Street, built a camouflaged underground shelter on his lot after the Germans entered Warsaw and created the ghetto, in which more than 40 Jewish people—Wolski's acquaintances or their relatives—were hiding, the known names include Epsztein, a baker from Siewierska Street. They were wealthy people, who did not work anywhere, living in the shelter and paying for themselves with their own funds.[67] In 1943, the hiding place was discovered by the Germans by undetermined means and liquidated. The Gestapo took away all the people in hiding and none of them returned. Mieczysław Wolski and Janusz Wolski, his nephew, were also arrested and did not return. After the Jews in hiding were taken away, the shelter was destroyed with grenades, and the house was set on fire.... Persons who are still alive and were present at the time of the liquidation of the shelter, include Wolski's mother, residing on Grójecka Street, as well as Wolski's sisters, who were, however, elsewhere at the time of the liquidation. Also alive is a relative of Wolski's, Maria Czakajewska, living at 4 Siewierska Street, apt. 16. During the liquidation of the shelter, the area was surrounded by German gendarmes from the student residence on Narutowicza Square. The liquidation of the hideout was carried out by Gestapo officers, in the company of plainclothes agents. The liquidation took several hours. [illegible signature][68]

Thus, the postwar report stated that the hiding place was discovered by "undetermined means." The report of the Blue policemen clearly indicated that the raid on the Krysia bunker was, as usual, the result of a betrayal. According to Kassow, it is possible that the raid was caused by the denunciation of a betrayed woman or by

67 It is worth noting that neither the *Kronika policyjna* nor the postwar investigations recorded the presence of Emanuel Ringelblum in the hiding place on Grójecka Street. Only the *Kronika policyjna* quoted in the text, in an entry dated March 15, 1944, gave an incorrect account of the arrest of "Dr. Ringelblum" as one of the of "those taking care of the bunker."

68 Report, January 26, 1950, AIPN, GK 317/248, pp. 67–67v.

a report from a collaborator, Jan Łakiński.[69] However, the latter's involvement in the discovery of Emanuel Ringelblum can probably be ruled out, since Jan Łakiński was executed on February 25, 1944, ten days before the discovery of the Krysia bunker. Police sources mention an informer's report, and it is difficult for a historian today to know more beyond such a general statement. However, the witnesses, the victims, and the militia officer who conducted the investigation after the war had no idea that the fall of the Krysia bunker and the deaths of its inhabitants were primarily the direct result of the actions of the Polish Criminal Police.

Kriegsfahndungskommando: The Commando for Wartime Manhunts

Following the outbreak of the ghetto uprising, the hunt for hidden Jews in and around Warsaw intensified. Thousands of escapees who had crossed over to the Aryan side during the *Grossaktion* between July and September 1942 were joined by hundreds more from the burning and liquidated ghetto. For the Jewish survivors, it was a suffocating and terrifying time. Finding a new hiding place became more and more difficult, and the fear of Polish friends and rescuers grew day by day. Teams of blackmailers combed the city in search of new victims, and the dense network of informers made the work easier for the various police units—secret and uniformed, Polish and German.

In the summer or fall of 1943, a plan was conceived at the Directorate of Criminal Police to create a specialized unit whose primary task would be to track down and arrest any hidden Jews. Until that time, catching Jews had been the responsibility of several different organizations: the Blue Police, the Gestapo, the Security Service, the Schupo, the Gendarmerie, and the Polish Criminal Police. Richter's previously mentioned commando took care of

69 See also Marian Hanasz, "Sprawa Łakińskiego," in Marian Hanasz, ed., *Goldmanka: W kręgu szkoły* (Warsaw: Praca zbiorowa, 2005), pp. 82–94. This case is discussed in more detail in Libionka, *Polska Podziemna wobec szantażystów i szmalcowników w Warszawie.*

the Jews "after hours" in addition to its regular duties. After all, the Sonderstreife's main task was to investigate underground organizations, not to hunt down Jews. It is also difficult to determine today how much the German supervisors knew about the search for Jews carried out by the Polish Kripo officers from the Sonderstreife. Indeed, the arrest and subsequent release of Adolf Berman points to the considerable agency of the Polish agents. The Germans must have known that the Polish Criminal Police were moonlighting after hours, pursuing "Jewish matters." This was to be remedied by a unit specializing exclusively in the tracking down and apprehending of Jews in hiding. It cannot be ruled out that the losses sustained as a result of underground reprisals were an additional incentive for some of the German policemen—and their Polish subordinates—to engage in a line of duty that was not only less dangerous but also much more lucrative. The establishment of a unit tasked exclusively with hunting down Jews indicates that the German authorities considered the situation in Warsaw alarming and the hunt for Jews in the former Polish capital had become a priority.

The formation of a special police unit to fight Jews was by no means an original idea of the security authorities in the Generalgouvernement. From the beginning of 1943 in France, a special unit had been operating within the Préfecture de Police in Paris to track down Jews who had escaped *Opération Vent printanier* (Operation Spring Wind), as the manhunts organized in the summer of 1942 were called. Fellow policemen dubbed members of that unit "*les mangeurs des Juifs*" (devourers of the Jews). Other "special-purpose" police groups operated within the office of the General Directorate for Jewish Affairs (commissariat general aux questions juives), while others were part of the militia (milice française) that collaborated with the Germans. Aside from those essentially French organizations, there were also groups that were directly dependent on and inspired by the Gestapo and the Kripo.[70] The situation was similar in the Netherlands, where

70 For more on the subject, see Jean-Marc Berlière, *Les Policiers français sous l'Occupation: D'après les archives inédites de l'épuration* (Paris: Perrin, 2001); Laurent Joly, *L'Antisémitisme de bureau: Enquête au coeur de la préfecture de Police de Paris et du commissariat général aux Questions juives (1940–1944)*

between 1943 and 1944, an extremely powerful police group was active called the Kolonne Henneicke (Henneicke Column), which victimized at least several thousand Jews from Amsterdam. The operational tactics of both the police officers and the Kolonne Henneicke relied heavily on denunciations. It was a strategy as uncomplicated as it was effective.[71] It was no different in the East, and in recent years, researchers have begun to describe the activities of special police and collaborationist formations in both Ukraine and Belorussia.[72]

In light of the historians' findings, it is clear that in all occupied countries, special squads and units were formed with the main purpose to catch hidden Jews. One can argue about their different inspiration and motives. Some members justified their actions by ideology, others by religion, others by simple greed, or any combination of these factors. But, one cannot deny the very existence of elaborate police structures whose aim was the final destruction of European Jews. Therefore, the fact that special police units were established in Poland during the war to track down Jews is nothing unusual. What is unusual is the silence surrounding the participation of Poles involved in the fight against the Jews.

The plan to establish a special police unit in Poland was put into effect in late summer 1943. The newly formed Polnische Kriminalpolizei section was euphemistically named Kriegsfahndungskommando (Commando for Wartime Manhunts).[73] According to one testimony, there was a plaque on the door of the room where the commando's undercover officers were stationed,

(Paris: Bernard Grasset, 2011); Tal Bruttmann, *La logique des bourreaux, 1943–1944* (Paris: Hachette Litterature, 2003).

71 Ad van Liempt, *Hitler's Bounty Hunters: The Betrayal of the Jews* (New York: Berg, 2005).

72 Martin Dean, *Collaboration in the Holocaust: Crimes of the Local Police in Belorussia and Ukraine, 1941–44* (New York: St. Martin's Press, 2000); John-Paul Himka, "The Lviv Pogrom of 1941: The Germans, Ukrainian Nationalists, and the Carnival Crowd," *Canadian Slavonic Papers*, 53:2–4 (2011), pp. 209–243; Gabriel N. Finder and Alexander V. Prusin, "Collaboration in Eastern Galicia: The Ukrainian Police and the Holocaust," *East European Jewish Affairs*, 34:2 (2004), pp. 95–118.

73 Maria Dzięgielewska testimony, January 3, 1950, AIPN, GK 317/248, pp. 52–53.

with the telling inscription Oberstreifkommando (Main Office for Manhunts).[74] Polish staff of the Warsaw Kripo simply called this office the "Jewish branch." Little is known about the method of establishment, the mode of work, and the personnel of the newly created Judenreferat. The few references extracted from postwar investigations and from intelligence reports at the time of the occupation indicate that the Kriegsfahndungskommando was a "mixed" unit. In addition to a dozen or so undercover officers from the Polish Criminal Police brought in from various commissariats, it included several German policemen, a few *Volksdeutsche*, and two Ukrainians.

SS-Untersturmführer and *Kriminalkommissar* Werner Balhause.
Photo Collection, YVA, 5044.

The Kriegsfahndungskommando was a separate unit assigned to special tasks, and it was not part of any of the seven Polnische Kriminalpolizei commissariats but reported directly to the German command. The Kriegsfahndungskommando was headed by *SS-Untersturmführer* and *Kriminalkommissar* Werner Balhause. Little

74 Bronisław Chudzikowski testimony, January 13, 1950, AIPN, GK 317/248, pp. 57–57v.

is known about Balhause.[75] In the fall of 1942, he was apparently involved in the liquidation of the Ostrowiec ghetto. He probably came to the Warsaw Kripo in the first half of 1943 and became the German supervisor of Commissariats II and III (theft) in the Directorate of Criminal Police in Warsaw. The work in Warsaw must have brought Balhause considerable profits, as mentioned in the underground *Kronika wydarzeń* in the entry dated January 19, 1944: "A number of German employees with the Kripo dir[ector] (Balhausen, Nusperling and others) are sending looted furniture and valuables to the Reich or storing them in houses occupied by the army, on Rozbrat Street."[76]

Balhause accepted volunteer policemen to his new section—usually men with experience in tracking down Jews. It was not a coincidence that he recruited, among others, two detectives from Commissariat II who were prewar undercover agents with an extensive network of informers in the city. Balhause's deputy in the Judenreferat was *Kriminalsekretar* Schuhardt, and completing the list of German officers were *Kriminalassistent* Henel (or Henkel) and a policeman from Silesia named Bomisch. The Germans from the Kriegsfahndungskommando had one room at their disposal in the Kripo headquarters, while the other room was occupied by their Polish subordinates and associates. Initially, Wacław Stroka was in charge of the Polish team in the section, but after his death—he was killed in early 1944 in an accidental shootout on Krochmalna Street—he was succeeded by Zygmunt Głowacki, a detective from Commissariat II.

Głowacki is a mysterious figure. According to the documents of the Special Court in Lwów (*Sondergericht* Lemberg) in 1942–1943, he was serving in Commissariat II of the local Kripo, and

75 Werner Balhause (aka Ballhause or Balhausen) was born in Berlin on March 27, 1903. He was employed with the KdS in Ostrowiec Świętokrzyski—rank of criminal commissioner (*Kriminalkommissar*). He was assigned to Department V of KdS Warschau. The criminal records are located at the Hamburg Public Prosecutor's Office, reference number 147 Js 34/65 (Zentrale Stelle Ludwigsburg, 206 AR-Z 23/64).

76 *Kronika wydarzeń*, entry dated January 19, 1944, AAN, Delegatura Rządu na Kraj, 202-II-44.

he was specializing in "Jewish matters." In the spring or summer of 1943, he appeared in the Directorate of Criminal Police in Warsaw, and soon afterward in the Balhause commando. He undoubtedly brought with him a wealth of experience acquired in Lwów, as will be discussed a little further on. Also working in the section was Detective Władysław Nowiński who transferred from the theft commissariat just like Głowacki, as well as other detectives such as Władysław Olszewski, a certain Sybilski, and two younger policemen, Jerzy Gzel (also known as Gezell or Gsell), and Paluchowski, whose first name is unknown. The first translator of the section was a Pole named Adamiec, and after his death in a shootout in Mińsk Mazowiecki in January 1944, he was replaced by the *Volksdeutscher* Bąk. Janina (Irena) Oleszuk, a prewar employee of the Investigative Service, became the secretary in the Jewish branch. Another important figure in the branch was Detective Leszek Tuszpiński who became the liaison between the Polish and German staff.

However, the daily work of the Jewish branch was based primarily on close cooperation with its network of informers. Each detective had his own agents who infiltrated different groups or different districts of the city. The secretary of the Warsaw police who dealt with the police officers daily also mentioned "a whole mass of informers" working for the Kriegsfahndungskommando.[77] We know that one of the policemen "had confidants among his contacts, he constantly received phone calls from the city."[78] Sergeant Głowacki was in charge of ten informers, one of whom—Mieczysław Jankowski, codename "Borys"—"had a perfect command of German and English and, as he said, also spoke French."[79] Also important for the Jewish branch were anonymous letters sent to the police and then forwarded to Balhause for further investigation.[80]

One could join the Jewish branch either by invitation or at one's own request. Working in the new section facilitated the establishment of closer contact with German superiors, which

77 Maria Dzięgielewska testimony, January 3, 1950, AIPN, GK 317/248, p. 52.
78 Władysław Nowiński hearing, February 24, AIPN, GK 317/248, pp. 14–15.
79 Zygmunt Głowacki hearing, January 14, AIPN, GK 317/248, pp. 21–22.
80 Władysław Nowiński hearing, March 13, 1950, AIPN, GK 317/248, p. 48v.

could prove very helpful in one's professional career. One of the volunteers, a prewar corporal from the theft brigade, attained the rank of senior sergeant in the Judenreferat, while others even attained the rank of commissioned officers. It is worth mentioning that Polish detectives employed in this section had previously received solid training. As early as 1941, two of them had completed a special three-week course in criminal law, investigation service, and investigative technique.[81] Such courses were held in Rabka at the Security Police and Security Service School (*Führerschule der Sicherheitspolizei und des SD*), which was established in 1939–1940, and was divided into two sections: German and Polish. It was where the previously mentioned Blue Police officer Colonel Wojciech Stano from Kraków was in charge of the training program for Polish officers.

In terms of the methods of investigative work, it is known that detectives went out into the city on patrol, usually in groups of two or three. According to Karol Frankowski, a policeman from the theft brigade:

> The branch [Kriegsfahndungskommando] was under the full command of the Germans. This branch was tasked [with carrying out] special reconnaissance and arrests. I saw with my own eyes how Zygmunt G[łowacki] brought the arrested to the [Directorate of Criminal Police] Office. He always went on those actions in the company of two men, and he worked in Warsaw, most often in the ghetto. Sometimes they went there by car. It was said that this branch earns a lot of money. The opinion about this branch was the worst...particularly trusted people were assigned to this unit, there was even an incident with one of the employees who could not bear the work emotionally and committed suicide.[82]

81 Zygmunt Głowacki hearing, January 31, AIPN, GK 317/248, pp. 29–30.

82 Karol Frankowski witness examination, January 10, 1950, AIPN, GK 317/248, pp. 55–55v.

Sometimes, the patrol was headed by one of the Germans, but as a rule, the command was given to one of the Polish Kripo agents. Patrols were directed to addresses that had been earlier identified and where Jews were said to be hiding.

The arrested Jews were then taken to the Criminal Police headquarters, where they were interrogated. According to one of the testimonies, "Detective G[łowacki] was brutal with the detainees. He would interrogate the Jews, shouting and speaking harshly to them."[83] After the initial interrogation, victims were transferred to Szucha Avenue into the hands of the Gestapo, or they were taken to Pawiak Prison. As one of the interrogated policemen claimed, "From the Gestapo, it was said, the Jews were transported to the concentration camps in Treblinka, Auschwitz and others."[84] In fact, in 1943 and 1944, Jews were taken to the nearby ghetto ruins, where the Germans carried out mass executions, which were reported every few days by the underground press. It is noteworthy that Blue policemen and criminal police officers from other commissariats also brought the city's captured Jews to the offices of the Section of Wartime Manhunts.

It is difficult to say anything specific about the first months of activity of the Kripo's Jewish branch as only scraps of information have survived in AK reports and postwar testimonies. It is also unclear at which point the arrests made by police officers "on their own" ended and where their actions as part of official duties began. It is known, however, that one of the first Kriegsfahndungskommando operations related to Jews—albeit not directly—was the trip to Treblinka taken by several officers and led by Balhouse in the fall of 1943. The purpose of the expedition was to investigate an attack on local residents by Ukrainian camp guards. It is unclear whether the Kripo officers visited the death camp, which was being liquidated at that time, or the nearby labor camp of Treblinka I, but several photographs have survived from the trip. One such photograph

83 Władysław Nowiński hearing, February 24, 1950, AIPN, GK 317/248, pp. 14–15.

84 Władysław Nowiński hearing, March 2, 1950, AIPN, GK 317/248, pp. 45–45v.

appears below and shows a Polish Kriegsfahndungskommando officer in front of a police car with a machine gun in his hands. In the late fall of 1943, the Kriegsfahndungskommando developed its own style of operation and began locating Jews both on its own volition and on orders from other institutions. According to Głowacki, who in his postwar testimony made obvious attempts to downplay the scale of his own involvement, "arrests of Jews were carried out frequently, on average once or twice a week."[85]

Zygmunt Głowacki, Polish Kripo agent, during a visit to Treblinka to investigate crimes committed by a Ukrainian camp guard, fall 1943. AIPN, GK 317/247.

The arrests were usually made in apartments where the Jews were hiding. Today, the scarce source base makes it impossible to determine—even approximately—the scale of the anti-Jewish actions of the Warsaw Kripo. The vast majority of victims of the

85 Interrogation of Zygmunt Głowacki, February 9, 1950, AIPN, GK 317/248, pp. 31–32.

Polish policemen will remain nameless forever, and their ashes have vanished in the ruins of the ghetto without a trace. This makes it all the more important to list those few names, addresses, or dates that can be found in the documents and help a historian bring at least a handful of specific victims out of anonymity and oblivion.

In January 1944, two of the commando's detectives and the translator Adamiec went to one of the streets between Podwale and the Old Town Market Square. "In an apartment on the second floor we found two elderly women of Jewish nationality. They were probably a mother and a daughter. We detained them and escorted them to the Directorate."[86] After some time, the translator Adamiec returned to the empty apartment and took bed and linen and undergarments, which were then distributed among the officers. Both Jewish women were hiding with false papers, but during the interrogation, they admitted to the Kripo agents that their real name was Fajans.

Several months later, in the early spring of 1944, agents appeared on Twarda Street, between Złota and Pańska Streets, where a twenty-year-old Jewish woman lived in a sublet room. She was arrested, but her Polish landlords avoided any unpleasant consequences, presumably thanks to the oft-used argument that they had rented the room to the Jewish woman "in good faith," unaware of the true ethnicity of their subtenant, and "none of the belongings were taken," the Kripo agent added by way of excuse.[87] Another arrest occurred in Warsaw's Powiśle district, where Kriegsfahndungskommando workers found "an elderly woman, a Jewess, living alone, in miserable conditions," and perhaps why this time also "none of the belongings were taken," as the former policeman assured.[88]

In a house on Hoża, Wilcza, or Wspólna Streets, the agents arrested a Jew in his thirties. Like the others, he was first brought to the Directorate of Criminal Police headquarters. Another elderly Jewish woman was caught in a Żoliborz district villa. As before, the

86 Ibid., pp. 34–34v.

87 Ibid.

88 Ibid.

Polish landlords were allegedly unharmed. However, it is difficult to believe this part of the testimony. The former Kripo officer interrogated after the war apparently found it easier to admit to capturing Jews than arresting Poles or stealing the victims' property. In the spring of 1944, another Jewish woman was arrested in a house on the corner of Puławska and Rakowiecka Streets, a whole Jewish family were dragged out of an apartment on Wronia Street, and a Kripo patrol arrested Jews in a building on one of the side streets off Belwederska Street. Members of the commando would also raid outside Warsaw. In May 1944, policemen Bomisch, Tuszyński (Tuszpiński), Nowiński, Henkel, Głowacki, and Gzel went to Świder, where a Jewish family was said to be hiding. In this case the trip did not bring the expected results. However, there is no doubt that the most memorable operation of the Kripo agents was the discovery and liquidation of the Krysia bunker in Warsaw.

March 7, 1944: The Krysia Bunker

The beginning of 1944 was a period of intensified work for the members of the Polnische Kriminalpolizei's Judenreferat. A handful of information on the subject may be found in the oft-cited *Kronika policyjna*, which contains reports by Blue policemen collected from various Warsaw precincts that were then sent to the intelligence units of the resistance. This information was reliable as far as the Blue Police officers themselves were concerned, quite reliable for the Polish Kripo, and much less reliable for the German police and Gestapo, where the Blue policemen had fewer "snitches" and less access to trustworthy sources. On February 29, 1944, Ludwik Landau, an employee of the Bureau of Information and Propaganda of the Main Headquarters of the Polish Armed Forces, was captured under mysterious circumstances. The following day the police detained his wife and daughter, who both committed suicide shortly after their arrest. On March 1, in Mińsk Mazowiecki, one of the Żegota leaders Julian Grobelny was arrested following a denunciation regarding his involvement in helping Jews. On March 2, Kripo agents arrested Jan Jaworski, a "member of the Committee for the Protection of Jews"—most likely a reference to Żegota—in a sweetshop on Mokotowska Street. He had gone there to give the agents a ransom for the release of previously detained Jews. A notebook with names and a false ID issued under the name Zygadlewicz was found on Jaworski.[89] A day later, the agents found a larger group of Jews hiding in a house on Kozia Street, and four days later the Krysia bunker—where Ringelblum was hiding—was raided. It is not known whether the capture of Jan Jaworski contributed to Ringelblum's arrest, but the coincidence surrounding the dates is striking.[90]

A reasonably accurate account of the operation itself can be reconstructed from the testimony given by two participants involved in Ringelblum's arrest. On March 7, 1944, early in the morning, as soon as the policemen came to work, *Untersturmführer* Balhause sounded the alarm in the section. After a short briefing, all officers were told to get into cars:

> Balhause ordered everyone to go with him. We went by car to Grójecka Street, I don't recall the number, it was on the section between Narutowicza Square and the last streetcar stop going in the direction of Okęcie. After our arrival, we found several Germans from the Gestapo already there. Through the gate, we entered the premises where the hothouse was located, surrounded by the Gestapo men and us. As I realized there, the gardener, who owned the hothouse, and his son, a teenage boy, were detained. On the order of one of the Germans, the gardener's son went into the bunker located under the hothouse and explained to the Jews there that any resistance was futile and that everyone should come out. The Jews from the bunker came out one by

89 *Kronika wydarzeń*, entry dated March 2, 1944, AAN, Delegatura Rządu na Kraj, 202-II-44. Both names are presumably false.

90 *Kronika wydarzeń*, entry dated March 3, 1944, AAN, Delegatura Rządu na Kraj, 202-II-44. The police report mentions the arrest of as many as thirty Jews on Kozia Street, but I would treat this figure with caution as it is not confirmed by other sources.

> one; there were twenty-some people and they were stopped by the Gestapo. Those Jews were of various genders and ages, there were even children among them. After being detained, the Jews and the gardener and his son were taken to the Gestapo, and we returned to the Directorate.[91]

As the cited detective from the Kriegsfahndungskommando testified: "In the spring of 1944, on orders from the Gestapo *Kriegsfahndung* section, I went to liquidate a Jewish bunker. Two Germans, Ballhause, the translator Bąk, and another German went there. As for the Poles, Jan Puszyn went there to help liquidate the bunker, and the Germans also had detectives from other brigades."[92] Polish policemen interrogated after the war understandably tried to downplay their participation in the operation:

> I took part in capturing Jews at 81 Grójecka St. There were already Germans there when we arrived.... it was only there that we found out Jews were hiding there. I only saw the Germans taking the Jews out. When they took them away, they told us we could go back to the Directorate, because they didn't need us. At that time I didn't hear or know that the gardener had been taken away. I only found out about it at the Directorate.[93]

Nevertheless, their testimony demonstrates that the Kripo mobilized considerable resources for the raid on the Krysia bunker, including groups of Blue policemen from various stations:

> As I recall...during the liquidation of the bunker with the Jews in Ochota, on Grójecka Street.... almost everyone from the section and many detectives from the Directorate and other commissariats were involved...**We were assigned to Gestapo officers, one each** [emphasis added, JG]. There was a shelter

91 Zygmunt Głowacki hearing, February 10, 1950, AIPN, GK 317/248, pp. 33–34.
92 Ibid., pp. 20–21.
93 Ibid.

> under the hothouse on the property. The Germans took some people out of this shelter. There was a dozen or so of them. They were taken by the Gestapo and driven away in a car. I don't know where to—we didn't do anything there. We were just present there.[94]

However, it is hard to believe that officers from the section for exterminating Jews were "just present" during their unit's most important operation. Concerning the aftermath of the operation, it is worth referring again to the preliminary investigation report, drawn up in January 1950 by an anonymous militia officer from the Ochota station. As a result of questioning the witnesses, he stated that after the Jews had been taken away "all Wolski's and the hiding people's belongings were taken away by the XXIII police commissariat,[95] while rags of no value that the police left behind were later stolen by the locals."[96] That day must have been special in the lives of Grójecka Street residents. The discovery of the bunker, the concentration of the Polish and German police, the robbery in the Wolski's house, and finally, as we read in the last sentences of the report, "all tenants of Wolski's house fled during the liquidation of the shelter, taking their most valuable belongings with them, unhindered by uniformed policemen from the XXIII Commissariat, who surrounded Grójecka Street, where crowds of local residents had gathered."[97]

On March 15, 1944, the discovery of the Krysia bunker was briefly mentioned—with errors—in the *Kronika policyjna*: "In

94 Władysław Nowiński hearing, March 2, 1950, AIPN, GK 317/248, pp. 45–45v.

95 The XXIII Blue Police Commissariat covered the area of Grójecka, Kopińska, and Kaliska Streets.

96 Report, January 26, 1950, AIPN, GK 317/248, pp. 67–67v. As I have already mentioned, the discovery of the Krysia bunker and the subsequent murder of its inhabitants was of little interest to the militia. This is best demonstrated by the fact that of all the witnesses of the liquidation of the bunker who were alive at the time (listed in the report), only the mother of the gardener (Wolski) was interviewed. In her short testimony, the mother of the murdered gardener stated that two Germans and two Polish policemen came to search her house. See Małgorzata Wolska, AIPN, GK 317/248, pp. 62–62v.

97 Report, January 26, 1950, AIPN, GK 317/248, pp. 67–67v.

connection with the discovery of the shelter with the Jews at 81 Grójecka Street, Dr. Ringelblum, Mrs. Melman, Zenia Panari, and Dr. Steinbok of the Scholl company, who were hiding under false documents, were arrested."[98] According to the Pawiak Prison chronicle, Ringelblum, the Warsaw ghetto historian, and all the other victims of the Kripo operation were killed on March 10, 1944.[99]

The discovery of the bunker on Grójecka Street must have resonated with the Warsaw District Police Board because on that same day, the German authorities applied for cash rewards for fifteen Kripo officers for their loyalty and zeal in their work. While there can be no absolute certainty that those rewards were definitely connected with the discovery of the Krysia bunker, it nevertheless seems unlikely that the coincidence of dates was by chance.[100] The operation described above was not the last "success" of the Warsaw Kripo. An entry from the *Kronika policyjna* dated March 15 mentions further arrests of people linked to the inhabitants of the bunker on Grójecka Street discovered a week earlier. On March 22, the police liquidated another hiding place, this time at 12 Orla Street. From March and April 1944, the Warsaw Kripo took part in blockades in Żoliborz in which forty Jews were caught, and on April 2, the unit under Balhause's command made further arrests, this time in restaurants.

"Jewish Gold"

Having learned about certain elements of the Kriegsfahndungskommando's activities, one may wonder about the motives that guided its employees. Police discipline and obeying orders undoubtedly played a large role here, but at least in some cases, the candidates came to Balhause of their own free will. Ideology,

98 *Kronika wydarzeń*, AAN, Delegatura Rządu na Kraj, 202-II-44.

99 Regina Domańska, *Pawiak—więzienie gestapo: Kronika 1939–1944* (Warsaw: Książka i Wiedza, 1978), p. 432.

100 *Kronika wydarzeń*, entry dated March 15, 1944, AAN, Delegatura Rządu na Kraj, 202-II-44.

however, does not seem to have been an important factor there. Perhaps antisemitic prejudice facilitated the decision to join the ranks of the catchers—a previous dislike of Jews certainly made the "job" itself easier—but the primary motive was the desire to get rich quick.[101] According to the secretary of the Directorate of Criminal Police, "in general, this whole section was engaged in exterminating Jews and robbing their property."[102] The belief that the lust for robbery was an important motivating factor for the policemen is confirmed by other sources. The desire to get the "Jewish gold" was characteristic not only of the employees of the Jewish branch but also the officers of other Polish Criminal Police departments in Warsaw.

According to AK intelligence reports, in late 1942 and early 1943, representatives of a special committee of the Warsaw Polnische Kriminalpolizei appeared in the ghetto, which was now half-empty after the *Grossaktion*. The committee consisted of policemen Mikołaj Gruca,[103] Tadeusz Wojtulski, and Edward Sierpacki, and was headed by former legionnaire and holder of the Cross of Independence, Second Lieutenant Michał Olczyk,[104] who had been in charge of the Commissariat II (theft) from the beginning of the occupation. The AK report reads:

> Olczyk, using an official pass, searched all the apartments in the houses assigned to Kripo employees and took not just the more valuable items, such as libraries, paintings, antiques,

101 Maria Dzięgielewska testimony, minutes of the main hearing, July 14, 1950, AIPN, GK 317/247, pp. 91–91v.

102 Maria Dzięgielewska testimony, January 3, 1950, AIPN, GK 317/248, p. 52v.

103 Policeman Gruca worked in the head office of the Directorate of Criminal Police in Warsaw. See Maria Dzięgielewska interrogation report, December 28, 1949, AIPN, BU 0423/3402, p. 43.

104 Undated report, AIPN, BU 0423/4889, p. 8. Before the war, Sierpacki worked in the political department of the Investigative Service in the national minorities brigade; in the "theft" brigade during the occupation; and after the war, among other things, in communications in the Department of Roads. In his own resumé written after the war, he stated that while working for the Kripo, he was in the underground organization Wiciarz and in the People's Party, where he used the codenames "Prałat" and "Wolski". See letter to the head of WUBP in Wrocław, January 4, 1953, AIPN, BU 0423/4902, p. 13.

> stamp albums, but almost all the furniture, gas stoves, etc. He has already sold some of those things and is slowly selling off the rest. In search for gold and foreign currency, he smashed walls and stoves, and demolished almost all those apartments.[105]

The enterprising policeman developed his activities on a large scale. He hired special teams to demolish apartments, sold former Jewish businesses located on "his" territory along with their stocks of raw materials, and finally came into conflict with the Polish *Treuhänders* (trustees managing "former Jewish property" on behalf of the Germans). The *Treuhänders* had to withdraw, however, because Second Lieutenant Olczyk threatened them with the intervention of the Security Police. According to the information collected by "Pleban"—the codename of Bolesław Kozubowski, head of counterintelligence of the II Department of the AK Warsaw District Command—Olczyk threatened people with German Sipo, and he also claimed to have useful contacts in the Polish underground.[106]

Returning to the subject of so-called trade within the Kriegsfahndungskommando, the property of arrested Jews was usually delivered to the section's offices, where the staff sorted the loot. All the tastier morsels went to the Germans, but Polish detectives also received their cut. This is very similar to the modus operandi of the Sonderstreife of Richter and Kaiser. A former section employee testified as follows:

> Only valuable things were taken from the Jewish property, and later, after they were brought to the section, they were segregated by the Germans. The Germans kept most of the valuables for themselves and the rest was distributed among the Polish employees. I personally received bed linen two or three times. When money was found on arrested Jews,

105 Undated report, AIPN, BU 0423/4889, p. 8.

106 Report "Plebana," undated, AIPN, BU 0423/4889, p. 9. For more about the "Odwet" group, loosely affiliated with the AK but directly connected with the Polish People's Army, see Notatka 992/BO.11, July 17, 1944, AAN, AK, 203-III-108, p. 6.

> section head Ballhause kept it and after some time paid certain sums to the Polish detectives as a bonus for their work. I also received such bonus several times; as I recall, once it was 2,000 zlotys, 1,000 zlotys, 800 zlotys, etc., sums in the range of about 1,000 zlotys. I also sold the bed linen I had received from the former Jewish property, I received about 2,000 zlotys for it. In two cases I participated in taking things from apartments that were probably formerly Jewish.[107]

Moreover, Jewish apartments allocated to members of the commando were not to be sneezed at either. One such apartment in a building at 16 Solna Street was given to Detective Niziński in the fall of 1943. In addition to the funds obtained either on orders or with the knowledge of their German superiors, there were also proceeds from operations carried out by Polish detectives independently. In such cases, it is difficult to say whether and how often they engaged in blackmail—the line between a Kripo agent and a *szmalcownik* was, after all, elusive—but the records preserve the testimony of Henryk Wileński, a Pole and reasonably wealthy businessman, who was arrested by one of Balhause's subordinates. The way to earn extra income was simple: After the arrest, the family was given the opportunity to buy the victim out of jail for a certain sum. The sums involved were often exorbitant—tens or even hundreds of thousands of zlotys—but the prospect of the arrested person being transported to a camp or shot had a mobilizing effect.[108]

The End of the Kriegsfahndungskommando

The Kriegsfahndungskommando operated until the outbreak of the Warsaw Uprising in August 1944. The success—and relative impunity—of Balhause's men was primarily due to the anonymity

107 Zygmunt Głowacki hearing, February 11, 1950, AIPN, GK 317/248, pp. 35–37.

108 Interrogation of the witness Wileński, February 13, 1950, AIPN, GK 317/248, pp. 60–60v; Henryk Wileński testimony, July 14, 1950, AIPN, GK 317/247, pp. 92v–93.

of the detectives, which in turn was the result of the Polish underground's lack of interest in operations aimed exclusively against the Jews. As long as the section kept out of the activities of the underground organization and they did not interfere with "political affairs," they remained outside the sphere of interest of the Polish Underground State. If their names appeared in intelligence reports, it was in connection with other operations that were of interest to the Polish conspirators. Hence, there is no point in searching AK materials for information about death sentences handed down to members of the section or orders to investigate Polish detectives. An example of this is one of the few references to Zygmunt Głowacki from AK intelligence reports dated April 3 and 17, 1944, a month after the raid on the Krysia bunker. This report had nothing to do with the hunt for Jews or with Balhause's section. It concerned an ordinary shootout in a café in which Głowacki together with another Polish Kripo officer shot a man named Bąba-Bąbiński. And it was Bąba-Bąbiński, a known provocateur and snooper, and not the Polish Kripo agents who was the object of the underground's interest.[109] Głowacki, in turn, was shot at on May 28, 1944, but according to the detective, it was a matter of some bandits' retribution.[110] Until the end of the occupation, Głowacki and his companions who "dealt" with the Jews were not of interest to the underground justice system. There could hardly be a greater contrast with detectives from Richter's Sonderstreife, who were often sentenced to death by underground courts and decimated by Kedyw fighters.

Detective Głowacki ultimately deserted from the Kripo but not until June or July 1944, when he obtained a false identity card under the name Euzebiusz Piąty. The ridiculous name—literally

109 Report 993, April 3, 1944, AAN, AK, 203-III-111, p. 10. It reads as follows: "Bąba-Bąbiński, former detective of XI Blue Police Com[missariat], was shot dead on March 30 [1944] in a cafe by Kripo detectives: Jan Paradowski and Zygmunt Głowacki." Two weeks later detectives reported that at the end of 1943, Bąba-Bąbiński incited the denunciation of a dozen or so policemen from the XI Commissariat. See Report 993, April 3, 1944, AAN, AK, 203-III-111, p. 40.

110 Władysław Suchodolski testimony, January 9, 1950, AIPN, GK 317/248, pp. 52–52v.

translated as Eusebio the Fifth—on the forged document must have embarrassed the Polish Kripo agent to such a degree that after the war, during the investigation, he saw fit to explain, "I would like to state that this name was chosen without consulting me."[111] Other officers of the commando withdrew along with the Germans from the uprising-stricken Warsaw to Sochaczew on August 8, 1944, and in January 1945 to Poznań. Most of them disappeared. Unlike the Gestapo or SD employees whose complicity in the crimes was obvious, Kripo officers successfully defended themselves after the war, arguing that the institution in which they had worked had no political objectives. Edward Podgórniak of the Kripo in Węgrów testified the following:

> The criminal police during the occupation...was tasked with detecting and combating criminal offenses, such as murders, thefts, and the like. Moreover, we were ordered to provide assistance to the uniformed police. We did not deal with political crimes because we were forbidden to do so, the Gestapo dealt with them....
>
> The criminal police did not participate in operations specifically organized to capture Jewish people. I personally took part in three operations. However, these operations were organized to combat bandits. Every day, police stations in the rural areas reported on the robberies, and, as they found out about growing banditry in particular areas, the German Gendarmerie together with the Gestapo organized sweeps and operations. We usually surrounded the forest and searched it. The criminal police took part in those operations because we were particularly interested in banditry.[112]

German Kripo employees also defended themselves in the same way, emphasizing their successes in the fight against common crime and shifting the responsibility for the persecution of Poles—and Jews—onto officers from other Sipo departments, most often

111 Zygmunt Głowacki hearing, undated, AIPN, GK 317/248.
112 Edward Podgórniak testimony, February 20, 1950, AIPN, GK 318/131, p. 422.

those from the Gestapo. Commissioner Tewes, who worked in the Warsaw Kripo, emphasized the professionalism of both the German and Polish officers and their completely apolitical character that was expressed in the fight against common crime.[113] *SS-Rottenführer* Hans Gundlach, criminal commissioner assigned to *Osteinsatz* (the so-called mission in the East) in the Kraków and Rzeszów Kripo, testified as follows after the war:

> At that time, together with the Polish police, I took part in combating banditry...it was not about political crimes, but about ordinary criminal cases. At the beginning of 1940, I was sent to Kraków as a criminal commissioner. I stayed there until Christmas 1940. Both in Rzeszów and in Kraków, I served under the head of the Kripo in Poland, *Oberregierungsrat* Schräpel. In the summer of 1940, another senior Kripo officer, Criminal Director Fleischer, arrived in Kraków from Berlin, and I reported directly to him. Our tasks in Kraków were the usual duties of any police force not involved in political affairs. These included the investigation of criminal cases according to the criminal code (theft, robbery, murder, fraud, etc.), as long as there were no political motives involved. I, like all other Kripo officers, never took part in investigations of a political nature, such as forced deportations, liquidations of Jewish ghettos, political interrogations, or the shipment of Polish workers to the Reich. All of this was handled by the Gestapo.[114]

In Commissioner Gundlach's case, such an obvious defense strategy had the desired effect. He was cleared of suspicion and released from a US internment camp. In his testimony, Commissioner Hans Gundlach forgot to add that in December 1940, he had been arrested by the Kraków Gestapo on suspicion of stealing "Jewish gold" from a Kripo police locker and was sentenced by an SS court in Berlin to fourteen months' imprisonment.[115]

113 Interrogation protocol of Wilhelm Tewes, questioned by the British occupation authorities in Germany, August 23, 1946, AIPN, GK 164/3754, pp. 2–4.

114 Interrogation of Hans Gundlach, August 13, 1946, AIPN, GK 164/2928, p. 1.

115 Interrogation of Hans Gundlach, August 22, 1946, AIPN, GK 164/2928, p. 4.

Emanuel Ringelblum with his son Uri before the war.
Ghetto Fighters' House Museum, Israel, Photo Archive, 19212.

Emanuel Ringelblum along with his wife and son were murdered in the ruins of the former ghetto a few days after his arrest. And what was the fate of the Polish policemen who shared responsibility for his capture? Zygmunt Głowacki and Władysław Nowiński were arrested in January 1950 during an investigation into the activities of the prewar Political Police (Defensywa) but not for their involvement with the Kriegsfahndungskommando. On July 14, 1950, the Warsaw Court of Appeals found both former officers of the Jewish branch guilty of the charges against them. Głowacki was sentenced to ten years in prison and Nowiński to seven. Both the prosecution and the two convicts appealed the sentence. During the review hearing on February 16, 1951, the Supreme Court upheld the sentence on Głowacki but reduced Nowiński's sentence to four years imprisonment. Nowiński was released from prison not long after that and so was Głowacki, right after the amnesty of 1956. Other members of the Kriegsfahndungskommando were never brought to justice.[116]

Gundlach served ten months, after which he was paroled and conscripted as a rank-and-file soldier into the SS police division.

116 The Polish amnesty of April 1956 set free thousands of prisoners, mostly those sentenced on political grounds during the Stalinist period.

Was the Commando for Wartime Manhunts the only cell established by the German criminal police in Warsaw for tracking Jews?[117] It is very doubtful, since scattered testimonies in archival materials indicate the existence of other groups of this kind. According to one Kripo employee, such a cell most probably existed within Commissariat VI:

> I found out about the existence of this unit by accident in 1941 or 1942, when, having come to the jail with some detainee, in front of the entrance I met Mr. Michał Wodnicki, known to me personally, who lived at 100 Pańska Street, in the same house where I lived at the time. When I asked Wodnicki what he was doing there, he said that he had been arrested on suspicion of harboring people of Jewish nationality or Jewish items and that the investigation in his case was carried out by a special section specializing in finding Jews, located on the first floor [of the police headquarters building on Daniłowiczowska Street]. Knowing the layout, I found out that the section was part of the Commissariat VI.[118]

With its multitude of Jews in hiding, the question is whether Warsaw constituted an exception and thus required the Germans to adopt a special hunting strategy. Were counterparts of the Kriegsfahndungskommando also established in other cities of the Generalgouvernement such as in Kraków, Lublin, Lwów, or Radom?[119] There is no doubt, however, that from the autumn of 1942, the Gendarmerie in conjunction with the Blue Police established a number of special units whose sole task was to track down and murder Jews. These were the previously discussed

117 Of course, there is no mention here of the better-researched Gestapo Judenreferat, i.e., the IV B (Jewish Affairs) section on Szucha Avenue, headed by *SS-Untersturmführer* Karl Brandt.

118 Zygmunt Głowacki hearing, January 25, 1950, AIPN, GK 317/248, pp. 25–28; Minutes of the main hearing, AIPN, GK 317/247, p. 88v.

119 A good deal of information about the search for Jews by Polish officers of the Lwów Kripo can be found in files in the criminal case of Włodzimierz Wyszyński, AIPN, GK 317/616.

Rollkommandos or Jagdkommandos that operated mostly in the rural areas of the Generalgouvernement and usually consisted of one or two German gendarmes and several Polish policemen.[120]

"I Saw Him Take Part in a Raid against the Jewboys": Sergeant Antoni Dziamski's *Einsatz*

While the Directorate of Criminal Police in Warsaw had nearly 700 officers who were more or less supervised by their German superiors, the Polnische Kriminalpolizei in small towns enjoyed a significantly larger degree of independence. In Gródek Jagielloński, Polnische Kripo agents Stanisław Laburda, Bronisław Czaban, Włodzimierz Moskal, and Kazimierz Bania took part in the liquidation of the secondary ghetto. There were no Germans in the local branch (*Aussenstelle*) of the Kripo.[121] Regarding the relative autonomy of the Polish Kripo units, it is worth taking a look at the composition of these units in the Kraków district.

In the fall of 1942, the Tarnobrzeg post was staffed by two Poles—sergeants of the Investigative Service—without any German supervision. The situation was the same in Mielec, Pruchnik, Brzesko Nowy, and Dąbrowa Tarnowska, except for the fact that three Polish investigators served there. One Polish police officer was assigned to the Kripo units in Gorlice, Łańcut, Przeworsk, and Dukla. In all the cases mentioned above, Polish Kripo officers worked together with the Blue Police, serving at the same post. German liaison officers came to smaller outposts on assignment in order to carry out specific orders. The daily routine of a Kripo station was determined by the Polish commander. Only in larger centers or in places considered strategic by the Germans did Polish plainclothes detectives work under German supervision. Thus, in *Aussenstelle* Jarosław (then renamed Jaroslau), six Poles worked

120 Jan Grabowski, *Hunt for the Jews: Betrayal and Murder in German-Occupied Poland* (Bloomington: Indiana University Press, 2013), pp. 101–121.

121 Kazimierz Bania interrogation report, September 18, 1947, AIPN, BU 688/194, p. 31.

under the command of two agents of the German Criminal Police, and the same was true in Miechów, where two Germans supervised the work of eleven Polish investigators. This was also the case in the small town of Dębica, where two Germans also worked. However, with labor camps as well as large Wehrmacht and SS training grounds in Dębica, it was of special importance from the point of view of the occupying authorities. Finally, it is worth noting that in the important Przemyśl station, which boasted a large staff of eighteen Polish officers, there was not even one German.[122]

Before the war, there were 16,000 inhabitants in Międzyrzec Podlaski (Mezrich in Yiddish), 12,000 of whom were Jews. It was a typical *shtetl* where the Germans had concentrated the Jewish population already by 1940, pushing it into the poorest district of town. It was not yet an official ghetto, which was not established until after the first deportation in the summer of 1942, but the conditions in the area inhabited by the Jews were no different from the extremely harsh conditions in other ghettos of the Podlasie region. In 1942, on the eve of the deportation to the extermination camps, the Jewish community of Międzyrzec numbered nearly 18,000 people, including more than 6,000 people who had been displaced from other areas of the Generalgouvernement, from areas annexed to the Reich, and even from Slovakia.[123] In Międzyrzec, there was a Blue Police station and a Kripo post. As previously seen, in smaller centers such as Międzyrzec where the German presence was not as strong as in Warsaw or other large cities, the Blue and Criminal Police were governed by their own rules, and local police chiefs enjoyed a lot of freedom, which also applied to the supervision and implementation of the occupation's regulations against the Jews.

From the point of view of the persecuted Jews, however, this did not mean that the relative independence of Polish officers translated into greater tolerance or empathy. In fact, quite the opposite. A great deal depended on the commander, who could try to protect "his" Jews but could also mobilize his subordinates

122 The Criminal Police, 1941–1942, AIPN Kr, 075/1, vol. 47, unpaginated.

123 "Międzyrzec Podlaski," in Megargee, *The United States Holocaust Memorial Museum Encyclopedia of Camps and Ghettos, 1933–1945*, pp. 684–687.

to introduce a reign of terror that went further than any German instructions dictated. In Międzyrzec Podlaski, the commanding officer of the Polnische Kriminalpolizei was Senior Sergeant Antoni Dziamski, who enthusiastically and with zeal joined the extermination policy of the occupying authorities.

Until the outbreak of war, Dziamski served as a detective in his hometown of Grudziądz. In 1940, after Grudziądz had been incorporated into the Reich and all Polish policemen had lost their employment, Dziamski was offered a relocation to the Generalgouvernement, and that is how he ended up in Międzyrzec. After the war, the authorities wanted to investigate him as a national renegade who had signed the *Volksliste*. His activities as a Kripo agent did not come to light until much later. Eyewitnesses of Antoni Dziamski's activities while on duty at the Międzyrzec police station can be seen through the following testimony given three years after the war. Moszek Kaufman testified that sometime before the deportations, he had witnessed Commander Dziamski shooting Jews "and even Poles…then I saw how the Jews were getting out of the ghetto looking for bread, and the aforementioned encountered them and shot them right on the spot," and he also recalled a Jew killed by Dziamski at the moment when he was "tearing a plank off the fence around the ghetto."[124] In both cases, this happened before the deportations but after the introduction of the death penalty for attempting to leave the ghetto.

Another testimony concerning the same early period of ghetto life was given by Fajwel Boruchowski, who recalled the following about Dziamski:

> [Dziamski] beat and shot people on the spot. I know that in 1942, in May, he shot a woman who was walking down the road. The woman was carrying milk, her name was Cyrla Szwarc, she resided in Międzyrzec on Jatkowa Street at number 9. Then, in 1941, I saw how Dziamski and Czarnowski, his colleague, it was in a forest near Dąbrówka,

124 Moszek Kaufman testimony, files in the criminal case of Antoni Dziamski, AIPN Lu, 328/20, vol. 2.

> encountered five escaped Soviet prisoners of war. I was herding cows for a farmer nearby and I heard Dziamski take out a pistol and shoot three of them, while his colleague Czarnowski shot the two remaining ones. They were a captain, a senior lieutenant, a major—these were the ones shot by Dziamski, and Czarnowski shot a senior sergeant and a sergeant, and I know this because I was grazing cows by the forest and those prisoners approached me before. Dziamski asked me what I was talking to them about and I said that they wanted to eat and he ordered me to drive the cows away, or else I would shoot you, so Dziamski said. And also in 1941, near Międzyrzec, I saw how Dziamski shot two Jews on the road, one was from Międzyrzec and the other from Nasielsk, the one from Międzyrzec was called Jankiel Brykols, and in the ghetto in 1942 I saw him take part in a raid against the Jewboys. It was the first action against Jews and he was dressed in civilian clothes. At that time I saw that Dziamski was the first one to start shooting and after him other gendarmes started shooting, so Dziamski shot that day, together with children and women, I don't know exactly, but no fewer than fifteen. Another time he came to the ghetto and said that he came to hunt, he took gold rings and whatever there was and he could find, next I know that he took one Jew named Barzemut, whom he transported for gold to Radzyń, for which he received several dozen golden ducats.[125]

Reading Fajwel Boruchowski's testimony, one can conclude that the killing of the escaped Soviet prisoners of war may have been somewhat of a turning point in the transformation of a simple detective into a mass murderer, which Dziamski had become by the end of 1942. Even before the liquidation of the ghetto, the sergeant was universally feared. According to Lejbko Rochman, "when the Polish locals saw him [Dziamski] walking down the street, they hid wherever they could, and as far as the Jews were

125 Fajwel Boruchowski testimony, files in the criminal case of Antoni Dziamski, AIPN Lu, 328/20, vol. 2.

concerned, there was no way they could have been seen on the street where Dziamski passed."[126] While in 1941 and early 1942 Sergeant Dziamski allowed himself to commit acts of incredible cruelty, later on he became the undisputed master of life and death of Międzyrzec's Jews. And this is without any metaphor or exaggeration. Leiron Fiszbein, another survivor of the Międzyrzec ghetto, testified as follows:

> I witnessed how he [Dziamski] shot the painter Abram with his entire family in the yard, in Międzyrzec, at 65 Piłsudskiego Street. The family consisted of seven people, that is, the parents, four sons and the mother-in-law named [illegible] Mnich were shot. On October 10, 1942, Dziamski came in with his colleague Czarnowski, who was later killed in Warsaw by an underground organization, and nine people were killed on that day, i.e., Tajwie Angielczyk and his five sons and two daughters. Dziamski found this family in a hideout and shot them all on the spot. Then, on November 15, 1942, Dziamski shot Jankel Idew, his wife, three sons and two daughters, one of the daughters had three children under ten years of age, that is ten people altogether, a fact I saw with my own eyes, because I am a Jew and I was interested in everything, and I don't look like a Jew at all, that's why I wasn't persecuted by them, I was considered a Pole.[127]

As can be seen in Fiszbein's testimony, Dziamski took part in every liquidation and showed incredible cruelty.

After the deportations in the summer of 1942, a remnant ghetto was established in Międzyrzec, which was liquidated in stages. In the first days of May 1943, the ghetto was finally liquidated, and the remaining few hundred Jews were told to clean the area and collect any abandoned goods to be sold at auction. Throughout this time, Sergeant Dziamski participated in the

126 Lejbko Rochman testimony, files in the criminal case of Antoni Dziamski, AIPN Lu, 328/20, vol. 2.

127 Leiron Fiszbein testimony, files in the criminal case of Antoni Dziamski, AIPN Lu, 328/20, vol. 2.

murders and mobilized his men for further acts of terror. It was in connection with the final liquidation of the ghetto that Lejbko Goldberg testified the following:

> In the first days of July 1943, near the gate of the ghetto in Międzyrzec Podl[aski], while I and my two friends were standing next to the aforementioned gate outside the ghetto and selling things that used to belong to Jews to the (Polish) residents, Antoni Dziamski unexpectedly approached us with a pistol in his hand and shouted, "Hands up!" Noting the imminent danger, I managed to run away. At that time, I heard him call them "bandits from the forest." I saw Dziamski leading the two detainees in the direction of the "Blue" police station. Then, after about one hour, I saw Jewish gravediggers carry the bodies of my two friends who had been captured by Dziamski. I was very close to the cart carrying them to the cemetery, and I recognized without a doubt that they were the same men whom he had just taken to the station. He was hostile toward Jews, and whenever he noticed a Jew outside the barbed wire, he either took him to the post or killed him on the spot.[128]

Goldberg's testimony is worth noting not only because of the information regarding the fate of the Jewish victims but also because of the close link between the activities of the Polish Kripo commander and the local Blue Police station. In Międzyrzec, as in other small towns in the Generalgouvernement, it was difficult to separate the activities of the Polish Kripo officers from those of their uniformed colleagues with whom they shared official space and participated in the same operations. Jews intercepted outside the ghetto were usually taken to a Polish police station. "Often one could see trucks transporting bloodied corpses from the police station to the Jewish cemetery. This is how Mrs. Miriam

128 Lejbko Goldberg testimony, files in the criminal case of Antoni Dziamski, AIPN Lu, 328/20, vol. 2.

Listgarten with her daughter Itke Platt were killed, as well as Lea Kniżnik," another account reads.[129]

In 1944, shortly before the Soviet army marched into Poland, Dziamski fled Międzyrzec and headed for Grudziądz, and then, as two neighbors testified, he apparently made his way to Łódź. Shortly after the war, the Kripo agent was arrested, but managed to escape from prison. In 1947, an arrest warrant was issued for Dziamski but to no avail. In 1949, a court in Biała Podlaska sentenced Dziamski in absentia to death. Like many other detectives, Dziamski vanished without a trace in the postwar chaos.

Meanwhile in Lwów: Directorate of Criminal Police in Lemberg

In August 1941, after the district of Galicia was incorporated into the Generalgouvernement, Lwów (Lemberg in German) acquired its own police structure like the capitals of the other four districts. It was not, however, the Blue Police known from all the other districts of the Generalgouvernement but the Ukrainian police (Ukrainische Hilfspolizei), known as the Black Police because of the color of their uniforms.

The Ukrainian police had six precincts in Lwów as well as stations scattered throughout the district, but the training of its officers left much to be desired. There were few Ukrainians in the prewar Polish police, thus those who were recruited from the wartime draft often did not meet the minimum professional and moral criteria, such as having no criminal record.[130]

Manpower shortages could not be compensated for by these Ukrainian policemen, who were trained before the attack on the Soviet Union in police schools in the Generalgouvernement.[131] Whereas the uniformed police was dominated by Ukrainians,

129 Feigenbaum, *Slaughter in Podlasie*, p. 103.

130 Christoph Mick, "Incompatible Experiences: Poles, Ukrainians and Jews in Lviv under Soviet and German Occupation, 1939–44," *Journal of Contemporary History*, 46:2 (2011), pp. 336–363.

131 See Finder and Prusin, "Collaboration in Eastern Galicia," pp. 95–118.

Officers of the Ukrainian Auxiliary Police. Courtesy of Jeffrey Burds.

Poles dominated the ranks of the criminal police. Most of the plainclothes detectives serving under the newly formed Directorate of Criminal Police in Lwów were recruited from among the members of the prewar Criminal Investigative Service. During the Soviet occupation, many Polish detectives were arrested, deported, or killed, but beginning in the fall of 1941, the Germans supplemented their staff by bringing in Polish officers from the Generalgouvernement and the territories annexed to the Reich.

One of the primary sources of information on the activities of the Polish Kripo in Lwów are the files of the local German Special Court (*Sondergericht* Lemberg). Careful reading of these documents allows for a better understanding of the specificity of local Kripo work. Unlike in other districts of the Generalgouvernement, the Lwów Kripo carried out its own investigations of so-called Jewish cases until the very end of the occupation. Moreover, surviving materials demonstrate that the Kripo was fully involved in those operations, from arrest to execution, with the latter usually taking place in the labor camp and concentration camp on Janowska Street. In addition, unlike the Directorate of Criminal Police in

Warsaw, which after arresting Jews turned the case over to the Gestapo for further investigation, Polish policemen in Lwów also conducted investigations against Poles and Ukrainians accused of helping Jews.[132]

While the task of catching Jews in hiding was carried out by the staff of all the police stations in Lwów, Commissariat III was given special power in that regard. On June 16, 1944, Master Corporal Michalski and two other officers from Commissariat II of the Directorate of Criminal Police in Lwów detected a Jewish hiding place:

> By way of confidential information, I learned that there were Jews in the house of Roman Dabrowski, residing at 19 Łyczakowska Street, apartment number 7 in Lwów. Therefore, I went together with Cpl. Makohon and Cpl. Bielec to the place where, during a search, we found a hidden shelter (camouflaged with wallpaper) in which there were five Jews, who were brought to the loc[al] Directorate.[133]

At the Directorate of the Criminal Police, the investigation was immediately handed over to the officers of Commissariat III. It seems that at least from 1943, all "Jewish matters"—mainly investigations concerning hidden Jews—were automatically transferred to Commissariat III for further action. The following note provides an example of this:

> V Commissariat, Lwów, January 28, 1944.
>
> Note: On January 27, 1944, a five-year-old Jewish child named Marcus, surname unknown, was found in the street in Lwów and brought to the police station. The child said that he was living at 3/7 Felsenstr. On January 28, 1944, the Fink family,

132 In 1944, Jewish affairs in Lemberg were also handled by the local SD. See Examination report, May 25, 1944, DALO, Sondergericht Lemberg, file 1279, p. 14.

133 Report, June 16, 1944, DALO, Sondergericht Lemberg, file 847, report, June 16, 1944, p. 2.

> that is Piotr Fink, Katarzyna Fink (born Socha) and Helena Fink, were arrested on suspicion of hiding Jews. Since in this case it was a question of hiding a Jewish child, the case was handed over to the III Commissariat.[134]

Based on the surviving records of the Lwów Special Court, one can reconstruct a fragmentary list of the officers of Commissariat III. In light of preserved interrogation protocols and internal correspondence, it seems that during the 1942–1944 period, the following officers worked there: Senior Sergeant Mikołaj Czernik; Corporal Karol Krajewski; the previously mentioned Corporal Zygmunt Głowacki, who transferred to the Directorate of Criminal Police in Warsaw in the spring or summer of 1943; Corporal Robakowski; *Kriminalassistent Feldwebel* Tadeusz (Stefan) Mroziewicz, who will be discussed further; and *Feldfebel* Józef Wawrzyniak. The records also include two Germans who signed their names on official commissariat correspondence as *Kriminalsekretär* Grabow and *Kriminalsekretär* Schiller (Schilling). The interpreter at the commissariat was someone called Stroszyński, although his signatures are so illegible that it is impossible to decipher his name beyond doubt. In addition to the detectives, the documents show traces of the activities of secret collaborators—informers who were in constant contact with the Kripo agents. One of them, nicknamed "Nóż" (Knife) was paid a bonus of 1,000 zlotys for catching Jews, whereas another, recorded in the documents as "a Pole, Mikołaj Kositiuk, working at *Werbeinstitut Galizien*," also earned a monetary reward for catching Jews (*Judenergreifung*).[135]

In addition to the Kripo, the Gestapo (KdS, Section IV-B-4), which had several outposts in Galicia, also dealt with Jewish matters in Lwów, as it did in other districts of the Generalgouvernement. During their investigations, officers of Commissariat III paid special attention to Jewish valuables, even going as far as digging

134 Note, January 28, 1944, DALO, Sondergericht Lemberg, file 1350, p. 20.

135 Interrogation of Dr. David Ehrlichhof, May 22, 1944, DALO, Sondergericht Lemberg, file 1279, p. 12. As for Kostiuk, see Report, May 23, 1944, DALO, Sondergericht Lemberg, file 1227, p. 3.

through the cellars of houses where Jews were found hiding, in the hope of finding "Jewish gold."[136]

In the archives of the Polish postwar courts, however, records of only one case have been preserved, and it concerns the direct tracking of Jews by officers of Commissariat III in Lwów. After the war, Włodzimierz Wyszyński, a Kripo agent who specialized in "solving the Jewish question" in the district's capital, faced the court. Wyszyński belonged to a group of agents who closely collaborated with the detectives of Commissariat III. Working with him were Poradzki and Kocek, other Polish Kripo agents from Directorate of the Criminal Police in Lemberg. One of Wyszyński's victims was Elżbieta Brodzianka-Pechnik, who was hiding under the Aryan name of Janina Milant and worked in the hospital for infectious diseases on Franciszkańska Street until January 1943. Seeing suspicions growing around her and fearing impending disaster, Brodzianka-Pechnik decided to quit her job. On the last day, as she was filling out her work card, she was stopped by Wyszyński, who told her to wait in one of the rooms while he himself called the police. The captured Jewish woman remembered that moment very well. After the war, she testified the following at the trial:

> [Wyszyński] then said into the telephone: "Send one man, Adamszyn." After a few minutes a man in civilian clothes came in and ordered me to leave with him. After leaving the room he demanded that I show him my ID; I showed him my ID, which he kept, and then he took me to the "Kripo." There I was led into a small room where a man in civilian clothes was sitting and talking in clear Polish. In the room I was first personally searched and then the man speaking in fluent Polish started to ask me if I was Jewish. I categorically denied, and the man told me that the authorities of the hospital where I worked knew that I was Jewish, to which I demanded a confrontation with Dr. Popadiuk. During the confrontation, Dr. Popadiuk said that he thought I was Jewish because I was alone and had no family. I do not recall whether Adamszyn came in at

136 Note, June 14, 1944, DALO, Sondergericht Lemberg, file 1279, p. 20.

> the time or whether he spoke to the accused. I was released on the day I was detained, except that I was given some kind of a paper to report in two days. After I was released, I went back to the hospital, because I was still on night duty, and in a conversation with Popadiuk, he told me: "You've been through some unpleasantness today," to which I did not respond.[137]

Another witness in the case against Wyszyński was the aforementioned Tadeusz Mroziewicz, deputy head of Commissariat III in Lwów. The presence of a Kripo sergeant as a witness at the trial of his own agent seems surprising, but we can assume that the Polish postwar court had little idea about the profile of the commissariat headed by Mroziewicz. Besides, the Kripo sergeant had a so-called certificate of morality from the underground. Mroziewicz testified the following:

> I lived in Lwów from 1941 to 1943, and I worked for the Kripo on behalf of an underground organization. During my work in the Kripo, I recall that a woman named Brodzik [Brodzianka] was brought in and that I interrogated her on the grounds that she was Jewish. I recall that before Brodzik entered my room I went out into the hall and asked who was there to see me, and then who had brought Brodzik to me, and a reply came from a group of men standing in the hallway, "Brodzianka was brought in by Wyszyński." During the interrogation of the woman, I immediately realized that Brodzik was Jewish.... I went to the chief of our station and told him that the detained woman was not Jewish, at which point the head came down to the room with me and, after taking a look at the suspect, agreed with me. On the way to the chief, I warned the suspect not to speak German in case he came to see her, and I warned her because I knew that almost all Jews could speak German and with that she could reveal herself. During the release of the suspect I kept her documents and told her to come back in two days to collect

137 Elżbieta Brodzianka-Pechnik (Janina Milant), files in the criminal case of Włodzimierz Wyszyński, AIPN, GK 317/616.

> the documents, which she did not do. If [illegible; most likely Czernik, the station commander] had been present, the matter would have been taken to the Gestapo.[138]

It is difficult to say how much truth there is to Mroziewicz's assurances about his cooperation with the underground. It certainly cannot be ruled out. However, there is no doubt that the Kripo sergeant, realizing that the detained woman had the "wrong" ancestry and for reasons known only to himself, decided to release her. It will never be known whether it was a bribe, a personal acquaintance, or some impulse of decency that was at work there. However, regardless of the individual case of Elżbieta Brodzianka, it is obvious that Mroziewicz, as the deputy commander of Commissariat III, bears full responsibility for the hunt for the hidden Jews of Lwów. As for Wyszyński, he was sentenced to five years' imprisonment by the Provincial Court for the city of Warsaw in 1954. The sentence was upheld on appeal by the Supreme Court.[139]

The vast majority of the Polish Kripo agents from Lwów vanished without a trace after liberation, just like their fellow detectives from Warsaw. Some lived under assumed identities, others passed away, surrounded by the love of their family and the respect of their friends, never having paid for their crimes committed during the war.

138 Tadeusz Mroziewicz testimony, files in the criminal case of Włodzimierz Wyszyński, AIPN, GK 317/616.

139 Justification of the verdict, April 30, 1954, files in the criminal case of Włodzimierz Wyszyński, AIPN, GK 317/616., pp. 89–90.

Chapter Eight

On Rescuing

The myth of the nation's innocence during the occupation enjoys an enormous and still growing popularity in Poland. An essential part of this myth is the conviction that altruistic attitudes toward Jews were common in Polish society. The multitude of publications, commemorations, medals, coins, exhibitions, and conferences have consolidated in public consciousness the belief that Jews could count on the kindness, help, and understanding of their Aryan fellow citizens during the Holocaust. And this belief is evidence of the power of a myth that, in fact, has rather tenuous roots, as endeavored to demonstrate in this volume. As Piotr Forecki aptly put it:

> The Righteous ceased to be flesh and blood people with independent biographies and became a fetishized figure in the discourse on Jewish issues. An argument "for" or "against." A shield and a sword, a fig leaf and a visor. The dominant narrative about them is nothing but a fable woven from frozen clichés and phantasms, created and told in Poland for years in order to lift people's spirits.[1]

As it happens, however, rescue cannot be discussed without reflecting on denunciations and persecution because both were

1 Piotr Forecki, *Po Jedwabnem: Anatomia pamięci funkcjonalnej* (Warsaw: IBL, 2018), pp. 255–256.

painfully intertwined. Nevertheless, the attempts—so frequent today—to describe the heroism of people rescuing Jews as something obvious in Polish society not only falsifies the history of the Holocaust but also diminishes their extraordinary deeds and courage, the pursuits of people who were prepared not just to make a stand against the German extermination policy but, above all, to face the hostility of their own neighbors, for whom rescuing Jews was unacceptable and an act of betrayal of the peculiarly defined concept of national community.

In 2009, thanks to the efforts of the French foundation Mémoire de la Shoah (The Shoah Memorial), an exhibition was opened in Paris titled "They Disobeyed to Save: French Policemen and Gendarmes, Righteous Among the Nations." It told the story of fifty-four French police officers who, while saving Jews, disobeyed their superiors and were awarded the Yad Vashem honor of Righteous Among the Nations. Help provided by French policemen and gendarmes took many forms, though most often, the decorated officers warned the would-be victims of impending arrests, helped them escape, or offered shelter under their own roofs. Some rescued for religious reasons, others had personal motives, others still were driven by a humanitarian impulse, and there were also those who rescued for profit, although such cases are less frequently mentioned in postwar accounts. One might ask whether fifty-four policemen recognized as Righteous Among the Nations is few or many? Everything depends on the point of view: For the Jews threatened with arrest and deportation, every rescuer had existential significance—in the literal sense of the word. However, from the point of view of the 20,000 police officers serving in and around Paris where the vast majority of French Jews lived, this was a small and certainly unrepresentative group. And even if we add to those fifty-four brave men a number of police officers whose deeds have not been recognized and commemorated by posterity, the decision to save Jews still remains the choice of the minority.

Can the choices and decisions of the French policemen provide any point of reference for the discussion of the attitudes of the Blue policemen serving in the Generalgouvernement?

After all, the measures applied by the occupation regime in the countries of Western Europe were much less harsh than the terror introduced by the Germans in the public sphere in the East. Still, is there no conceivable way to compare the motivations of people who provided help despite the risk, even if the risks they faced were vastly different? French policemen were not threatened with death, but they faced the risk of punitive investigation, imprisonment, and the loss of their jobs. As is well known, the prospect of the death penalty is not necessary to enforce conformist behavior. This has been convincingly demonstrated, among others, by Christopher R. Browning, who studied the attitudes of German policemen. The mere threat of a reprimand, critical evaluation, or peer pressure was enough to make them join their comrades in genocidal killings.

To begin with, of the less than 20,000 Polish officers who rose through the ranks of the Blue and Criminal Police during the war, only a handful were awarded the honor of Righteous Among the Nations. Fifteen, to be exact. Is that many or few? Fortunately, it is not the historian's role to answer such questions. It is our duty, however, to attempt to outline the realities of the period as faithfully as possible and put the scattered pieces of the historical puzzle together in such a way as to create a coherent picture that will allow the reader to draw their own conclusions.

Against the background of the bleak picture that emerges from the study of the Polnische Polizei im Generalgouvernement, the question of aid provided to Jews by its members may seem marginal, even insignificant. Should the historian focus just on those fifteen Righteous ones? Of course, such an approach would be too rigorous and unfair. There were certainly more rescuers than those who have been honored, and more importantly, there were also other, less obvious forms of help that deserve to be included in the broadly defined category of rescue. Among the Blue policemen, as among other members of Polish society, several attitudes toward Jews developed during the period. Today, it is difficult to establish what proportion of people demonstrated one of such attitudes, even more so because the attitudes of the policemen—and the rest of society—evolved as the situation developed, in direct correlation with the rhythm of increasing German pressure and the growing desperation of the Jews. From a report of the Radom Sipo from the fall of 1943, based on estimates of several local Blue Police posts, we learn that about 10 percent of Blue policemen could then be described as "actively collaborating with the underground."[2] The author of the report, *SS-Obersturmbannführer* Illmer, added that this was an underestimation, since a much higher percentage of officers were probably involved in underground activity. Warsaw police commander Lieutenant Colonel Reszczyński estimated that half of his subordinates were part of the resistance. As for the number of police officers who openly collaborated with the occupier, Polish researchers—based on equally incomplete data—estimated it at 10 percent.[3]

Can we conclude from this that at least 10 percent of policemen, who were actively engaged in underground work, would have been willing to offer help to the Jews? And can we also assume that another 10 percent of the officers actively collaborated with the enemy and joined in with the persecution of Jews, while the other 80 percent of their colleagues were indifferent to the Jews, neither helping nor harming them? As demonstrated in previous chapters, such calculations would be unjustified and unfounded. All of the above estimates, which, by the way, raise obvious methodological objections, are of little significance in deliberations on this subject. Numerous examples indicate that patriotic underground involvement was by no means a measure of any given Blue policeman's attitude toward the Jews. Moreover, in some cases, people who openly collaborated with the Germans helped outlawed Jewish survivors, whether out of calculation, personal affection, or other reasons.

It is no coincidence that the chapter devoted to the policemen honored as Righteous Among the Nations concludes this book. Only now, after learning about the scale and the different forms of involvement of both the Blue and Criminal Police in the process of the "Final Solution to the Jewish Question," is it possible to

2 Hempel, *Pogrobowcy klęski*, pp. 229–230.

3 Marek Mączyński, "Polskie formacje policyjne w stolicy Generalnego Gubernatorstwa 1939–1945," *Rocznik Krakowski*, 59 (1993), p. 159; Hempel, *Pogrobowcy klęski*, p. 204.

appreciate the heroism and determination of those few courageous and usually very isolated individuals who decided to help the Jews.

As Jan Tomasz Gross wrote in one of his most insightful—not to mention ahead of its time—texts devoted to the Holocaust:

> Underground work and helping Jews were fundamentally different, not in terms of the more or less severe criminal sanctions meted out by the Nazis to those found guilty of practicing one or the other of these forms of activity. The most important difference between the two was that participation in the resistance was generally respected and that it was carried out by a great many people, while only a handful of people were involved in helping the Jews, and they lacked social support for their activity.[4]

If rescuing Jews was the most dangerous form of conspiracy in Poland, then the "Blues" who chose to embark upon such a journey put themselves at the epicenter of risk. By extending a helping hand to the Jews, not only were the police officers defying German regulations and German supervisors, but more importantly, they were challenging the police *esprit de corps* and had to be ready for a confrontation with their colleagues involved in tracking down and murdering the Jews in hiding.

The story of Captain Piotr Kruk, head of the XVII Commissariat in Warsaw, will serve as an illustration of this kind of confrontation. The annals of history are silent about Captain Kruk, and in this volume, he has been mentioned only once in reference to the reports of the Warsaw commissariats concerning the number of captured Jews. Some of these reports were signed by Captain Piotr Kruk in accordance with the regulations of his service. One of Kruk's subordinates was Michał Wojciechowski, a long-serving officer who had been in the police force since 1928. Wojciechowski joined the "Blues" at the end of 1939 and was soon assigned to the

4 Jan Tomasz Gross, "Ten jest z ojczyzny mojej…, ale go nie lubię," in Jan Tomasz Gross, *Sąsiedzi i inni: Prace zebrane na temat Zagłady* (Kraków: Austeria, 2018), p. 54. The text was first published in the émigré magazine *Aneks*, 41–42 (1986), pp. 13–35.

XVII Commissariat. As early as 1941, underground reports referred to him as a blackmailer and robber who specialized in tracking down Jews, and in 1943, the AK counterintelligence accused him of collaboration with the Gestapo. Kruk and Wojciechowski often clashed. Despite his superior rank, the commissariat commander was unable to threaten his subordinate, who had strong ties to the German overseers.

After a failed blackmail attempt—the blackmailed Jew turned to the police for help—Wojciechowski and his accomplice ended up in police custody. "It was at that time when Wojciechowski disclosed that he was a German. At the personal intervention of the police director he was released from custody."[5] As we read in the AK counterintelligence reports, Kruk's quarrels with Wojciechowski concerned precisely the Jews. "Kruk often drew Wojciechowski's attention to his exploits with the Jews, whom Wojciechowski was handing over to the Germans."[6] It was against this background that a denunciation took place in late autumn 1943, as a result of which the Germans arrested and executed Captain Kruk. If the AK counterintelligence reports are to be believed, the head of the Warsaw Blue Police Commissariat was the only officer of the Blue Police on record who paid with his life for trying to defend the Jews.

It is unknown, and will probably never be known, what arguments Wojciechowski used to incriminate his superior in the eyes of the Germans. He could have accused him of having connections with the armed underground, but there is no doubt that the conflict between the two policemen was based on different views surrounding the "Jewish question." It also shows how saving the Jews—or as the oft-quoted Sergeant Franciszek Banaś from Kraków put it, "playing the Jewish uncle"—was very dangerous. In both these cases, namely of Kruk and Banaś, it was not the Germans but their Polish colleagues who posed a direct threat. Banaś, who tried to dampen the enthusiasm of younger policemen eager to

5 Report, investigation of Wojciechowski of the Blue Police, AIPN, BU 380/30, vol. 3, pp. 187–188.

6 Ibid.

kill the Jews during the liquidation of the Kraków ghetto, was threatened by his colleagues with denunciation to the Germans. One of them even reported "the Jewish uncle," and the whole thing could have ended very badly indeed for Banaś had it not been for the intervention of a friendly Schupo officer.

Regarding the police *esprit de corps*, or rather the part thereof which concerned the attitude of officers toward the ongoing genocide, the Blue Police officer Tadeusz Krasnodębski, author of a published memoir, must be mentioned. Krasnodębski, a policeman serving in small towns close to Tarnów and a clandestine Home Army officer, said the following about Jews: "Jews were cowardly"; "they had no instinct for self-preservation"; "they did not resist"; "apart from attempts to bribe German officials and policemen, Jews did not think about other forms of saving themselves, perhaps because they would require will and courage to resist the occupier, which they, except for a few individuals, could not find in themselves."[7] According to him, the Jews abandoned their hiding places, prepared with so much effort and expense, at the first call of the Germans:

> Even if the AK or other patriotic organizations had rushed to help the Jews, the Jews would still have remained passive and fallen into the hands of the Germans. All that was left of the Jews were the treasures carefully hidden in their homes, which were later discovered by enterprising Polish peasants after the deportations. After the war, the rescued Jews returned home, took back the "post-Jewish property," joined the communist security apparatus and oppressed the Poles, falsely accusing them of delivering and murdering the Jews.[8]

These are a handful of quotations from the diary of a Blue policeman, a patriot, a Home Army officer, and a conspirator. As we know, Banaś, who was awarded the honor of Righteous Among

7 Tadeusz Stefan Krasnodębski, *Policjant konspiratorem: Szesnaście lat na muszce Gestapo i bezpieki* (Kraków and Międzyzdroje: Przedsięwzięcie Galicja and Wydawn. Arkadiusz Wingert, 2008), pp. 389–419.

8 Ibid.

the Nations, also spoke about the Jews in a similar tone, and other officers' opinions shown earlier in the example of postwar court testimonies were even less flattering.

The policemen who, against all odds, decided to help the Jews, were initially threatened by their colleagues who had a different opinion on the "Jewish question," followed by their direct German supervisors. Refusal to collect ransom from Jewish merchants, turning a blind eye to illegal presence outside the ghetto, or tardiness in arresting any discovered Jews were all offenses that could have provoked someone to report such a police officer. The report was then forwarded to the German commissioned officer or the NCO assigned to the given commissariat. Moreover, occupation authorities sent local *Volksdeutsche* or Sonderdienst members to certain Blue Police commissariats. According to police reports and reports of the AK intelligence, the presence of officers from the lands annexed into the Reich—mainly from the Poznań region and Pomerania—was particularly dangerous. Strangers, outsiders in the new territory, and poorly integrated with the rest of the police collective, they often took up—or were suspected of taking up—the role of paid informants for the enemy. German surveillance was further strengthened by mixed patrols composed of Blue policemen and gendarmes as well as Schupo officers in cities. It was in these patrols, created by the regional Orpo commanders, that the risk of exposure for those who wanted to help was correspondingly greater.

Different Shades of Help

One has to emphasize and reiterate that helping the Jews took various forms, and due to their function, the Blue policemen had more opportunities than civilians to both harm and aid the Jews. As we know, the implementation of the Nazi's anti-Jewish decrees was the responsibility of Polish officers from the early days of the occupation. It was the "Blues" who escorted Jews to forced labor, arrested Jews captured without a pass after curfew, and made sure that Jews wore armbands, to name just a few of the dozens of the occupation's regulations and orders, whose enforcement was left to the Blue Police. Subsequent tasks, such as taking part in executions and liquidations or enforcing the occupation's increasingly brutal regulations, had an impact on the work ethos of the Blue Police officers. Unlike other Generalgouvernement inhabitants, the Blue policemen often came into direct contact with the Jews because of their duties and, more importantly, they quickly gained virtually unlimited power over their fellow non-Aryan citizens who had been deprived of their rights. Only German supervision could restrain the extent of the Polish policemen's arbitrary actions. In smaller towns and rural areas, such contact was more frequent and less formal than in the cities. In Warsaw, Lublin, or Kraków, only the staff of some stations served in or around the ghettos, whereas in Węgrów, Opoczno, Miechów, Sokołów Podlaski, Wodzisław, Kałuszyn, or the hundreds of other smaller towns with Jewish communities, all police officers were involved to some degree in the policy of surveillance, repression, and terror.

Returning to the various forms of assistance provided, the criteria for division, as is usually the case, are neither clear nor obvious and do not lend themselves to easy classification. To start with "indifferent" attitudes, can various cases of inaction be regarded as assistance? Ordinary people who spotted Jews on the street could pretend not to have noticed or recognized them, however police officers could not afford that luxury. The following is an example of Staszek, a chauffeur from Tarnów, who boasted that he had rescued Jews he knew during the occupation:

> I came across him one day and wanted to hear on what basis he was building his fantasies [about rescue]. "What do you mean?" he was quite genuinely surprised. "Don't you remember how many times I met you in Tarnów, even when there were no more Jews in the city? But I didn't sell you out to the Germans…" That was the rescue he bragged about.[9]

9 Maria Hochberg-Mariańska and Mieczysław Mariański, *Wśród przyjaciół i wrogów: Poza gettem w okupowanym Krakowie* (Kraków: Wydawn. Literackie, 1988), p. 11.

The very thing that Staszek the chauffeur boasted about—not telling the Germans about a Jew he recognized—would have had official consequences for police officers. For example, perhaps there would have been a denunciation of such actions by a vigilant colleague, reporting a "failure to perform police duties," to use the official language. Nonetheless, numerous accounts of ghetto liquidations feature a recurring theme of Polish policemen turning a blind eye to escaping Jews, which was possible because Blue Police officers were usually the ones who formed an outer cordon sealing off the ghetto during liquidation operations. In September 1942, during the liquidation of the ghetto in Dąbrowa, seven-year-old Cyla Braw was escaping together with her mother through the fields. Just beyond the ghetto's border stood a cordon made up of Blue policemen and Baudienst youths. "When we crossed the road, there was a Polish policeman, but he didn't do anything to us," the girl testified after the war.[10]

A more active form of support was warning of impending deportations, arrests, or other dangers. Blue Police stations and commissariats received information about planned deportations some time in advance. Full mobilization was announced many hours ahead of time, and sometimes policemen found out about the operation the day before. This knowledge could be used in many ways. As Calel (Calek) Perechodnik, a Jewish policeman from the Otwock ghetto, wrote:

> In Otwock there was a group of several score Polish citizens who knew exactly what would happen the following morning. Because around five o'clock in the evening a recent telephone message arrived at the Polish police station, asking that they reserve fifty freight cars for seven in the evening on Wednesday, August 19. It was also ordered that at seven that morning there be a roll call of uniformed and criminal police to take part in the *Aktion* to deport Jews.... Polish policemen...took advantage of this information, if only to remove from Jewish tailors or shoemakers items that were

10 Cyli Braw account, ŻIH, 301/2342.

> ordered, whether they were finished or not. In other towns policemen felt that it was the obligation to inform the local Jews about the impending liquidation. The Otwock police did not consider it their obligation and did nothing.[11]

It is important to add at this point, however, that Lieutenant Bronisław Marchlewicz, commander of the police station in Otwock, helped several Jews after the liquidation, for which he was later awarded the honor of Righteous Among the Nations. Nevertheless, while Commander Marchlewicz was helping, the underground intelligence reported that his subordinates were guarding the Jews who had been captured during an attempt to escape from the liquidated ghetto and later handed them over to the Germans to be shot.[12] As one can see, it is extremely difficult to discuss the phenomenon of rescue in isolation from denunciation and murder. In nearby Falenica, the Blue Police officers acted differently than their colleagues in Otwock: They informed their Jewish friends about the planned liquidation, a result of which was that some of the Jews managed to escape. Similarly, on August 11, 1942, in Jodłowa near Pustków in the Małopolska region, policemen warned their Jewish acquaintances about the upcoming operation, and as a result, over 100 Jews were able to escape.[13]

Tolerating smuggling can also be counted as a peculiar form of aid effort, provided the definition is appropriately flexible. There is no question, after all, that without smuggling from the Aryan side, ghetto inhabitants would have starved to death long before the deportations began. In his diary, Adam Czerniaków frequently stressed the importance of the illegal exchange of goods, which, according to him, provided the ghetto with almost 80 percent of its food. That exchange was made possible primarily by the ubiquitous corruption among the Blue policemen guarding the ghetto gates. However, even though corruption was built into the German administrative system and was a necessary component

11 Perechodnik, *Am I a Murderer?*, p. 30.

12 Liquidation of the ghetto, undated, AAN, Delegatura Rządu na Kraj, 202-II-29, p. 54.

13 Jakub Schenker account, ŻIH, 301/1694.

of it, from time to time the occupier ordered ostensive "clearing" operations to restore a semblance of discipline among the ghetto guards. Among the testimonies from the Warsaw ghetto, there is no shortage of those that describe the so-called hierarchy of bribery in such explicit terms: A Jewish policeman collected half of what was given to a Polish policeman, while a German gendarme demanded twice as much as received by his Polish colleague. The corruption that was prevalent at all levels of the Blue Police is also the subject of extensive accounts in the Oneg Shabbat Archive.[14] As previously mentioned, it is true that letting smugglers into the ghettos involved certain risk, but in most cases, the only consequence was the arrest of one or more of the policemen who had the misfortune to take a bribe at the very moment when the Germans had ordered increased scrutiny.[15]

But could tolerating food smuggling, albeit in exchange for exorbitant bribes, be considered a form of assistance? After all, the corruption among officers guarding the ghetto was one of the causes of the dramatic high prices inside the closed Jewish district. One of the reasons for the fact that almost 90,000 Jews died of starvation and associated diseases in the Warsaw ghetto alone was the extreme poverty of its inhabitants to which the bribes collected at the gates also contributed. In peacetime, bribery in the police force or among government officials in general is often a trivial though reprehensible matter. However, bribery during wartime and even more so at the ghetto borders or within the ghettos themselves, was more than just exploitation and corruption. It was complicity in a crime. A policeman extorting tribute from those condemned to death becomes an accomplice to murder. Yet without the smuggling, ghetto inhabitants would have starved to death within months at the most. Was the susceptibility of

14 Notes on smuggling in the Warsaw Ghetto, June 13, 1942 (unknown author), ŻIH, Ring I/157.

15 Sylwia Szymańska-Smolkin, "Rola policji granatowej jako pośrednika w utrzymywaniu łączności między gettem a stroną aryjską," in August Grabski and Artur Markowski, eds., *Narody i polityka: Studia ofiarowane profesorowi Jerzemu Tomaszewskiemu* (Warsaw: Inst. Historii Uniw. Warszawskiego, 2010), p. 223.

Polish policemen to corruption therefore a form of violence or assistance? Again, it is fortunately not the historian's job to answer such questions as a historian's primary duty is to present historical realities as accurately as possible and leave the moral judgment to the reader.

Direct Assistance: Kraków

Submitted just after the war to the Jewish Historical Commission in Kraków, the testimony of Franciszek Banaś includes an intriguing paragraph concerning an Austrian national from Vienna, a Schupo *Wachtmeister* Oswald (Maksymilian) Bousko. *Wachtmeister* Bousko deserves some attention because, as can be inferred from the handful of accounts, he was an extraordinary man who was directly involved in a police conspiracy that aimed to save Jews. Not just that but Bousko was also the organizer of the system of help that included several Blue policemen operating in the Kraków ghetto. The testimony of Sergeant Banaś is particularly significant since it was given shortly after the described events. In 1945, Banaś wrote the following:

> There was one Bosko [*sic*] in the German police. He saved many Jews. I trusted him and collected his letters from a Jewish woman named Landau. I would bring them to one officer who sent Jews to Switzerland. If any of the lucky ones returned, let them admit how they got to the land of happiness. It was a pity about Wachmeister Bosko [*sic*]. He was from Vienna—and he was shot for hiding Jews. He is a martyr for the great Jewish cause. The Jews in the ghetto know this man.[16]

Helena Birnfeld, who was hiding near Kraków, also mentions the mysterious policeman: "I was saved from death because I knew a German policeman named Bosko [*sic*], who always warned

16 "Stefana" account, ŻIH, 301/2058.

me in time and I would go into hiding at the house of my Polish acquaintances."[17]

Interestingly, while Banaś writes at length about the brave Austrian in his account given to the Jewish Commission in 1945, he does not mention him at all in his memoir written a quarter of a century later.

Austrian police officer Oswald Bousko, 1927.
Courtesy of the Vienna Police Archive.

According to records compiled by Yad Vashem, Bousko assembled several policemen—all Austrian nationals and colleagues from Vienna—and began smuggling Jews from the Kraków ghetto across the border. Sergeant Banaś thought that Bousko was sending Jews to Switzerland but, in fact, the smuggling network that was created by the enterprising Viennese directed Jews via Tarnów to Slovakia and then to Hungary. Bousko himself was indeed sentenced to death and shot in 1944, although not for helping Jews but for deserting his post. The same version of events can be found in the memoir of Tadeusz Pankiewicz, owner of a

17 Heleny Birnfeld account, ŻIH, 301/3428.

pharmacy located in the Kraków ghetto. According to Pankiewicz, Bousko was deputy head of the Schupo in the Podgórze district, an area covering the Jewish quarter, during the war. During the liquidation of the ghetto and later, he was said to have helped many Jews. The pharmacist himself met with him many times in the ghetto and witnessed his deeds. Contrary to what Banaś writes—and in accordance with the findings of Yad Vashem—Pankiewicz states that *Wachtmeister* Bousko was shot as a deserter in the fall of 1944.[18]

Particularly important from our point of view are *Wachtmeister* Bousko's ties to the Blue Police or, more precisely, to the Polish officers serving in the Kraków ghetto. As Franciszek Banaś himself writes, Banaś remained in close contact with Bousko, and Bousko got him out of trouble at least once after the Pole had been denounced by his own colleagues. Another Blue policeman who cooperated with the Austrian was Corporal Stanisław Śliżewski. Śliżewski lived at 21 Zielona Street, less than 2 kilometers from the perimeter of the Kraków ghetto. Hiding in his apartment were two Jews, Adolf Żabner and Zofia Korngold. At some point, Żabner's brother, for whom Śliżewski had risked his life to get him out of the Rzeszów ghetto, also showed up at Zielona Street. The last tenant of Śliżewski's was *Wachtmeister* Oswald Bousko himself, "who worked in the ghetto in Kraków."[19] Both Banaś and Śliżewski, in cooperation with Bousko, smuggled forged papers into the ghetto, arranged hideouts for Jews on the Aryan side, and facilitated their escape from the closed Jewish district. The third policeman who saved Jews in the Kraków ghetto was Władysław Szałek, a young man who was born in Kraków's Kazimierz district and was raised with and among Jews.[20] When contact with his Jewish friends became very difficult after the establishment of the ghetto in Podgórze, Szałek decided to join the Blue Police, having discussed the matter with his Jewish acquaintances:

18 Tadeusz Pankiewicz, *Apteka w getcie krakowskim* (Kraków: Wydawnictwo Literackie, 2017), pp. 77, 100–103.

19 Adolf Żabner affidavit for the Department of the Righteous, December 4, 1995, ŻIH, 349/24/2208.

20 Władysław Szałek file, YVA, M.31.2/1580.

> The Jews, in conversation with me, suggested that I should join the abovementioned police, which they believed would give me personal protection from the repressions awaiting young people, as well as a chance to provide significant help to the Jews, especially since they could arrange for me an assignment to the precinct inside the ghetto through officers of that police they knew.[21]

It is quite likely that the officer who could have arranged for Szałek to be assigned to the ghetto was Oswald Bousko himself. Indeed, Szałek soon arrived there as a policeman and began supplying Jews with well-crafted documents. One of the forgers, Leon Singer, even set up his workshop in the policeman's apartment. Then, with the help of some other officers, Szałek set up illegal passages at several points in the Jewish quarter, through which food was delivered to the ghetto, and "served as an opportunity for those Jews whom necessity forced them to leave the ghetto illegally and where they were forced to move without the obligatory armbands, risking their lives," Szałek wrote many years after the war.[22] What is more, by coordinating with Jewish police officers in the ghetto, Polish policemen were able to crack down—at least for a time—on the mass of blackmailers prowling around the ghetto walls. One of Szałek's associates was Eugeniusz Śliwa. From the end of 1943 to October 1944, Śliwa smuggled packages and information into Schindler's factory and later hid a Jewish woman in his house in Mikluszowice near Bochnia after she had escaped from the camp.[23]

In 1964, Oswald Bousko was posthumously recognized as Righteous Among the Nations. Władysław Szałek was awarded the honor in 1979. Stanisław Śliżewski had to wait longer and was not honored until 2008. As one can infer from the records, the twenty-year delay in awarding this honor to the heroic policeman was presumably the result of an unfortunate mistake. Officials who verified the information at one point consulted the personnel file

21 Letter from Władysław Szałek to Yad Vashem, March 30, 1967, YVA, M.31.2/1580.

22 Ibid.

23 Bronisław Scheidelberg account, ŻIH, 301/2308.

of a man named Slischewsky, an officer in the SS Security Police who served in the Lublin region in 1944, and who, of course, had nothing to do with our Śliżewski. Years passed before the mistake was rectified, and Śliżewski received the honor posthumously.

Constable Oswald Bousko during the war.
Photo Collection, YVA, Righteous Among the Nations Collection.

The network involved in helping Jews that was created by *Wachtmeister* Bousko, his fellow Austrian gendarmes, and Polish Blue policemen was quite unique in the history of the police in the Generalgouvernement. What is striking is its noble motives and honorable aim rather than its international composition, of which, after all, we know many examples when Polish and German policemen cooperated within criminal groups. It is difficult to say why such a group was established in Kraków. I would agree with Max Bergholz who, in his book on violence in the Balkans during World War II, attributes the fundamental role in the formation of such attitudes to individuals.[24] It was individuals, specific people,

24 Max Bergholz, *Violence as a Generative Force: Identity, Nationalism, and Memory in a Balkan Community* (Ithaca: Cornell University Press, 2016).

usually prominent residents such as village leaders, clergymen, policemen, and merchants, who could and did change the course of events at decisive moments, so that while a massacre was taking place in one village, people were living peacefully in another one nearby, despite the same ethnic, religious, and social composition. Bergholz suggests that this was possible because such people could inspire others to follow them at any critical moment. There are many indications that the Austrian *Wachtmeister* Oswald Bousko was just such an exceptional man, able to encourage his subordinates and friends to act for a good cause.

Direct Assistance: Warsaw

Unlike in Kraków, attempts to rescue Jews made by policemen were organized individually and in absolute secrecy in Warsaw. For a better understanding of this, a return to the well-known Blue Police Railway Commissariat in Jerozolimskie Avenue is required. This Blue Police post was last mentioned here in regard to the arrest of Frieda Verstandig, who had managed to survive the ordeal after paying an enormous ransom. At around the same time as this incident in mid-1943, a Jewish woman captured in the city along with a Polish woman who had helped her were brought to the police post by Blue Police officers:

> We were terrified. They took us to the Blue Police, which—as we all know—collaborated with the occupier. Polish Blue Police. That police was located, I think it was the railway police station, it was located across the street, on Jerozolimskie Avenue. They brought us to some room and a detective came in and asked who we were. I said, "I am Helenka Falkowska, and this is my aunt, Aniela Krzystoszek." And [later], "Where are you two going?" "We've come on a trip to Warsaw, we live in Kraków." He said, "Oh, you've come on a trip to Warsaw, but tell me, aren't you Jewish by any chance?" I said, "I'm not." "And your aunt, she's not Jewish?" And the horrible questioning began. They just started beating us, that detective, me and Anielcia,

> and he beat her, and he beat me. I couldn't watch her suffer. This poor innocent woman was looking at me with those poor eyes and at that time we could see through the window, it was on the ground floor, how the trucks were driving past, covered with tarpaulin, transporting captured people to the Gestapo. The investigator said, "Can you see these people?" I could see them, there were some Jewish faces. I recognized that those were Jews. "They're taking them away to deal with them once and for all, so you have to admit who you really are." At that time I couldn't bear it any longer, and it was a fatal mistake of mine. It could have been a fatal mistake of mine. And I said that I was a Jew and that Anielcia was not. She just wanted to help me, because there were good people who wanted to help. And then the detective left the room. It didn't matter to me anymore, because I couldn't take the pain any more. I was broken, I was without my mother. I knew that something had happened to my mother, she didn't come. I had no contact with my brother or my father. I was wandering aimlessly, I was hungry, I didn't want to, life was no longer important to me. And then the detective left the room. After a while another officer appeared. I remembered his features for many years.
>
> [Question:] A Pole too, right?
>
> A Pole, without that detective. An officer of that police force. He looked at me and said, "I have a daughter your age. What a shame to waste such young life. I am going to open the spare door. You both run away immediately. I was not here at all." So we did what he said.[25]

We do not know the name of the brave policeman nor the true identity of the Jewish woman he saved. However, considering the atmosphere, the style of work, and the general attitude toward the Jews at the railway commissariat in Jerozolimskie Avenue, we can fully appreciate the scale of the heroism of that unnamed officer.

25 Hanną Gdalewicz-Nielsen interview, VHA, 7970.

Another anonymous hero in a blue uniform saved the life of Helena Landsberg, who was hiding in Warsaw. The woman was handed over to the police by the concierge of the house where she was living. In a dramatic account recorded for the VHA, she described her experience as follows:

> They dragged me downstairs and a patrol came, two gendarmes and a Blue policeman, and they ordered me to go with them. I went with them. I had my purse with me. There was a photograph of my mother and my brother, they didn't look Jewish at all. And that's why I let myself keep those photographs. And that policeman started talking to me. He asked me who was in the photographs and who I had, what I had and what I was going to do. Later he said, "They are taking you to the Powazki cemetery, to be shot." Because that's what they did with everyone found there. "But I'll try to arrange something with them. Do you have any money?" I told him, "I have 3,000 zlotys." I had even more hidden, but the 3,000 I had at hand. So I gave it to him. We entered the cemetery. He talked to those Germans. After some time he came back. He told me to sit on some bench by the grave and gave me 1,500 and said to me, "You remind me of my daughter. I don't want you to die so miserably. I took care of them with 1,500 zlotys. You will need this money more than I will. You just have to give me a word of honor that you will never come here again. Because I work here and they know me. And I will only take you somewhere in the center of Warsaw. Please don't ever come here again." I got on the streetcar with him. Two other guys got on behind us. One of them said to him, "I want to talk to this lady." He says, "This lady is under arrest. I'm escorting her." That man says, "I know the tricks. You've just taken her out of the ghetto." So he says, "She didn't come out of any ghetto and she's arrested for smuggling." So that man followed us. At Bankowy Square…It was different. He jumped out, pulled me with him. That other one managed to jump out after us.

> [Question:] But who jumped out?
>
> The policeman. And me with him. So we get into some doorway. He suddenly says to that guy, "Who are you exactly? Please, identify yourself." And he shakes his hand, signaling me to run away. A streetcar was just passing by. I ran, jumped into the moving streetcar and rode away. Earlier, he had told me at the cemetery when he was giving me the money, "Remember my service number: 387." I remember it to this day. "If you survive, you will testify that I helped you." And that was the last time I saw him. I later searched for him through newspapers, because I worked in the Office of Press Control, so I had contacts, I had influence, I searched everywhere. There was a special commission to look at the former Blue Police—I was looking for him there. I placed ads. Nothing. Not a trace. I've never found him.[26]

Despite many years of studying Blue Police records, the identity of the brave Warsaw policeman, service number 387, is still unknown to this author. This is a great pity because the list of policemen who saved Jews with similar dedication, risking their lives, is quite short. Another Warsaw policeman, who after long deliberations and with hesitation released the arrested Pola Kaplan and her husband, also remains anonymous.[27]

One of the most extraordinary Righteous policemen was Jan Kubicki, who also served in Warsaw.[28] Kubicki, who lived in great poverty in Warsaw's Marymont quarter in a one-room apartment with his daughter and wife, saved Jews in various ways. As several documented cases demonstrate, he hid several of them under his roof despite the cramped conditions, sometimes obtained clothes and papers for those in hiding, and also smuggled a Jew out of a labor camp and later helped him find shelter. There were times

26 Helena Landsberg interview, VHA, 16637.

27 Pola Kapłan interview, VHA, 27634.

28 Jan and Zofia Kubicki file, YVA, M.31.2/1075. Documentation in the Kubicki file at Yad Vashem includes the testimonies of Ms. Sawicka, Ms. Heinsdorff, Mrs. Nissenbaum with her daughter, and Ms. Gertler.

when Kubicki received reports about the whereabouts of Jews in hiding. In such cases, Kubicki went to the indicated address to warn the victims of the denunciation. The Warsaw policeman did it all selflessly, as proven by testimonies of the rescued submitted right after the war and thus deserves special attention since they were written long before the Israeli authorities established the title of Righteous Among the Nations, which made selflessness one of the conditions for awarding this honor.[29] How far Kubicki's case deviated from the norm and the extent of how his behavior was unusual is evidenced by the fact that this policeman learned to read Hebrew during the war, and one of the books he read was Simon Dubnow's *History of the Jews*, which he had brought home from the ghetto. In her testimony for the VHA, Kubicki's wife Zofia recalled that her husband never spoke to her about the details of his aid activity. On one occasion, for example, he brought home two Jewish women named Marecka whom he was supposed to arrest following a denunciation. Instead of taking them to the police station, he invited them to his house and then helped them find shelter where they could stay longer.[30]

Sergeant Wacław Nowiński, who served at the Blue Police River Commissariat in Warsaw and was already mentioned in the chapter about the Warsaw police, became similarly involved in rescuing Jews. Several officers worked there who were considered by the underground as exceptional pests and German lackeys, not to mention the fact that several others were actively involved in tracking down hidden Jews, as evidenced by reports submitted to the Warsaw police commander in the summer of 1943. Providing help under such circumstances was extremely risky, even if Sergeant Nowiński was a ranking officer and a shift leader. One of those saved by Nowiński was Aleksander Bronowski, a resident of Lublin who was hiding on the Aryan side. Bronowski fell into the hands of Polish undercover Kripo officers on April 9, 1943. The Kripo agents tracked down their victim on a streetcar on its way to the Praga district. After an unsuccessful attempt to extort a ransom—

29 Kiry Heinsdorf account, ŻIH, 301/2232.

30 Zofia Kubicka interview, VHA, 37628.

Bronowski had only 500 zlotys on him at the time—the agents led the captured Jew to the nearest Blue Police station, which happened to be the River Commissariat, where he was locked in a holding pen.[31] Sergeant Wacław Nowiński was on duty overnight and after a long conversation with the detainee, he agreed to protect him:

> He told me that the matter was successfully resolved, that at 7:00 AM agents would come, to whom I would hand 5,000 zlotys. Wacław Nowiński handed me that sum and when I asked how he could be sure I would return it, he told me I owed him nothing and I shouldn't return the money to him.[32]

Indeed, once the ransom was handed over, the agents released Bronowski. It is worth adding here that in his testimony given in Warsaw in April 1960, Bronowski emphasized the dedication of Sergeant Nowiński, who apparently also helped other Jews hiding in Warsaw.[33] Wacław Nowiński and his wife Janina were awarded the title of Righteous Among the Nations in 1970, as were Jan and Zofia Kubicki six years later.

Characteristic of the help provided by the Warsaw policemen was the fact that they kept their secret well guarded. They told only their wives, who in any case had to know about the Jews arriving at their apartment. Over the course of this author's many years of research, a single mention of any activity that even remotely resembles the aid network organized by the Kraków policemen has not been found. The examples of Kubicki, Nowiński, or the few anonymous rescuers do not exhaust the list of heroic policemen. We can add to this group Eliasz Pietraszka, who helped ten-year-old Irma Grundland escape from the ghetto in February 1943. Then he placed the girl in his own apartment in Grochów—among his

31 Aleksandr Bronowski account, ŻIH, 301/5910.

32 Ibid. See also the statements of Józef Szarbel and others attached to the account of Kazimiera Sadzikowska in ŻIH 301/6306; and the account of Janina Pańska, saying that Wacław Nowiński helped many Jews including Dr. Aleksander Wertheim, YVA, O.3/2198.

33 Aleksandr Bronowski account, ŻIH, 301/5910. Among others, Bronowski mentioned Janina Pańska, the Rapaport family, and Dr. Berłowicz.

own children—and a little later, fearing that the neighbors might denounce her, he took her to a relative near Tarnopol (Ternopil), where she survived until the arrival of the Russians.[34]

The list should also include another Warsaw policeman called Jan Fakler. He arranged with Halina Rubinstein's parents in the ghetto that he would help them transport their child to the Aryan side. The parents died, but the Faklers took care of the girl who lived with them until the end of the war. After liberation, she was taken from them by Captain Yeshayahu Drucker, one of the Jews who traveled around Poland after the war searching for Jewish children entrusted to Polish families for safekeeping during the occupation.[35]

Outside Warsaw, we should also mention the brave policeman Stanisław, who hid the daughter of a rabbi from the Tarnów region under his roof. Officer Stanisław, whose surname we do not know, was also prepared to rescue and hide in his house Rywka Szenker, who was being escorted to prison. Distrustful of the policeman and afraid of being raped, Rywka rejected the offer, however, and it was only after the war that she found out that the policeman Stanisław was not lying and that he had indeed rescued Jews.[36]

Another figure worth mentioning is Sergeant Jan Kostrzewski, the brave head of the post in Targowisko near Bochnia, who protected his friend Dawid Infeld for a long time. Sergeant Kostrzewski also helped several other Jews, providing them with accommodation and directing them to safe places as well as warning them of planned manhunts.[37] Such activities were difficult and dangerous because not all the policemen at the station in Targowisko shared Sergeant Kostrzewski's philosemitic views. Unfortunately, in January 1943, Dawid Infeld visited a Polish woman he knew to collect some things with which he had entrusted her "for a rainy day." He did not expect that his acquaintance, who

34 Irma Grundland account, ŻIH, 301/5543.

35 Jan and Maria Fakler file, YVA, M.31.2/839.

36 See Rywka Szenker's recollections in Grabowski, *Szczęście posiadać dom pod ziemią…*, p. 192.

37 The entire case can be reconstructed based on the investigation against Jan Kostrzewski, AIPN Kr, 502/3575.

in the meantime had become attached to those few items, would call the police. Two of Sergeant Kostrzewski's subordinates arrived and promptly executed Infeld. The commanding officer, who only learned about the situation after the fact, could not rebuke his subordinates for what they had done out of fear for his own life.

The list of "good policemen" is certainly much longer, but this does not change the fact that those brave men in no way conformed to the police norm. By rescuing Jews, they placed themselves outside the Blue collective, and there is no doubt that the greatest danger for them was their own colleagues, so many of whom had joined the German extermination campaign. Today, the commemoration of people who saved Jews is often done in the name of a trivial and shallow sense of conceived patriotism or for the sake of defending the ill-understood "good name of the nation." However, if one wants to understand the horrible dilemmas facing those who decided to help Jews during the occupation, we need look no further than the handful of examples from the lives of the Blue policemen who, having found themselves in the very heart of darkness, decided to help those facing imminent death.

Conclusion

Shortly before he fell into the hands of the Polish Criminal Police, Emanuel Ringelblum wrote the following:

> It is, however, the anti-Semites as a whole, infected with racialism and Nazism, who created conditions so unfavourable that it has been possible to save only a small percentage of the Polish Jews from the Teuton butchers. Polish fascism and its ally, anti-Semitism, have conquered the majority of the Polish people. The blind folly of Poland's anti-Semites, who have learnt nothing, has been responsible for the death of hundreds of thousands of Jews who could have been saved despite the Germans. The guilt is theirs for not having saved tens of thousands of Jewish children who could have been taken in by Polish families or institutions. The fault is entirely theirs that Poland has given asylum at the most to one percent of the Jewish victims of Hitler's persecutions.[1]

Always very well informed, Ringelblum was not wrong in his estimate of the losses of the Jewish nation. Indeed, of the Polish Jews who found themselves under German rule, excluding those who had escaped to the Soviet Union, less than 30,000—or around 1 percent—survived. As argued in this book, a significant role in the murder of the Jews who had initially managed to escape the "Teuton butchers" was played by Poles, officers of the Blue and Criminal Police, members of volunteer fire brigades, and gawkers—that is neighbors—and they all made their own contribution to the German genocidal policies.

1 Ringelblum, *Polish-Jewish Relations*, pp. 247–248.

The question is whether the presented evidence allows us to draw general conclusions about the behavior of the Polish detectives and their uniformed colleagues in the entire Generalgouvernement. There are times when after many years of research and analyzing a great deal of archival evidence, one can conclude that it is possible to say we know "*wie es eigentlich gewesen*" (what really happened), to quote Leopold von Ranke. Although further research can clarify certain aspects of the issue and bring to light more details, it is the prerogative of the historian to propose hypotheses. In this case, the hypothesis that has been formulated in various ways throughout the pages of this book strongly emphasizes the criminal nature of the activities of the Blue and Criminal Police during the occupation. Those organizations, established and commanded by the Germans but composed mostly of prewar Polish policemen, morphed into criminal formations that became one of the most important elements of the strategy of the "Final Solution to the Jewish Question" in Poland.

There were about 1,000 Blue Police stations and commissariats in the Generalgouvernement during the war. The evidence presented in this book involves cases of the murderous practices of Polish officers serving at 124 posts scattered throughout every district of the Generalgouvernement. Is this a fairly representative and large enough sample of the behavior of Polish policemen? Can any general conclusions be drawn based on it? I see no reason why not.

Returning to the reflections of the Warsaw ghetto historian Ringelblum on the causes of the radicalization of anti-Jewish attitudes, antisemitism played the primary and most sinister role in the motivation, legitimization, and fueling of the murderous aggression. In his book on the Holocaust, British historian David Cesarani quoted one of the bystanders who claimed that for the Germans, the execution of 300 Jews in Ponary meant eliminating 300 enemies of humanity. For the Lithuanian volunteers who also took part in the massacre, the murdered Jews were simply the source of 300 pairs of trousers and 300 pairs of shoes.[2] In

2 David Cesarani, *Final Solution: The Fate of the Jews, 1933–1949* (New York: St. Martin's Press, 2016), p. 394.

light of the murderous actions of the Blue Police, the claim of the "bystander" quoted by Cesarani can be called into question. Is mere greed, a lust for loot, a sufficient explanation for the zeal, initiative, and entrepreneurship of the murderers in blue uniforms? It is rather doubtful, and all the more so, despite the rampant terror, not all shoes and not all trousers could be considered as due loot. Christopher R. Browning, one of the most insightful researchers of *die Täter* (the perpetrators) and often quoted in this book, concluded that for Germans, killing Jews involved following orders and was done under pressure from colleagues, their brothers in arms. In the case of the Polish policemen and Polish firemen—and, I believe, Lithuanian volunteers—the murders of Jews had deeper roots. The killings, often committed dispassionately, were made possible by a deep, well-rooted hatred that grew out of antisemitism and fueled for centuries by the Catholic Church as well as nationalist indoctrination that had been gaining strength from the beginning of the twentieth century. Greed and plunder undoubtedly had an impact on attitudes, but in the case of the Poles that murdered their Jewish neighbors, they were not the most important factors.

There is a question that troubles historians researching the history of genocides—not only Holocaust historians but also scholars who study the Armenian genocide or that of the Tutsi. The question is simple: Why and how do seemingly normal people turn into mass murderers? Looking through tens of thousands of pages of archival documents, listening to recorded accounts, talking to survivors, and reading books and articles on the subject, one would hope to come closer to finding an answer to the question that has been bothering so many scholars of the Holocaust. Unfortunately, despite the mounting weight of evidence, the goal grows more elusive. For instance, let us take a closer look at the following issue. Many witnesses pointed out the exceptional harmfulness of those young people who joined the Blue Police during the war. Some underground reports also note this phenomenon and condemned young police recruits who carried out the occupiers' most barbaric orders without hesitation. Many young policemen from the wartime enlistment appear in the pages of this book, and it is clear that they were capable of cruel acts. However, the majority of policemen who murdered Jews in large numbers were mature people, fathers, officers who often had twenty years of experience in the prewar police service under their belts. How does one explain such an evolution of attitudes? Why and how did a guardian of the law, a defender of public order, become a murderer of his fellow citizens, all within the space of two or three years? It seems that the young recruits along with veterans with prewar police careers committed murder alike. Furthermore, in both cases, unlike the German policemen who murdered anonymous victims far from their hometowns, the Polish policemen killed people they knew well, often their schoolmates.

Witnesses to the events, including the authors of the underground intelligence reports, all pointed out the toxic influence of the policemen who were resettled in the Generalgouvernement from territories incorporated into the Reich. Captain Wraubek wrote about this phenomenon, Sergeant Banaś also wrote about it, and so did the anonymous Home Army informers. According to them, police officers transferred to the Generalgouvernement from northern or western Poland, operated in unfamiliar territory, and therefore felt little connection with the local population but often felt a certain affinity with the Germans. They were fluent in German, and some had served in the German army during World War I. To a certain extent, sources confirm such observations: Among the zealots who ruthlessly collected grain and cattle quotas from the peasants and who tirelessly pursued Poles wanted for labor in the Reich, one could indeed find many so-called *poznaniaks*, or people hailing from the Poznań area in western Poland. However, there was no significant difference between the indigenous and resettled policemen's behavior on the "Jewish front." Both groups took part—with comparable engagement—in the implementation of the "Final Solution to the Jewish Question," tracking down, robbing, and murdering their Jewish co-citizens.

In discussions about Polish complicity, co-perpetration or Polish participation in the Holocaust, one often mentions the death penalty that threatened Poles for even minor violations of the occupiers' orders. Unfortunately, in this case, the threat of the death penalty does nothing to explain the participation of Polish policemen in the extermination of Jews, and it certainly has very little explicative value in the cases of policemen who murdered outside German control and without German supervision. More importantly, the death penalty was often applied by the Germans to members of the Blue Police who cooperated with the Polish underground, as previously mentioned in the case of the execution of Kraków officers in 1943, and yet this had little dissuasive effect on the policemen's willingness to continue supporting the underground. On the other hand, as has been emphasized, there is no record of even a single case of a Polish policeman shot for refusing to murder Jews. On the contrary, as demonstrated in the case of the Racławice post or in the case of the liquidation of the Kraków ghetto, a Polish policeman could refuse to carry out the order of a German officer and suffer no consequences. The point is that in the case of both German and Polish policemen, it was easy to find volunteers to carry out the order to kill. To put it bluntly, in the archives and in the literature on the subject, one finds no trace of any serious consequences incurred by a Polish policeman for refusing to shoot the Jews.

After the War

With the end of the war approaching, the Blue policemen were faced with difficult decisions. Some who had been involved with the resistance movement for a long time could count on the support of their underground organizations. Others tried even harder to establish contacts with the underground after gauging the political climate. At the beginning of 1944, the scale of desertions increased. Hundreds of Blue policemen, especially east of the Vistula River, were fleeing posts with their weapons and joining the resistance. The Germans tracked down deserters and often shot them, but in the last months of the war, the terror apparatus was not as efficient as it had been in previous years. The draconian regulations—deportation to a concentration camp—that extended criminal responsibility to the families of Polish policemen accused of desertion did not change much. Among the deserters were also officers who had previously distinguished themselves as notorious hunters of Jews. In many cases, the policemen who murdered Jews continued their activity in the underground as members of partisan units or other resistance structures. To a certain extent, the dilemmas of the Blue policemen in 1944 were not unlike those faced by the policemen in Ukraine a year earlier. There, between March and April 1943, thousands of officers of the so-called Ukrainian Black Police abandoned their service and joined partisan units. The difference was that the Ukrainians deserted having received an explicit order from the Ukrainian nationalist OUN-UPA.[3] In the Generalgouvernement, the underground authorities did not order police officers to desert, but Blue policemen nevertheless fled en masse from their service and joined the underground.

While some policemen deserted, others tried to provide themselves with an alibi for the uncertain postwar years. One Jewish woman hiding in Warsaw described the last months of the occupation as follows:

> It was in May 1944. Everyone knew that the defeat of Germany was near. And those *szmalcowniks* and those Poles who worked for the Germans somehow changed then. And a policeman came to us, a Blue policeman, who worked for the Germans. The janitor told him that my mother was hiding there. And there was one boy hiding there, who had lost his parents. I was taking care of him, and they thought he was my son. So the policeman wanted to take us. And then he says to me, "I'll save you because the war is ending, and you'll testify that I saved Jews." And I asked him, "Will you save the boy, too?" He said, "I'll save the boy, too." And he let us go. He gave me his address and his name. I threw it out right away. Such a scoundrel, who worked for the Germans and captured everyone, Jews and non-Jews, I will

3 John-Paul Himka, "Former Ukrainian Policemen in the Ukrainian National Insurgency: Continuing the Holocaust outside German Service," in Wendy Lower and Faulkner Rossi, eds., *Lessons and Legacies, vol. XII, New Directions in Holocaust Research and Education* (Evanston: Northwestern University Press, 2017), pp. 141–162.

> not be a witness for him after the war. But in any case, he left me alone, and that boy, too.[4]

On August 15, 1944, the new Communist authorities that were established in the eastern part of liberated Poland—Polish Committee for National Liberation (Polski Komitet Wyzwolenia Narodowego, PKWN)—dissolved the Blue Police, recognizing it as a collaborationist formation in service of the enemy. In practice, however, the verification of police personnel and the review of former Blue Police officers did not begin until mid-1946. Although the PKWN decree disbanded the Blue Police, the former policemen had no problem finding their way into the ranks of the security and police forces of the new regime. This transition to the service of the new authorities was a logical step for the former Blue policemen, who had no other "sellable" skills apart from their police experience.

The presence of Blue policemen in the Communist militia and security forces was not without significance for the Jewish survivors coming out of hiding. For many Jewish Holocaust survivors, those first months of freedom did not mean the end of the danger. The atmosphere in Poland was tense, and the first signs of civil war were visible all around the country. In the atmosphere of generalized and continuing violence, the returning Jews often fell victim to the hatred of their former neighbors and the armed underground. The situation at that time is well illustrated by the following remark made by Ber Ryczywoł, a Jewish survivor from Łuków:

> It was beyond my comprehension—how can this be? The Russians are here, and they are going to beat the Jews? I stayed in the villages until the beginning of 1945, because I couldn't go to Warsaw. I kept passing myself off as a Pole. It wasn't much fun. I heard that they were murdering Jews. This happened, for example, in Kołbiel, Garwolin County. I also visited towns, usually Łuków. **I was afraid to go to the villages because it was**

4 Janina Żurawicka interview, VHA, 17885.

> **worse than back under the German rule** [emphasis added, JG]. If I did go to a village, it would have to be one where no one knew me. Near Siedlce, but I don't know the name of that town, a few Jews were killed. In Kałuszyn, too.[5]

On Easter Sunday, March 31, 1945, in the small village of Kańczuga near Przeworsk, a mass murder of Jews took place.[6] At least thirteen people died there—children, women, and men, whose only crime was that they were Jewish and that they had returned to claim back their own houses. In time, some of the murderers from Kańczuga were caught, brought to trial, and sentenced. According to a journalist researching the history of this crime:

> If we take a closer look at the affiliations of those who murdered the Jews in Kańczuga, it would turn out that they were a strange bunch indeed: wartime Home Army soldiers, postwar "Radwan" [anti-communist partisans] soldiers, a "Blue" policeman, a postwar Militia officer, an MO lieutenant, a member of the Polish Workers' Party (PPR), and in later years—the Polish United Workers' Party (PZPR). Thus, the entire social cross-section was represented: from the right to the left.[7]

From our point of view, the fact that militia officers—one of whom had served in the Blue Police—took part in planning and carrying out the crime in Kańczuga is particularly important. The phenomenon of former members of the Blue Police infiltrating the enforcement structures of the new government apparatus soon became ubiquitous. The presence of former "Blues" in the ranks of the Kielce police has recently been documented by Joanna Tokarska-Bakir.[8] In her moving study of the Kielce pogrom, she outlined the social dynamics that preceded and contributed to

5 Ber Ryczywół testimony, *Majne iberlebungen*, ŻIH, 302/43.

6 The case was investigated by reporter Wojciech Piecuch. See "Wielka Noc w Kańczudze," *Gazeta Wyborcza*, March 2–3, 2002.

7 Piotr Lipiński, "Nikt ich nie tykał," *Gazeta Wyborcza*, August 30, 2002.

8 Joanna Tokarska-Bakir, *Pod klątwą: Społeczny portret pogromu kieleckiego* (Warsaw: Czarna Owca, 2018).

the events of July 4, 1946. An analysis of biographies of militia and security officers responsible for organizing the military and militia response to the pogrom and those who took part in the pogrom itself was revealing, and it seems that former members of the Blue Police, *Volksdeutsche*, and murderers of Jews during the war quickly infiltrated the security forces of the new regime. There, they often continued with what they had been doing during the war: namely, they continued to murder Jews. There is no doubt that the personal, social, and professional relationships that had been established and reinforced during the war continued after liberation, with disastrous consequences for the Jews.

As mentioned, it was only later that the personnel verification began. The process started in mid-1946 and was completed by the end of the following year. By that time, a considerable group of Blue policemen—some researchers estimate that it was around 1,000 officers—had taken up employment in the Citizens' Militia.[9] Such calculations definitely underestimate the number of "Blues" in the ranks of the police in the initial postwar years. In Kraków alone, a census of former members of the police force prepared by order of the central authorities on July 24, 1945, showed that there were 101 former Blue Police officers working in the local police stations.[10] Considering that there were approximately 400 policemen serving in Kraków during the occupation, it is easy to calculate that 25 percent of them found their way into the ranks of the Communist militia. One of them was Henryk Mika, who in 1943 had completed training at the police school in Nowy Sącz and was serving in Kraków. Although he was listed in the AK records as a Gestapo agent, he served as chief of the investigative brigade in one of the Kraków precincts after the war. He was dismissed from the militia only in 1948.[11] The initial postwar years seem to have offered a safe haven to former Blue policemen who threw their lot in with the new authorities.

9 Piotr Majer, "Okupacyjne i powojenne losy polskich policjantów," *Przegląd Policyjny*, 1–2 (1990), pp. 101–120.

10 Lists of former Blue policemen working in the Citizens' Militia, 1945–1946, AIPN, BU 155/3098, pp. 33–35.

11 Note, August 22, 1950, AIPN Kr, 010/3437, p. 49.

The situation changed only after a special Rehabilitation Qualification Commission for former policemen began to work in earnest. Established on August 29, 1945, the commission started to verify the applications of former Blue policemen in the middle of 1946 and continued to examine them until the end of October 1947. During that time, the commission examined 8,247 applications submitted by former policemen of which 556 applicants were denied rehabilitation.[12] One could assume that former members of the Blue Police who had committed the most severe wartime crimes—including crimes against Jews—did not apply for rehabilitation for fear of being discovered. However, such an assumption would be incorrect. Out of over 500 Blue policemen who had committed crimes against Jews during the war—a working list that was established for the purposes of this study—as many as forty-three submitted rehabilitation applications to the committee. Perhaps they thought that their wartime activities had been forgotten by then, or perhaps that crimes against Jews would no longer be an obstacle to rehabilitation. Of those who applied, only three were approved, although most of the others were denied rehabilitation solely because they failed to meet the statutory application deadlines. In several cases, the Rehabilitation Qualification Commission received information from the National Councils—one of the bodies who was reviewing the applications—that became the basis for subsequent criminal investigations. Sometimes, the commission received reports about simultaneous trials of former police officers who were applying for rehabilitation.

Memory

Although many years have now passed, Polish memorial battles surrounding the war and occupation have not spared the history of the Blue Police. However, from the point of view of the Polish history policy—the official state narrative based on defending

12 See Robert Litwiński, "Komisja rehabilitacyjno-kwalifikacyjna dla byłych policjantów (1945–1952)," *Dzieje Najnowsze*, 1 (2004), pp. 117–134.

the myth of "innocent Poland"—the issue is controversial, inconvenient, and poses a problem. After all, it is difficult to dispute the fact that the Blue policemen served the occupier. They rounded up Poles slated for forced labor in the Reich, arrested members of the underground, and ruthlessly collected grain quotas from peasants, not to mention the many smaller and larger crimes against the ethnically defined Polish national community. Until recently, there were hardly any references and literature to their crimes against the Jews. In the only historical monograph of the Blue Police so far—and the book was published more than thirty years ago—the author had practically nothing to say about the policemen's involvement in the "Final Solution to the Jewish Question." Furthermore, he came to the conclusion that there were no reasons to hold Polish policemen responsible for anything particularly damaging in that area.[13] Finally, the author went as far as to say that if Polish policemen "with their excellent knowledge of the area" had really applied themselves in their work, then so many Jews would certainly not have survived in hiding until liberation.[14]

Nevertheless, from the standpoint of historical politics, the problem of crimes committed by members of the Blue Police against their fellow countrymen remain unresolved. The simplest explanation, to which the defenders of an idealized version of Polish history often resort, assumes that the Blue Police was an alien element in Polish society, that Poles who wore the Blue uniform became German lackeys and, as such, automatically excluded themselves from the national community.

Such an assertion explains a lot: Poles who in these circumstances harmed other Poles could simply no longer be considered Polish. This explicative model is quite simple, it removes unpleasant cognitive dissonance, and it can be applied to many other uncomfortable issues in the history of the occupation. Following the same line of reasoning, one can explain, for example, that all *szmalcowniks* and informers who gave away the Jews to

13 Hempel, *Pogrobowcy klęski*, pp. 170–179.

14 Ibid., p. 180. Incidentally, the author cites the figure of 150,000 survivors, which is not consistent with the state of knowledge both then and now.

their deaths, were simply criminals and dregs of society, people who excluded themselves from the Polish *Volksgemeinschaft*. This kind of easy explanation, however, triggers resistance among the supporters of "innocent history" who would like to preserve the memory of Blue policemen as heroes of the underground, members of resistance groups, people who made indisputable contributions in the struggle against the occupation and in many cases paid for it with their lives.

The second memorial defense ploy is to relativize the issue. As claimed by the defenders of historical myths, Blue policemen committed many crimes, but did the Jewish police behave any better? After all, both organizations were set up by the Germans, both served the Germans, and both had some vile, some less vile, and some noble people as members. Although Polish historians, in service to the state, have honed this type of narrative in recent years, the explanatory formula based on the analogy of the Jewish police has been present in historical polemics for a long time and has become something of an automatic, defensive response used by supporters of Polish myths. The point is that any attempt to compare the Jewish police with the Blue Police immediately leads us into the territory of Holocaust denial. Is it possible to compare victims with their killers? In the end, almost all Jewish policemen shared the fate of other Jews. Some outlived them by a day, others by a few weeks until the liquidated ghettos were cleared, and then they too went to their deaths. Their choices can in no way be compared to those of Polish officers who, throughout the occupation, retained agency and had a distinct ability to shape their own fates.

This kind of argument in its purest form can be found in the official position of the Polish authorities responsible for the state-approved interpretation of history. The communiqué of the Institute of National Remembrance (IPN) reads as follows:

> Exercising ruthless rule inside and outside the ghettos, the German Reich looked for various groups within the population that, in exchange for special treatment, would become tools used in the implementation of its criminal orders. It found such collaborators both among the Poles

> outside the ghettos and among the Jews in the ghettos. In the ghetto reality created by the Germans, some of the latter wanted to save their lives and those of their families that way. For its own purposes, the German Reich established new German police formations consisting of Poles (the "Blue" Police), and in the ghettos—consisting of Jews (Jüdischer Ordnungsdienst). Like any totalitarian state, the German Reich made extensive use of informers and collaborators. It protected those who, through denunciation and loyalty to the imposed German laws, indulged their criminal instincts, wanted to take advantage of an opportunity to acquire material goods, or saw a chance of survival.[15]

What more can be added? Here are the Poles, there are the Jews, above them the German terror, the same dilemmas, the same dramas, and the same choices—so claims the message of the institution charged by the Polish state with the supervision of Polish memory. For researchers of Holocaust history, this is an unacceptable position. From here, it is only a step toward claiming that things were not so bad for the Jews during the occupation because the Germans allowed them to set up the Jewish Councils, or "Jewish self-governments," as recently put by the head of the Office of Education at the Lublin IPN.[16] Can victims be made co-responsible for their own deaths? Apparently so. Going back to the quoted statement, can we compare the dilemmas of Jews condemned to death with the choices of officers of the uniformed police? Is it possible to suggest that the fates of Poles and Jews under the occupation were similar, that the threats faced by both nations were comparable? I hope that readers of this book agree that such

15 See "Zbrodniczy wymiar okupacji niemieckiej na ziemiach polskich 1939–1945: Stanowisko IPN," Instytut Pamięci Narodowej, February 19, 2018, https://ipn.gov.pl/pl/dla-mediow/komunikaty/47461,Zbrodniczy-wymiar-okupacji-niemieckiej-na-ziemiach-polskich-19391945-Stanowisko-.html (accessed September 2019).

16 "Historyk z IPN: hitlerowcy dali Żydom samorządy, A Polakom nie," https://strajk.eu/historyk-z-ipn-hitlerowcy-dali-zydom-samorzady-a-polakom-nie/ (accessed December 2023).

comparisons are fundamentally unjustified. Placing murderers and their Jewish victims on the same footing is a form of falsification of Holocaust history that Holocaust scholars have dubbed Holocaust equivalence. After all, one must not forget that on the one hand we have a nation that survived the war and which at no point during the occupation faced total physical extermination, and on the other, a nation of Polish Jews who ceased to exist as a community with its own language, customs, history, and traditions.

Monument to commemorate the Polish Blue policemen on the grounds of the former Płaszów concentration camp.
Courtesy of Dagmara Swałtek-Niewińska.

Then there is a third, most radical, attitude toward the history of the Blue Police. It may be called an affirmative approach. This position is well illustrated by the following statement:

> We are glad that we have lived to see the moment when we can restore the good name of the "Blue" policemen. We remove

> the blank spot on the "Blue" policemen's record of service, infusing it with their heroic deeds and ample evidence of fight against the occupier in the underground structures of Polish resistance. Today, we restore their memory by paying homage to them.[17]

This is an excerpt from a speech given by the chairwoman of the Kraków branch of the national association Rodzina Policyjna 1939 (Police Family 1939) on November 13, 2012, during the ceremony of the unveiling of an obelisk commemorating the Blue policemen who were executed by the Germans in the fall of 1943. There is no doubt that Blue policemen who died serving the cause of Polish independence can and should be commemorated, as can be seen in this volume with the discussion of the tragic history of the policemen in Kraków. When it comes to commemoration, however, the exact location where the commemoration is held plays an enormous role. Increasingly often in Poland, the sites are chosen in such a way as to challenge a contending or alien historical narrative. Examples of this include the Karski bench and the Irena Sendler alley near the POLIN Museum of the History of Polish Jews in Warsaw, or the Sendler Square strategically located on Planty Street in Kielce. Irena Sendler, the courageous Polish woman who devoted her life to saving Jewish children had no connection to Kielce during the war, but it was decided that a square named after her would have an alleviating effect on the memory of the pogrom that began in that very place.

Returning to the monument to the heroic Blue policemen, the obelisk could have been placed in front of the police headquarters in Kraków or in front of any of the over 120 churches in Kraków. However, it was placed on the grounds of the Płaszów concentration camp, a place where in 1943, some of the patriotic Blue policemen were executed by the Germans. A place that until now has been

17 "Pomnik Granatowych Policjantów rozstrzelanych przez Niemców," Świętokrzyskie Stowarzyszenie Rodzina Policyjna 1939 r. w Kielcach, https://osrp-swietokrzyskie.policja.gov.pl/rp1/aktualnosci/3689,Pomnik-Granatowych-Policjantow-rozstrzelanych-przez-Niemcow.html?search=683241511 (accessed September 2019).

identified primarily—if not exclusively—with the martyrdom of the victims of the Holocaust, with the 10,000 Jews who died in the Płaszów camp. Placing a monument there was a symbolic gesture that both paid homage to the murdered policemen and re-appropriated the site of the camp for the purposes of Polish memory and Polish martyrdom.

As can be seen from these few examples, the history of the Blue Police is not a closed chapter. On the contrary, the fate of the policemen under occupation has returned as one of the elements of the struggle for memory and historical myths on which Polish history politics is based. It is characteristic that the crimes committed by the Blue policemen against other Poles do not provoke such emotions anymore: After all, as one may think, these are "internal Polish matters" that only Poles care about. It is completely different in the case of the history of the Holocaust, the only part of Polish history that has universal significance and sparks interest around the world. It is also the only part of Polish history over which Polish authorities have absolutely no control, hence the anxious, often aggressive actions such as the Polish Holocaust Law of 2018, which time and again astonish the international public. However, it so happens that the Blue Police had an important role to play in the murder of Polish Jews and thus entered the field of interest of Holocaust researchers. Furthermore, the Blue Police were an essential, sometimes indispensable, element of the German strategy for the extermination of European Jews. In addition, Polish policemen often murdered Jews on their own, showing great initiative. It is only regrettable that in the dispute over Polish innocence, few people remember the tens or hundreds of thousands of Jewish victims of the Blue Police, people who could have been saved, people who had a decent chance of surviving the war, people whose memory Emanuel Ringelblum unsuccessfully tried to preserve.

APPENDICES

Administrative Police Structures in the Generalgouvernement

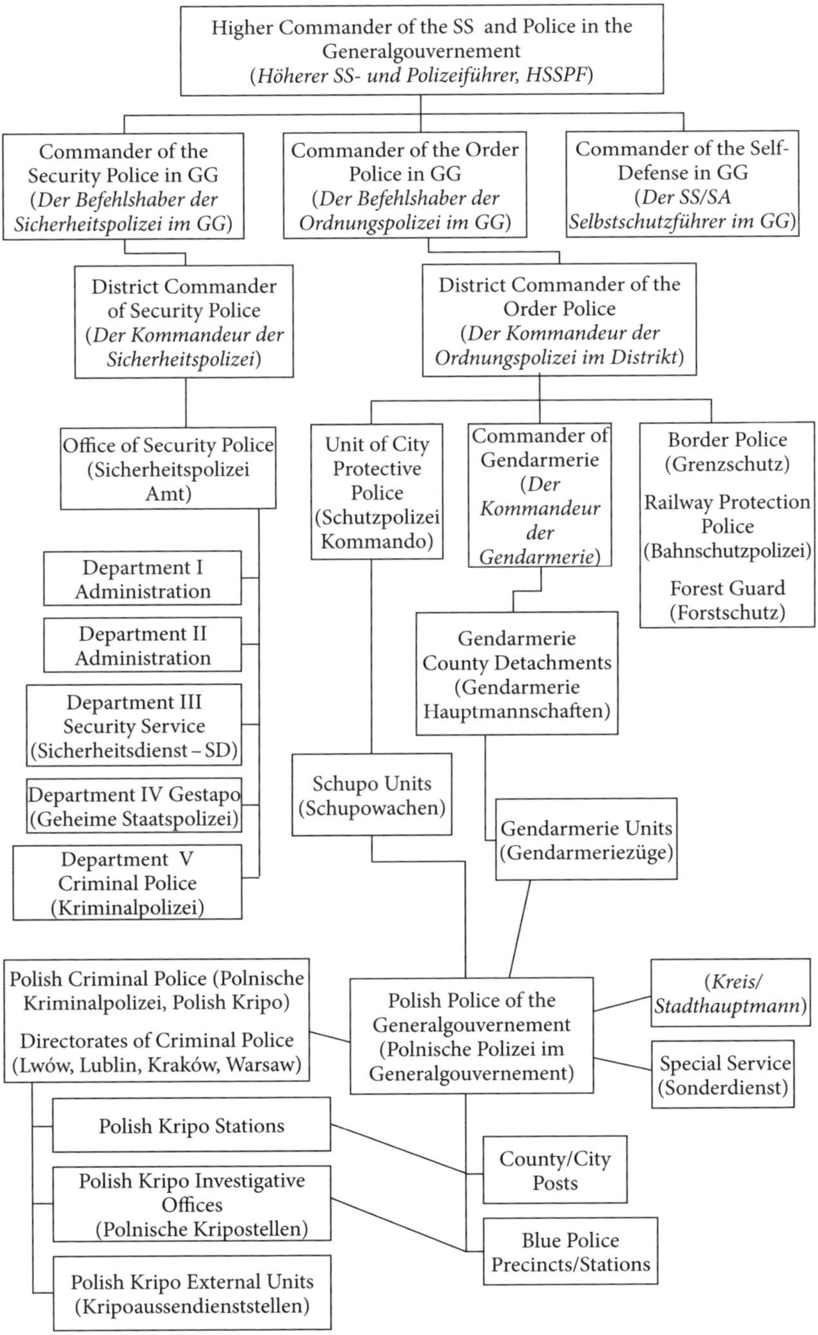

File 301/4660: Anonymous Testimony about the Inhabitants of the Lublin Province Guilty of Collaboration with the Germans and Murdering Jews[1]

Aleksander Lipiński—from Osiny Górne, Skupie Commune—murdered Jews and Russians.

Skóra—from the village of Dziegietnia near Sokołów Podlaski. He had eight Jews hiding in his house. One evening a boy who was a member of this group came out of the barn to look for food. During his absence, Skóra and an acquaintance of his murdered the seven remaining Jews. When the boy returned to the barnyard, Skóra invited him into the house, treated him to vodka and snacks, and when the boy entered the barn, one of the bandits slammed him on the head with the thick end of an axe, and the boy fell. The bandit thought the boy was dead, so he said to his friend: "He is already dead, take...with...let's harness the horse and cart them away." When they both went out to harness the horse, the boy escaped from the barn. He is still alive to this day.

There was a former village leader named Księżepolski from the village of Dmochy-Mingosy, Skupie Commune. At his place there were three Jews: two men and one woman. The village leader gathered fifteen men armed with police weapons, and they surrounded the place where the Jews were staying. One of them, Avram Ajnemer, was immediately shot dead. They also killed Aron Ajnemer, and Henia Ajnemer, who said she would point out the place in the forest where the money was buried, was led by one of the bandits to be shot. The woman managed to get away from him and fled. The bullets shot from the automatic machine did not reach her. She is alive.

Stefan Zając, from the village of Przywory Duże, Domanice Commune, Siedlce County, is now a militiaman in Domanice. His

1 Testimonies relating to the murders in which Blue policemen were involved, 1942–1944, ŻIH, 301/4660.

associates: Wyrębek Kazik; A. Gajowy aka Żak; Cabaj Zdzisław from Przywory; Mróz Stefan; Mróz Mundek from Przywory Małe; the two Bednarczyk brothers; Lutek from Przywory Duże; Stanisław Akninski from Drupia, Skórzec Commune, Siedlce County. Stanisław Akninski, son of Lucjan, Ludwik Czarnacki, Jan Wiancek from Drupia—all those listed are members of the same gang. Stanisław Wiendza from Drupia—[is] also [one] of them. And one of them—Żak—was an overt Gestapo agent. They all trained their dogs to look for hiding places where Jews, Russians were staying. They also eliminated Polish partisans or handed them over to the Gestapo. They searched the forests of Wiśniew, Jagodne, Drupia. They organized ambushes. On one occasion, they shot two Jews in the Wiśniew Forest, Szlojma Gutowski and Aszer Tuchczer who came from Siedlce. The gang, headed by Zając, found a hiding place with the Russians in the Wiśniew Forest. They sent gendarmes there who killed those hiding. Three Russians were killed on the spot and another one escaped and died alone from his wounds. The same gang made an ambush in the Drupia Forest where Jankiel Gażelinski and Cywia Gażelinski were shot dead, and Elia Gażelinski was wounded in the left leg. He is alive...

Cabaj and Wyrębek caught a Jew—Federman Lajzer—tied him to a tree and beat him with logs until he died. This happened near the alder wood, close to the village of Przywory Małe.

Stefan Zając used to capture Jews and Russians and deliver them to the police. Once he caught some Jews and took them there, but since the Polish police did not want to kill them, Zając did it himself. He was assisted by Stefan Mróz. Those killed were: Naftali Gażelinski; Chaja-Sara Gażelinska; Izrael Gażelinski. In total, about forty Jews were murdered at that time. The [witness?] does not know the names of all those killed.

From the same gang: Stanisław Akninski from Drupia. He reported on Jews and Polish workers to the Gestapo. There were Jews and Poles working in the manor in Drupia. Akninski reported everything he heard about the Polish laborers: that they were stealing and working poorly. Because of him, Polish men and women were sent to labor in Germany. These included: Sadowski Roman and the two Gizak brothers—one of them called Wacek from Drupia, the woman Skłodowska Kazia from Drupia. Akninski threatened the Polish poor. He also handed over Zylbersztejn Szolem to the Gestapo. Zylbersztejn Szolem is alive...

Akninski also reported to the Gestapo on a Pole, Witold Kordaszewicz from Drupia. He was interrogated there until he fell seriously sick and died. At the Gestapo, Elia Gażelinski's naked body was beaten for three hours without a break until he passed out; his hair was pulled out of his head. Szloma Zylbersztejn was also beaten at the Gestapo. All this was because of Akninski. Zofia from Drupia, the wife of the peasant Kordyszewicz, whom Akninski handed over to the Gestapo, is alive. She may be a witness. Elia Gażlinski will also testify. Akninski also handed over to the Gestapo Woźniak from Wólka Wisniewska, Wiśniew Commune, Siedlce County.

On the same day, March 10, 1942, Stanisław Mendże and his father Julian Mendże of Drupia, Zając's gang—Cabaj, Czarnacki, Wiandek, Wyrębek, Akninski Stanisław, "Żak"[?], Stefan Mróz—together with the police found the hiding place of eleven Jews, men and women, threw grenades and poured gasoline on it. Lejbl Frejman, a Jew from Węgrów, tried to save himself by escaping, but they shot him. They were all burned alive. The same gang in the Stany Colony surrounded the house of the farmer Strzelinski from Stany and threw grenades there. Three Russian partisans who were in the house died. This happened at night. The next day, in the morning, this gang came again and set fire to Strzelinski's house.

The house burned down along with a badly wounded partisan. Eight days later, the same bandits, together with the Germans, carried out a raid in the forest and shot Strzelinski, a farmer, and his wife. [The] Strzelinskis' son and daughter—two small children orphaned as a result of the bandits' actions—are alive because they were not in the forest at the time. The manhunt took place on November 8, 1943, in the Stany Forest (Stany, Skórzec Commune,

Siedlce County). These two little orphans know exactly who is to blame for the deaths of their parents, brothers, and sisters. The story is told by Elia Gażelinski of Drupia. His relative Gażelinski Josef was also shot during this manhunt. Srul Cudakiewicz and Rywka Gażelinska were also killed then.

On September 16, 1943, the same gang led a raid in the Burekta [Borekta?] Forest near Drupie. At the head of the gang—bandit Stanisław Akninski, son of Franciszek.... During this raid those murdered were: Frejman; Cytrynbojm; Zylbersztejn Zlata; and five Russian prisoners. Elia Gażelinski saw all this and how the gang prepared for the raid and how they positioned themselves. He saw where the bandits kept their weapons.

Kiszelinski Zygmunt from Tymianki, Niwiski Commune, collaborated with the Germans. The Home Army set a reward for killing Kiszelinski, who had many Polish partisans on his conscience. It was in 1943. Kiszelinski shot one of the partisans who was a lieutenant. Between Chojeczne and Gałki, he also shot three Jewish families that came from Geszki[?].

Felek Faciski, Męczyn Colony, Skupie Commune. A Russian prisoner of war lived and worked at his place for a piece of bread. Once, a friend came to visit the Russian, and then Felek Faciski broke his arms and legs, threw him into the granary, and sent for the police. He was shot in a meadow in the spring of 1943, while the laborer and four more Russians were shot in the fall of 1943 across from his cottage in Tadeusz Sikorski's meadow.

Stanisław Kurabiak was a policeman with the Germans. He murdered both Jews and Russians. He murdered the Jew Motl Feferkranc in Wólka Proszewska in Wiśniew Commune, and it was witnessed by Szalwar from Wólka Proszewska. The story goes like this: When Szalwar saw a policeman coming, he warned two Jews about it. One of them, Chaim Mordechaj Piaskowski, hid in Szalwar's shed, whereas the other, Motl Feferkranc, got nervous and ran out onto the road. As he ran away, Kurabiak shot him, pulled out his gold teeth, and removed the corpse's boots from his feet. Kurabiak and other policemen from Skupie went to the railroad tracks and murdered all the Jews who had saved themselves by jumping off the trains to Treblinka. In short, Kurabiak and his gang murdered almost 100 Jews. In a hiding place near the village of Zaliwie Szlacheckie, Niwiski Commune, there were seven [*sic*] Jewish women: Naska Góra, Naska Goldfarb, Szajndla Piaskowska with her eighteen-year-old daughter, Dwojra Feferkranc with her seven-year-old child, a girl. Together with Kurabiak Stanisław, the policemen Skanecki, Zimnacha, and Wichalak came, rallied peasants with axes and pitchforks, surrounded the hiding place, took out the Jewish women and brought them to the jail in Mokobody. They stayed there all day. The next day the men took them, led them to the cemetery and shot them. Two women with children did not want to leave the jail, so they were killed on site. The bodies were taken outside the town on a wheelbarrow by Andrzej Gajowniczek from Mokobody and by Zwoliński Józef. They were buried there as well. The latter two could be witnesses in this case. In Osiny Górne, Skupie Commune, Stanisław Wojewódzki and the son of Jastrzębski from Osiny Górne caught Dawid Rużawa-Kwiata and his daughter, tied them up, and took them to the police station in Mokobody, where the police shot them. Józef Zwoliński buried them. His payment was the clothes he could take off the dead. It was in March 1943...

In December 1944 in the hamlet of Zaliwie Szlacheckie, Niwiski Commune, Juda Widenbojm from Mokobody, his brother Berko Widenbojm, sister Sara with her fiancé, the miller's son from Kaluszyn, all stayed in a hideout in Lowiecki's farm. Skanecki Heniek, a policeman from Mokobody, found the hideout of the abovementioned Jews. Dzidek Domański together with Skanecki shot the hidden Jews. One of them, Jehuda Lejb, was shot twelve times. There was also one boy from Treblinka. Jehuda Lejb had rabbinical authority. During his stay in the hideout, he ate only kosher, he ate only sweet things.

Józef Babrik from the Smolaki Colony, Skupie Commune. His father-in-law's name was Rybowski. Rywka Sadownik from Mokobody and her fiancé, the tailor Josl, and a six-year-old boy who had escaped from Treblinka and whose name was Abram Kasten [Kosten?], sold something to Józef Babrik. Babrik told them to come for the money in a few days. When the three of them came to collect the debt, the peasant, upon meeting them outside, told them not to enter because there were strangers there. He told them to go into the cellar next to his house.

Little Abramek did not enter the cellar but hid in the bushes. From a distance he saw the peasant looking for him and heard him say in Polish: "Where the hell did he go?" Abramek understood that it was not good, so he hid deeper in the bushes, and from a distance, he saw the peasant close the cellar where the Jews were and ride his bicycle to Bielany. He brought the Bielany police who dragged the Jews out of the cellar and shot them in the forest on Babrik's land. The child saw how the peasant Babrik and his father-in-law stripped the Jews of their clothes and buried their bodies in the forest.... Abramek told this story to everybody who he has met: Christians and Jews. He came to us, in the hamlet of Niemenczyn, at Góra's place. Motl Goldfarb from Mokobody left things with Babrik. Motel Goldfarb's grandson Jankiel Rydel (who survived the war) went to Babrik after the liberation to claim the things belonging to his grandfather. Babrik told him: "If you keep asking for these things, you will die." Jankiel told us immediately about it.

He asked Abram Rzepa from Mokobody and Mosze Mendel Góra from Mokobody whether he should take these items away because he was threatened with death. Mosze Mendl told him to leave these things behind. Despite this, on March 9, 1945, Goldfarb's grandson was murdered in Mokobody. Stanisław Dydamski, Osiny Dolne Commune. Judl Solarz and his brother Mordka were hiding at this place. There also was a deportee by the name of Wróbel. Dydamski went to fetch the gendarmes, and they were all shot in the middle of the day. November 1943.

Janek Gąsiorek and his brother Franek from Mokobody took under their roof a Jewish tailor and his fiancée Sara Groszek. For two weeks, the Jews were working for them, and then the Gąsioreks called policeman Michalak from Mokobody, and he killed the Jews. That's how their work has been rewarded.

Adaś Grzymowski, Heniek Ostaś, and Heniek Lewicki from Kapuściaki. Adaś on the horseback, Lewicki, and Tadek Gałecki with a whole posse chased after three Jews who had fled the police arrests in Mokobody: Herszl Rużawa and his brother and one more unknown fellow who had fled the train destined for Treblinka. The posse caught these three Jews, beat them up, and delivered them to the Polish police, who shot them. They were killed in Olek Talach's field, and he buried them (he can be the witness). December 1942.

Zygmunt Fifa from Zaliw Szlachecki, Niwiski Commune, with his friend, February 10, 1943. Two boys from Kalisz, aged twelve and thirteen, used to sleep in a barn with hay. When the weather was poor, the boys stayed in the barn. Zygmunt Fifa with his friend went to the Mokobody police and reported that two Jewish boys are hiding at the farm of peasant Stansław Jański. The police arrived with the cart driver Bolek Król from Mokobody. When the police arrived, Zygmunt Fifa left his smithy, and together with his friend, they guarded the barn so that the children could not leave it. One of them managed to escape. They pursued the boy for 3 kilometers, and once he sagged, the policeman Wasikiewicz shot him.

Marcel Dymański from the hamlet of Ostrożany, Mokobody, living close to the Liwiec Bridge in the Skupie Commune. There were five Russian POWs in his orchard. One of them, Arik, was a doctor, another one, Aleksy, was a lieutenant, and there were three more. Sokół Damian from Ostrożany, Dymański's neighbor, reported them to the police in Mokobody. Karbik Stach, Heniek Skanecki, and Maszukiewicz killed the five Russians one morning in September 1943. At the same time as these five Russians were being murdered, the peasants denounced a Jew who had been strolling on that side of the Liwiec [River], and the policemen shot him too. His name was Szmulek Kiwedarbiuk. His mother, brother, and sister live in America. Kiwedarbiuk was buried at the foot of the bridge, on the field of Heniek Giżański. The peasant Giżański, who buried Szmulek, is a decent man and does not plough close to the murdered Jew.

Abramek, lovely child, who escaped from Treblinka when he was six, since May 29, 1944, has hidden in the hamlet of Ostrożany, close to the Liwiec [River], Skupie Commune, Siedlce County. He was together with fifteen-year-old girl Dina Goldfarb and a boy called Szymon Gruszka, age fourteen. There was one more ten-year-old boy who had left earlier. So, they slept at Kazik Dymowski's place in the hamlet of Ostrożany. Mosze Goldfarg, the boy who survived and who now is in Munich, said that he saw the armed Czesław Kozieł, Czesław Popowski, armed too, Lutek Antoniak, armed, Damian Sokół from Ostróżany, Zygmunt Fifa from Zaliw, and some others whose names he did not know, entering Dymowski's house. They saw the sleeping children, [and] they took two sacks, filled them with stones, put the fifteen-year-old girl into one of the sacks, both boys into the other one, tied the sacks, and started to hit them with the rifle butts. Then, they shot their rifles at these sacks. It happened next to the Liwiec, so after the murder, they threw the sacks into the river.

Krasnodębski—Dziegietnia close to Sokołów. Toba Warszawska from Kisielany hid at his place, and that is where she was murdered by the peasant Krasnodębski. One needs to ask him where she [her body] is today. Toba's sister Sabina was hiding at the peasant Piotr Grabowski's place in the village of Kudelczyn, Bielany Commune, Sokołów County. In June 1943, the peasant Krasnobdębski came to Grabowski and asked whether Sabina is a Jewess too. Grabowski answered: "Don't tell anyone. One will stay with you, and the other one with me." Since then, both sisters have disappeared.

Czepelewicz from Sokołów with a girl were hiding in the village of Korabie, Kudelczyn Commune, Sokołów County. Initially, they stayed at Jan Dymowski's place, close to Sokołów. Jan Dymowski found them a place to stay with Janeczek from Korabie, and Czepelewicz had to pay him 60,000 zlotys for three months. On Friday, June 16, 1943, about 7 PM, Janeczek woke up Czepelewicz and told him: "Get up and run, a band has arrived." Czepelewicz stood up and left the room. As soon as he left, he was shot. The bullet wounded him seriously, and so he lay next to the house for four days. He had to chase away the dogs. He hoped for someone to help him, but from among the villagers, no one gave assistance. And so, he died. It had been later established that Janeczek sent for his brother who lived in the village of Świniary, Skupie Commune. Janeczek's brother shot Czepelewicz. The brothers later circulated news that a band had killed him. When Czepelewicz was shot, the girl from a print shop in Sokołów who stayed with him fled into the fields and hid there. The next day, she came back to Janeczek who told her to go back to hide again in the fields, because they are afraid. Janeczek repaired to Bielany to inform the police, and when one of the policemen arrived in Korabie, Janeczek pointed out where the girl was hiding, and the policeman shot her.

On May 26, 1944, three Jews who had escaped from Treblinka [Treblinka I labor camp] appeared near the villages of Paczuski, Sikory, Wiechetki, Sokołów County. The peasants with the help of the Bielany police surrounded the Jews and captured them. They first beat them until they bled and then told them they could go. When the Jews started to run away, the policemen threw grenades at them, and all that was left of the Jews were shreds of flesh. After the bloody job was done, the policemen approached their victims and were very pleased. They buried them in the village of Wiechetki. Wandering in the villages close to Sokołów, a Jewish woman met two children: a sixteen-year-old girl and a ten-year-old boy, and some other Jews. In the woods close to Wańtuchy, six other men and one Russian were hiding. On April 16, 1943, the peasants from the village brought the police from Bielany, and the policemen shot those in hiding. In the forest, in that place, there is a mound. The Russian survived the winter in Kosierady Forest. He was in the forest when the Jews brought him some straw and a bottle of milk. He died together with the Jews.

Three girls, sisters, one aged eighteen, the second one fifteen, and the youngest who was eight, were wandering around the villages. One played Polish songs on fiddles, and the other one sang together with her. That's how they made their living. Before the peasants learned that these were Jewish children, they treated them well because they were very impressed. One of the peasants from Krynice said that these must certainly be Jewish children, so the peasants... [text breaks off].

Wacek Halędzki in the village of Kukawki, Tarków Commune, Siedlce County. April 1943, At that time, there were Jews in this village: Warszawczyk Elie; Awram Warszawczyk; a woman Fajnzylber with three small children; Icchak Finkelsztejn; and Jankiel Smolarz. The aforementioned people stayed with Wacek Halendzki for three months, and then he drove us out. Two weeks later, he took the Fajnzylber woman with her children again. He arranged a hiding place for them in the bushes, not far from his house. Pinkus Grindland and Chane [Chaim?] from the village of Ostrowik and Elie Warszawczyk were also in the same hideout. Halędzki Wacek and a few more peasants raided that shelter with axes and other tools and killed everyone. And I escaped. The dead bodies are still in the same place now.

There was a manhunt for Jews in the woods in Stopki[?] Colony, Czuryły Commune, Siedlce County, on May 4, 1943. Eleven Jews and five Russians were murdered.

Wisakinski from this colony—a Jew [Federman] who managed to escape the manhunt came to his supposed friend Wisakinski Michał, asking him to give him a shirt to change into, as his was covered in blood due to a wound he had suffered. Instead of helping, Wisakinski summoned another peasant, Czerski from Stopki[?] Colony, and both beat Federman with pegs until they murdered him. Wisakinski paid an acquaintance for his help in murdering the Jew by giving him two trees. Federman Awram had his belongings at Wisakinski's house—clothes, grain, etc. Since Federman Awram from Siedlce was a grain trader and, at the same time, had a pass as a laborer, he collected debts from others and brought the grain to Wisakinski in the latter's wagon.... Małka Federman, Awram's sister, fled in another direction.

Szemanko. He lived until 1944, until the liberation of Poland, in Siedlce, [at] 2 Kosciuszko Street. He now lives in Białystok. During the German occupation, he was a policeman. During the liquidation of the labor camp, he shot Jews who worked there clearing the Liwiec River. He shot many Jews in the ghetto. In the ghetto, the tailor Srul saw, in 1942, how the militiaman Dawid Blausztejn[?] from Siedlce beat old Jews on the head with a riding crop. He treated Jews with cruelty. This is recounted by citizens of Siedlce who saw it.

Głuchowski Jan from Chlewiski, Zeliszew Commune, Siedlce County. He handed over five Russian partisans to the Germans. The Polish partisans wanted to kill Głuchowski, but the Jews urged them not to because he had a Jewish boy with him. Then he killed the boy anyway.

Franek Bednasiak from the Zeliszew Colony, Zeliszew Commune, Siedlce County handed over a Jewish family of five to the Gestapo. They were all shot dead.

Szastek Stanisław from Kotuń, who is said to have taken part in the murder of the Jew Chanelewicz in the fall of 1945. He is currently in the Wałbrzych prison. He needs to be brought to Siedlce and put in touch with the leadership of NSZ gangs such as [text missing].

Wasiak Stanisław from Kotuń, the leader of the gang, and Woznicki from Kotuń, mentioned in numerous records. It is suspected that he is hiding under another name as a clerk in the local administration. He is even said to be a *starost* in Siedlce. His wife is a teacher in Broszków. He lives with Mrs. Szykar in Broszków. The same Woźnicki questioned the peasants of Broszków about when Cesia Cegłowska, a Jewish woman, was returning to Broszków. He regretted that he had moved to Kotuń so late. If he had arrived in

Broszków a little earlier, not a single Jew would have left the town alive. Apparently he moved to Kotuń in 1945 (or to Broszków).

Also, Stefan Nowakowski from Kotuń is the leader and friend of the whole gang. An eighteen-year-old girl, Jadzia Pisarkówna from Broszków, who works at "Rolnik" and knows a lot about the whole gang, needs to be arrested. Mrs. Mechel—a mother of two children, as a clerk writes notes on a typewriter about the underground organization because she has no money to live on. Her husband died in Auschwitz, but she needs to be interrogated so she can talk about Woźnicki, this whole gang, the peasant from Broszków, and also the farmer from Siedlce.

Stanisław Wasiak from Kotuń, who belongs to the same gang, now lives in Zielona Góra, was the leader of this gang, [and] today he is gathering support for the Kotuń bandits who murdered Chanelewicz, a Jew from Kotuń or Broszków. The son of Jan Kruk, the former voit from the time of the German occupation, he is now in a military unit in Skierniewice as a second lieutenant. His name is Kazik Kruk. He rents a room. Also, his father Jan Kruk is a member of the NSZ gang.

Kendzer, a foreman in Broszków during the German days, is now a county official somewhere in the Poznań region. The following people can speak about Kendzer: Kiszelinski Rafał from Opole; Łukaszek; Niszcza; Kiszelinski from the village of Tymianki, Niwiski Commune, Siedlecki County; two Karczaniak brothers from Czarnowąż, Wyszków Commune, Węgrów County; Wiliński Józef, 8 Dimek [Dymek]; Tadeusz with his brother Waldek; Piotrkowski Józef; Dzik Jan from Wilczonek Colony, Bojmie Commune, Węgrów County; Lengas from Zagacz and Sabiek, son-in-law Fiuk from Zagacz, Sankowski, a blacksmith from Broszków station. Lakaszek's son-in-law lives in the Kotuń Colony next to the railroad tracks.... And Wojewodka with his son-in-law, from the Poliaki Colony, Bojmie Commune, Węgrów County.

The village elder from Poliaki saw how they murdered seven Jews from the village of Tymianki. They should all have weapons. They are currently working with the NSZ organization. Owszaniak Władysław from Pabianice Colony, Skupie Commune, Siedlce County. He delivered three Jews into the hands of the Gestapo. He transported them bound with a rope. Two Jews came to him—Srul Gwiazda and Josł Makowski—to collect a debt of 2,000 zlotys for a fox fur collar, and he killed them. Owszaniak took part in the murder of three Russians—one of them was a shoemaker, another a doctor, his name was Damen, and one more. Now Owszaniak is the leader of the NSZ gang.

The Karabon brothers from the village of Hołubla, Krześlin Commune, Siedlce County, Jecki Jakub, and a former Polish policeman with the German occupier—Zumak—and others. On one occasion, they carried out a raid on Jews in the field in the colony next to Hołubla. They attacked five Jews sleeping in the rye and started shooting at them. One of the Jews tried to escape, but Stanisław Karabon, who had brought a horse specifically for this bloody job, pursued the fleeing Jew and shot him. After completing this bloody task, the participants dropped in on their friend and said: "You can serve vodka, because we have already dealt with the problem. You won't have to give them bread anymore!" One day, Jecki Jakub from the village of Hołubla was traveling from the village of Bartków to Hołubla. On the way, he met a young Jewish boy. He tied him up like a ram led to the slaughter, put him on the wagon, and drove him to the Polish police, who were serving the occupier. Handing the boy over to the policemen, he said this: "Here you have a Jew. Take him away from me. He must be killed." Naturally, there was no persuading them, and they murdered him. This was not an isolated incident.

Translated from the Yiddish by Sara Arm and Agata Reibach

Bibliography

Archival Material

Yad Vashem Archives (YVA)

JM – Microfilm Collection
M.9 – The Jewish Historical Documentation Center (Simon Wiesenthal Collection)
M.10 – Ringelblum Archive ("Oneg Shabbat")
M.31 – Righteous Among the Nations
O.25 – M. Silberberg Collection about the Polish Government in Exile in London
O.3 – Collection of Testimonies
O.33 – Testimonies, Diaries, and Memoirs Collection

Archiwum Akt Nowych (Archive of Modern Records, AAN)

AK:
203-VIII-2; 203-X-68; 203-III-105; 203-III-108; 203-III-109; 203-III-110; 203-III-111; 203-III-112; 203-III-214; 203-III-115; 203-III-118; 203-III-119; 203-III-123; 203-III-124

Delegatura Rządu na Kraj (Government Delegation for Poland):
202-II-11; 202-II-23; 202-II-28; 202-II-29; 202-II-31; 202-II-36; 202-II-37; 202-II-44; 203-III-122

Ministerstwo Sprawiedliwości (Ministry of Justice):
1656

Rząd GG (Government of the Generalgouvernement):
111

Archiwum i Muzeum Pomorskie Armii Krajowej oraz Wojskowej Służby Polek (Archive of General Elżbieta Zawacka)
Renata G. Hamerska file

Archiwum Instytutu Pamięci Narodowej (Archive of the Institute of National Remembrance, AIPN)
BU 155/3098; BU 380/30; BU 688/194; BU 0255/327; BU 0330/236; BU 0423/3402; BU 0423/4447; BU 0423/4889; BU 0423/4902; BU 0423/4999; BU 0423/5006

GK 104/3; GK 104/4; GK 104/24; GK 164/2928; GK 164/3754; GK 196/336; GK 209/57; GK 209/250; GK 317/28; GK 317/100; GK 317/133; GK 317/134; GK 317/247; GK 317/248; GK 317/616; GK 318/126; GK 318/131; GK 318/134; GK 318/460; GK 318/505; GK 318/568; GK 453/465; GK 453/1291; GK 652/48, vol. 1; GK 656/1; GK 656/2; GK 656/3; GK 656/6; GK 658, vols. 1–52; GK 695/1; GK 695/2; GK 714/17; GK 714/19; GK 714/20

Gestapo-Zichenau

Archiwum Instytutu Pamięci Narodowej Oddział w Katowicach (Archive of the IPN in Katowice, AIPN Ka)
566/10

Archiwum Instytutu Pamięci Narodowej Oddział w Kielcach (Archive of the IPN in Kielce, AIPN Ki)
128/206; 128/207; 128/209; 128/210; 128/211; 128/212

Archiwum Instytutu Pamięci Narodowej Oddział w Krakowie (Archive of the IPN in Krakow, AIPN Kr)
010/3437; 075/1, vol. 41; 075/1, vol. 47; 502/3575

Archiwum Instytutu Pamięci Narodowej Oddział w Lublinie (Archive of the IPN in Lublin, AIPN Lu)
326/161; 328/20

Archiwum Instytutu Pamięci Narodowej Oddział w Rzeszowie (Archive of the IPN in Rzeszow, AIPN Rz)
353/113

Archiwum Narodowe w Krakowie (National Archive in Kraków, ANKr)
Sąd Apelacyjny w Krakowie (Appellate Court in Kraków) (SAKr)
Komenda Policji Polskiej w Krakowie (Polish Police Headquarters in Kraków)
Starosta Miasta Krakowa (Commissionary Mayor of Krakow) (SMKr)
Posterunek Policji Polskiej w Brzesku Nowym (Polish Police Post in Brzesko Nowe) (PPPBrzN)

Archiwum Państwowe Miasta Stołecznego Warszawy (Warsaw City Archive, AMSW)
Komenda Policji Polskiej "Obwod Praga" 1939–1944 (Polish Police Headquarters "Praga District" 1939–1944)
Starostwo Powiatowe Warszawskie (Warsaw County Office)
Burmistrz Komisaryczny m. Warszawy (Mayor Commissioner of the city of Warsaw)
Prokuratura przy Sądzie Specjalnym w Warszawie (Staatsanwaltschaft bei dem Sondergericht Warschau, SSW) (Prosecutor's Office at the Special Court in Warsaw)
Sąd Niemiecki (Deutsches Gericht) (German Court)
Sondergericht Warschau (Special Court, Warsaw)
II Komisariat PP
Amt des Gouverneurs des Distrikts Warschau, SS- und Polizeifuhrer fur den Distrikt Warschau, 1939–1944 (Office of the Governor of the Warsaw District, SS and Police Leader for the Warsaw District, 1939–1944)
Komenda Policji Polskiej Miasta Warszawy (Polish Police Headquarters of the City of Warsaw)

Archiwum Państwowe w Kielcach (State Archive in Kielce, AP Kielce)
Posterunek Policji Polskiej w Opocznie (Polish Police Post in Opoczno)

Archiwum Państwowe w Lublinie (State Archive in Lublin, AP Lublin)
Posterunek Policji Polskiej w Staninie (Polish Police Post in Stanin)

Bundesarchiv Berlin-Lichterfelde (Federal Archives Berlin-Lichterfelde)
SS- und Polizei Gericht VI, Krakau (SS and Police Court VI, Kraków)

Bundesarchiv Ludwigsburg (Federal Archives Ludwigsburg, BAL)
B162/2149; B162/2158; B162/3749

Derżawnyj Archiw Lwiwskoj Obłasti (State Archives of Lviv Oblast, DALO)
Sondergericht Lemberg (Special Court, Lemberg)

Ghetto Fighters' House Museum Archive (GFH)
Adolf Berman Collection

Instytut Zachodni (Institute for Western Affairs)
I-21

United States Holocaust Memorial Museum (USHMM)
RG 15.026 M; RG 15.174 M; RG 15.180 M; RG 15.207 M

USC Shoah Foundation Visual History Archive (VHA)
Interviews:
Sevek Fishman, 18608
Maria Wanda Gadomska, 26215
Hanną Gdalewicz-Nielsen, 7970
Alfred Górny, 22077
Łucja Jurczak, 36453
Władysław Iwaszczukiewicz (Adam Gelbard), 43591
Pola Kapłan, 27634
Paweł Koper, 12706
Zofia Kubicka, 37628

Helena Landsberg, 16637
Józefem Tkaczykie, 34989
Janina Żurawicka, 17885

Zentrale Stelle, Ludwigsburg (Central Office, Ludwigsberg)
211 AR-Z; 77/66 BI/a

Żydowski Instytut Historyczny (Jewish Historical Institute, ŻIH)
301 – Testimonies of survivors of the Holocaust
302 – Memoirs of survivors of the Holocaust
349 – Department of the Documentation of Awards for Yad Vashem 1979–2004
Ring – Oneg Shabbat Ringelblum Archive

Research Literature: Books and Articles

Ajenstat, Charles, *Hermann Höfle: L'Autrichien artisan de la Shoah en Pologne* (Paris: Berg, 2007).

Arendt, Hannah, *Eichmann in Jerusalem: A Report on the Banality of Evil* (London: Penguin, 2022).

Banaś, Franciszek, *Moje wspomnienia*, ed. by Michał Kalisz and Elżbieta Rączy (Rzeszów: Instytut Pamięci Narodowej, Komisja Ścigania Zbrodni przeciwko Narodowi Polskiemu, Oddział w Rzeszowie, 2009).

Bańkowska, Aleksandra, and Tadeusz Epsztein, eds., *Archiwum Ringelbluma: Konspiracyjne Archiwum Getta Warszawy, vol. 11, Ludzie i prace "Oneg Szabat"* (Warsaw: Wydawnictwa Uniwersytetu Warszawskiego, 2013).

Bartoszewski, Władysław, *1859 dni Warszawy* (Kraków: Znak, 1974).

Bergholz, Max, *Violence as a Generative Force: Identity, Nationalism, and Memory in a Balkan Community* (Ithaca: Cornell University Press, 2016).

Berlière, Jean-Marc, *Les Policiers français sous l'Occupation: D'après les archives inédites de l'épuration* (Paris: Perrin, 2001).

Bernatt-Reszczyński, Maciej, *Niewygodny Polak* (Poznań: Wydawnictwo Poznańskie, 2017).

Bielawski, Feivel Shraga, *The Last Jew from Wegrow* (New York: Praeger, 1991).

Biernacki, Stanisław, *Okupant a polski ruch oporu: Władze hitlerowskie w walce z ruchem oporu w dystrykcie warszawskim 1939–1944* (Warsaw: Glowna Komisja, 1989).

______, "Organizacja i metody działania policji hitlerowskiej w dystrykcie warszawskim," in *Stan i perspektywy badań w zakresie zbrodni hitlerowskich: Materiały z konferencji naukowej w dn. 27–28 kwietnia 1970*, vol. 1 (Warsaw, 1973).

Biernacki, Stanisław, and Jerzy Stoch, "Działania władz okupacyjnych (policji i administracji) w dystrykcie warszawskim przeciwko ruchowi oporu w latach 1939–1944," *Najnowsze dzieje Polski: Materiały i studia z okresu II wojny światowej*, 10 (1966), pp. 47–76.

Black, Peter, "Indigenous Collaboration in the Government General: The Case of the Sonderdienst," in Pieter M. Judson and Marsha L. Rozenblit, eds., *Constructing Nationalities in East Central Europe* (New York: Berghahn Books, 2005).

Böhler, Jochen, Klaus-Michael Mallmann, and Jürgen Matthäus, *Einsatzgruppen w Polsce* (Warsaw: Bellona, 2008).

Borodziej, Włodzimierz, *Terror i polityka: Policja niemiecka a polski ruch oporu w GG 1939–1944* (Warsaw: Instytut Wydawniczy Pax, 1985).

Browning, Christopher R., *Ordinary Men: Reserve Police Battalion 101 and the Final Solution in Poland* (New York: Harper Perennial, 2017).

Bruttmann, Tal, *La logique des bourreaux: 1943–1944* (Paris: Hachette Litterature, 2003).

Büchler, Yehoshua R., "'Unworthy Behavior': The Case of SS Officer Max Täubner," *Holocaust and Genocide Studies*, 17:3 (2003), pp. 409–429.

Bühler, Josef, ed., *Das Generalgouvernement: Seine Verwaltung und seine Wirtschaft: Sammlung von Vorträgen der ersten wissenschaftlichen Vorträgsreihe der Verwaltungsakademie des Generagouvernements* (Krakow: Burgverl, 1943).

Bussgang, Fay, and Julian Bussgang, eds., and tr., *Działoszyce Memorial Book* (New York: Jewishgen.Inc, 2012).

Canin, Mordechaj, *Przez ruiny i zgliszcza: Podróż po stu zgładzonych gminach żydowskich w Polsce* (Warsaw: Nisza, 2019).

Cesarani, David, *Final Solution: The Fate of the Jews, 1933–1949* (New York: St. Martin's Press, 2016).

Chętnik, Adam, *Wspomnienia z lat okupacji* (Warsaw: Muzeum Historii Polskiego Ruchu Ludowego, 2014).

Ciałowicz, Anna, ed., *Archiwum Ringelbluma: Konspiracyjne Archiwum Getta Warszawy, vol. 32, Pisma Rabina Szymona Huberbanda* (Warsaw: Żydowski Instytut Historyczny im. Emanuela Ringelbluma, 2017).

Ciesielska, Maria, "Lekarze wykonujący operacje plastyczne i zabiegi likwidujące skutki obrzezania w Warszawie w czasie II wojny światowej," in Alicja Bartuś and Piotr Trojański, eds., *Cena odwagi: Między ocaleniem życia a ocaleniem człowieczeństwa* (Oświęcim: Fundacja na Rzecz MDSM, Wydawnictwo Naukowe Uniwersytetu Pedagogicznego im. Komisji Edukacji Narodowej, 2019), pp. 209–223.

Cukierman, Icchak ("Antek"), *Nadmiar pamięci (Siedem owych lat): Wspomnienia 1939–1946* (Warsaw: PWN, 2000).

Curilla, Wolfgang, *Der Judenmord in Polen und die Deutsche Ordnungspolizei 1939–1945* (Paderborn: Schöningh, 2011).

Czubaszek, Krzysztof, "Stanisław Żemis—świadek zagłady Żydów w Łukowie," *Zaglada Zydow Studia i Materiały*, 14 (2018), pp. 279–311.

Dean, Martin, *Collaboration in the Holocaust: Crimes of the Local Police in Belorussia and Ukraine, 1941–44* (New York: St. Martin's Press, 2000).

______, "Jewish Survival in Forced Labor Camps for Jews: The Agricultural Camps in Czortków County of Eastern Galicia, 1942–1944," in Alexandra Garbarini and Paul B. Jaskot, eds., *Lessons and Legacies, vol. XIII: New Approaches to an Integrated History of the Holocaust. Social History, Representation, Theory* (Evanston: Northwestern University Press, 2018).

Domańska, Regina, *Pawiak – więzienie gestapo: Kronika 1939–1944* (Warsaw: Książka i Wiedza, 1978).

Dreifuss, Havi (Ben-Sasson), *Relations between Jews and Poles during the Holocaust: The Jewish Perspective* (Jerusalem: Yad Vashem, 2017).

Dworzecki, Jacek, "Policja w Polsce we wrześniu 1939 roku," *Zeszyt Naukowy*, 4 (2010), pp. 75–88.

Dziurok, Adam, "23 lata, 6 miesięcy i 22 dni Salomona Morela," *Biuletyn Instytutu Pamięci Narodowej*, 6–7 (2004), pp. 42–45.

Engelking, Barbara, ed., *Sny chociaż mamy wspaniałe…Okupacyjne dzienniki Żydów z okolic Mińska Mazowieckiego* (Warsaw: Stowarzyszenie Centrum Badań nad Zagłada Żydów, 2016).

______, "*Szanowny panie gistapo!*": *Donosy do władz niemieckich w Warszawie i okolicach w latach 1940–1941* (Warsaw: IFiS PAN, 2003).

Engelking, Barbara, and Jan Grabowski, eds., *Dalej jest noc: Losy Żydów w wybranych powiatach okupowanej Polski*, vols. 1 and 2 (Warsaw: Stowarzyszenie Centrum Badań nad Zagładą Żydów, 2018).

Engelking, Barbara, and Jacek Leociak, *The Warsaw Ghetto: A Guide to the Perished City* (New Haven: Yale University Press, 2008).

Finder, Gabriel N., and Alexander V. Prusin, "Collaboration in Eastern Galicia: The Ukrainian Police and the Holocaust," *East European Jewish Affairs*, 34:2 (2004), pp. 95–118.

Fligelman, Daniel, "Diary, May 28–June 22, 1942," in Katarzyna Person, ed., *Archiwum Ringelbluma: Konspiracyjne Archiwum Getta Warszawy, vol. 5, Getto warszawskie: życie codzienne* (Warsaw: Żydowski Instytut Historyczny im. Emanuela Ringelbluma and DiG, 2011).

Forecki, Piotr, *Po Jedwabnem: Anatomia pamięci funkcjonalnej* (Warsaw: IBL, 2018).

Getter, Marek, "Policja granatowa w Warszawie 1939–1944," in Krzysztof Dunin-Wąsowicz et al., *Warszawa lat wojny i okupacji, 1939–1944*, vol. 2 (Warsaw: Państwowe Wydawn. Naukowe, 1972).

______, "Policja polska w Generalnym Gubernatorstwie 1939–1945," *Przegląd Policyjny*, 1–2 (1999), pp. 74–91.

Goldhagen, Daniel Jonah, *Hitler's Willing Executioners: Ordinary Germans and the Holocaust* (New York: Vintage, 1997).

Górski, Józef, "At the Turn of History," ed. by Jan Grabowski, *Holocaust Studies and Materials: Journal of the Polish Center for Holocaust Research* (2008), pp. 300–312.

Gozdawa-Gołębiowski, Jan, "Powiat Węgrowski w latach okupacji hitlerowskiej 1939–1944," in Arkadiusz Kołodziejczyk and Tadeusz Swat, eds., *Węgrów: Dzieje miasta i okolic w latach 1441–1944* (Węgrów: Towarzystwo Miłośników Ziemi Węgrowskiej, 1991).

Grabowski, Jan, "German Anti-Jewish Propaganda in the

General-gouvernement, 1939–1945: Inciting Hate through Posters, Films, and Exhibitions," *Holocaust and Genocide Studies*, 23:3 (2009), pp. 381–412.

______, *Hunt for the Jews: Betrayal and Murder in German-Occupied Poland* (Bloomington: Indiana University Press, 2013).

______, *"Ja tego Żyda znam!": Szantażowanie Żydów w Warszawie 1939–1943* (Warsaw: IFiS PAN, 2004).

______, "Józef Górski, Na przełomie dziejów," *Zagłada Żydów, Studia i materiały*, 2 (2006), pp. 280–291.

______, *Judenjagd: Polowanie na Żydów 1942–1945: Studium dziejów pewnego powiatu* (Warsaw: Stowarzyszenie Centrum Badań nad Zagładą Żydów, 2011).

______, "Powiat węgrowski," in Barbara Engelking and Jan Grabowski, eds., *Dalej jest noc: Losy Żydów w wybranych powiatach okupowanej Polski*, vol. 1 (Warsaw: Stowarzyszenie Centrum Badań nad Zagładą Żydów, 2018).

______, "Rural Society and the Jews in Hiding: Elders, Night Watches, Firefighters, Hostages and Manhunts," *Yad Vashem Studies*, 40 (2012), pp. 49–74.

______, *Szczęście posiadać dom pod ziemią… Losy kobietocalałych z Zagłady w okolicach Dąbrowy Tarnowskiej* (Warsaw: Stowarzyszenie Centrum Badań nad Zagładą Żydów, 2016).

______, "Tropiąc Emanuela Ringelbluma: Udział polskiej Kriminalpolizei w 'ostatecznym rozwiązaniu kwestii żydowskiej,'" *Zagłada Żydów, Studia i materiały*, 10 (2014), pp. 27–56.

______, "Zarząd Powierniczy i nieruchomości żydowskie w Generalnym Gubernatorstwie: 'Co można skonfiskować? W zasadzie wszystko,'" in Jan Grabowski and Dariusz Libionka, eds., *Klucze i kasa: O mieniu żydowskim w Polsce pod okupacją niemiecką i we wczesnych latach powojennych 1939–1950* (Warsaw: Stowarzyszenie Centrum Badań nad Zagładą Żydów, 2014).

Grabowski, Jan, and Barbara Engelking, eds., *Night without End: The Fate of Jews in German-Occupied Poland* (Bloomington and Jerusalem: Indiana University Press and Yad Vashem, 2022).

Grabowski, Jan, and Dariusz Libionka, "Anatomia donosu księdza Stanisława Trzeciaka na księdza Tadeusza Pudra," *Zagłada Żydów, Studia i materiały*, 13 (2017), pp. 641–675.

______, "Bezdroża polityki historycznej: Wokół Markowej, czyli o czym nie mówi Muzeum Polaków Ratujących Żydów podczas II Wojny Światowej im. Rodziny Ulmów," *Zagłada Żydów, Studia i materiały*, 12 (2016), pp. 619–642.

______, "Distorting and Rewriting the History of the Holocaust in Poland: The Case of the Ulma Family Museum of Poles Saving Jews During World War II in Markowa," *Yad Vashem Studies*, 45:1 (2017), pp. 29–61.

______, "Meldunki Obwodu 'Praga' Policji Polskiej o zatrzymaniach Żydów w Warszawie w okresie maj–lipiec 1943 r.," *Zagłada Żydów, Studia i materiały*, 10 (2014), pp. 592–621.

Grabowski, Waldemar, *Polska tajna administracja cywilna 1940–1945* (Warsaw: Instytut Pamięci Narodowej, 2003).

Grabowski, Zbigniew Ryszard, *W skorodowanym zwierciadle pamięci* (Warsaw: Żydowski Instytut Historyczny im. Emanuela Ringelbluma, 2018).

Gross, Jan Tomasz, *Sąsiedzi i inni: Prace zebrane na temat Zagłady* (Kraków: Austeria, 2018).

Hanasz, Marian, "Sprawa Łakińskiego," in Marian Hanasz, ed., *Goldmanka: W kręgu szkoły* (Warsaw: Praca zbiorowa, 2005).

Hempel, Adam, *Pogrobowcy klęski: Rzecz o policji "granatowej" w Generalnym Gubernatorstwie 1939–1945* (Warsaw: Państwowe Wydawnictwo Naukowe, 1990).

Hilberg, Raul, *Sprawcy, ofiary, śiadkowie. Zagłda Żdó 1933–1945* (Warsaw: Centrum Badań nad Zagładą Żydów and Cyklady, 2007).

Himka, John-Paul, "Former Ukrainian Policemen in the Ukrainian National Insurgency: Continuing the Holocaust outside German Service," in Wendy Lower and Faulkner Rossi, eds., *Lessons and Legacies, vol. XII: New Directions in Holocaust Research and Education* (Evanston: Northwestern University Press, 2017).

______, "The Lviv Pogrom of 1941: The Germans, Ukrainian Nationalists, and the Carnival Crowd," *Canadian Slavonic Papers*, 53:2–4 (2011), pp. 209–243.

Hirszfeld, Ludwik, *Historia jednego życia* (Warsaw: Czytelnik, 1946).

Hochberg-Mariańska, Maria, and Mieczysław Mariański, *Wśród przyjaciół i wrogów: Poza gettem w okupowanym Krakowie* (Kraków: Wydawn. Literackie, 1988).

Janczewska, Marta, ed., *Archiwum Ringelbluma: Konspiracyjne Archiwum Getta Warszawy, vol. 12, Rada Żydowska w Warszawie (1939–1943)* (Warsaw: Wydawnictwa Uniwersytetu Warszawskiego and Żydowski Instytut Historyczny im. Emanuela Ringelbluma, 2014).

Janicka, Elżbieta, "Obserwatorzy uczestniczący zamiast świadków i rama zamiast obrzeży: O nowe kategorie opisu polskiego kontekstu Zagłady," *Teksty Drugie*, 3 (2018), pp. 131–147.

Joly, Laurent, *L'Antisémitisme de bureau: Enquête au coeur de la préfecture de Police de Paris et du commissariat général aux Questions juives (1940–1944)* (Paris: Bernard Grasset, 2011).

Kaplan, Chaim A., *Scroll of Agony: The Warsaw Diary* (New York: Macmillan, 1965).

Kassow, Samuel D., *Who Will Write Our History? Emanuel Ringelblum, the Warsaw Ghetto, and the Oyneg Shabes Archive* (Bloomington: Indiana University Press, 2007).

Klemp, Stefan, *Vernichtung—Die deutsche Ordnungspolizei und der Judenmord im Warschauer Ghetto 1940–43* (Berlin: Prospero, 2013).

Königsberg, Wojciech, *AK 75: Brawurowe Akcje Armii Krajowej* (Kraków: Znak Horyzont, 2017).

Kornbluth, William, *Sentenced to Remember: My Legacy of Life in Pre-1939 Poland and Sixty-Eight Months of Nazi Occupation* (Bethlehem, PA: Lehigh University Press, 1994).

Krasnodębski, Tadeusz Stefan, *Policjant konspiratorem: Szesnaście lat na muszce Gestapo i bezpieki* (Kraków and Międzyzdroje: Przedsięwzięcie Galicja and Wydawn. Arkadiusz Wingert, 2008).

Kubalski, Edward, *Niemcy w Krakowie: Dziennik 1 IX 1939–18 I 1945*, ed. by Jan Grabowski and Zbigniew R. Grabowski (Kraków and Budapest: Austeria, 2010).

Landau, Ludwik, *Kronika lat wojny i okupacji*, vols. 1–3 (Warsaw: Państowe Wydawnictwo Naukowe, 1962–1963).

Lasman, Noach, *Wspomnienia z trzech światów*, ed. by Andrzej Niziołek (Poznań: Wydawnictwo Miejskie Posnania, 2018).

Lewin, Abraham, *A Cup of Tears: A Diary of the Warsaw Ghetto*, ed. by Antony Polonsky (Oxford: Basil Blackwell and the Institute of Polish-Jewish Studies, 1988).

Libionka, Dariusz, ed., *Akcja Reinhardt: Zagłada Żydów w Generalnym Gubernatorstwie* (Warsaw: Instytut Pamięci Narodowej, 2004).

______, "Polska konspiracja wobec eksterminacji Żdó w dystrykcie warszawskim," in Barbara Engelking, Jacek Leociak, and Dariusz Libionka, eds., *Prowincja noc: Żcie i zagłda Żdó w dystrykcie warszawskim* (Warsaw: IFiS PAN, 2007).

______, "Polska Podziemna wobec szantażystów i szmalcowników w Warszawie: Korekta obrazu," *Zagłada Żydów, Studia i materiały*, 14 (2018), pp. 115–164.

______, "Powiat miechowski," in Barbara Engelking and Jan Grabowski, eds., *Dalej jest noc: Losy Żydow w wybranych powiatach okupowanej Polski*, vol. 2 (Warsaw: Stowarzyszenie Centrum Badań nad Zagładą Żydów, 2018), pp. 64–108.

______, "Zapisy dotyczące Żydów w warszawskich kronikach policyjnych z lat 1942–1944," *Zagłada Żydów, Studia i materiały*, 10 (2014), pp. 592–621.

Libionka, Dariusz, and Laurence Weinbaum, *Bohaterowie, hochsztaplerzy, opisywacze: Wokoł Żydowskiego Związku Wojskowego* (Warsaw: Stowarzyszenie Centrum Badań nad Zagładą Żydow, 2011).

Litwiński, Robert, "Komisja rehabilitacyjno-kwalifikacyjna dla byłych policjantów (1945–1952)," *Dzieje Najnowsze*, 1 (2004), pp. 117–134.

______, *Korpus policji w II Rzeczpospolitej. Służba i życie prywatne* (Lublin: UMCS, 2007).

______, "Policja granatowa w okupacyjnej Warszawie w obronie bezpieczeństwa i porządku publicznego: Od podległości wobec okupanta do współpracyz Polskim Państwem Podziemnym," in Robert Spałek, ed., *Porządek publiczny i bezpieczeństwo w okupacyjnej Warszawie* (Warsaw: IPN, 2018).

Mączyński, Marek, "Polskie formacje policyjne w stolicy Generalnego Gubernatorstwa 1939–1945," *Rocznik Krakowski*, 59 (1993), pp. 153–160.

Madajczyk, Czesław, *Polityka III Rzeszy w okupowanej Polsce*, vol. 1 (Warsaw: Państwowe Wydaw. Naukowe, 1970).

Majer, Piotr, "Okupacyjne i powojenne losy polskich policjantów," *Przegląd Policyjny*, 1–2 (1990), pp. 101–120.

Majer, Piotr, and Andrzej Misiuk, eds., *Losy policjantów polskich po 1 września 1939* (Szczytno: Wydawnictwo Wyższa Szkoła Policji, 1996).

Makower, Henryk, *Pamiętnik z getta warszawskiego: Październik 1940–styczeń 1943* (Wrocław: Ossolineumm 1987).

Marat, Emil, and Michał Wójcik, *Made in Poland: Opowiada jeden z ostatnich żołnierzy Kedywu Stanisław Likierni* (Warsaw: Wielka Litera, 2014).

Margolis-Edelman, Alina, *Tego, co mówili, nie powtórzę…* (Wrocław: Siedmioróg, 1999).

Markiel, Tadeusz, and Alina Skibińska, *"Jakie to ma znaczenie, czy zrobili to z chciwości?": Zagłada domu Trynczerów* (Warsaw: Stowarzyszenie Centrum Badań nad Zagładą Żydów, 2011).

Marszalec, Janusz, "Morderstwo na Makowieckich i Widerszalu: Stara sprawa, nowe pytania, nowe wątpliwości," *Zagłada Żydów, Studia i materiały*, 2 (2006), pp. 23–53.

Marszałek, Józef, *Obozy pracy w Generalnym Gubernatorstwie w latach 1939–1945* (Lublin: Państwowe Muzeum na Majdanku, 1998).

Matusak, Piotr, *Straż pożarna* (Warsaw: Fundacja "Warszawa Walczy 1939–1945," 2014).

Megargee, Geoffrey P., ed., *The United States Holocaust Memorial Museum Encyclopedia of Camps and Ghettos, 1933–1945, vol. 2: Ghettos in German-Occupied Eastern Europe* (Bloomington: Indiana University Press, 2012).

Meier, Rudolf, *Soldaten-führer durch Warschau* (Warsaw: Deutsche Buchh, 1941).

Mick, Christoph, "Incompatible Experiences: Poles, Ukrainians and Jews in Lviv under Soviet and German Occupation, 1939–44," *Journal of Contemporary History*, 46:2 (2011), pp. 336–363.

Misiuk, Andrzej, *Policja Państwowa 1919–1939: Powstanie, organizacja, kierunki działania* (Warsaw: Wydawnictwo Naukowe PWN, 1996).

Misiuk, Andrzej, and Andrzej Pepłoński, eds., *Organizacja instytucji policyjnych w II Rzeczpospolitej 1918–1926: Wybor źrodeł i dokumentow* (Szczytno: Wyższej Szkoły Policji, 1992).

Najberg, Leon, *Ostatni powstańcy getta* (Warsaw: Żydowski Instytut Historyczny w Polsce, 1993).

Obremski, Tadeusz, *Wśród zatrutych noży: Zapiski z getta i okupowanej Warszawy*, ed. by Agnieszka Haska (Warsaw: Stowarzyszenie Centrum Badań nad Zagładą Żydów, 2017).

Opoczyński, Perec, "Dom numer 21," in Monika Polit, ed., *Reportaże z warszawskiego getta* (Warsaw: Stowarzyszenie Centrum Badań nad Zagładą Żydów, 2009).

______, "Księga parówki," in Monika Polit, ed., *Reportaże z warszawskiego getta* (Warsaw: Stowarzyszenie Centrum Badań nad Zagładą Żydów, 2009).

Pachter, Mietek, *Umierać też trzeba umieć…*, ed. by Barbara Engelking (Warsaw: Stowarzyszenie Centrum Badań nad Zagładą Żydów, 2015).

Pankiewicz, Tadeusz, *Apteka w getcie krakowskim* (Kraków: Wydawnictwo Literackie, 2017).

Panz, Karolina, "Powiat nowotarski," in Barbara Engelking and Jan Grabowski, eds., *Dalej jest noc: Losy Żydów w wybranych powiatach okupowanej Polski*, vol. 2 (Warsaw: Stowarzyszenie Centrum Badań nad Zagładą Żydów, 2018).

Perechodnik, Calel, *Am I a Murderer? Testament of a Jewish Ghetto Policeman,* ed. and trans. by Frank Fox (Boulder: Westview Press, 1996).

Person, Katarzyna, *Assimilated Jews in the Warsaw Ghetto, 1940–1943* (New York: Syracuse University Press, 2014).

______, *Policjanci: Wizerunek Żydowskiej Służby Porządkowej w getcie warszawskim* (Warsaw: Zydowski Instytut Historyczny im. Emanuela Ringelbluma, 2018).

Piątkowski, Sebastian, "Mięzy obowiązkiem a kolaboracją Policja 'granatowa' w dystrykcie radomskim w latach 1939–1945," in Edyta Majcher-Ociesa, ed., *Z dziejów policji polskiej w latach 1919–1945* (Kielce: KTN, 2010).

______, "Oprawcy, prześladowcy, ratownicy: Problematyka Zagłady w aktach radomskiej ekspozytury Prokuratora Specjalnego Sądu Karnego w Lublinie," *Zagłada Żydów, Studia i materiały*, 4 (2008), pp. 484–498.

Piotrowski, Stanisław, ed., *Dziennik Hansa Franka* (Warsaw: Wydawnictwo prawnicze, 1956).

Pohl, Dieter, "Znaczenie dystryktu lubelskiego w 'ostatecznym rozwiązaniu kwestii żydowskiej,'" in Dariusz Libionka, ed., *Akcja Reinhardt: Zagłada Żydów w Generalnym Gubernatorstwie* (Warsaw: Instytut Pamięci Narodowej, 2004).

Ringelblum, Emanuel, *Kronika getta warszawskiego: Wrzesień 1939–styczeń 1943* (Warsaw: Czytelnik, 1983).

______, *Polish-Jewish Relations during the Second World War* (Evanston: Northwestern University Press, 1992).

Rotem, Simcha ("Kazik"), *Wspomnienia bojowca ŻOB*, ed. by Iwona Śledzińska-Katarasińska (Warsaw: PWN, 1993).

Rufeisen-Schüpper, Hela, *Pożegnanie Miłej 18: Wspomnienia łączniczki Żydowskiej Organizacji Bojowej* (Kraków: Beseder, 1996).

Rybicka, Hanna, ed., *Obwodowe oddziały dywersji bojowej Okręgu AK Warszawa: Dokumenty warszawskiego Kedywu z lat 1943–1945* (Warsaw: Wydawnictwa Uniwersytetu Warszawskiego, 2010).

Rzędowska, Anna, and Dina Feldman, *Getto żydowskie w okupowanym Piotrkowie* (Piotrków Trybunalski: Biblioteki Piotrków 800, 2014).

Siebert, Friedrich Wilhelm, "Die Verwaltung im Generalgouvernement unter besonderer Berücksichtigung der Tätigkeit der Hauptabteilung Innere Velwaltung," in Josef Bühler, ed., *Das Generalgouvernement: Seine Verwaltung und seine Wirtschaft. Sammlung von Vorträgen der ersten wissenschaftlichen Vorträgsreihe der Verwaltungsakademie des Generagouvernements* (Krakow: Burgverl, 1943).

Siemak, Zbigniew, "Policja kryminalna II Rzeczypospolitej: Powstanie, organizacja, kadry i metody pracy," *Zagadnienia Społeczne*, 1 (2014), pp. 184–205.

Skibińska, Alina, "'Dostał 10 lat, ale za co?': Analiza motywacji sprawców zbrodni na Żydach na wsi kieleckiej w latach 1942–1944," in Barbara Engelking and Jan Grabowski, eds., *Zarys krajobrazu: Wieś polska wobec Zagłady Żydów 1942–1945* (Warsaw: Stowarzyszenie Centrum Badań nad Zagładą Żydów, 2011).

______, "Powiat biłgorajski," in Barbara Engelking and Jan Grabowski, eds., *Dalej jest noc: Losy Żydów w wybranych powiatach okupowanej Polski*, vol. 1 (Warsaw: Stowarzyszenie Centrum Badań nad Zagładą Żydów, 2018).

Skrodzki, Wojciech, "Żydzi z Wodzisławia," *Tygodnik Powszechny*, 28 (2006).

Stangneth, Bettina, *Eichmann Before Jerusalem* (New York: Vintage Books, 2014).

Stankowski, Albert, and Piotr Weiser, "Demograficzne skutki Holokaustu," in Feliks Tych and Monika Adamczyk-Garbowska, eds., *Następstwa zagłady Żydów. Polska 1944–2010* (Lublin and Warsaw: Wydawn. Uniwersytet Marii Curie-Skłodowskiej and

Żydowski Instytut Historyczny im. Emanuela Ringelbluma, 2011).

Stroop, Jurgen, *Żydowska dzielnica mieszkaniowa w Warszawie już nie istnieje!*, ed. by Andrzej Żbikowski (Warsaw: Instytut Pamięci Narodowej and Żydowski Instytut Historyczny, 2009).

Swałtek-Niewińska, Dagmara, "Powiat bocheński," in Barbara Engelking and Jan Grabowski, eds., *Dalej jest noc: Losy Żydów w wybranych powiatach okupowanej Polski,* vol. 2 (Warsaw: Stowarzyszenie Centrum Badań nad Zagładą Żydów, 2018).

Szurek, Jean-Charles, "Powiat łukowski," in Barbara Engelking and Jan Grabowski, eds., *Dalej jest noc: Losy Żydów w wybranych powiatach okupowanej Polski,* vol. 1 (Warsaw: Stowarzyszenie Centrum Badań nad Zagładą Żydów, 2018).

Szyfman, Arnold, *Moja tułaczka wojenna* (Warsaw: Ministerstwa Obrony Narodowej, 1960).

Szymańska-Smolkin, Sylwia, "Rola policji granatowej jako pośrednika w utrzymywaniu łączności między gettem a stroną aryjską," in August Grabski and Artur Markowski, eds., *Narody i polityka: Studia ofiarowane profesorowi Jerzemu Tomaszewskiemu* (Warsaw: Inst. Historii Uniw. Warszawskiego, 2010).

Tenenbaum, Joseph E., *Legacy and Redemption: A Life Renewed* (Washington, DC: United States Holocaust Memorial Museum and Holocaust Survivors' Memoirs Project, 2005).

Tokarska-Bakir, Joanna, *Pod klątwą: Społeczny portret pogromu kieleckiego* (Warsaw: Czarna Owca, 2018).

Van Liempt, Ad, *Hitler's Bounty Hunters: The Betrayal of the Jews* (New York: Berg, 2005).

Vanagaitė, Rūta, and Efraim Zuroff, *Our People: Discovering Lithuania's Hidden Holocaust* (Lanham, MA: Rowman & Littlefield, 2020).

Verstandig, Mark, *I Rest My Case* (Evanston: Northwestern University Press, 2002).

Wangrat, Tadeusz, *Polska i powiat węgrowski w przededniu i w czasie II wojny światowej* (Węgrów: Światowy Związek Żolnierzy AK Obwód "Smoła," 2010).

Weinreich, Max, *Hitler's Professors: The Part of Scholarship in Germany's Crimes against the Jewish People* (New Haven: Yale University Press, 1999).

Wenklar, Michał, "Polacy w niemieckiej policji pomocniczej. Schutzmannschaftsbataillon 202 w świetle zeznań jego członków," *Studia nad Autorytaryzmem i Totalitaryzmem*, 34:4 (2012), pp. 35–50.

Westermann, Edward B., "'Friend and Helper': German Uniformed Police Operations in Poland and the General Government," *The Journal of Military History*, 58:4 (1994), pp. 643–662.

Wiatr, Ewa, "'Turning Jews Over': The Participation of 'Blue' Policemen in Deportations of Jews Illustrated with the Example of the Radomsko County" (English edition), *Zagłada Żydów, Studia i materiały*, 10 (2014), pp. 302–314.

Willenberg, Samuel, *Bunt w Treblince* (Warsaw: Res Publica, 1991).

Wulf, Josef, *Das Dritte Reich und seine Vollstrecker—Die Liquidation von 500 000 Juden im Ghetto Warschau* (Berlin: Arani, 1961).

Wyleżyńska, Aurelia, *Kroniki wojenne, 1939–1944*, 2 vols. (Warsaw: Państwowy Instytut Wydawniczy, 2022).

Wyszyński, Franciszek, *Dzienniki z lat 1941–1944*, ed. by Jan Grabowski and Zbigniew Ryszard Grabowski (Warsaw: Mowią Wieki-Bellona, 2007).

Zamorski, Kordian Józef, *Dzienniki (1930–1938)*, ed. by Robert Litwiński and Marek Sioma (Warsaw and Łomianki: Inst. Józefa Piłsudskiego and Wydawn LTW, 2011).

Żbikowski, Andrzej, "'Night Guard': Holocaust Mechanisms in the Polish Rural Areas, 1942–1945, Preliminary Introduction into Research," in Jan T. Gross, ed., *The Holocaust in Occupied Poland: New Findings and New Interpretations* (Frankfurt am Main: P. Lang, 2012).

Żelaśkiewicz, Jerzy Michał, *Społeczność żydowska w Książu Wielkim do 1942 r.* (Warsaw: Jerzy Żelaśkiewicz, 2010).

Zimmerman, Joshua D., *Polskie Pańtwo Podziemne i Żydzi w czasie II wojny śiatowej* (Warsaw: Wydawnictwo Naukowe PWN, 2018).

Newspaper Articles and Online Materials

"Aufruf des Höheren SS- und Polizeiführers im Generalgouvernement für die besetzen polnischen Gebiete" (Announcement for [the residents of] the Occupied Polish Territories by the Higher SS- and Police Leader in the Generalgouvernement), *Verordnungsblatt des Generalgouverneurs für die Besetzten Polnischen Gebiete*, November 2, 1939.

Cęckiewicz, Stanisław, "Prześladowania nowobrzeskich Żydów," *Internetowy Kurier Proszowicki*, https://www.24ikp.pl/skarby/felietony/wydarzenia/20120421zydzi_nb/art.php (accessed July 2016).

"Dalszy wykaz współpracowników gestapo!!!" *Małopolska Agencja Prasowa*, June 4, 1943.

"Erlass des Führers und Reichskanzlers über die Verwaltung der besetzten polnischen Gebiete" (Führer and Reich's Chancellor's Decree concerning the Administration of the Occupied Polish Territories), *Reichsgesetzblatt*, part 1, October 24, 1939.

"Erste Verordnung über den Aufbau der Verwaltung der besetzten polnischen Gebiete" (First Decree on the Establishment of an Administration for the Occupied Polish Territories), *Verordnungsblatt des Generalgouverneurs für die Besetzten Polnischen Gebiete*, October 26, 1939.

"Four Kraków Policemen Sentenced to Death," *Małopolska Agencja Prasowa*, August 1, 1943.

Lipiński, Piotr, "Nikt ich nie tykał," *Gazeta Wyborcza*, August 30, 2002.

"Na nienoszących oznak żydów kary więzienia i grzywny nieograniczonej wysokości," *Nowy Kurier Warszawski*, March 15, 1940.

Piecuch, Wojciech, "Wielka Noc w Kańczudze," *Gazeta Wyborcza*, March 2–3, 2002.

Poliakiewicz, Simche, *Dzień w Treblince: Kronika żydowskiego życia*, https://sokolow.jewish.pl/simche-polakiewicz/dzien-w-treblince/ (accessed July 2019).

"Pomnik Granatowych Policjantów rozstrzelanych przez Niemców," Świętokrzyskie Stowarzyszenie Rodzina Policyjna 1939 r. w

Kielcach, https://osrp-swietokrzyskie.policja.gov.pl/rp1/aktualnosci/3689,Pomnik-Granatowych-Policjantow-rozstrzelanych-przez-Niemcow.html?search=683241511 (accessed September 2019).

"Równia pochyła," *Biuletyn Informacyjny*, December 4, 1941.

"Salomon Morel," Wikipedia entry, https://en.wikipedia.org/wiki/Salomon_Morel (accessed August 2019).

"Verordnung über den Feuerschutz im Generalgouvernement," (Decree on Fire Protection in the Generalgouvernement), *Verordnungsblatt für das Generalgouvernement*, April 29, 1941.

"Verordnung über die Kennzeichnung der Juden und Jüdinnen im Generalgouvernement" (Decree about the Marking of Jews and Jewesses in the Generalgouvernement), *Verordnungsblatt des Generalgouverneurs für die Besetzten Polnischen Gebiete*, November 30, 1939.

"Verordnung über die Pflicht zur Anmeldung jüdischen Vermögens im Generalgouvernement" (Decree on the Obligatory Duty to Register all Jewish Assets in the Generalgouvernement), *Verordnungsblatt des Generalgouverneurs für die Besetzten Polnischen Gebiete*, January 29, 1940.

"Współpraca policji niemieckiej z polską," *Dziennik Radomski*, March 13, 1940.

"Zbrodniczy wymiar okupacji niemieckiej na ziemiach polskich 1939–1945: Stanowisko IPN," Instytut Pamięci Narodowej, February 19, 2018, https://ipn.gov.pl/pl/dla-mediow/komunikaty/47461,Zbrodniczy-wymiar-okupacji-niemieckiej-na-ziemiach-polskich-19391945-Stanowisko-.html (accessed September 2019).

Private Collections and Unpublished Manuscripts

Feigenbaum, Mosze Józef, *Slaughter in Podlasie: Notes from the Holocaust*, tr. by L. M. Zell (unpublished manuscript), courtesy of Amir Feigenbaum.

Grabowski, Tadeusz Wacław, *Wspomnienia* (manuscript in the author's possession).

Mikulski, Jan, *Myśli, wspomnienia, uwagi, refleksje…* (Biłgoraj: n.p., 1970) (typewritten manuscript available in the Biłgoraj Public Library).

Pędowski, Karol, *Pamiętnik: Powrót do mojego miasta* (handwritten manuscript), Biblioteka Narodowa (BN), Magazyn Rękopisów, ref. 12254 (mf 104106).

Wraubek, Józef, *Na Podhalu* (author's archive, undated manuscript).

Index

Names and Organizations

Page numbers in italics refer to photographs.
Page numbers ending with "t" refer to tables.

Places

Page numbers in italics refer to photographs.